GW00771262

Max Rafferty

Detail in
Contemporary
Timber
Architecture

LAURENCE KING

Published in 2010 by
Laurence King Publishing Ltd
361–373 City Road
London
EC1V 1LR
e-mail: enquiries@laurenceking.com
www.laurenceking.com

A catalogue record for this book is
available from the British Library

ISBN: 978 1 85669 641 8

Designed by Hamish Muir
Illustrations by Advanced Illustrations
Limited
Picture Research by Sophia Gibb

Printed in China

Detail in Contemporary Timber Architecture

Virginia McLeod

Laurence King Publishing

Contents

Timber is recognized as one of the oldest building materials used by humans for their shelter, with its softness, warmth and versatility proving to be of almost universal importance in cultures across the world. The sheer quantity of timber buildings through the ages reflects the degree to which the planet was forested – from the softwoods that create a ring below the Arctic Circle and furnish Russia, Canada and Scandinavia with building timber (typically fir, spruce, pine and larch), to the hardwood forests of North America, Central and Eastern Europe, China and Japan, which furnish these countries with an abundance of oak, beech, birch, maple and chestnut trees, and in South America, Central Africa, South-East Asia and Australia where ample sources of hardwoods flourish in the sub-tropical rainforest environments of these areas.

While timber succeeded as the dominant building material for many millennia, the eighteenth century witnessed a paradigm shift in building technology with the introduction of cast and wrought iron which could be mass produced in large quantities and enabled the construction of buildings with larger structural spans. The subsequent boom in the use of reinforced concrete and steel as dominant structural materials in the twentieth century saw timber relegated for use in small, domestic-scale buildings where its relatively low-tech, low-cost properties were appreciated.

In recent decades, however, timber has been rediscovered, especially in industrial countries where the realization that the indiscriminate plundering of natural resources and the use of vast quantities of energy to manufacture building materials is both unsustainable and inconsistent with contemporary attitudes towards energy conservation, pollution and recycling. Timber, unlike many high-tech, man-made building materials, is completely recyclable. In addition, in the form of a tree it regulates our climate, stabilizes the soil and is one of the primary contributors to a balanced biosphere. In its cut form, whether through rotting or combustion, timber is returned to the natural cycle without contributing additional energy.

And, of course, it is now widely recognized that timber out-performs many other building materials not only in terms of its renewability, but also its malleability, adaptiveness and its ability to be used in widely varying climates and conditions. It is an excellent insulator in colder climates and can be used to create light, open structures that encourage cross ventilation in hot climates. It is also structurally versatile, with a very high strength to weight ratio. Pine, for example, can provide the same degree of strength as steel with a structure that is 16 times lighter, and as concrete with a structure five times lighter.

While the tradition of building in timber is uninterrupted in domestic contexts, it has only relatively recently reappeared in larger public buildings. This development is in no small part due to recent technological developments aimed at improving the structural performance of timber. For example, bonding pieces of timber together results in beams that eliminate the 'negative' qualities of solid timber elements – they do not split or warp and possess uniform properties in both tension and compression. Large laminated timbers (such as Glu-lam beams) and smaller components such as veneer-laminated wood panels are able to be used to create previously unattainable spans which would otherwise only be possible using steel or reinforced concrete.

The use of high-tech timber products has opened up the possibility of employing timber in building types as diverse as sports halls, bridges, educational buildings and high-rise offices, all of which are represented in this book. Hérault Arnod Architectes' Cultural, Sports and Congress Centre in France (page 30) uses timber to create a full-size indoor sports centre using a large span timber structure, while celebrating a long and proud history of timber craftsmanship in the French Alps in the beautifully crafted screen panels that adorn the exterior of the building.

In Norway, architects Saunders & Wilhelmsen have designed an astonishing lookout bridge in Aurland (page 166) that employs pressure-treated pine that echoes the pine forests in which it stands above a fjord on the west coast of the country. In a breathtaking change of scale, Francis-Jones Morehen Thorp's Chancellery and Business School in Perth, Australia, (page 18) uses jarrah, a species of eucalyptus, in geometrically complex and aesthetically dramatic screens to create an iconic new building that exemplifies the aspirations of the Edith Cowan University. Again in Australia, this time in Melbourne, DesignInc have designed a mould-breaking high-rise office building in the city that is the recipient of numerous awards for design and sustainability (page 180). Here, the timber facade rises through 12 storeys and functions as one of the key climatic moderators, screening the interior from the sun and filtering cooling breezes.

Larger buildings and public structures such as these are now being designed and built all over the world – works such as Bohlin Cywinski Jackson's Grand Teton Discovery Centre in the USA, Cowper Griffiths' Anglesey Abbey Visitor Centre in the UK and Matteo Thun's Hugo Boss Industries Building in Switzerland are representative of a new wave of timber architecture. It is in the domestic sphere, however that timber architecture continues to be the material of choice for architects and their clients.

This book illustrates how construction details are as vital a part of timber architecture as its external form and interior layout. Whether so subtle as to be invisible, or revealed as extraordinarily complex, details determine the quality and character of a building. Good detailing entails exercising the utmost care and attention at the junctions between materials, between the different elements of a building and where a material changes direction. Through details, the myriad parts that make up a building come together to form a whole – joints, connections, seams, openings and surfaces are transformed via a combination of technology and invention into a building.

We are accustomed to being presented with photographic representations of architecture in books, magazines and on-line, with the inspiring image continuing to be the focus of the two-dimensional representation of architecture. Increasingly these images are now often accompanied by floor plans to provide a better understanding of the way a building works. The availability of floor plans is, of course, of enormous assistance in helping us to understand the spatial sequences, the extent and scale of a building. However it is not inherent in the purpose of a plan or a photograph, even if accompanied by a section, to reveal the individual elements – literally the nuts and bolts – that go together to make up a wall, a floor, a roof, a window, a staircase, a kitchen and so on. Construction details, however, do just this, and this book unites the photograph, the plan and section, as well as the details to bring to the reader a comprehensive insight into the true workings of the building.

Architects draw details specifically to reveal the inner workings of a building – primarily, of course, they are used by the builder in order to construct the building. Readers of architectural publications, however, are all too rarely given the opportunity to examine the details – the 'real' representation of how a building is put together. This book aims to remedy that and provides a guide to the inner workings of 50 of the most inspiring examples of contemporary timber architecture, exposing to the reader what has previously remained hidden behind the facade. These details reveal not only an 'x-ray' of the buildings presented, but an insight into the cognitive processes of the architects who brought them into being.

Architectural details account for up to 95 per cent of the sometimes hundreds of drawings produced to describe the way a building is put together. They act as the means by which architects communicate their intent to builders, engineers and other participants in the building process. They also act as one of the most challenging intellectual and technical exercises for any architect, producing, as they must, a series of what are essentially graphic representations of every single junction and connection in a building. Almost exclusively made up of two-dimensional representations (plan and sectional drawings), the challenge resides in the architect's ability to imagine the most complex of junctions, assemblies and components in three dimensions – as they will actually be built on site – and transfer them on to paper, or on to a screen, into two dimensions, into the conventional drawn representations that have been used in the construction industry for decades, even centuries.

While the selection of details presented for each of the buildings in this book is necessarily limited by space, they nonetheless go a long way towards deconstructing the image of the finished building. They not only inspire, they also help us to understand the thought that went into the making of the building and perhaps the technical problems that were solved along the way.

Timber has been, and remains today, one of the most user-friendly of building materials. It suggests warmth and contact with nature as well as being a harbinger of hope for a new, more environmentally friendly approach for the building industry. It is my hope that these 50 projects, in their diversity, experimental spirit and architectural excellence, illustrate the potential of this oldest, and newest, of building materials.

Virginia McLeod

Notes

US and Metric Measurements
Dimensions have been provided by the architects in metric and converted to US measurements, except in case of projects in the US, where dimensions have been converted to metric.

Terminology
An attempt has been made to standardize terminology to aid understanding across readerships, for example 'wood' is generally referred to as 'timber' and 'aluminum' as 'aluminium'. However materials or processes that are peculiar to a country, region or architectural practice that have no direct correspondence are presented in the original.

Floor Plans
Throughout the book, the following convention of hierarchy has been used – ground floor, first floor, second floor, and so on. In certain contexts, terms such as basement level or upper level have been used for clarity.

Scale
All floor plans, sections and elevations are presented at conventional architectural metric scales, typically 1:50, 1:100 or 1:200 as appropriate. An accurate graphic scale is included on the second page near the floor plans of every project to aid in the understanding of scale. Details are also presented at conventional architectural scales, typically 1:1, 1:5 and 1:10.

8

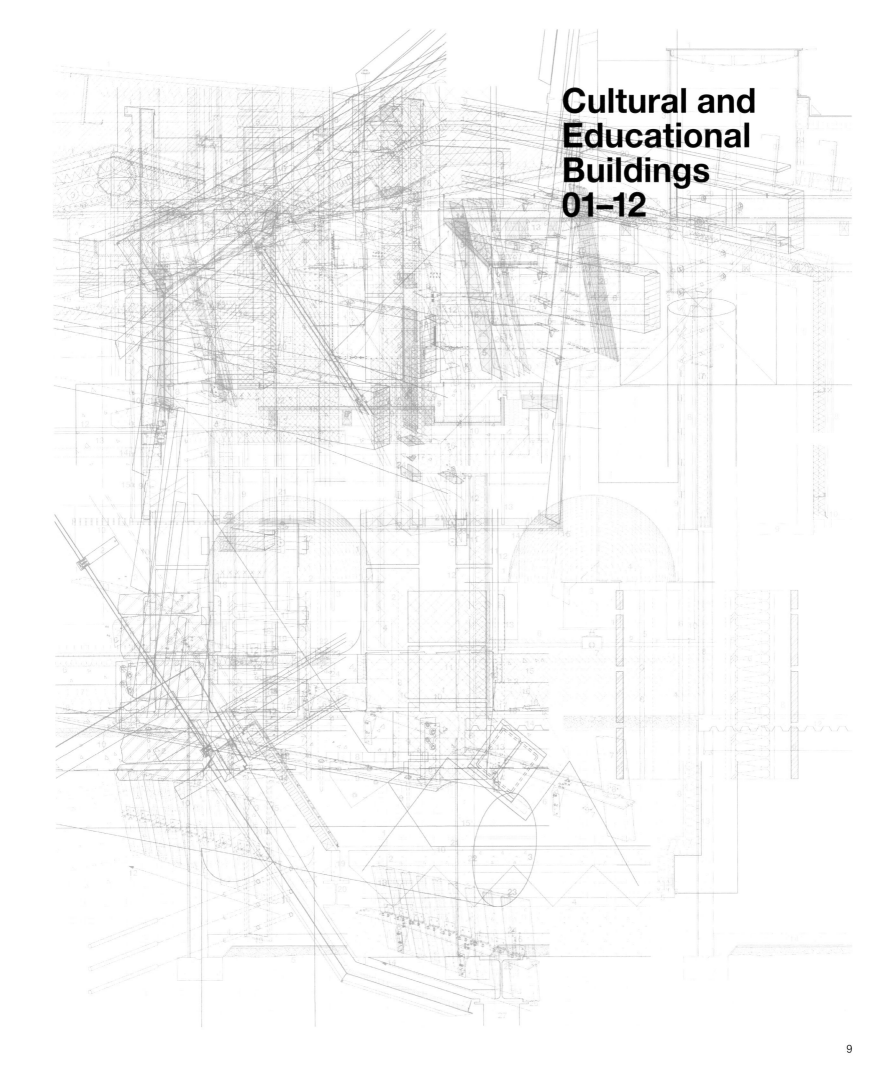

Cultural and Educational Buildings
01–12

**Grand Teton Discovery and Visitor
Center
Moose, Wyoming, USA**

Client
National Park Service, Grand Teton
National Park Foundation, Grand
Teton Association

Project Team
Peter Q. Bohlin, Raymond S. Calabro,
David Miller, Jessica O'Brien, Christian
G. Evans, Mark Adams, Daniel Ralls,
Zeke Bush, Michelle Evans

Structural Engineer
Beaudette Consulting Engineers

The Grand Teton Discovery and Visitor
Center is sited between a sagebrush
meadow and a riparian forest along
the Snake River. Approaching through
a grove of spruce, cottonwood and
aspen trees, visitors are drawn into a
courtyard that provides an intimate
setting that accommodates groups of
people for gatherings and orientation.
A colonnade of Douglas fir logs
surrounds the courtyard while the roof
tilts upward and away from the
courtyard. Entering at the north end of
the courtyard, visitors are drawn into
the heart of the building. Located here
is a large gathering hall with
magnificent views of the Teton Range,
where a large concrete and stone
fireplace acts as the focal point of the
room. Tall Douglas fir log frames
support a raft of engineered timber
beams that radiate from the centre of
the building and cantilever past the
windows. The log frames are placed
to minimize the span of the glue-
laminated timbers while allowing
circulation through the exhibit spaces.

The exhibits are fully integrated with
the architecture of the Visitor Center.
Exhibition panels tilt out of the floor
slab and video screens embedded in
the floor show dramatic film footage of
the park's geography and wildlife. The
new building features passive solar
strategies such as building orientation
and the extensive use of windows for
natural light. The use of Forest
Stewardship Council (FSC) certified
timber, storm and snow melt water
management strategies, mechanical
cooling using groundwater, the
extensive use of recycled materials
and low-consumption plumbing
fixtures all contribute to this building's
sustainable design.

1 View of the large gathering hall where the jagged edges of the timber roof celebrate the peaks of the Teton Range beyond.
2 A massive stone and concrete chimney rises above a fireplace which takes centre stage in the hall.
3 Douglas fir log frames support a raft of engineered wood beams that radiate from the centre of the plan. These are placed to allow circulation through the exhibit spaces.
4 View of one of the timber log columns, the large scale of which is matched by the walls of glazing that bring the dramatic Wyoming landscape into the building.

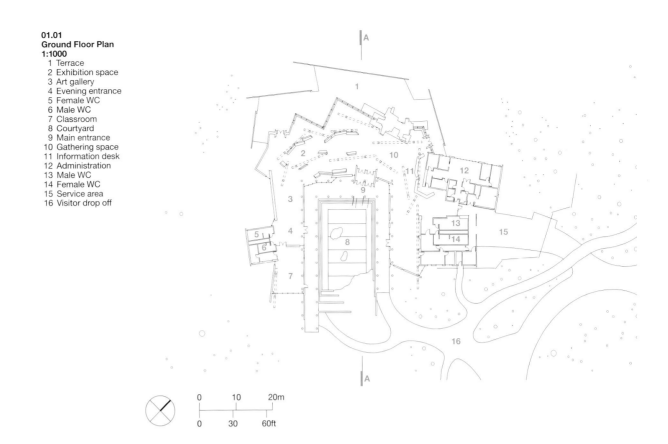

01.01
Ground Floor Plan
1:1000
1 Terrace
2 Exhibition space
3 Art gallery
4 Evening entrance
5 Female WC
6 Male WC
7 Classroom
8 Courtyard
9 Main entrance
10 Gathering space
11 Information desk
12 Administration
13 Male WC
14 Female WC
15 Service area
16 Visitor drop off

0   10   20m
0   30   60ft

01.02
South-East Elevation
1:500
1 WC
2 Classroom
3 Courtyard
4 Main entrance to
  gathering space
  and galleries
5 Roof
6 Chimney
7 Bookshop
8 Service area

01.03
Section A–A
1:500
1 Classroom
2 Courtyard
3 Roof to art gallery
4 Roof to exhibition
  and gathering
  spaces
5 Gathering space
6 Glazing to terrace
7 Terrace

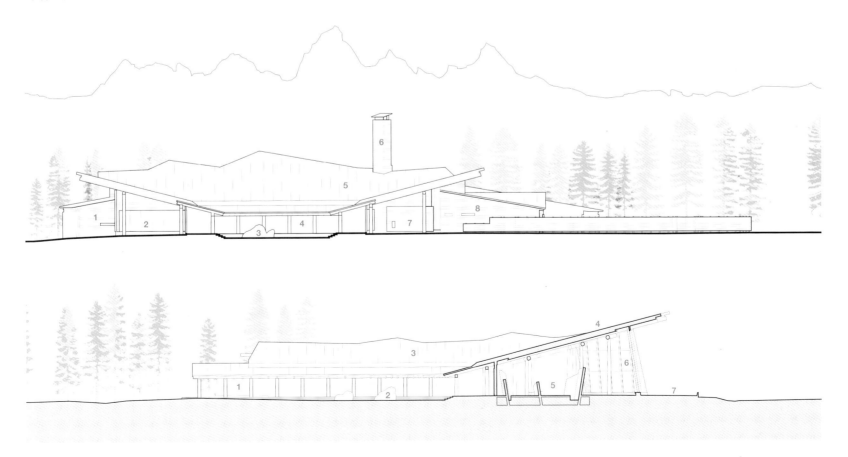

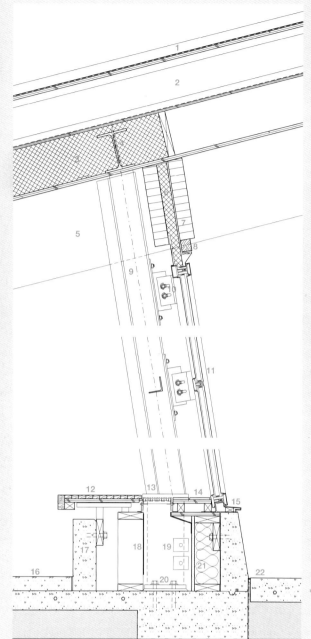

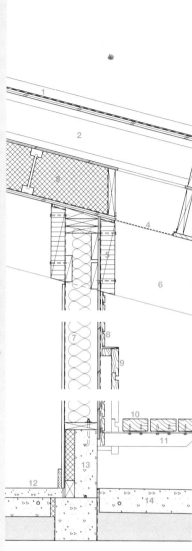

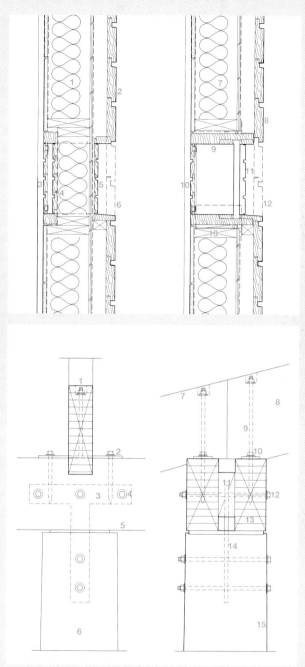

01.04
Custom Curtain Wall Section Detail at Timber Bench
1:20
1 Pre-finished metal standing seam roof system over sheet membrane waterproofing over 19 mm (3/4 inch) sheathing
2 240 mm (91/2 inch) cold roof space over building felt over 12 mm (1/2 inch) sheathing
3 Spray-in foam insulation over 19 mm (3/4 inch) ACX plywood sheathing
4 Perimeter steel beam
5 Glu-laminated beam beyond
6 Rigid insulation
7 Glu-laminated blocking over self-adhered membrane flashing

8 Notched blocking at curtain wall head
9 Steel column assembly
10 Custom curtain wall anchor
11 Custom aluminium curtain wall system
12 Built up maple bench
13 Anodized aluminium linear grating
14 Blackened steel panels
15 Pre-finished metal sill flashing
16 Concrete slab with hydronic heating system
17 Concrete curb
18 Sheet metal baffle
19 Fin tube heating system
20 Steel column base plate
21 Batt insulation over vapour barrier over 15 mm (5/8 inch) gypsum wall board

22 Washed aggregate concrete slab

01.05
Detail Section at Courtyard Wall
1:20
1 Pre-finished metal standing seam roof system over sheet membrane waterproofing over 19 mm (3/4 inch) sheathing
2 240 mm (91/2 inch) cold roof space over building felt over 12 mm (1/2 inch) sheathing
3 Spray-in foam insulation
4 Cold roof vent with metal pest screen
5 Glu-laminated blocking
6 Glu-laminated beam beyond
7 Batt insulation over vapour barrier over 15 mm (5/8 inch) gypsum

wall board
8 Cedar siding over drainage mat over moisture barrier over 12 mm (1/2 inch) sheathing
9 Cedar siding over pressure-treated furring
10 Ipe timber bench
11 Painted steel T-beam
12 Concrete slab with hydronic heating system
13 Concrete curb
14 Washed aggregate concrete slab with snow melt system

01.06
Detail at Courtyard Slot Window With Sliding Shutter
1:20
1 Batt insulation over vapour barrier over 15 mm (5/8 inch) gypsum wall board
2 Cedar siding over

pressure treated furring over moisture barrier over 12 mm (1/2 inch) sheathing
3 Cedar sliding door with stainless steel track and hardware
4 Cedar siding
5 Cedar siding over drainage mat over moisture barrier over sheathing
6 Cedar siding beyond
7 Batt insulation over vapour barrier over 15 mm (5/8 inch) gypsum wall board
8 Cedar siding over pressure treated furring over moisture barrier over 12 mm (1/2 inch) sheathing
9 Cedar window frame with removable stop
10 Cedar sliding door with stainless steel track and hardware
11 25 mm (1 inch)

thick insulated glass unit
12 Cedar siding beyond
13 Pre-finished metal jamb flashing

01.07
Log Column to Double Glu-Lam Connection Detail
1:20
1 19 mm (3/4 inch) threaded rod with 19 mm (3/4 inch) hex nut and washer
2 19 mm (3/4 inch) lag bolts with washer
3 T-shaped steel knife plate
4 19 mm (3/4 inch) threaded rod with 19 mm (3/4 inch) hex nut and washer
5 380 x 130 mm (15 x 51/8 inch) Glu-laminated beam
6 Peeled log column
7 380 x 130 mm (15 x 51/8 inch) Glu-

laminated beam
8 460 x 130 mm (181/10 x 51/8 inch) Glu-laminated beam
9 19 mm (3/4 inch) threaded rod with 19 mm (3/4 inch) hex nut and washer
10 19 mm (3/4 inch) lag bolts with washer
11 Continuous Douglas fir blocking
12 19 mm (3/4 inch) threaded rod with 19 mm (3/4 inch) hex nut and washer
13 380 x 130 mm (15 x 51/8 inch) Glu-laminated beam
14 T-shaped steel knife plate
15 Peeled log column

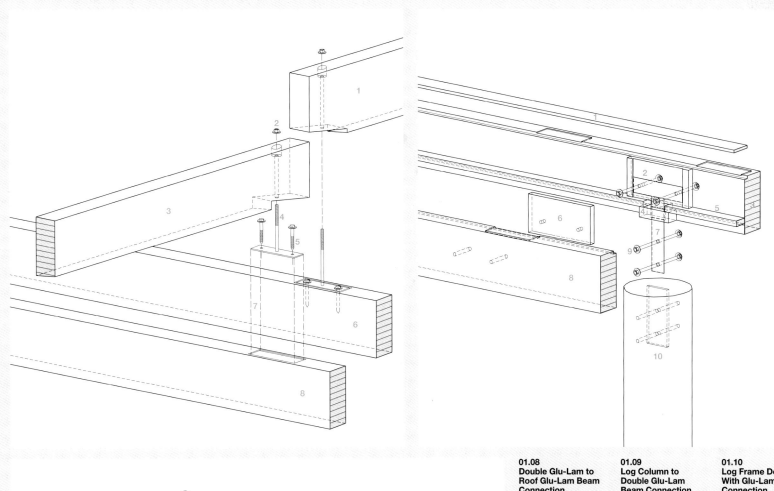

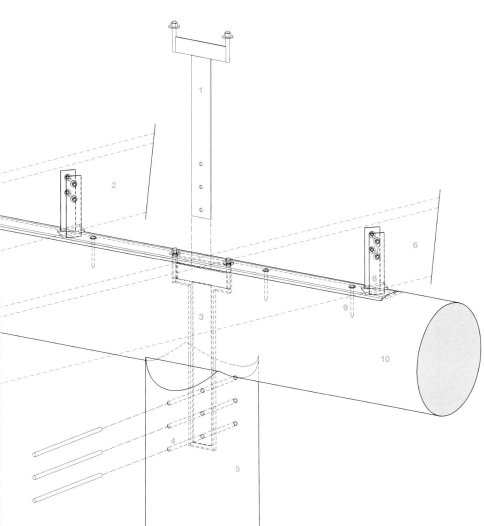

01.08
Double Glu-Lam to Roof Glu-Lam Beam Connection
Not to scale
 1 460 x 130 mm (18 x 5^1/$_8$ inch) Glu-laminated beam
 2 Hex nut and washer
 3 380 x 130 mm (15 x 5^1/$_8$ inch) Glu-laminated beam
 4 19 mm (^{3}/$_4$ inch) threaded rod and steel plate assembly
 5 19 mm (^{3}/$_4$ inch) lag bolts with washer
 6 380 x 130 mm (15 x 5^1/$_8$ inch) Glu-laminated beam
 7 Routed Glu-laminated beam to accept threaded rod and steel plate assembly
 8 380 x 130 mm (15 x 5^1/$_8$ inch) Glu-laminated beam

01.09
Log Column to Double Glu-Lam Beam Connection Detail
Not to scale
 1 Continuous Douglas fir blocking
 2 Douglas fir blocking
 3 380 x 130 mm (15 x 5^1/$_8$ inch) Glu-laminated beam
 4 Douglas fir spacer with slot for knife plate
 5 Continuous Douglas fir blocking
 6 Douglas fir blocking
 7 T-shaped steel knife plate
 8 380 x 130 mm (15 x 5^1/$_8$ inch) Glu-laminated beam
 9 19 mm (^{3}/$_4$ inch) threaded rod with 19 mm (^{3}/$_4$ inch) hex nut and washer
10 Peeled log column with routed knife plate slot

01.10
Log Frame Detail With Glu-Lam Connection
Not to scale
 1 Custom steel knife plate, threaded rod and steel drift pin assembly
 2 460 x 130 mm (18 x 5^1/$_8$ inch) Glu-laminated beam
 3 Custom steel knife plate and threaded rod assembly installed, shown dashed
 4 25 mm (1 inch) steel drift pin, shown dashed
 5 Peeled log column
 6 460 x 130 mm (18 x 5^1/$_8$ inch) Glu-laminated beam
 7 19 mm (^{3}/$_4$ inch) thru-bolts
 8 Custom rafter beam bearing plate assembly, shown dashed
 9 19 mm (^{3}/$_4$ inch) lag bolts with washer
10 Peeled log beam

02
Dannatt, Johnson Architects

Battle Visitor Centre
Battle, East Sussex, England, UK

Client
English Heritage

Project Team
David Johnson, Julian Mowbray

Structural Engineer
Michael Barclay Partnership

Project Manager
Turner & Townsend

The new visitor centre for the site of the Battle of Hastings replaces previous facilities at Battle Abbey which had become dilapidated at this world-famous English Heritage battlefield site. The new two storey building houses a cafe, interpretation and audio-visual display, and visitor facilities. The building emerges from an existing stone wall that encompasses the site. It forms a protective screen between the abbey and the car park, and improves the landscaping of a formerly untidy area along the route to the battlefield. A local palette of materials has been used, employed with modern construction techniques. Each of the main walls of the building employs a different material. Tonbridge Green Sandstone, laid in split courses, merges with the existing stone wall. This wall overlaps with a wall of Sussex hand-made bricks, set back from the road and running around to face the car park.

The primary element is a curved wall of sawn green oak sections. The timbers alternate in an off-set stagger, with the inset oak pieces compressed between the adjacent outer sections, which are bolted together using stainless steel fixings. This results in a deep saw-tooth profile internally and externally. The green oak has been allowed to dry slowly, enhancing the texture of the wall surface. The wall curves to avoid the root systems of two walnut trees, anchoring the building into the site, and is evocative of a Norman palisade. Oak is used in other ways throughout the building, notably in the curtain wall, where the oak mullions allow continuous areas of glass to follow the complex geometry of the overlapping walls and ceilings. Spaced oak battens in the café ceiling and auditorium seating have been used to soften the reverberation in these areas.

1 The textured green oak wall acts as a screen to the south-east. Double height slots of glazing allow views out to the walnut trees that were protected during the construction of the building.
2 View of the Visitor Centre with Battle Abbey in the background. The timber wall curves around a low grass bank, avoiding the two walnut trees.
3 View of the main stair which connects the entrance lobby on the upper level to the interpretation area and auditorium below.
4 Detail view of the interior face of the rough sawn oak wall and slot windows.

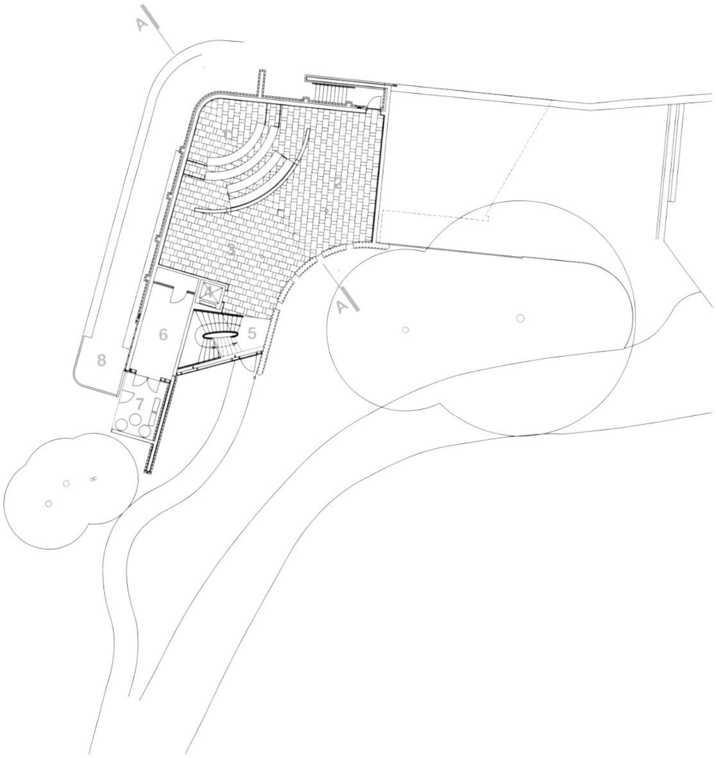

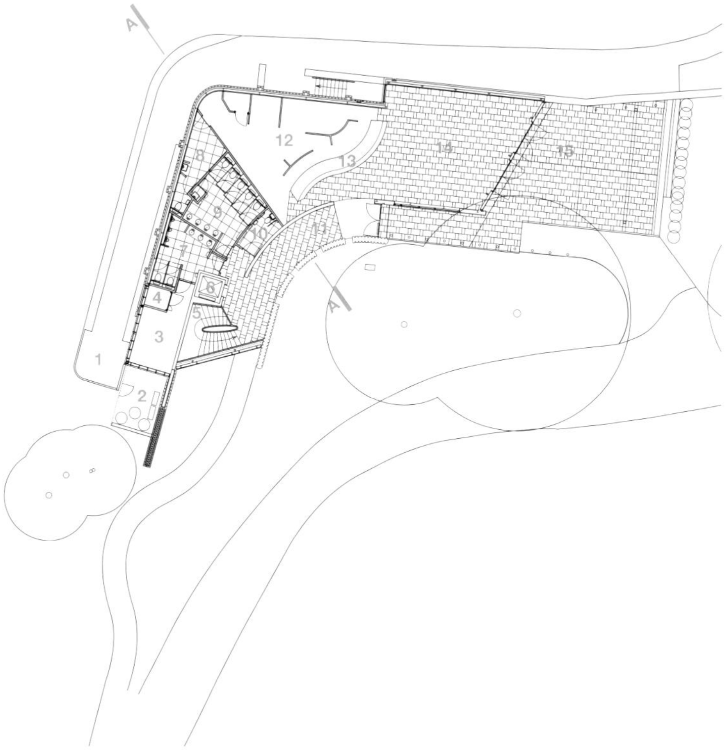

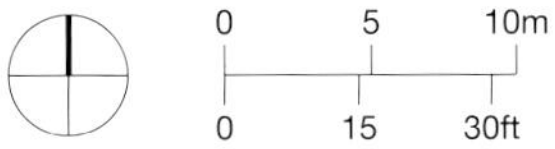

0
5
10m
0
15
30ft

02.01
Lower Ground Floor Plan
1:500

1 Audio-visual auditorium
2 Interpretation area
3 Interpretation area
4 Elevator
5 Stair
6 Plant room
7 Storage
8 Path to Battle Abbey

02.02
Upper Ground Floor Plan
1:500

1 Path to Battle Abbey
2 Storage
3 Plant room
4 Cleaner's store
5 Stair
6 Elevator
7 Male WC
8 Staff WC
9 Female WC
10 Disabled WC
11 Entrance lobby
12 Kitchen
13 Cafe servery
14 Cafe
15 Cafe terrace

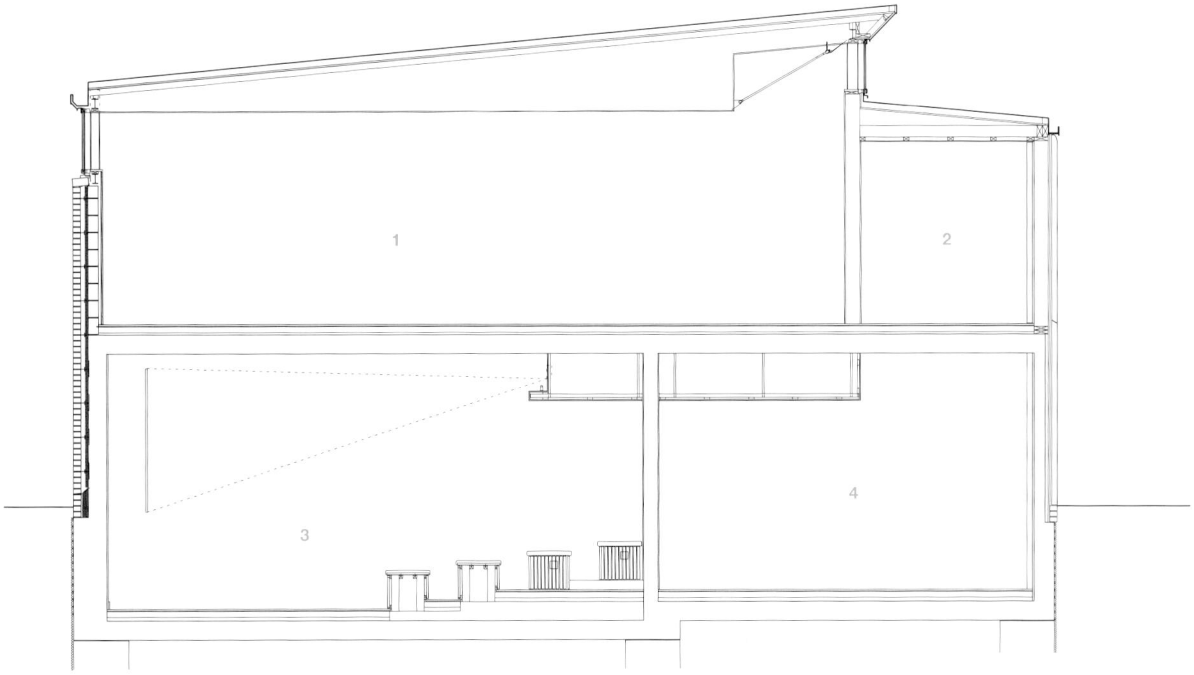

02.03
Section A–A
1:100

1 Kitchen
2 Entrance
3 Audio-visual auditorium
4 Interpretation area

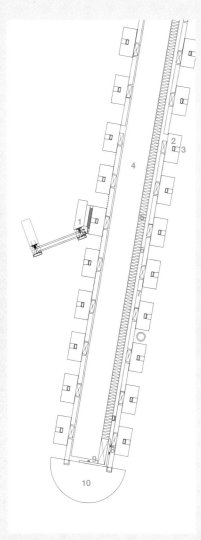

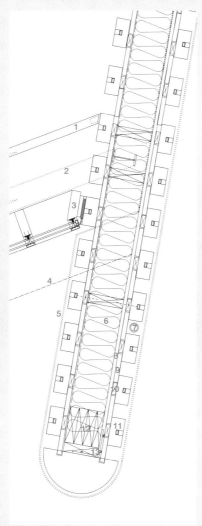

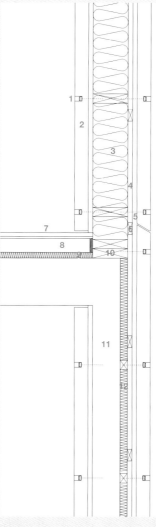

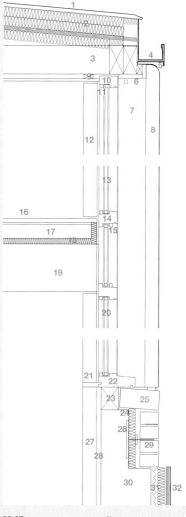

02.04
Oak Palisade Wall
Low Level Plan Detail
1:20
 1 Oak framed curtain
walling system
 2 150 x 75 mm (6 x 3
inch) sawn green oak
 3 Seasoned oak
pellet
 4 Reinforced
concrete wall
 5 40 mm (1¹/₂ inch)
polystyrene insulation
 6 25 mm (1 inch) air
gap
 7 22 x 150 mm (⁴/₅ x
6 inch) sawn green oak
 8 Chem-fix bolt
 9 150 x 150 x 10 mm
(6 x 6 x ²/₅ inch)
stainless steel fixing
angle
10 Half round green
oak bull nose

02.05
Oak Palisade Wall
High Level Plan
Detail
1:20
 1 45 mm (1³/₄ inch)
diameter oak handrail
 2 Line of steel wind
post
 3 Oak framed curtain
walling system
 4 Line of roof above
 5 Line of structural
gutter above
 6 200 mm (7⁹/₁₀ inch)
lightweight glass fibre
insulation
 7 48 mm (1⁹/₁₀ inch)
diameter galvanized
metal rain water pipe
 8 25 mm (1 inch) air
space
 9 Breather paper
10 125 mm (5 inch)
stainless steel coach
screw
11 150 x 75 mm (6 x 3
inch) sawn green oak
12 Timber framing
13 150 x 150 x 10 mm
(6 x 6 x ²/₅ inch)
stainless steel fixing
angle

02.06
Oak Palisade Wall
Section Detail
1:20
 1 Chem-fix bolt
 2 150 x 75 mm (6 x 3
inch) sawn green oak
 3 200 mm (7⁹/₁₀ inch)
lightweight glass fibre
insulation
 4 25 mm (1 inch) air
space
 5 22 x 150 mm (⁴/₅ x
6 inch) sawn green oak
 6 125 mm (5 inch)
stainless steel coach
screw
 7 Stone tiling on
mortar bed
 8 Cement screed
 9 30 mm (1¹/₅ inch)
rigid insulation
10 Timber framing
11 Reinforced
concrete wall
12 40 mm (1¹/₂ inch)
polystyrene insulation

02.07
Oak Palisade Wall
Window Section
Detail
1:20
 1 Terne-coated
stainless steel roofing
 2 Rigid insulation
 3 150 x 50 mm (6 x 2
inch) timber joist
 4 5 mm (¹/₅ inch)
thick structural gutter
curved to radius
 5 Lead flashing
 6 22 mm (⁴/₅ inch)
thick oak wall lining
 7 22 mm (⁴/₅ inch)
thick oak reveal
 8 150 x 75 mm (6 x 3
inch) oak wall lining
 9 50 x 25 mm (2 x 1
inch) timber batten
10 100 x 63 mm (4 x
2¹/₂ inch) oak window
frame
11 18 x 18 mm (⁷/₁₀ x
⁷/₁₀ inch) oak bead
12 Wax finished 150 x
75 mm (6 x 3 inch) oak
wall lining
13 28 mm (1¹/₁₀ inch)
double glazing unit
14 Oak window frame
15 Oak glazing bead
16 Stone tiling on
mortar bed
17 Cement screed
18 30 mm (1¹/₅ inch)
rigid insulation
19 Exposed reinforced
concrete slab
20 28 mm (1¹/₁₀ inch)
double glazing unit
with opaque laminated

film
21 25 mm (1 inch) oak
sill
22 Oak window sill
23 Timber sub frame
24 Damp proof course
25 Brick sill
26 Cast-in wall tie
27 150 x 75 mm (6 x 3
inch) oak board
28 25 mm (1 inch) oak
board
29 Face brickwork
30 Reinforced
concrete retaining wall
31 Hydroduct sheet,
damp proof membrane
and tanking
32 Lost in place ply
formwork

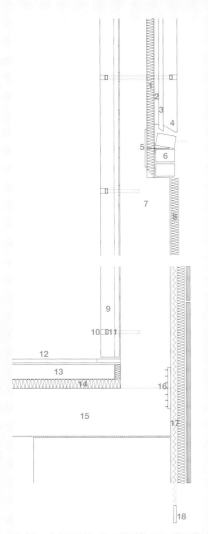

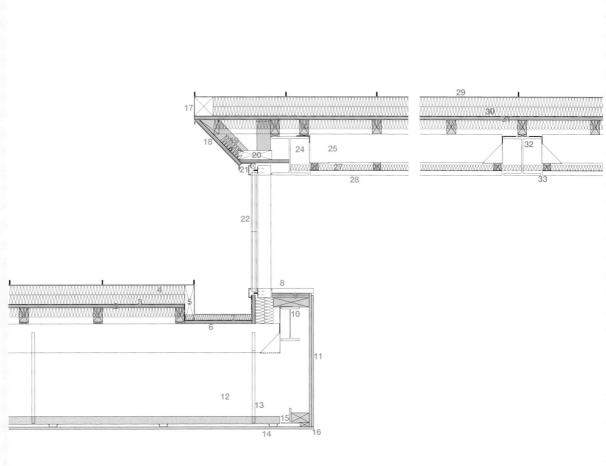

02.08
Oak Palisade Wall Base Section Detail
1:20
  1 40 mm (1¹/₂ inch) polystyrene insulation
  2 25 mm (1 inch) timber batten
  3 25 mm (1 inch) oak board
  4 Oak weather board with chamfered underside at 30 degrees and preservative sealed
  5 Cast-in wall tie
  6 Brickwork
  7 Reinforced concrete retaining wall
  8 50 mm (2 inch) Claymaster polystyrene ground heave prevention
  9 Oak wall lining
  10 Pellet / bolt fixing
  11 Packers as required
  12 Stone tiling on mortar bed
  13 Cement screed
  14 50 mm (2 inch) rigid insulation
  15 Reinforced floor slab
  16 Serviseal waterstop
  17 Damp proof membrane
  18 Hydrocoil drainage outlet located at base of foundation

02.09
Clerestory Glazing Detail
1:20
  1 Timber rafters on packing to suit curvature of roof deck
  2 Plywood sheathing
  3 Insulation and vapour barrier
  4 Stainless steel sheet
  5 Timber framing
  6 Plywood sheathing
  7 Stainless steel sheet to form gutter
  8 Timber sill
  9 Plywood packing
  10 Universal beam
  11 Plasterboard lining
  12 Ceiling void
  13 Metal ceiling hanger
  14 Plasterboard ceiling
  15 Metal ceiling rail
  16 Edge stop bead
  17 Stainless steel roof sheet
  18 Plywood sheathing
  19 Timber framing
  20 Timber packing
  21 Proprietary glazing frame
  22 Fixed double glazed unit
  23 75 x 50 mm (3 x 2 inch) timber rafters
  24 203 x 203 mm (8 x 8 inch) universal beam
  25 150 x 50 mm (6 x 2 inch) timber purlins
  26 40 x 40 mm (1³/₅ inch) timber battens
  27 Acoustic liner and

black tissue
  28 38 x 25 mm (1¹/₂ x 1 inch) oak battens to form ceiling
  29 Stainless steel roof sheet
  30 80 mm (3¹/₈ inch) rigid insulation board
  31 Vapour control layer
  32 Paint finished universal beam
  33 10 mm (²/₅ inch) gap between beam and oak batten ceiling

03
Francis-Jones Morehen Thorp

**Chancellery and Business School,
Edith Cowan University
Perth, Western Australia, Australia**

Project Team
Richard Francis-Jones, David Haseler,
Elizabeth Carpenter, Lance White,
Justin Wong, Jason Wedesweiler,
Olivia Shih, Johnathan Redman,
Matthew Todd

Structural Engineer
Bruechle Gilchrist & Evans

The new Chancellery and Business
School is sited on a gentle rise, set
amongst bushland and eucalyptus.
The forms and character of the
buildings have been drawn directly
from the landscape. The Chancellery
buildings are like two giant plants,
their branches fanning out and rising
up from the ground. The curving
form is assembled from jarrah struts
that begin almost parallel to the
ground then fold up and out, framing
a new ceremonial open space. The
jarrah screen provides shelter, shade
and structural support to work areas,
courtyards, cafe and gallery spaces
over three levels. Between the timber
screen and the main enclosure
stairways and lifts are placed in this
shaded zone open to the view to
create informal meeting places.

Positioned either side of the central
space, are located the Council
Chamber and the executive offices
of the Vice Chancellor. In counterpoint
with the Chancellery building is the
linear structure that accommodates
the School of Business teaching and
office spaces. In another interpretation
of the landscape, the ground plane
has been extended and bent up into a
gentle slope that looks back to the
rising forms of the Chancellery. This
form is made from clay brick and
concrete packed together to create an
enclosing bowl-like open space with
seating for events or informal
gatherings. Intersecting this sloped
artificial landscape are metal
enclosures accommodating the
academic offices. These orthogonal
forms look back towards the
Chancellery and city beyond through a
metal veil of automatic louvres. The
organic forms of the architecture have
been developed to appear to rise
almost naturally out of the landscape
itself and to embody the values and
aspirations of the University.

1 The rising structure
of the Chancellery
gives form to Edith
Cowan University's
desire to embrace the
place and landscape
of Joondalup, and
present an iconic and
contemporary identity
to the community.
2 Central to the design
is the notion of
buildings drawn from
the landscape framing
a new collegiate space
which can be seen,
and function, as the
heart of the campus.
3 The jarrah screen
uses paired laminated
beams from managed
timber sources
connected to universal
beam columns, which
in turn connect to
universal beam
outriggers in the floor
and roof planes.

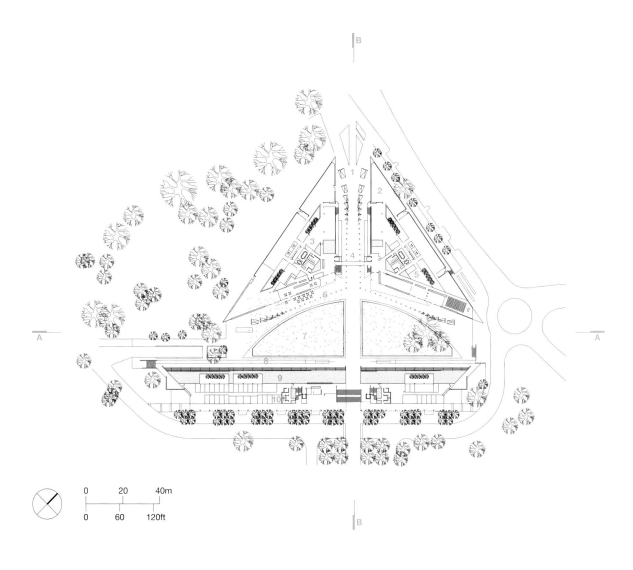

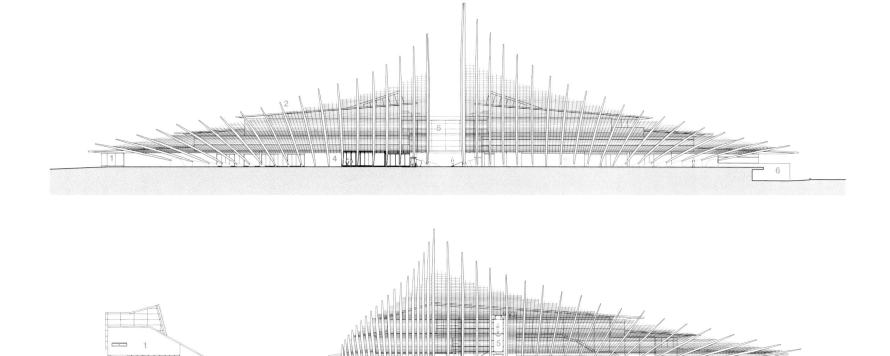

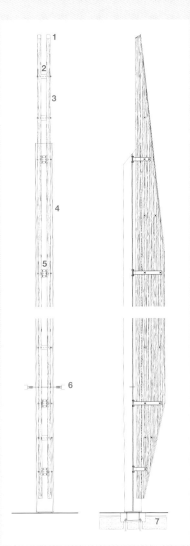

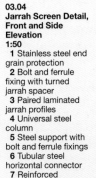

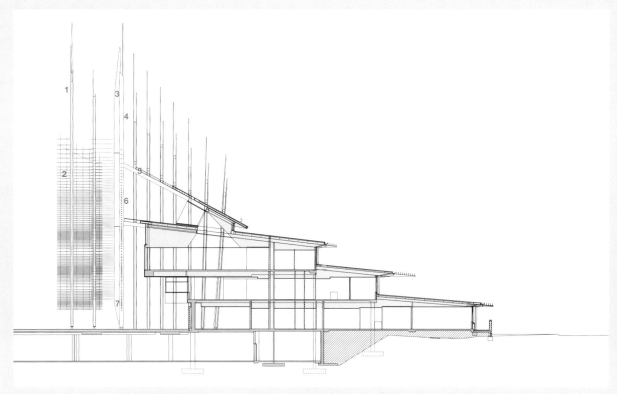

03.05
Jarrah Screen Detail Section
1:500
 1 Composite steel and timber spar
 2 Recycled jarrah batten screen
 3 Paired laminated jarrah profiles
 4 Universal steel column
 5 Steel outrigger connection to primary

structure
 6 Recycled jarrah batten screen
 7 Paired laminated jarrah profiles

03.04
Jarrah Screen Detail, Front and Side Elevation
1:50
 1 Stainless steel end grain protection
 2 Bolt and ferrule fixing with turned jarrah spacer
 3 Paired laminated jarrah profiles
 4 Universal steel column
 5 Steel support with bolt and ferrule fixings
 6 Tubular steel horizontal connector
 7 Reinforced concrete footing

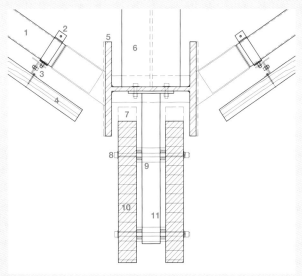

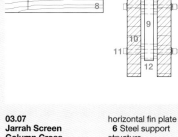

03.06
Jarrah Screen Column Cross Section Detail 1
1:20
 1 Structural steel horizontal connector
 2 Strap connector
 3 Vertical batten frame
 4 50 x 75 mm (2 x 3 inch) recycled jarrah batten

 5 Steel support structure
 6 Steel outrigger
 7 Profile of laminate jarrah at higher part of colonnade, shown dotted
 8 Galvanized mild steel fixings
 9 Washer / packer
 10 Laminated jarrah profile
 11 100 x 50 mm (4 x 2 inch) rectangular

hollow section steel galvanized mild steel timber support stub

03.07
Jarrah Screen Column Cross Section Detail 2
1:20
 1 Structural steel outrigger
 2 Strap connector
 3 Structural steel horizontal connector
 4 Vertical batten frame
 5 Structural steel

horizontal fin plate
 6 Steel support structure
 7 Laminated jarrah above top outrigger
 8 50 x 75 mm (2 x 3 inch) recycled jarrah batten
 9 100 x 50 mm (4 x 2 inch) rectangular hollow section steel galvanized mild steel timber support stub
 10 Laminated jarrah

 11 75 mm (3 inch) diameter turned jarrah spacer to intermediate fixings between stubs supports
 12 Capped end to rectangular hollow section timber support stub ground to a smooth finish

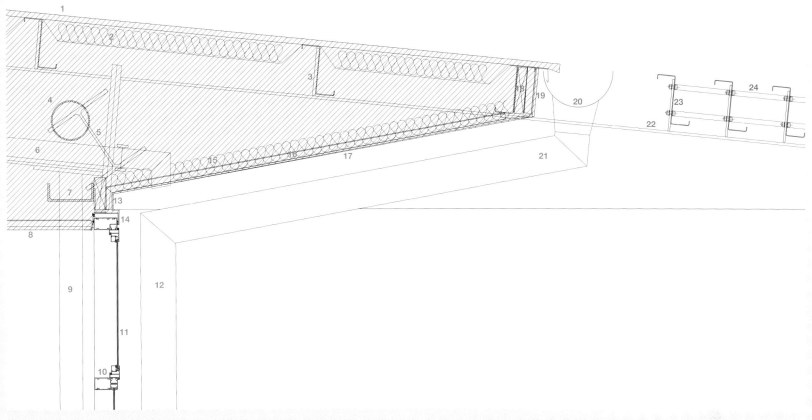

03.08
Detail Eaves Section
1:20
 1 Pre-finished metal
sheet roofing
 2 Insulation
 3 Steel Z-purlins
 4 Steel circular
hollow section roof
bracing
 5 Structural steel
outrigger beyond
 6 80 mm (3¹/8 inch)
diameter PVC

drainage pipe
 7 Structural steel
window head support
 8 Plasterboard ceiling
lining
 9 Circular hollow
section column
 10 100 mm (4 inch)
flush glazed aluminium
window system
 11 High level operable
window sash
 12 150 mm (6 inch)
diameter down pipe

13 Fibre cement soffit
14 Aluminium trim
15 Insulation
16 Vapour barrier
17 Fibre cement soffit
lining
18 Fascia support
19 Compressed fibre
cement sheeting
20 300 mm (11⁴/5 inch)
gutter
21 150 mm (6 inch)
diameter down pipe
22 Cantilevered

structural steel cut to
profile
23 Cold-formed
Z-purlins with
automotive paint finish
24 Steel purlin spacers
with automotive paint
finish

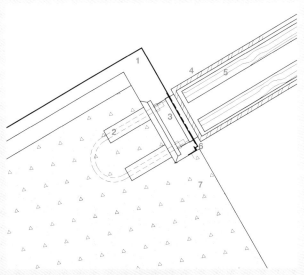

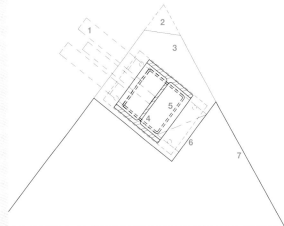

03.09
Typical Jarrah Screen
Column Plinth
Baseplate Section
Detail
1:20
 1 3 mm (¹/10 inch)
plate stainless steel
concealed fixed cover
plate / capping
 2 Masonry anchors
to pre-cast plinths
 3 25 x 25 x 3 mm
(1 x 1 x ¹/10 inch)

galvanized mild steel
angle collar all round
square hollow section
 4 Steel support
structure
 5 Laminated jarrah
 6 Square hollow
section
 7 Pre-cast concrete
plinth

03.10
Typical Colonnade
Column Plinth
Baseplate Plan Detail
1:20
 1 Laminated jarrah
above
 2 Removable 3 mm
(¹/10 inch) plate
stainless steel cover
plate / capping
 3 Pre-cast concrete
plinth
 4 Fixed 3 mm (¹/10

inch) plate stainless
steel cover plate
 5 Square hollow
section
 6 150 mm (6 inch)
deep rebate in plinth
for base plate
 7 Return, removable
3 mm (¹/10 inch) plate
stainless steel cover
plate / capping

**Médiathèque René Goscinny
Sainte-Luce-sur-Loire, France**

Client
Ville de Sainte-Luce-sur-Loire

Project Team
Jean-Louis Garcia, Xavier
Bouanchaud

Structural Engineer
E2C Atlantique

Landscape Architect
Jacques Lebris Paysagiste

This urban building – a new library and youth centre – is composed with respect for existing civic buildings and green spaces on the site. The design, rather than being composed of a single building, presents two distinct buildings. The functions of each are sufficiently different as to not require a common entrance. The youth service is placed around a patio to the north, and the library stretches along the length of the garden to the south. The building takes its shape from trees that have been kept on the site – at its heart is a pine tree, around which a curved patio is developed, acting as the joint of the building. On the ground floor this separates the public spaces from the work spaces and, on the first floor, the adults' library from the children's library. In addition, two imposing trees at the southern end guide the flow between the ground floor (toy library and function room) and the first floor (library). The layout was dictated by a wish to clarify how the space should be 'read' and used. The user intuitively discovers the space which fits his or her expectations.

Access is via the square through a covered walkway. The glass entrance hall overlooks the garden and also opens onto a patio. From the entrance hall, the public can directly access the library via a large centrally placed staircase. Particular attention has been paid to the management of movement. Access to the technical areas is at the rear of the buildings, so as not to interfere with the different flows. All the public spaces are found on the first floor of the building on one level. A protruding pod, clad in wood, forms the quiet alcove which is used for children's story time. This striking element stimulates the children's imagination and livens up the garden facade, giving the eye a focal point.

1 The concrete southern facade of the library is very closed in order to protect readers and books from the sun. Narrow windows offer views onto the green roof of the ground floor building.
2 The children's reading and story space is elevated over the garden on a forest of brightly coloured steel columns, giving it a distinctly different character to the more subdued library building.
3 View of the interior of the children's story space.
4 In the library, a wall of windows provides both natural light and views over the garden. The timber ceiling lends a warmth to the space.

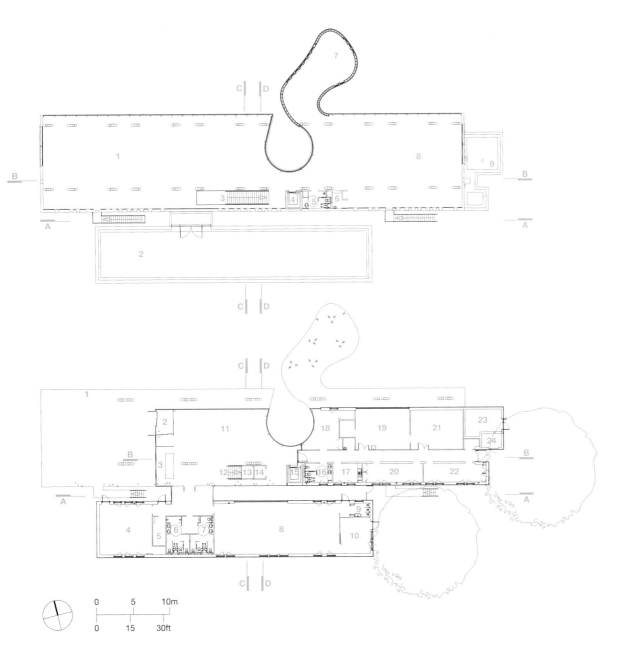

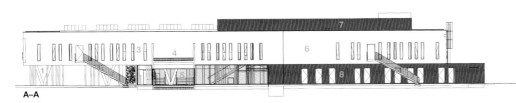

A–A

C–C

B–B

D–D

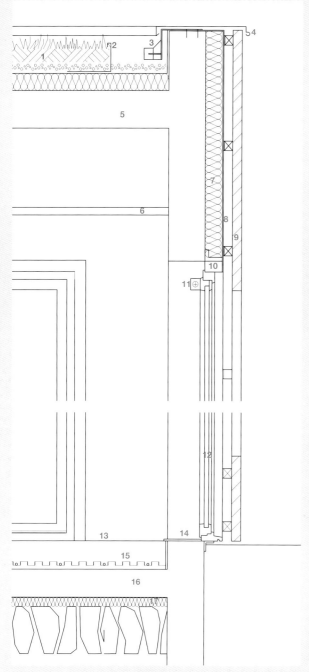

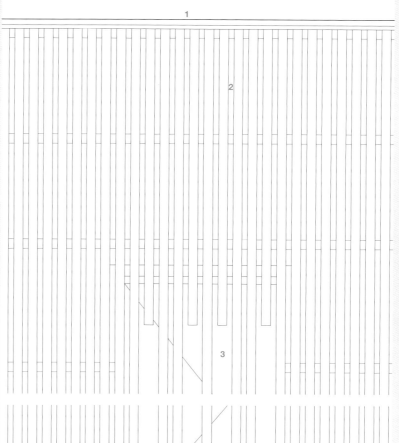

04.08
Timber Facade Screen Elevation Detail
1:20
1 Folded zinc parapet cover and drip profile
2 Untreated Douglas pine cladding on timber framework
3 Double glazing door unit
4 Timber screen support framework

04.09
Timber Facade Screen and Door Plan Detail
1:20
1 Untreated Douglas pine cladding on timber framework
2 Timber screen support framework
3 Insulation
4 Roller blind sun protection system side armature
5 Double glazing door unit
6 Timber door threshold and cover strip to heating trench
7 Stainless steel grille over heating trench

04.07
South Facade Typical Wall Section Detail
1:20
1 Vegetation to roof
2 Zinc angle separating vegetation and gravel drainage bed
3 Fall prevention system
4 Folded zinc parapet cover and drip profile
5 Reinforced concrete roof structure
6 Suspended painted plasterboard ceiling
7 Insulation
8 Waterproof membrane
9 Untreated Douglas pine cladding on timber framework
10 Timber door head
11 Roller blind sun protection system
12 Double glazing unit
13 Stainless steel grille
over heating trench
14 Timber door threshold and cover strip to heating trench
15 Underfloor heating
16 Reinforced concrete floor slab
17 Rigid insulation

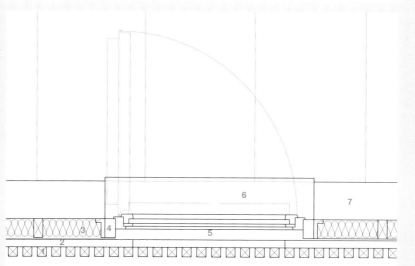

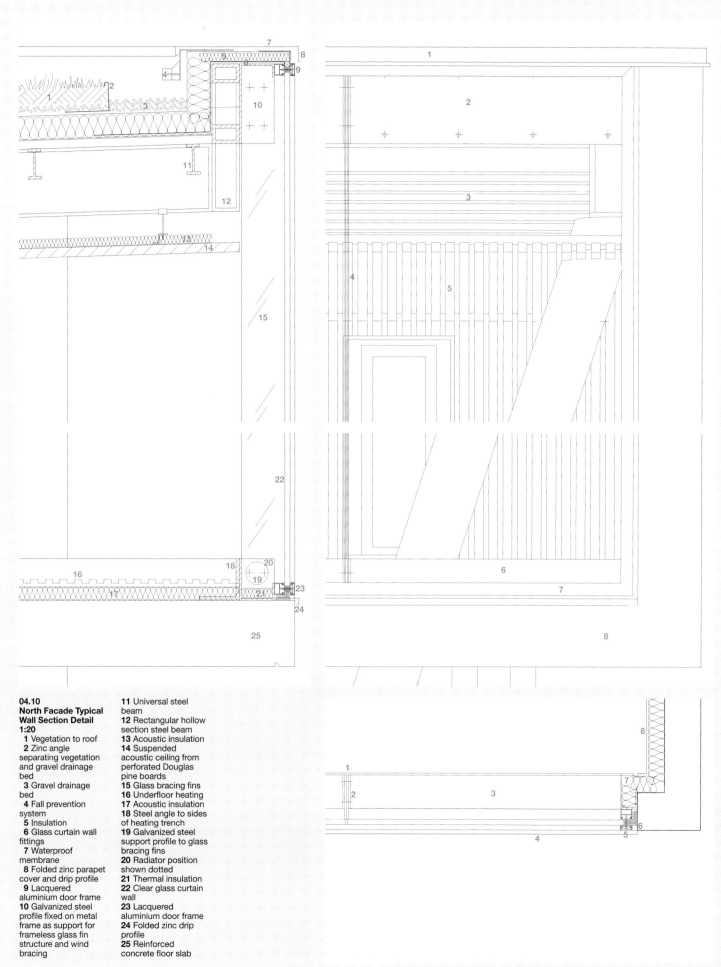

04.11
Timber Facade Screen Elevation Detail 2
1:20
1 Folded zinc parapet cover and drip profile
2 Galvanized steel profile fixed on metal frame as support for frameless glass fin structure and wind bracing
3 Metal louvred screen
4 Glass bracing fins
5 Suspended acoustic ceiling from perforated Douglas pine boards
6 Radiator position
7 Lacquered aluminium window frame
8 Reinforced concrete floor slab

04.12
Timber Facade Screen Plan Detail
1:20
1 Glass bracing fins
2 Galvanized steel support profile to glass bracing fins
3 Line of galvanized steel support profile to glass bracing fins
4 Folded zinc drip profile
5 Lacquered aluminium window frame
6 Stained concrete floor
7 Thermal insulation
8 Painted plasterboard interior wall

04.10
North Facade Typical Wall Section Detail
1:20
1 Vegetation to roof
2 Zinc angle separating vegetation and gravel drainage bed
3 Gravel drainage bed
4 Fall prevention system
5 Insulation
6 Glass curtain wall fittings
7 Waterproof membrane
8 Folded zinc parapet cover and drip profile
9 Lacquered aluminium door frame
10 Galvanized steel profile fixed on metal frame as support for frameless glass fin structure and wind bracing

11 Universal steel beam
12 Rectangular hollow section steel beam
13 Acoustic insulation
14 Suspended acoustic ceiling from perforated Douglas pine boards
15 Glass bracing fins
16 Underfloor heating
17 Acoustic insulation
18 Steel angle to sides of heating trench
19 Galvanized steel support profile to glass bracing fins
20 Radiator position shown dotted
21 Thermal insulation
22 Clear glass curtain wall
23 Lacquered aluminium door frame
24 Folded zinc drip profile
25 Reinforced concrete floor slab

**Culloden Battlefield Visitor Centre
Inverness, Scotland, UK**

Client
The National Trust for Scotland

Project Team
Gareth Hoskins, Thomas Bernatzky,
Nick Domminney, Thomas Hamilton,
Kathy Li, David Lindsey

Structural Engineer
David Narro Associates

Services Engineer
Max Fordham

Gareth Hoskins Architects won a
competition in 2004 to design the
National Trust for Scotland's new
Visitor Centre for Culloden Battlefield,
the site of the last battle to be
fought on mainland Britain which has
the status of a war grave and burial
ground for over 1,200 people. The
new building is three times the size of
the existing facilities it replaces and
is designed for up to 250,000 visitors
a year, housing an interpretation of
the battle along with educational and
conference facilities, a cafe and
restaurant, gift shop and staff
accommodation.

Whilst the existing visitor centre was
built on archaeologically sensitive
ground, the new centre is moved away
from the battlefield lines, ensuring that
the new building would not disturb
graves or artifacts. The new building
is anchored between an existing field
wall and a new gently rising berm,
screening visitor traffic from the
battlefield and delivering visitors onto
a planted roof terrace for a unique
view of the site. The building and
berm act as a portal to the site,
allowing visitors the choice of a stay
under the scalloped roofs of the
restaurant before or after an
interpretive journey through the
exhibition with views out to the
landscape at key points culminating
on the roof terrace. The building is
constructed using a steel frame
with concrete floor slab and highly
insulated timber walls and roofs.
External walls are mainly clad with
untreated Scottish larch from a nearby
estate; other areas are clad with local
Caithness Stone and field stones
salvaged from the site. Internal timber
linings are from untreated Scottish
larch with all other joinery made from
oiled British oak.

1 Four curved roof
elements are
orientated to bring
natural light into the
public spaces
including the education
suite (left) and the
restaurant (right).
2 View from the
battlefield. The long
larch-clad ramp and
bridge allow access to
the roof terrace on top
of the visitor centre.
3 View of the timber
brise soleil to the south
facing window of the
exhibition space.
4 The Caithness Stone
memorial wall offers a
visual interpretation of
the historic site and
forms the northern
facade of the building.

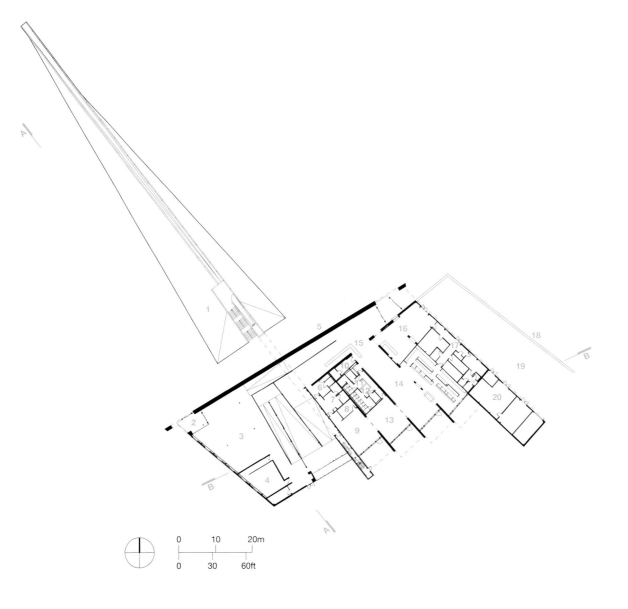

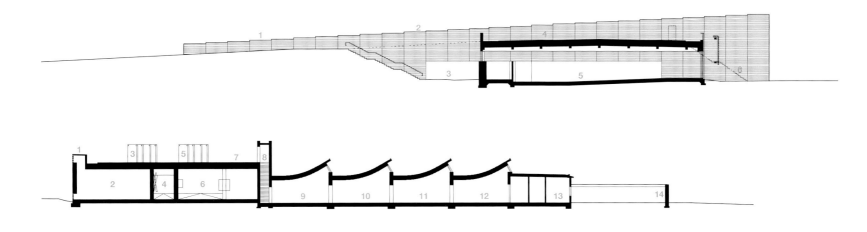

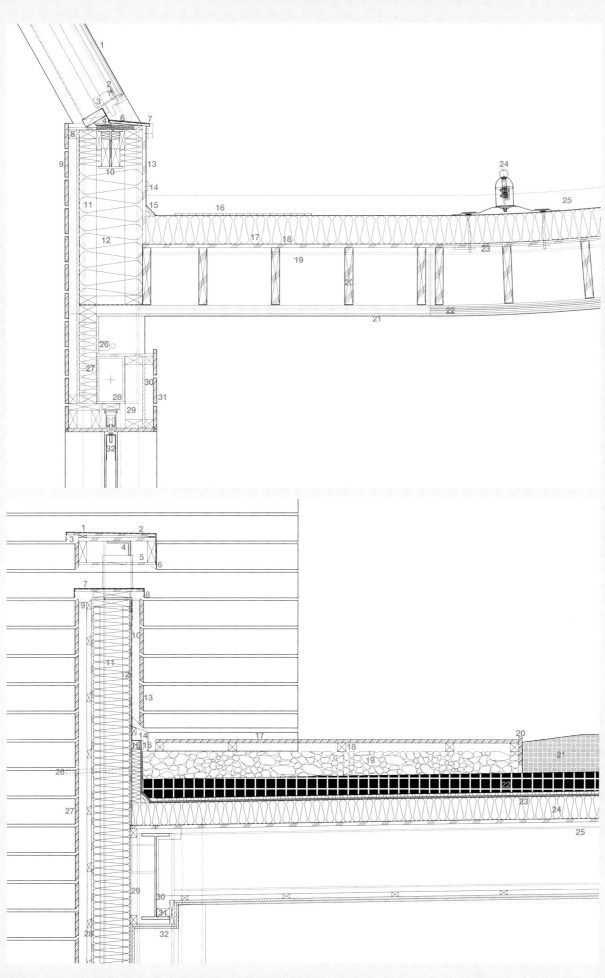

05.04
Skylight, Roof and Sliding Door Detail
1:20
1 Clerestory window
2 Steel plate stiffener with single point actuator
3 Micro XL window actuator
4 Tilting fillet to base of clerestory window
5 Soft wood packer at intervals
6 12 mm (1/2 inch) roof grade oriented strand board under geotextile underlay
7 Bent pressed mill finished flashing secured with clips
8 45 x 45 mm (13/4 inch) soft wood batten
9 135 x 19 mm (51/3 x 3/4 inch) square edged fire treated internal timber board cladding
10 Steel universal beam
11 Location of steelwork beyond
12 Mineral wool insulation to fully fill cavity
13 12 mm (1/2 inch) roof grade oriented strand board
14 Peel stop to roof membrane
15 50 x 50 mm (2 x 2 inch) soft wood angle fillet
16 750 mm (291/2 inch) wide Icopal roof walkway
17 Mineral wool insulation
18 Vapour control barrier to be continuous around external envelope
19 Location of steelwork beyond shown dotted
20 356 x 45 mm (14 x 13/4 inch) timber strand joists at 400 mm (153/4 inch) centres
21 Painted plasterboard ceiling
22 Five layers of 50 x 9 mm (2 x 1/3 inch) strips of plywood over curved sections
23 Two layers of 9 mm (1/3 inch) roof grade oriented strand board over curved sections
24 Fall arrest system

25 Proprietary profile strip to match membrane colour, adhesive fixed to top surface
26 Fluorescent batten fitting
27 100 mm (4 inch) mineral wool insulation to give acoustic separation
28 Steel rectangular hollow section
29 95 x 45 mm (33/4 x 13/4 inch) soft wood framing including studs at 600 mm (232/3 inch) centres
30 45 x 45 mm (13/4 inch) soft wood battens at 600 mm (232/3 inch) centres
31 135 x 19 mm (51/3 x 3/4 inch) square edged fire treated internal timber board cladding
32 Soft wood framed sliding door from interior grade plywood with hard wood lipping to all edges

05.05
Parapet and Roof Detail
1:20
1 12 mm (1/2 inch) roof grade oriented strand board
2 Bent pressed mill finished flashing secured with clips
3 Soft wood tilting fillet to form fall
4 Steel angle
5 Proprietary 100 mm (4 inch) circular plastic vent grille at 1,200 mm (471/4 inch) centres
6 Bent pressed mill finished flashing
7 12 mm (1/2 inch) roof grade oriented strand board
8 Bent pressed mill finished flashing
9 Bird mesh from 15 mm (3/5 inch) maximum mesh size
10 45 x 45 mm (13/4 x 13/4 inch) soft wood battens at 600 mm (232/3 inch) centres
11 Insulation
12 Breather membrane
13 147 x 19 mm (53/4 x 3/4 inch) open boarded rain screen cladding from Scottish larch
14 Peel stop to roof

membrane
15 45×45 mm ($1\frac{3}{4} \times 1\frac{3}{4}$ inch) soft wood batten
16 Peel stop to roof membrane
17 95×19 mm ($3\frac{3}{4} \times \frac{3}{4}$ inch) grip profiled timber boards with 10 mm ($\frac{2}{5}$ inch) gaps screwed to battens in oversized holes with self-tapping screws and washers
18 45×45 mm ($1\frac{3}{4}$ inch) soft wood battens at 600 mm ($23\frac{2}{3}$ inch) centres
19 20–40 mm ($\frac{3}{4}$–$1\frac{3}{5}$ inch) diameter washed gravel with minimum depth of 50 mm (2 inches)
20 200×38 mm ($7\frac{9}{10} \times 1\frac{1}{2}$ inch) retaining board
21 200 mm ($7\frac{9}{10}$ inch) intensive green roof soil mix
22 100 mm (4 inch) water reservoir layer
23 Roofing membrane and roof bar lapped up and secured to soft wood framing with peel stop bars
24 Insulation
25 12 mm ($\frac{1}{2}$ inch) roof grade oriented strand board
26 Overflow pipes (shown dotted) at regular intervals
27 147×19 mm ($5\frac{4}{5} \times \frac{3}{4}$ inch) open-boarded rain screen cladding from Scottish larch
28 45×45 mm ($1\frac{3}{4} \times 1\frac{3}{4}$ inch) fire-treated softwood battens and 45×25 mm ($1\frac{3}{4} \times 1$ inch) fire-treated and profiled counter battens
29 Vapour control barrier continuous around external envelope
30 Universal steel beam
31 Soft wood packer
32 Two layers of 12.5 mm ($\frac{1}{2}$ inch) thick plasterboard to achieve one hour fire rating

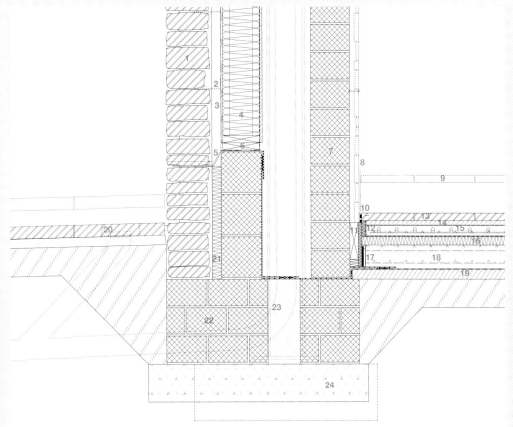

05.06
Wall Base Detail
1:20
1 250 mm ($9\frac{4}{5}$ inch) deep flat bonded Caithness Stone at random courses
2 Mechanical fixing to structure
3 50 mm (2 inch) ventilated void
4 200 mm ($7\frac{9}{10}$ inch) Timber I-beam stud wall with oriented strand board sheathing fully filled with mineral wool insulation
5 Damp proof course
6 200×38 mm ($7\frac{9}{10} \times 1\frac{1}{2}$ inch) sole plate
7 215 mm ($8\frac{1}{2}$ inch) thick brickwork
8 Caithness tiles fixed to blockwork with suitable adhesive
9 Floor finish at top of ramp shown dotted
10 Neatly gunned continuous mastic seal
11 195×45 mm ($7\frac{2}{3} \times 1\frac{3}{4}$ inch) timber fixed to front of blockwork wall 50 mm (2 inches) below finished floor level along length of ramp
12 25 mm (1 inch) thick high performance insulation
13 40 mm ($1\frac{3}{4}$ inch) Caithness Stone slabs
14 25 mm (1 inch) thick bedding to Caithness Stone slabs on separating layer of recycled polythene
15 65 mm ($2\frac{1}{2}$ inch) thick calcium-sulphate underfloor heating screed
16 50 mm (2 inch) thick rigid floor insulation of extruded polystyrene tongue and groove boards
17 Compressible isolation joint
18 125 mm (5 inch) thick reinforced concrete slab
19 Recycled polythene damp proof membrane secured with butyl adhesive tape
20 Rainwater pipe access pipe with cover to allow rodding of rain water pipe
21 50 mm (2 inch) thick high performance insulation
22 Blockwork
23 Rainwater pipe shown dotted set in grout to blockwork cavity
24 Concrete pad foundations to steelwork

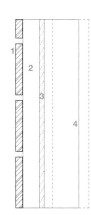

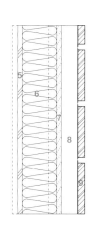

05.07
Caithness Stone Tile Detail
1:10
1 250 mm ($9\frac{4}{5}$ inch) flat bonded Caithness Stone outer face. Stone wall built up in portions approximately 300 mm ($11\frac{4}{5}$ inch) high against 50 mm (2 inch) thick polyfoam which is removed as the wall is built up to form the cavity
2 50 mm (2 inch) thick ventilated cavity
3 Breather membrane
4 9 mm ($\frac{1}{3}$ inch) thick external grade oriented strand board
5 200 mm ($7\frac{9}{10}$ inch) thick mineral wool insulation to fully fill cavity
6 Wall ties to fix stone back to timber stud wall
7 Vapour control layer continuous around external envelope
8 12.5 mm ($\frac{1}{2}$ inch) thick plasterboard
9 Steelwork beyond shown dotted
10 Wall ties to fix brickwork back to timber stud wall
11 215 mm ($8\frac{1}{2}$ inch) thick brickwork
12 Caithness tiles fixed to brickwork with suitable adhesive
13 12–25 mm ($\frac{1}{2}$–1 inch) thick Caithness tiles of varying width and finish at random lengths

05.08
Double Sided Timber Partition Detail
1:10
1 Stainless steel screw fixed 145×19 mm ($5\frac{7}{10} \times 3/4$ inch) fire treated timber boarding
2 45×45 mm ($1\frac{3}{4}$ inch) soft wood battens at 600 mm ($23\frac{2}{3}$ inch) centres
3 12.5 mm ($\frac{1}{2}$ inch) thick plasterboard
4 95×45 mm ($3\frac{3}{4} \times 1\frac{3}{4}$ inch) soft wood framing with studs at 600 mm ($23\frac{2}{3}$ inch) centres
5 12 mm ($\frac{1}{2}$ inch) proprietary oriented strand board sheathing
6 100 mm (4 inch) mineral wool insulation to give acoustic separation
7 12.5 mm ($\frac{1}{2}$ inch) plasterboard
8 45×45 mm ($1\frac{3}{4}$ inch) soft wood battens at 600 mm ($23\frac{2}{3}$ inch) centres
9 Stainless steel screw fixed 145×19 mm ($5\frac{7}{10} \times 3/4$ inch) fire treated timber boarding

Cultural, Sports and Congress Centre
Les Deux Alpes, Isère, France

Client
Mont-de-Lans Municipality

Associate Architects
François Deslaugiers

Structural Engineer
Batiserf

There was no ambiguity about the client's requirements for this project. It had to be 'traditional' in nature, bearing in mind that what is designed to be traditional Alpine architecture today is, in fact, a kitsch mixture of a wide variety of regional styles. The architects hesitated before accepting the commission, but eventually decided to embrace the challenge. Like many winter ski resorts built in the 1960s, Les Deux Alpes includes buildings with no design rationale that have chaotic relationships with the landscape. This mountain area is now looking for a new image to counter the expressions of a sometimes excessive modernity. As a result this new cultural centre is an experiment in divergence from the archetypal language of the chalet.

Due to regulatory requirements, the building is contained within a basic rectangular structure with dual-section roofs, akin to a barn. It has a telescopic structure split into three nested sections – the sports hall, the hall and communal spaces, and the theatre. The walls and roof are faced entirely with timber, an important cultural reference in these mountains. The whole of the sports hall is covered with timber lacework based on a motif sourced from an old chalet. The pattern, enlarged and multiplied to form a regular grid, changes its status and becomes a repetitive, abstract composition. The wall of the performance hall is faced with narrow, unjointed timber strips, with their edges cut at an angle to prevent water accumulating. Inside the sports hall and the communal spaces, the walls and ceilings are faced with boards, some in natural timber and others painted in bold colours.

1 The timber motif came into use in traditional regional architecture with the invention of the band saw and is becoming more popular today due to the development of automatic cutting systems and computer-controlled cutting. Reflecting the return of this technique, the sports hall is covered with a timber lacework motif.
2 The roof over the gable end to the sports hall is separated from the facade by a strip of glazing, adding a decidedly contemporary touch to the traditional chalet form.
3 View of the main entrance, which is located in the centre of the long facade, with the sports hall roof rising above the lattice work to the right.
4 One long wall of the sports hall is lined in timber boards, some painted in bold colours to create a striking sculptural quality to the space.

06.01
Ground Floor Plan
1:500

1 Performance and
conference hall
stage
2 Performance and
conference hall
seating
3 Reception hall
4 Public WC
5 Public WC
6 Storage and
maintenance area
7 Technical facilities
8 Referee changing
room 1
9 Referee changing
room 2
10 Coatroom
11 Team / shared
changing room
12 Team / shared
changing room
13 Team / shared
changing room
14 Team / shared
changing room
15 Female WC
16 Male WC
17 Hall
18 Office
19 Bin store
20 Kitchenette
21 Maintenance store
22 Storage
23 Heating plant
24 Sports hall

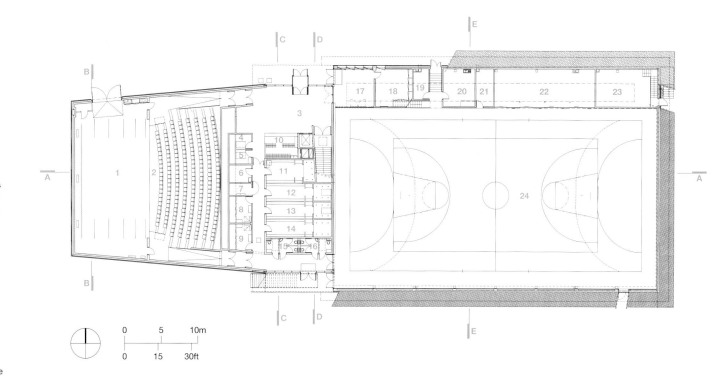

06.02
Section A–A
1:500

1 Performance and
conference hall
stage
2 Performance and
conference hall
seating
3 Reception hall
4 Foyer
5 Projection room
6 Sports hall

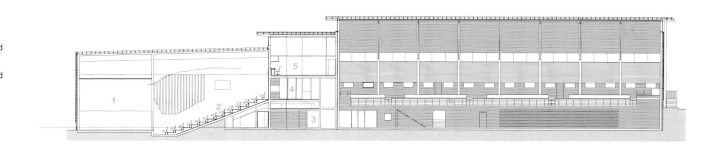

06.03
Section B–B
1:500

1 Performance and
conference hall

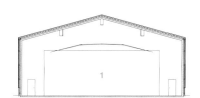

06.05
Section C–C
1:500

1 Changing and
cloakrooms
2 Reception hall
3 Entrance hall
4 Projection room

06.04
Section D–D
1:500

1 Changing and
cloakrooms
2 Reception hall
3 Entrance hall
4 Lobby to director's
office and
projection room

06.06
Section E–E
1:500

1 Sports hall

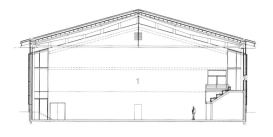

31

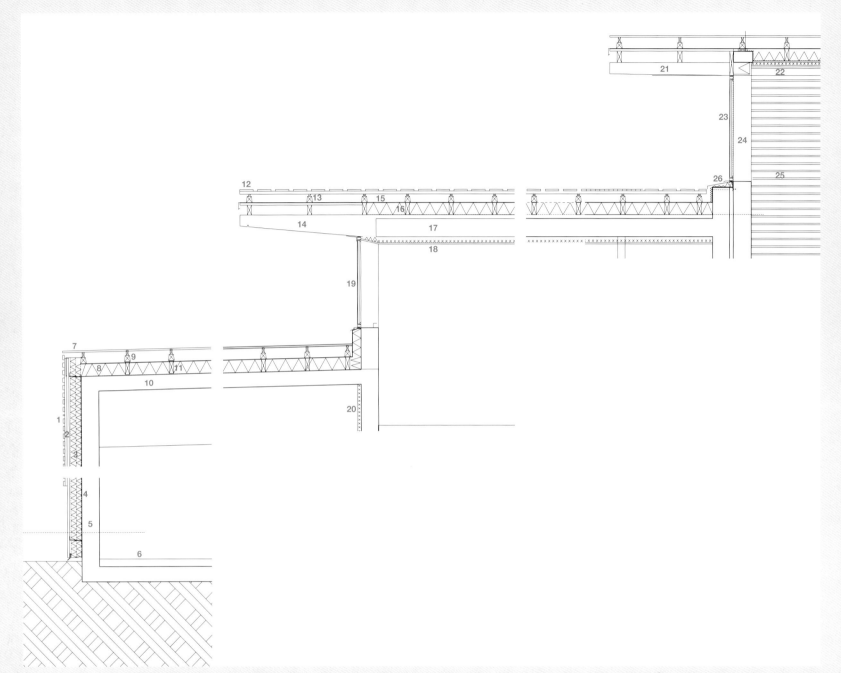

06.07
Detail Wall Section
1:50

1 Larch panels attached to steel wall panels with galvanized steel cleats
2 Ventilated cavity
3 Two layers of 75 mm (3 inch) thick insulation
4 Vapour barrier
5 Reinforced concrete column
6 Suspended timber floor over concrete slab
7 175 mm (6⁴/5 inch) larch roof panels fixed to eaves board

8 Sealing layer over thermal insulation
9 Continuous galvanized steel cleats fixed to timber battens
10 Vapour barrier over concrete beam
11 Timber joists
12 185 mm (7¹/4 inch) larch roof panels fixed to eaves board with galvanized steel cleats
13 Galvanized steel cleats fixed to timber battens
14 Tapered timber rafter
15 Sealing layer
16 Vapour barrier and compression layer

over thermal insulation
17 Absorbent phonic baffles placed between perforated concrete beams
18 False timber ceiling
19 Fixed double glazed window in timber frame
20 Absorbent phonic mural fabric over acoustic baffles
21 Laminated timber beam
22 False timber ceiling over absorbent material
23 Fixed double glazed window in timber frame

24 240 x 240 mm (9¹/2 x 9¹/2 inch) concrete pillar
25 Larch strips wall cladding
26 Larch cover strip

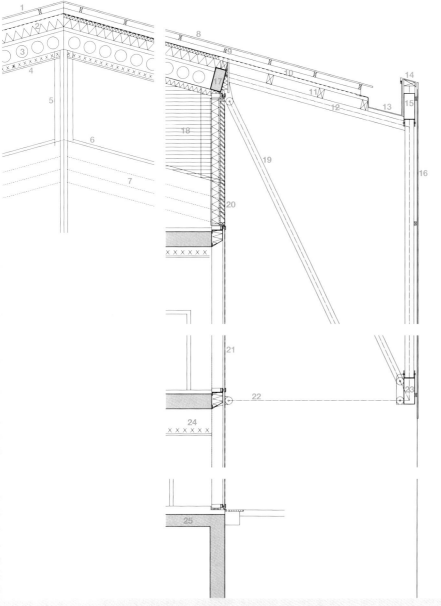

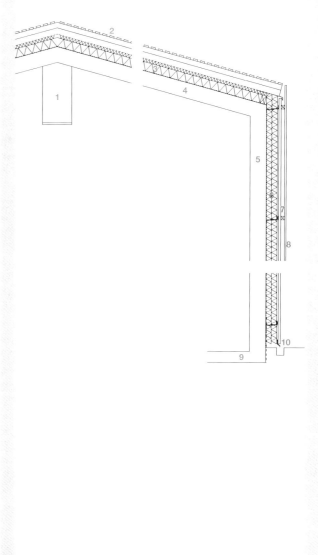

06.08
Detail Roof Section 1
1:50
1 185 mm (7¼ inch)
larch roof panels fixed
to eaves board with
galvanized steel cleats
2 Vapour barrier and
compression layer
over thermal insulation
3 Perforated steel
beam
4 False timber ceiling
over absorbent
material
5 Central glazing bar
6 Timber window
frame
7 Upper part of
climbing wall

8 185 mm (7¼ inch)
larch roof panels fixed
to eaves board with
galvanized steel cleats
9 Galvanized steel
cleats fixed to timber
battens
10 Sealing layer over
thermal insulation
11 80 x 120 mm (3⅛ x
4¾ inch) timber joists
12 Double articulated
timber rafters
13 Zinc gutter lining on
45 mm (1¾ inch) thick
timber support panels
14 Zinc cover to
upstand
15 Steel RHS beam
16 Timber screen

panels to exterior wall
17 Steel RHS
18 Larch strips wall
cladding
19 Steel strut
20 Angled larch strips
over insulated wall
panels
21 Glass curtain wall
22 Steel strut
23 Steel RHS
24 False timber ceiling
over absorbent phonic
material
25 Reinforced
concrete floor slab

06.09
Detail Roof Section 2
1:50
1 Concrete beam
2 185 mm (7¼ inch)
larch roof panels fixed
to eaves board with
galvanized steel cleats
3 Vapour barrier and
compression layer
over thermal insulation
4 Concrete beam
5 240 mm (9½ inch)
concrete column
6 Two layers of 75
mm (3 inch) insulation
with vapour barrier
7 Steel panel over
ventilated cavity
8 60 x 20 mm (2⅓ x

¾ inch) timber panels
attached to steel
panels with cleats
9 Reinforced
concrete floor slab
10 Zinc flashing over
drain

Crawley Down Primary School
Crawley, West Sussex, England, UK

Client
West Sussex County Council

Project Team
Leeza Aldis, Lee Johnson

Structural Engineer
Scott Wilson

Services Engineer
White Young Green

Quantity Surveyor
Grant Associates

This project involved a £1.8 million new extension complete with major internal alteration works and refurbishment to the existing Junior School, including the complete demolition of the original 1960s infant school. The new scheme not only provides modern and flexible facilities for staff, pupils and parents, but is also available to the local community, who can hire the hall after hours for events. The design worked towards creating a focal point for the village community, as well as being a place for children to grow in an environment without boundaries.

Each classroom has been designed for the pupils; nursery classes have no internal or external barriers, windows are placed at toddler height as well as adult height and strong colours are used on the walls. By Year Six, room heights are taller with higher ceilings and neutral colours, giving the classrooms a more 'grown-up' feel. The varied roof heights and ceiling pitches represent the 'growing-up' journey and give it a sense of gradual flow through the years. Externally, the timber-lined entrance canopy is a strong focal point and acts as a marker for the school. Circular cut-outs improve natural daylight and help to bond external and internal spaces. The extension has been successfully moulded to the old building and, once inside, it is difficult to distinguish between the old and the new.

1 A timber-lined canopy with angled timber prop supports gives the school a dramatic new entrance.
2 The entrance is flanked by staff offices on the left and the community room on the right, which is used by the community out of school hours.
3 The entrance canopy features both downlights and large circular skylights to bring natural light into the entrance area.

07.01
Ground Floor Plan
1:500

1 Class base room
2 Lobby
3 Boys WC
4 Girls WC
5 Reception
6 Reception
7 Library
8 Community room store
9 Community room disabled WC
10 Community room
11 Community room WC
12 Community room kitchen
13 School reception
14 Main entrance lobby
15 Entrance canopy
16 Head teacher's office
17 Office
18 Disabled WC
19 Staff room
20 Plant room
21 Class base room
22 Class base room
23 Class base room
24 Group room
25 Cloakroom and lockers
26 Boys WC
27 Girls WC
28 Cloakroom and lockers
29 Lockers
30 External courtyard
31 Class base room
32 Class base room
33 Utility room
34 Caretaker
35 Boys WC
36 Stock room
37 Main hall
38 Class base room
39 Class base room
40 Group room
41 Class base room
42 Computer room
43 Girls WC
44 Cloakroom and lockers
45 Staff WC
46 Hall store
47 Meeting and group room
48 Deputy head teacher
49 Staff room

```
0        5        10m
0        15       30ft
```

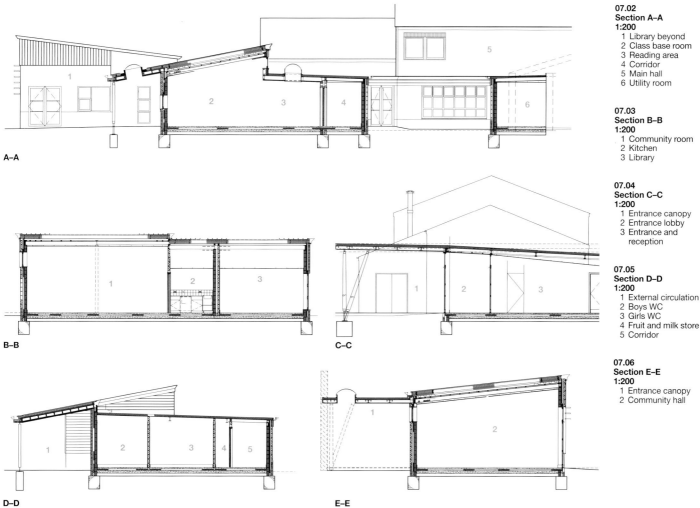

A–A

07.02
Section A–A
1:200
1 Library beyond
2 Class base room
3 Reading area
4 Corridor
5 Main hall
6 Utility room

B–B

07.03
Section B–B
1:200
1 Community room
2 Kitchen
3 Library

C–C

07.04
Section C–C
1:200
1 Entrance canopy
2 Entrance lobby
3 Entrance and reception

07.05
Section D–D
1:200
1 External circulation
2 Boys WC
3 Girls WC
4 Fruit and milk store
5 Corridor

D–D

E–E

07.06
Section E–E
1:200
1 Entrance canopy
2 Community hall

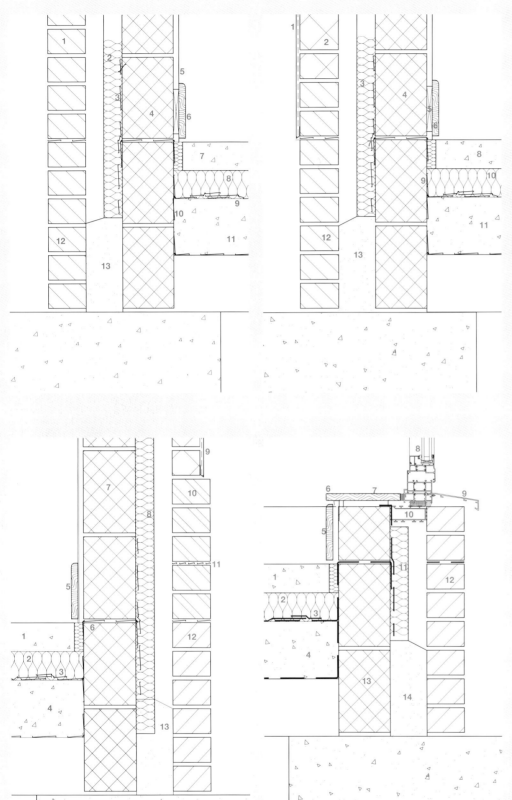

07.07
External Wall and Floor Slab Detail 1
1:10
 1 102.5 mm (4 inch) thick clay facing brickwork above damp proof course
 2 50 mm (2 inch) thick expanded polystyrene insulation boards
 3 Fully bonded bitumen damp proof membrane dressed up cavity side of blockwork and lapping damp proof course
 4 140 mm (5½ inch) thick medium density block work inner leaf
 5 Multicoat proprietary plaster to internal face of blockwork
 6 Painted timber skirting board on treated softwood timber packer
 7 75 mm (3 inch) sand and cement floating screed
 8 75 mm (3 inch) floorboard insulation
 9 Loose laid polythene damp proof membrane lapped and taped
 10 Flexible damp proof course
 11 150 mm (6 inch) thick ground bearing reinforced concrete slab on slip membrane
 12 102.5 mm (4 inch) thick clay facing brickwork below damp proof course
 13 Lean mix fill to cavity

07.08
External Wall and Floor Slab Detail 2
1:10
 1 Proprietary through colour external render system
 2 100 mm (4 inch) thick blockwork external leaf
 3 50 mm (2 inch) thick expanded polystyrene insulation boards
 4 140 mm (5½ inch) thick medium density blockwork inner leaf
 5 15 mm (3/5 inch) thick treated softwood timber packer
 6 Painted timber skirting board
 7 Fully bonded bitumen damp proof membrane dressed up cavity side of blockwork and lapping damp proof course
 8 75 mm (3 inch) sand and cement floating screed
 9 Flexible damp proof course
 10 75 mm (3 inch) floorboard insulation

11 150 mm (6 inch) thick ground bearing reinforced concrete slab on slip membrane
 12 102.5 mm (4 inch) thick clay facing brickwork below damp proof course
 13 Lean mix fill to cavity

07.09
External Wall and Floor Slab Detail 3
1:10
 1 75 mm (3 inch) sand and cement floating screed
 2 75 mm (3 inch) floorboard insulation
 3 Loose laid polythene damp proof membrane lapped and taped
 4 150 mm (6 inch) thick ground bearing reinforced concrete slab on slip membrane
 5 Painted timber skirting board on treated softwood timber packer
 6 Fully bonded bitumen damp proof membrane dressed up cavity side of blockwork and lapping damp proof course
 7 140 mm (5½ inch) thick medium density blockwork inner leaf
 8 50 mm (2 inch) thick expanded polystyrene insulation boards
 9 Proprietary through colour external render system
 10 102.5 mm (4 inch) thick clay facing brickwork above damp proof course
 11 Position of stepped damp proof membrane at level thresholds
 12 102.5 mm (4 inch) thick clay facing brickwork below damp proof course
 13 Lean mix fill to cavity

07.10
External Wall, Floor Slab and Window Detail
1:10
 1 75 mm (3 inch) sand and cement floating screed
 2 75 mm (3 inch) floorboard insulation
 3 Loose laid polythene damp proof membrane lapped and taped
 4 150 mm (6 inch) thick ground bearing reinforced concrete slab on slip membrane
 5 Painted timber skirting board on treated softwood timber packer
 6 Line of multicoat proprietary plaster to

internal face of blockwork beyond
 7 Painted timber sill board on treated softwood timber packer
 8 Polyester powder coated double glazed aluminium window
 9 Proprietary polyester powder coated aluminium sill section
 10 Cavity closers
 11 50 mm (2 inch) thick expanded polystyrene insulation boards
 12 102.5 mm (4 inch) thick clay facing brickwork above damp proof course
 13 140 mm (5½ inch) thick medium density blockwork inner leaf
 14 Lean mix fill to cavity

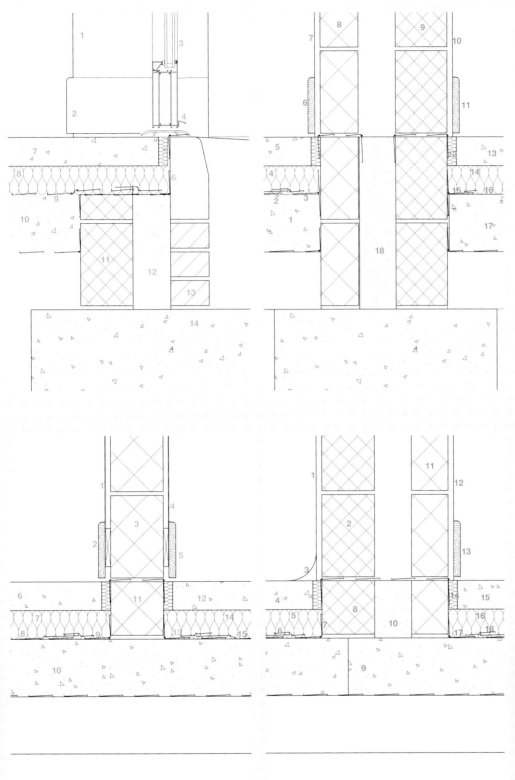

07.11
External Wall, Floor Slab and Door Detail 1:10
1 18 mm (7/10 inch) gyproc thermaline reveal
2 Painted timber skirting board on treated softwood timber packer
3 Aluminium double glazed external door
4 Proprietary aluminium seal bar fixed to threshold
5 Rigid insulation
6 Fully bonded bitumen damp proof membrane dressed up cavity side of blockwork and lapping damp proof course
7 75 mm (3 inch) sand and cement floating screed
8 75 mm (3 inch) floorboard insulation
9 Loose laid polythene damp proof membrane lapped and taped
10 150 mm (6 inch) thick ground bearing reinforced concrete slab on slip membrane
11 140 mm (5 1/2 inch) thick medium density blockwork inner leaf
12 Lean mix fill to cavity
13 102.5 mm (4 inch) thick clay facing brickwork below damp proof course
14 Reinforced concrete foundation

07.12
Internal Wall and Floor Slab Detail 1 1:10
1 150 mm (6 inch) thick ground bearing reinforced concrete slab on slip membrane
2 Loose laid polythene damp proof membrane lapped and taped
3 Flexible damp proof course
4 75 mm (3 inch) floorboard insulation
5 75 mm (3 inch) sand and cement floating screed
6 Painted timber skirting board on treated softwood timber packer
7 Multicoat proprietary plaster to internal face of blockwork
8 100 mm (4 inch) blockwork
9 140 mm (5 1/2 inch) thick medium density blockwork inner leaf
10 Multicoat proprietary plaster to internal face of blockwork
11 Painted timber skirting board on

treated softwood timber packer
12 Rigid insulation
13 75 mm (3 inch) sand and cement floating screed
14 75 mm (3 inch) floorboard insulation
15 Flexible damp proof course
16 Loose laid polythene damp proof membrane lapped and taped
17 150 mm (6 inch) thick ground bearing reinforced concrete slab on slip membrane
18 Lean mix fill to cavity

07.13
Internal Wall and Floor Slab Detail 2 1:10
1 Multicoat proprietary plaster to internal face of blockwork
2 Painted timber skirting board on treated softwood timber packer
3 140 mm (5 1/2 inch) thick medium density blockwork inner leaf
4 Multicoat proprietary plaster to internal face of blockwork
5 Painted timber skirting board on treated softwood timber packer
6 75 mm (3 inch) sand and cement floating screed
7 75 mm (3 inch) floorboard insulation
8 Loose laid polythene damp proof membrane lapped and taped
9 Flexible damp proof course
10 150 mm (6 inch) thick ground bearing reinforced concrete slab on slip membrane
11 First block cut to size to keep coursing of blockwork above
12 75 mm (3 inch) sand and cement floating screed
13 Flexible damp proof course
14 75 mm (3 inch) floorboard insulation
15 Loose laid polythene damp proof membrane lapped and taped

07.14
Internal Wall and Floor Slab Detail 3 1:10
1 Multicoat proprietary plaster to internal face of blockwork
2 140 mm (5 1/2 inch) thick medium density blockwork inner leaf
3 PVC safety

sheeting with full coving for skirting
4 75 mm (3 inch) sand and cement floating screed
5 75 mm (3 inch) floorboard insulation
6 Loose laid polythene damp proof membrane lapped and taped
7 Flexible damp proof course
8 First block cut to size to keep coursing of blockwork above
9 150 mm (6 inch) thick ground bearing reinforced concrete slab on slip membrane
10 Lean mix fill to cavity
11 100 mm (4 inch) thick medium density blockwork inner leaf
12 Multicoat proprietary plaster to internal face of blockwork
13 Painted timber skirting board on treated softwood timber packer
14 Rigid insulation
15 75 mm (3 inch) sand and cement floating screed
16 75 mm (3 inch) floorboard insulation
17 Flexible damp proof course
18 Loose laid polythene damp proof membrane lapped and taped

Svalbard Science Centre
Longyearbyen, Svalbard, Norway

Client
Statsbygg / Norwegian Directorate of
Public Construction and Property

Project Team
Einar Jarmund, Håkon Vigsnæs,
Alessandra Kosberg

Structural Engineer
AS Frederiksen

Landscape Architect
Grindaker AS

The project was commissioned to
create new administrative, research
and museum facilities in Svalbard
on a site with extremely harsh
environmental conditions. The
insulated copper-clad skin of the
new structure is wrapped around the
building, creating an outer shell that
relates aerodynamically to the flow of
wind and snow passing across the
site. The skin has been designed to be
flexible to both geometrical changes
in the climate and alterations to the
programme in the future. The building
is elevated on columns to prevent the
permafrost melting – this permanent
feature of the frozen landscape being
the only surface on which the building
is anchored. The primary structure is
timber, which facilitated minute on-site
adjustments to avoid cold bridges.
The outer copper cladding retains its
workability even at low temperatures,
thereby extending the construction
period further into the cold season.

An important consideration was to
create vital public spaces – an interior
campus environment providing warm
and light meeting places during
the dark and cold winter months.
The spruce-clad interior spaces have
complex geometries that relate
directly to the outer skin. The
effectiveness of the circulation is
maximized in the resultant flowing
spaces, while at the same time
offering varied vistas and experiences.
The immense north-facing glazed
aperture of the building's spruce-
panelled central atrium expresses the
centre's mission to study the arctic
environment. Spruce-clad corridors
radiate out from the atrium, providing
access to the faculty offices,
laboratories, and classrooms for
300 students and 50 staff.

1 Three dimensional
climatic modelling was
used to generate the
geometry of the
copper-clad facades.
The building is
elevated to keep it
from contributing to
the melting of the
permafrost.
2 In old Norse,
Svalbard means 'the
land of the cold
coasts'. Here, the
vastness of the
northern polar sky,
and the dark and cold
of the winter polar
night are apparent in
this Arctic archipelago
at 78 degrees north
latitude.
3 In the Arctic
landscape where
colour is scarce, bright
hues have been used
sparingly but
dramatically in the
interior to contrast with
the predominantly
timber finishes.
4 The central atrium
provides a point of
social focus for the
research community as
well as being at the
centre of the
circulation system.

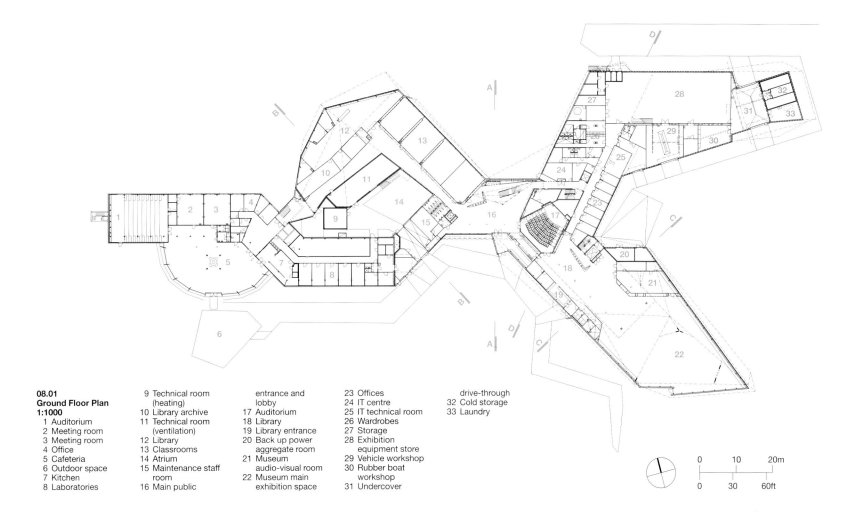

08.01
Ground Floor Plan
1:1000
1 Auditorium
2 Meeting room
3 Meeting room
4 Office
5 Cafeteria
6 Outdoor space
7 Kitchen
8 Laboratories
9 Technical room (heating)
10 Library archive
11 Technical room (ventilation)
12 Library
13 Classrooms
14 Atrium
15 Maintenance staff room
16 Main public

entrance and lobby
17 Auditorium
18 Library
19 Library entrance
20 Back up power aggregate room
21 Museum audio-visual room
22 Museum main exhibition space
23 Offices
24 IT centre
25 IT technical room
26 Wardrobes
27 Storage
28 Exhibition equipment store
29 Vehicle workshop
30 Rubber boat workshop
31 Undercover

drive-through
32 Cold storage
33 Laundry

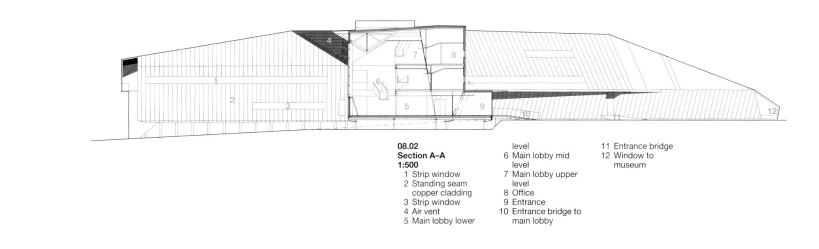

08.02
Section A–A
1:500
1 Strip window
2 Standing seam copper cladding
3 Strip window
4 Air vent
5 Main lobby lower

level
6 Main lobby mid level
7 Main lobby upper level
8 Office
9 Entrance
10 Entrance bridge to main lobby
11 Entrance bridge
12 Window to museum

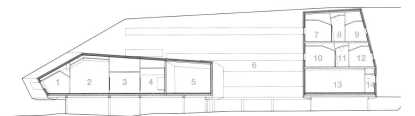

08.03
Section B–B
1:500
1 Office
2 Library
3 Library archives
4 Corridor
5 Technical room
6 Atrium
7 Office
8 Corridor
9 Office
10 Office
11 Corridor
12 Office
13 Maintenance staff room
14 Corridor

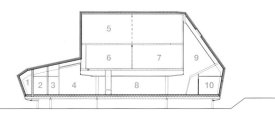

08.04
Section C–C
1:500
1 Technical room
2 Storage
3 Storage
4 Museum audio-visual room
5 Museum offices
6 Sysselmannen archives
7 Sysselmannen laboratories
8 Museum
9 Museum triple height space
10 Museum entrance

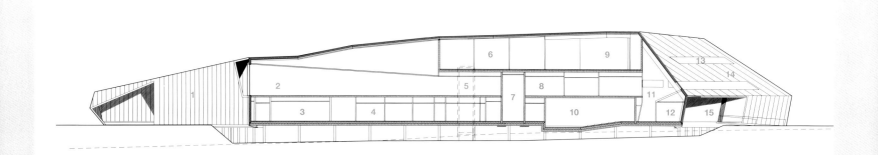

08.05
Section D–D
1:500
1 Standing seam copper cladding
2 Corridor
3 Storage
4 Office
5 Storage
6 Technical room
7 Stair
8 Office
9 Technical room
10 Auditorium
11 Triple height museum space
12 Office
13 Strip window
14 Standing seam copper cladding
15 Window to museum

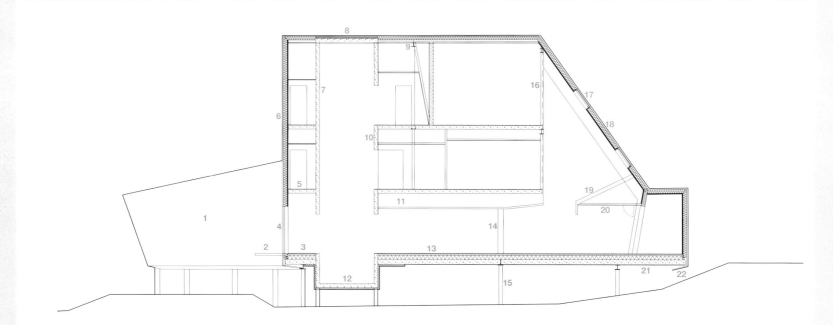

08.06
Typical Section Detail
1:200
1 Copper cladding with standing seams
2 Loading / unloading dock
3 Lift entrance
4 Copper-clad loading dock door
5 Storage
6 Copper-clad outer wall
7 Concrete construction to lift enclosure
8 Copper roof sheeting
9 Technical space for ventilation and lighting
10 Concrete construction to lift enclosure
11 Ceiling void for ventilation and lighting installations
12 Elevator pit
13 24 mm (1 inch) thick solid wood flooring to museum
14 Steel column
15 Steel column underneath building
16 Interior glass wall
17 Glazing to exterior wall
18 Copper-clad outer wall
19 Interior timber construction
20 Timber ceiling
21 Concrete floor slab
22 Copper cladding wrapped around the underside of the floor construction

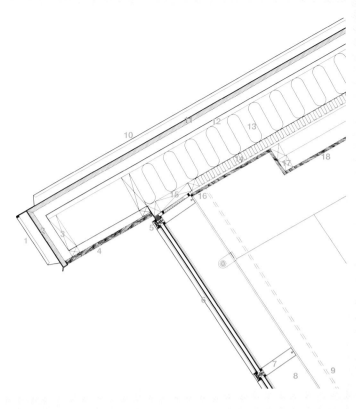

08.07
Roof Detail
1:20
1 Standing seam copper cladding
2 Plywood boarding
3 200 mm (7⁹/10 inch) insulation timber construction
4 Timber panelling
5 Metal window system
6 Fixed double-glazed window
7 Metal window system
8 Timber structure
9 Line of primary timber structure beyond shown dotted
10 Standing seam copper cladding
11 Plywood boarding
12 Plywood boarding
13 200 mm (7⁹/10 inch) insulation timber construction
14 50 mm (2 inch) insulation
15 Timber blocking
16 Timber panelling to ceiling soffit
17 Two 50 mm (2 inch) timber battens
18 Timber panelling to ceiling

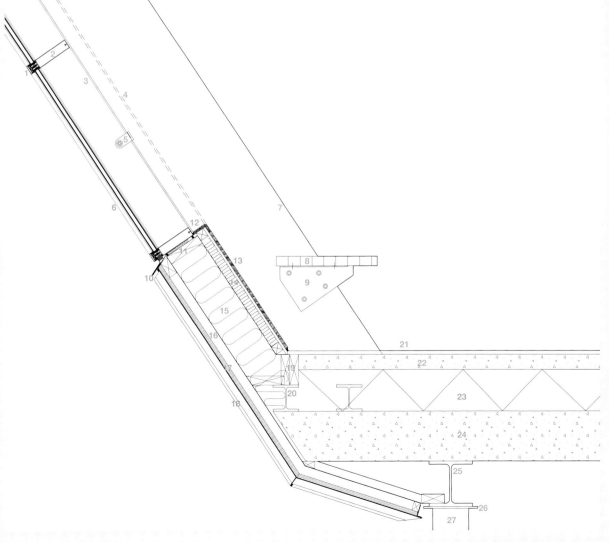

08.08
Window, Wall and Floor Detail
1:20
1 Metal window frame, exterior component
2 Metal window mullion
3 Metal window frame, vertical component
4 Line of primary timber structure beyond shown dotted
5 Fastening bracket
6 Fixed double-glazed window
7 Timber structure
8 Timber bench bolted to primary timber structure
9 Metal fixing bracket for timber bench
10 Copper window sill
11 200 mm (7⁹/10 inch) insulated timber construction
12 Timber panelling to inner sill
13 Timber wall panelling
14 50 mm (2 inch) insulation
15 200 mm (7⁹/10 inch) insulated timber construction
16 50 mm (2 inch) closed air space
17 Plywood boarding
18 Standing seam copper cladding

19 50 x 200 mm (2 x 7⁹/10 inch) timber floor structure
20 Steel beam to wall structure
21 Timber flooring
22 70 mm (2³/4 inch) concrete floor slab
23 200 mm (7⁹/10 inch) thick insulation
24 200 mm (7⁹/10 inch) thick concrete floor slab
25 Steel floor substructure beam
26 Steel bearing plate connection between steel beam and steel column
27 Steel column

Kärsämäki Church
Kärsämäki, Finland

Client
Parish of Kärsämäki

Project Team
Anssi Lassila

Structural Engineer
Jussi Tervaoja, Oulu University,
Department of Architecture, Wood
Studio

The first church in the parish of
Kärsämäki was completed in 1765.
However, by 1841 the church had
become dilapidated and was
eventually demolished. The idea to
build a new, modern church using
traditional eighteenth century methods
was conceived in 1998, and a
competition was organized within the
Department of Architecture at the
University of Oulu. The winning design
comprises two parts – a timber log
core and a black, tarred and shingle-
clad envelope. The building generates
an atmosphere of archaic simplicity
appropriate to an ecclesiastical
structure, as well as providing
optimal weather resistance in this
northern climate.

The space between the outer skin
and the church interior houses
secondary facilities such as
vestibules, vestry and a storeroom.
Visitors entering the church are led
through a dimly lit space and are
drawn towards the main space lit from
above by a lantern skylight. The logs
for the load-bearing log frame were
felled from forests owned by the
parish. The notched corner joints were
created with traditional hand tools
while the inner and outer surfaces of
the log frame were hewn with a broad
axe. The roof structure was
constructed on-site with notched
joints and timber dowels used to
secure it to the walls. All the work was
primarily carried out using traditional
tools or tools fabricated using old
models. 50,000 aspen shingles were
required for the roofing and cladding,
which were split and then finished by
whittling. Finally, the shingles were
dipped in hot tar prior to being fixed in
place. This delicate church is a
beautifully hand-crafted structure that
takes pride in resurrecting traditional
building techniques.

1 The south-west
corner of the church is
cut away to create the
entrance. To the left,
parishioners enter via a
small stair, and to the
right via a gentle ramp.
2 The other corners
feature vertical panels
of glazing covered with
adjustable shutters to
moderate light and air.
3 View of the shingled
facade and the
entrance. The
tar-dipped timber
shingles lend a
complex texture to the
facade and contrast
with the untreated
timber of the other
building elements.
4 The interior is
constructed as a
building within a
building. It is here that
the hand-built quality
of the church is most
readily apparent. All of
the timber is left
untreated so that the
natural warmth
contributes to the
calm quality of this
contemplative space.

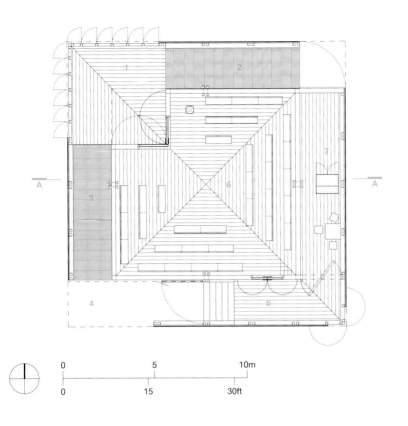

09.01
Ground Floor Plan
1:200
1 Entrance hall
2 Ramp
3 Ramp
4 Covered entrance
5 Hall
6 Church
7 Vestry

0   5   10m

0   15   30ft

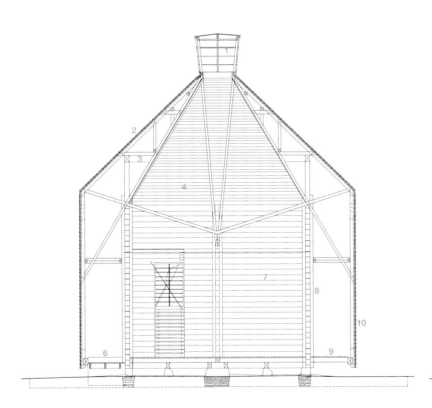

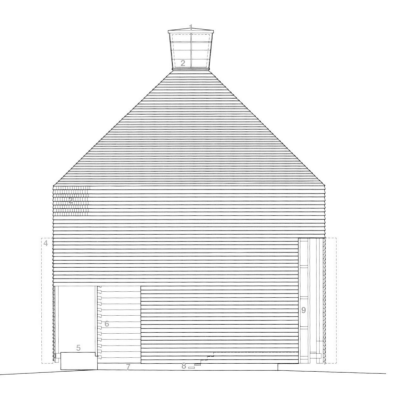

09.02
Section A–A
1:200
1 Skylight
2 Shingle-clad roof
3 Intermediate
timber structure
between envelope
and core
4 Inner surface of
log-framed interior
core
5 Centre joint to
stabilizing

structure
6 Ramp
7 Church hall
8 Outer surface of
log-framed interior
core
9 Vestry
10 Shingle-clad
exterior wall

09.03
South Elevation
1:200
1 Copper sheeting
to lantern roof
2 Clear glazing to
lantern
3 Tarred aspen
shingles to exterior
walls and roof
4 Line of open
timber shutter
shown dotted
5 Entrance ramp

6 Axe-hewn timber
log frame
7 Stone foundations
8 Entrance stair
9 Aspen-framed
glazed door

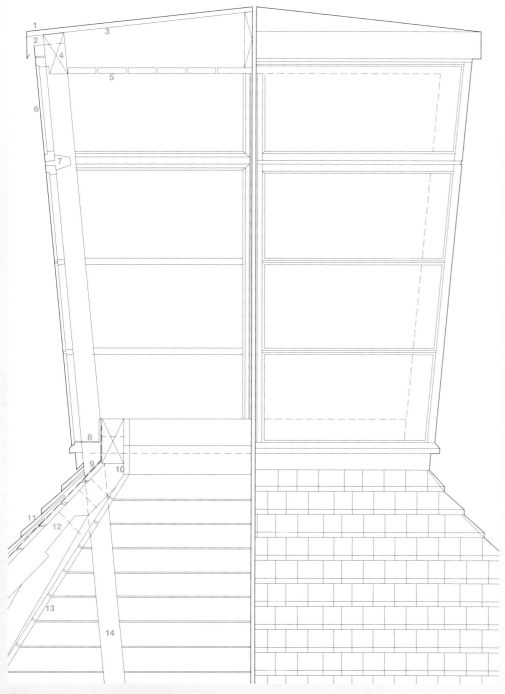

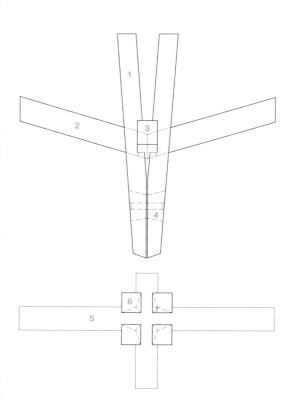

09.04
Lantern and Roof
Detail
1:20
1 Copper sheeting to roof lantern
2 Ventilation gap
3 152 x 25 mm (6 x 1 inch) timber board
4 100 x 200 mm (4 x 8 inch) timber blocking
5 152 x 25 mm (6 x 1 inch) timber board ceiling to lantern
6 Clear blown glass to lantern
7 Linseed oiled timber window frame

8 Hammered iron clamp
9 Birch bark waterproofing layer
10 Hammered iron bolt
11 Tar-dipped aspen shingles
12 125 x 125 mm (5 x 5 inch) timber structure
13 Hand-sawn timber interior wall and ceiling lining
14 100 x 100 mm (4 x 4 inch) timber structure

09.05
Middle Joint
Elevation and Plan
Detail
1:20
1 100 x 100 mm (4 x 4 inch) timber structure
2 125 x 125 mm (5 x 5 inch) timber structure
3 125 x 125 mm (5 x 5 inch) timber structure
4 Timber wedge joint
5 125 x 125 mm (5 x 5 inch) timber structure
6 100 x 100 mm (4 x 4 inch) timber structure
7 Dovetail joint

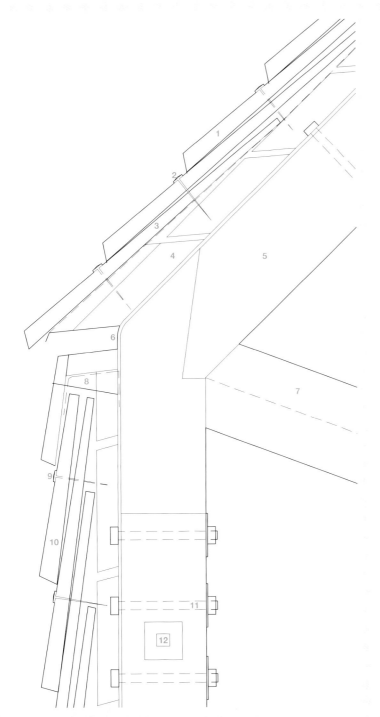

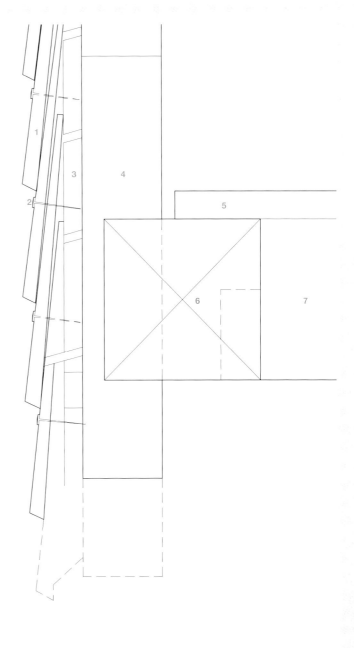

09.06
Eaves Detail
1:5
 1 Tar-dipped aspen
shingles to roof
 2 Tar-hardened
forged nail
 3 Birch bark
waterproofing layer
 4 38 x 152 mm (1¹/₂ x
6 inch) board
 5 125 x 125 mm (5 x
5 inch) timber roof
structure
 6 Hammered iron
clamp
 7 125 x 125 mm (5 x
5 inch) timber roof

structure
 8 Birch bark
waterproofing layer
 9 Tar-hardened
forged nail
10 Tar-dipped aspen
shingles to wall
11 Hammered iron bolt
12 Hammered iron bolt

09.07
Wall and Floor Detail
1:5
 1 Tar-dipped aspen
shingles to wall
 2 Tar-hardened
forged nail
 3 38 x 152 mm (1¹/₂ x
6 inch) board
 4 50 x 100 mm (2 x 4
inch) timber wall
structure
 5 Lye-washed timber
floorboards
 6 200 x 250 mm (8 x
10 inch) floor bearer
 7 200 x 250 mm (8 x
10 inch) floor joist

**Provincetown Art Association and
Museum (PAAM)
Provincetown, Massachusetts, USA**

Client
Provincetown Art Association and
Museum (PAAM)

Project Team
Jorge Silvetti, Rodolfo Machado,
Andrew Cruse, Michael LeBlanc, Kelly
Smith, Derek Johnson, John Clegg,
Chris Grimley

Structural Engineer
Richmond So Engineers

The renovation and expansion of the
Provincetown Art Association and
Museum (PAAM) is an attempt to
shape an architectural identity for
the institution within Provincetown's
unique urban context. It has also
dramatically improved the museum's
ability to store and display art, and
made the museum a leader in
sustainable design. The museum
acquired its current site in 1918 and,
over the years, several additions were
built onto the original building. By the
time PAAM selected Machado and
Silvetti for the project in early 2003,
the art storage space was woefully
inadequate, the galleries were
too small, and the museum school
consisted of a single classroom.

The project was realized in two
phases – the first involved the
renovation of Hargood House, the
Moffett, Hawthorne and Hofmann
Galleries, expanding the office
spaces, and creating a library. The
second phase involved the creation
of the new Patrons', Jalbert and Duffy
Galleries, as well as new art storage
areas and an expanded museum
school. The Jalbert and Patrons'
Galleries open towards Commercial
Street, the town's major pedestrian
thoroughfare, with a large sliding glass
door, making PAAM both literally and
symbolically more accessible to the
community. The museum is a
timber-framed building over a
concrete basement. The majority of
the floor framing is in engineered
timber. The old portion of the museum
is clad with white cedar shingles, and
the new portion with custom Spanish
cedar shingles and louvres, while
interior materials include heartpine
and Douglas fir floors, plaster walls
and white oak cabinetry.

1 The renovations and
expansion were
designed to rigorous
standards of
sustainable design.
Some of the building's
green elements are
visible, such as the
photovoltaic panels on
the roof and the many
natural materials seen
both inside and
outside the building.
2 On the building
elevations, both the
museum and school
entries are marked
with glass lanterns,
essentially cubic
skylights, whose
illumination denotes
the entrances to the
main building
activities.
3 Detail view of the
Spanish cedar louvres
(top) and Dutch lapped
timber shingles
(below).
4 In the painting
studio, the white
painted plasterboard
walls and ceiling, and
the white epoxy floor
are lit from above by a
glazed roof lantern.

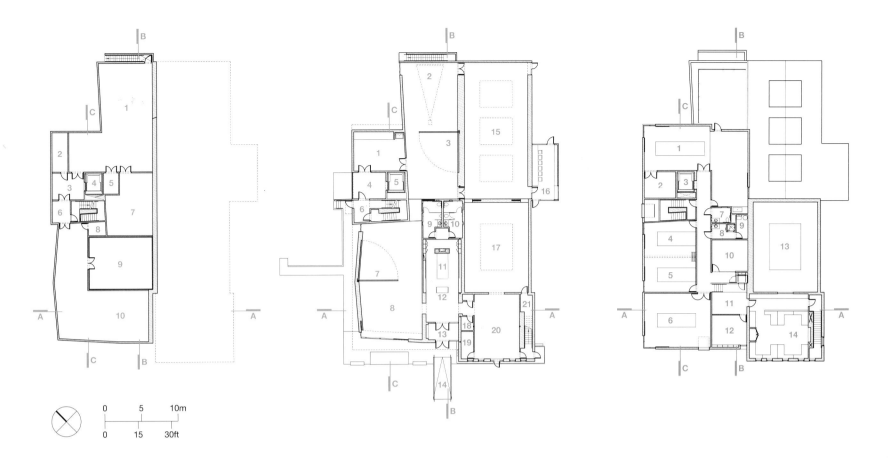

10.01
Ground Floor Plan
1:500
1 Temporary storage
2 Electrical room
3 Vestibule
4 Elevator
5 Elevator machine room
6 Hall
7 Mechanical room
8 Storage
9 Print storage
10 Permanent storage

10.02
First Floor Plan
1:500
1 Preparations area
2 Special exhibits gallery
3 Hinged moveable wall
4 Loading dock
5 Elevator
6 School vestibule
7 Hinged moveable wall
8 Gallery
9 Male WC
10 Female WC
11 Bookshop
12 Museum ticketing
13 Entrance vestibule
14 Entrance ramp
15 Gallery
16 Library
17 Gallery
18 Coatroom
19 Storage
20 Gallery
21 Storage

10.03
Second Floor Plan
1:500
1 Printing studio
2 Storage
3 Elevator
4 Drawing studio 1
5 Drawing studio 2
6 Painting studio
7 Restroom
8 Restroom
9 Janitor's closet
10 Conference room
11 Lobby
12 Director's office
13 Void over gallery below
14 Staff offices

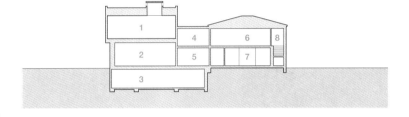

10.04
Section A–A
1:500
1 Painting studio
2 Gallery
3 Permanent storage
4 Director's office
5 Lobby
6 Office
7 Gallery
8 Stair

10.05
Section B–B
1:500
1 Director's office
2 Lobby
3 Stair
4 Conference room
5 Restroom
6 Restroom
7 Painting studio
8 Vestibule
9 Lobby
10 Bookshop
11 Restroom
12 Special exhibits gallery
13 Permanent storage
14 Print storage
15 Mechanical room
16 Temporary storage

10.06
Section C–C
1:500
1 Painting studio
2 Drawing studio 2
3 Drawing studio 1
4 Stair
5 Elevator
6 Printing studio
7 Gallery
8 Permanent storage
9 Print storage
10 Preparations area
11 Temporary storage

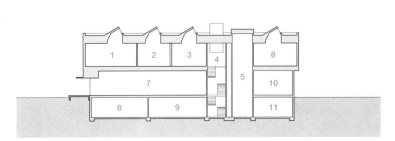

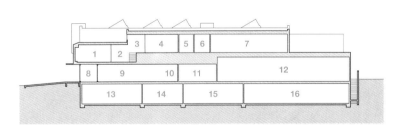

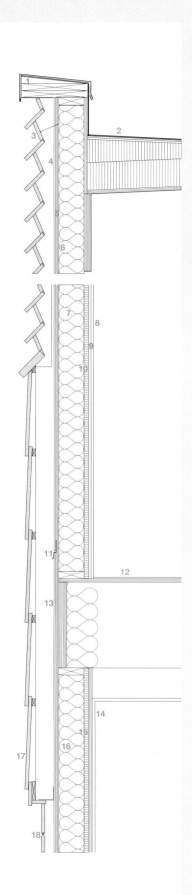

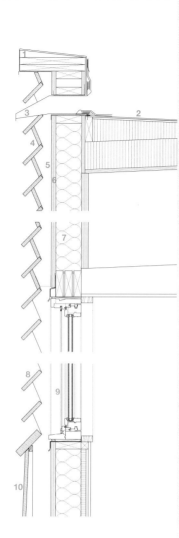

10.07
Detail Wall Section 1
1:10
1 Zinc-coated copper parapet
2 Single ply roofing membrane with insulation
3 Spanish cedar timber louvre with closer board on furring
4 Exterior grade plywood
5 Air barrier and furring
6 Structural sheathing
7 Platform frame with batt insulation
8 Homasote (recycled compressed wall board)
9 Gypsum wall board
10 19 mm (3/4 inch) thick plywood
11 Z-flashing at panel joints
12 Epoxy flooring
13 Engineered lumber floor framing
14 Gypsum wall board
15 19 mm (3/4 inch) thick plywood
16 Semi-rigid insulation
17 Dutch lap wood shingle assembly on furring
18 Horizontal tongue and groove sheathing

10.08
Detail Wall Section 2
1:10
1 Zinc-coated copper parapet
2 Single ply roofing membrane with insulation
3 Zinc-coated copper scupper
4 Spanish cedar timber louvre with closer board on furring
5 Exterior grade plywood
6 Air barrier and furring
7 Structural sheathing
8 Spanish cedar timber louvre with closer board on furring
9 Inward-swinging casement window
10 Dutch lap wood shingle assembly on furring

10.09
Detail Wall Section 3
1:20
1 Sheet metal parapet
2 Single ply roofing membrane with insulation
3 Platform framing with batt insulation
4 Exterior structural sheathing and air barrier
5 Timber louvre assembly on furring
6 Homasote (recycled compressed wall board) on gypsum wall board and semi-rigid insulation
7 Dutch lap wood shingle assembly on furring
8 Liquid epoxy flooring
9 Intake for natural ventilation system
10 Timber sun shade
11 Timber window wall assembly
12 Timber floor assembly
13 Structural concrete slab on steel framing
14 Concrete foundation wall with insulation and damp proofing
15 Concrete slab on grade with rigid insulation, vapour barrier, compacted gravel and geotextile

10.10
Detail Wall Section 4
1:20
1 Sheet metal parapet
2 Single ply roofing membrane with insulation
3 Timber louvre assembly on furring
4 Platform framing with batt insulation
5 Louvres without closer board at windows
6 Inward-swinging casement window
7 Homasote (recycled compressed wall board) on gypsum wall board and semi-rigid insulation
8 Exterior structural sheathing and air barrier
9 Dutch wood timber shingle assembly on furring
10 Liquid epoxy flooring
11 Gypsum wall board
12 19 mm (3/4 inch) thick plywood
13 Liquid epoxy flooring
14 Structural concrete slab on steel framing
15 Concrete foundation wall with insulation and damp proofing
16 Concrete slab on grade with rigid insulation, vapour barrier, compacted gravel and geotextile

10.11
Detail Wall Section 5
1:20
1 Single ply roofing membrane
2 Plaster ceiling at lantern
3 Insulated glazing
4 Edge of ceiling
5 Structural steel framing for glass lantern
6 Timber louvre assembly on furring
7 Platform framing with batt insulation
8 Exterior structural sheathing and air barrier
9 Dutch lap wood shingle assembly on furring
10 Exterior door
11 Fibre block flooring
12 Structural concrete slab on steel framing
13 Concrete foundation wall with insulation and damp proofing
14 Concrete slab on grade with rigid insulation, vapour barrier, compacted gravel and geotextile

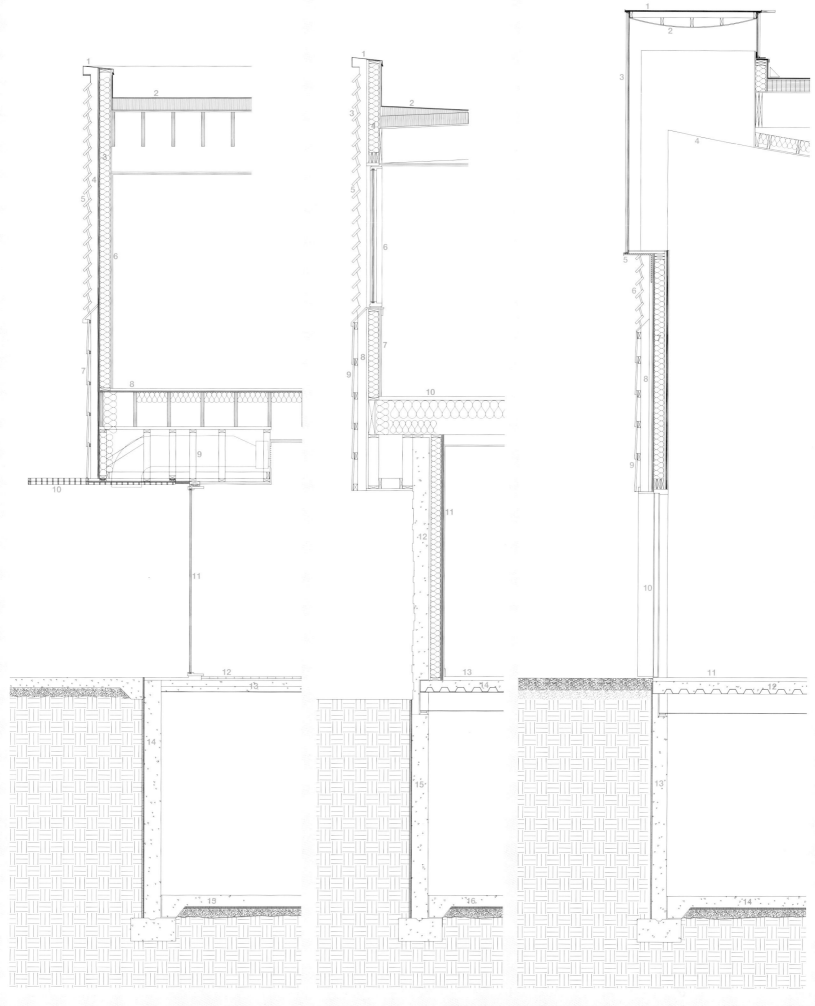

49

BEATFUSE!
Long Island City, New York, USA

Client
PS1 Contemporary Art Center and
The Museum of Modern Art

Project Team
Pablo Castro, Jennifer Lee, Shin Kook
Kang, Akira Gunji, Selin Semaan, Luis
Costa, Kaon Ko, Alice Bo-Wen Chang,
Dasha Khapalova, Tobi Bergman,
David Karlin, Kim Shkapich

Structural Engineer
Robert Silman Associates

Main Contractor
Site Assembly

Every Saturday in summer a popular
block party takes place celebrating
music, art and architecture, along with
the cosmopolitan diversity of the city's
population. This project transforms an
outdoor concrete-walled museum
courtyard gallery into a dynamic
space through the inventive use of
common materials and standard
building components. Entirely digitally
fabricated using CNC-milled wood
and laser-cut steel from emailed 3D
files in a completely paperless
process, the project was designed in
six weeks and constructed in less
than 12 weeks.

The Caldarium is designed with no
shade and an array of radial chaise
longues for sunbathing, with a large
soaking pool. In the large triangular
gallery of the Tepidarium, shade
structures, pools and misters cool the
air by evaporation. The small gallery of
the Frigidarium is lined with foil-
backed insulation to maintain the ice
block benches installed every
Saturday morning. The space is
partially covered by ten concertina
shells manufactured and assembled in
a workshop and later erected on site.
The shells were modelled and
manufactured digitally using a CNC
router to achieve their dynamic curved
form. The shells are then covered with
a skin of polypropylene mesh scales,
allowing wind and rain to move
through them without taxing the
structure with lateral or lifting loads.
Each concertina shell is unique, but
they fuse into each other to create a
realm that spans the entire courtyard
and creates multiple places of
distinctive mood and atmosphere.

1 View of the
Tepidarium where
shade structures,
pools and mist
fountains lower the
summer temperatures
by as much as five
degrees.

2 Just like the music
fused seamlessly by
the Warm Up DJ's,
thousands of New
Yorkers join together
without losing their
individuality. The
structure extends to

the boundaries of the
site to achieve the
most impact with
the least material.
3 The Tepidarium with
the mist fountains in
action.
4 The timber shells are

covered with mesh
scales that adjust to
the curved surfaces of
the frames while
overlapping in ways
that generate a
nuanced moiré texture.

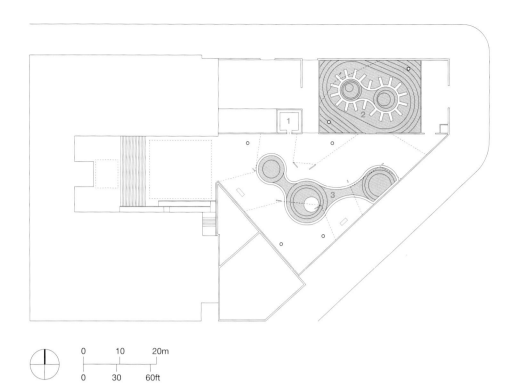

11.01
Site Plan
1:1000
1 Frigidarium
2 Caldarium
3 Tepidarium

0   10   20m
0   30   60ft

11.02
Timber Gridshell
Elevations
1:500
1 Gridshell A
   elevations
2 Gridshell B
   elevations
3 Gridshell C
   elevations
4 Gridshell D
   elevations
5 Gridshell E
   elevations
6 Gridshell F
   elevations
7 Gridshell G
   elevations

1

2

3

4

5

6

7

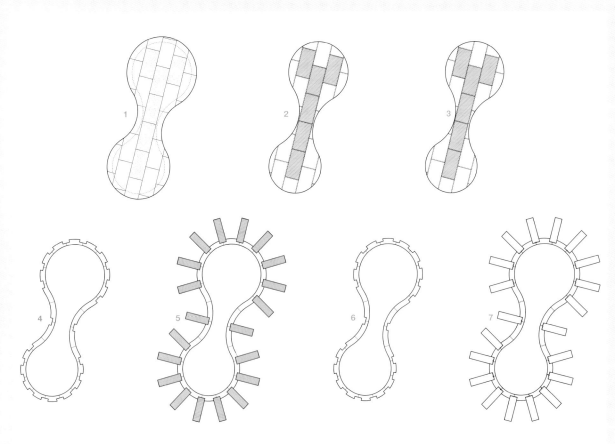

11.03
Tepidarium Pool Components
Not to Scale

1 Layer CB1 – base bottom of 76 mm (3 inch) thick foam cut from six whole sheets
2 Layer CB2 – base middle of 12 mm (1/2 inch) thick plywood cut from six whole sheets aligned to foam layer below
3 Layer CB3 – base top of 12 mm (1/2 inch) thick plywood cut from six whole sheets, displaced 50 mm (2 inches) from layer below for fastening
4 Layer CR4 – rim bottom from 76 mm (3 inch) thick foam cut from nine whole sheets
5 Layer CR5 – rim middle from 76 mm (3 inch) thick foam cut from nine whole sheets and layer of foam for recliners from 76 mm (3 inch) thick foam cut from 32 whole sheets and laid in eight layers to create reclining seats
6 Layer CR6 – rim middle from 12 mm (1/2 inch) thick plywood cut from nine whole sheets and aligned to foam layer below
7 Layer CR7 – rim top from 12 mm (1/2 inch) thick plywood cut from eight whole sheets, and top layer to recliners of 6 mm (1/4 inch) plywood cut from ten whole sheets displaced 50 mm (2 inches) from layer below for fastening

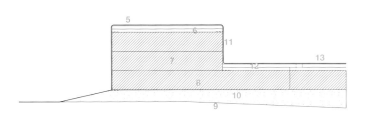

11.04
Caldarium Recliner Section and Pool Edge Detail
Not to Scale

1 50 mm (2 inch) minimum thickness of levelled sand bed
2 Eight vertical layers of 76 mm (3 inch) thick rigid foam insulation
3 6 mm (1/4 inch) plywood to top surface of recliner
4 Site installation to include fastening block together at 50 mm (2 inch) plywood overlap with 6 mm (1/4 inch) blocking placed at fasteners and joints covered and fastened with fibreglass tape and two coats of epoxy resin
5 Three layers of epoxy resin coating
6 Two layers of 12 mm (1/2 inch) plywood glued to foam with epoxy resin
7 Rigid foam insulation
8 Fibreglass fabric wrapped under plywood and foam
9 Existing ground level
10 50 mm (2 inch) minimum thickness of levelled sand bed
11 Single layer of fibreglass cloth on foam insulation to all vertical surfaces
12 Fibreglass fabric wrapped under plywood and foam
13 Site installation to include fastening block together at 50 mm (2 inch) plywood overlap with 6 mm (1/4 inch) blocking placed at fasteners and joints covered and fastened with fibreglass tape and two coats of epoxy resin

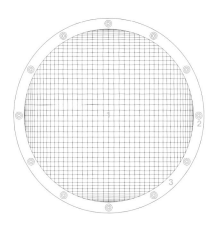

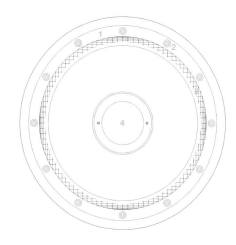

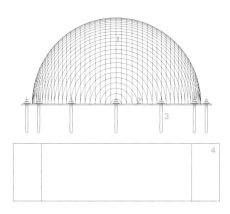

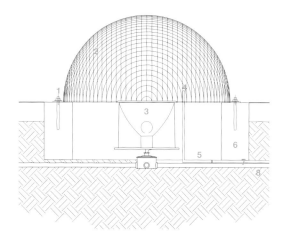

11.05
Light Strainer Cover
Plan 1
Not to Scale
 1 Moulded wire mesh welded to edge of 10 mm (2/5 inch) thick steel flange
 2 12 mm (1/2 inch bolt fixings
 3 10 mm (2/5 inch) thick steel flange

11.06
Light Strainer Cover
Plan 2
Not to Scale
 1 10 mm (2/5 inch) thick steel flange
 2 12 mm (1/2 inch bolt fixings
 3 Moulded wire mesh
 4 Uplighter

11.07
Light Strainer Cover
Elevation
Not to Scale
 1 Moulded wire mesh welded to edge of 10 mm (2/5 inch) thick steel flange
 2 10 mm (2/5 inch) thick steel flange
 3 12 mm (1/2 inch bolt fixings
 4 Concrete footing

11.08
Light Strainer Cover
Section
Not to Scale
 1 12 mm (1/2 inch bolt fixings
 2 Moulded wire mesh welded to edge of 10 mm (2/5 inch) thick steel flange
 3 Uplighter housing and waterproof J-box set in gravel bed
 4 Fog nozzle
 5 Gravel infill
 6 Concrete footing
 7 Braided hose for fog system
 8 Electrical conduit

Mitchell Park Camera Obscura
Greenport, New York, USA

Client
Village of Greenport

Electrical Contractor
Johnson Electric Construction Corp

Structural Engineer
Buro Happold

Main Contractor
Loduca Associates

Electrical Contractor
Johnson Electric Construction Corp

The Camera Obscura (in Latin 'dark room') is one of four buildings designed for Mitchell Park, a waterfront park for the Village of Greenport on Long Island, New York. Through an optical lens and a mirror, a live image of the Camera's surroundings is projected down onto a flat, circular table that is raised or lowered to adjust focal depth. The Camera Obscura was conceived as a research and development project that is small in size but not in scope. The goal was to construct a building entirely from digitally fabricated components. In the past, SHoP had utilized digital fabrication for individual trades, such as laser-cut metal panels or computer numerical controlled millwork. For the first time, the architects brought multiple processes together to test tolerance and co-ordination issues.

Designed entirely as a three-dimensional computer model, the construction of the Camera was communicated as a kit of custom parts accompanied by a set of instructions for assembling the components. Primary aluminium and steel components were laser-cut using digital files directly extracted from the computer model. Full-scale templates were provided for wall and roof sheathing using a black paper-resin board called Skatelite which is used primarily in skateboard and BMX freestyle parks and is noted for its ability to accept a high degree of curvature. The warped exterior skin is comprised of milled ipe hardwood planks, the same wood that is used throughout the Park structures.

1 Exterior view of the Camera, which is clad in milled ipe timber planks.
2 The roof, parapet and pivot door are constructed from zinc panels. The timber structure echoes its maritime context.
3 Detail view of the zinc roof and timber wall cladding.
4 The interior of the Camera's roof is made from a composite structure of steel ring beams and exposed timber joists. The curved walls incorporate aluminium shelves and a bench for visitors. Images from the Camera in the roof are displayed on the central circular table.

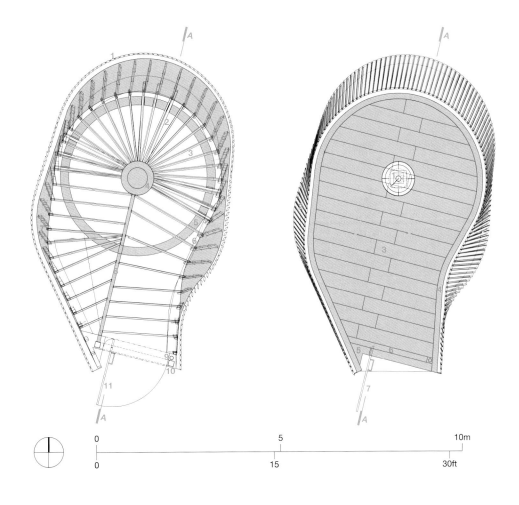

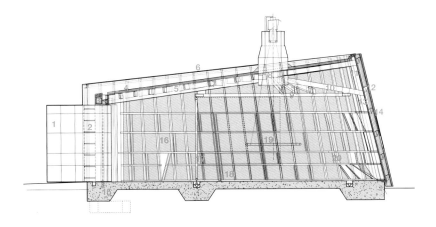

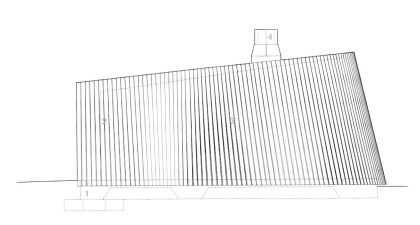

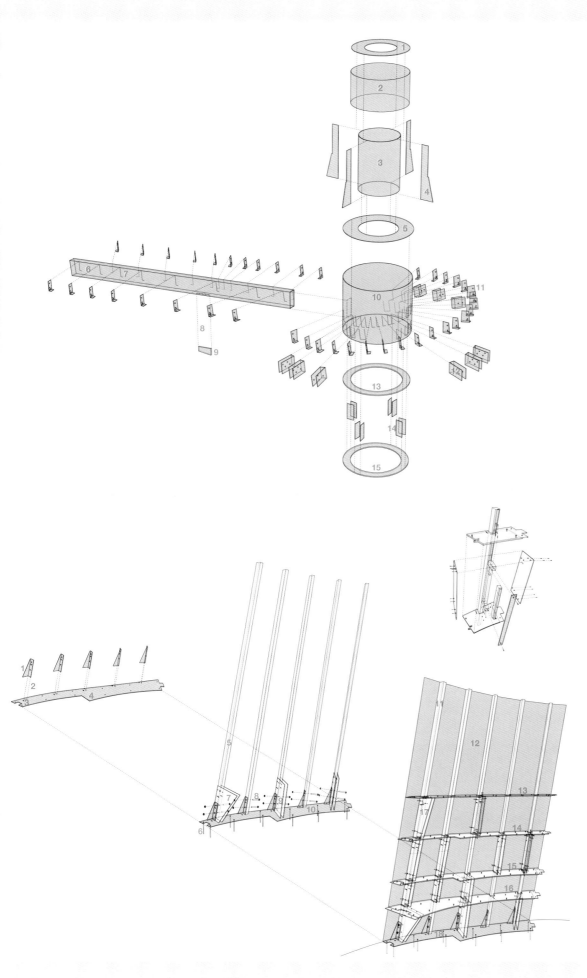

12.05
Compression Ring to Roof Assembly Detail
Not to Scale
1 6 mm (¼ inch) thick steel ring
2 4 mm (⅙ inch) steel cover plate for camera apparatus with lock pin, hasp and handle
3 6 mm (¼ inch) thick steel ring
4 6 mm (¼ inch) thick steel stiffening fin
5 6 mm (¼ inch) thick steel ring
6 254 x 101 x 12 mm (10 x 4 x ½ inch) thick steel rectangular hollow section beam
7 Continuous weld location
8 Line of typical continuous weld
9 12 mm (½ inch) thick steel plate
10 6 mm (¼ inch) thick steel ring
11 Steel tabs for 50 x 150 mm (2 x 6 inch) ipe roof joists with laser-cut tabs folded 90 degrees and continuously welded to steel compression ring beam
12 Steel compression saddles
13 6 mm (¼ inch) thick steel stiffening ring
14 6 mm (¼ inch) thick steel stiffening ribs
15 6 mm (¼ inch) thick steel stiffening ring

12.06
Sill Plate, Shelf Assembly, Aluminium Fins and Shelf Support Detail
Not to Scale
1 Folded sill tabs aligned with corresponding weld locations labelled on sill plate
2 Continuous welds between folded steel tabs and steel sill plate
3 Weld location labels etched onto steel during laser cutting production process
4 Sill plate with thermal spray finish applied after assembly
5 50 x 100 mm (2 x 4 inch) ipe wall structure
6 Steel anchor bolt
7 Aluminium shelf fin support
8 12 mm (½ inch) diameter stainless steel through bolts
9 Aluminium fin shelf support
10 Steel sill plate
11 50 x 100 mm (2 x 4 inch) ipe wall structure
12 Skatelite and plywood wall sheathing composite
13 Top shelf
14 Mid shelf
15 Desk shelf
16 Bench shelf
17 Aluminium fin shelf support
18 Steel sill plate

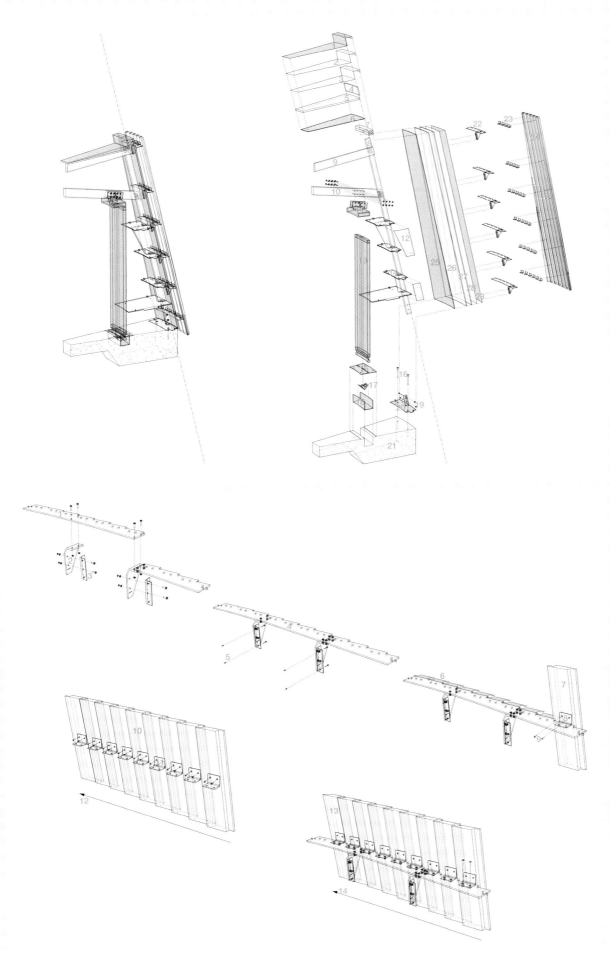

12.07
Floor, Wall and Roof
Assembly Detail
Not to Scale
 1 Flat beam zinc roof
 2 Plastic drainage
and ventilation sheet
 3 High temperature
ice and water shield
 4 19 mm (3/4 inch)
thick plywood parapet
sheathing screwed
through 6 mm (1/4
inch) Skatelite Pro into
50 x 152 mm (2 x 6
inch) ipe roof joists
below.
 5 19 mm (3/4 inch)
thick plywood roof
sheathing
 6 6 mm (1/4 inch)
thick black Skatelite
Pro with all seam lines
to match at roof joists
and screwed into ipe
roof joists at 152 mm
(6 inch) centres
 7 50 x 100 mm (2 x 4
inch) double timber
header
 8 50 x 100 mm (2 x 4
inch) ipe wall structure
 9 50 x 152 mm (2 x 6
inch) roof joist
 10 76 x 152 mm (3 x 6
inch) steel
compression chord
 11 Steel tension ring
assembly fastened to
ipe compression
chords with 12 mm (1/2
inch) stainless steel
through bolts
 12 Aluminium fin shelf
support
 13 Revolving metal
wall panel
 14 Aluminium shelf
 15 6 mm (1/4 inch)
thick steel cover plate

flush mounted into
finished concrete floor
 16 Anchor bolts
 17 38 mm (11/2 inch)
diameter transfer balls
mounted on steel
angle
 18 Steel mounting
plates as required for
level installation of
transfer balls and
revolving metal wall
assembly
 19 12 mm (1/2 inch)
diameter stainless
steel through bolt
 20 Steel sill plate
assembly
 21 Concrete
foundation pad
 22 Aluminium
sawtooth guide and
gusset assembly for
ipe cladding planks
 23 Mounting hinge for
ipe cladding planks
 24 Milled 50 x 152 mm
(2 x 6 inch) ipe
planking to exterior
wall
 25 6 mm (1/4 inch)
Skatelite Pro sheathing
screw fixed into ipe
wall structure with all
seam lines to match at
ipe columns and
aluminium shelves
 26 12 mm (1/2 inch)
plywood sheathing
screwed through to
Skatelite sheathing
 27 12 mm (1/2 inch)
plywood sheathing
screwed and glued to
adjacent plywood
sheet
 28 High temperature
ice and water shield
 29 Waterproof
membrane

12.08
Sawtooth Guide and
Ipe Plank Exterior
Wall Assembly
Procedure Detail
Not to Scale
 1 Laser-cut
aluminium sawtooth
guide with all bolt and
rivet holes
 2 Folded aluminium
sawtooth gusset
 3 Mounting hinge
 4 Sawtooth assembly
screwed through to
composite wall panels
 5 Screw locations to
screw through
waterproof membrane
into composite wall
panels
 6 Milled ipe planks to
form exterior cladding
 7 Profiled ipe plank
 8 Mounting hinge
 9 Mounting hinges
screwed to each
individual ipe plank
prior to final installation
 10 Profiled ipe plank
 11 Mounting hinge
 12 Ipe planks screwed
to mounting hinges
sequentially
 13 Profiled ipe plank
 14 Mounting hinges
bolted to sawtooth
guide assembly
sequentially

58

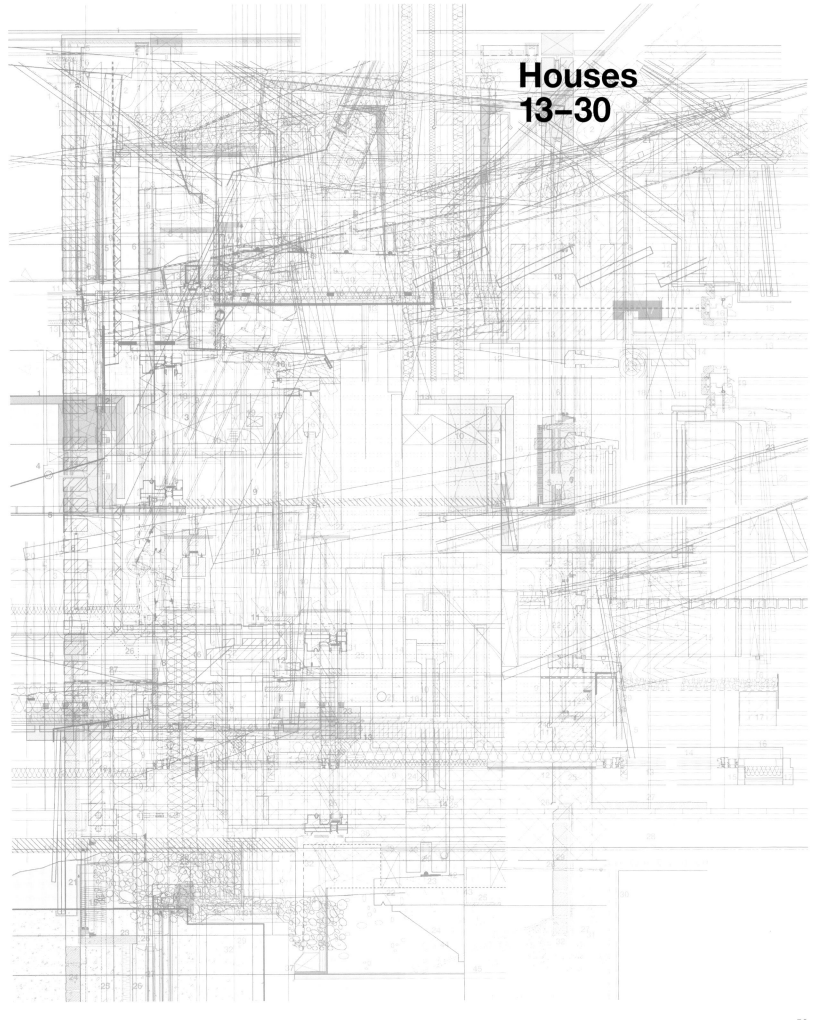

**Houses
13–30**

Salt House
St Lawrence Bay, Essex, England, UK

Project Team
Alison Brooks, Angel Martin Cojo, Juan Francisco Rodriguez

Structural Engineer
Price & Myers

Main Contractor
E.O.Jones + Sons

The Salt House, a contemporary weekend retreat, was built for a client who was interested in the atrium house typology, and in particular strong visual connections within the house due to the special needs of one of the children. The project had the added demand of fulfilling the requirements for new buildings in high-risk flood plains. The two-storey house is located at the end of a terrace of nineteenth century timber-boarded fishermen's houses sheltered by a sea wall. Floodproofing measures required lifting the house above the level of its neighbours, creating a 'bookend' to the terrace, which is balanced by the inn at the other end.

The form and geometry of the house reinterprets the local vernacular of hipped roof, bay windowed cottages. The facade 'bends' so that the highly glazed north and south elevations maximize sea views to the north and passive solar gain from the south. The exterior walls and decks are clad in ipe, a durable hardwood from sustainable forests, while the roof is finished in synthetic slates to match neighbouring roofs while enabling precision cutting. Inside, interconnected spaces are 'wrapped' by wall and ceiling planes. The ground floor is conceived as a continuous landscape that steps up from the entrance courtyard to the timber deck. Huge sliding doors lead to the slate floored central atrium, 'folded' staircase and a sunken living area with a fireplace wall that extends outside to the deck, garden and beach. Upstairs, a second living space and study is bathed in light from the central atrium rooflight. The space is framed by folded elements, including the timber balustrades of the mezzanine, which fold downward to create the staircase, while the facetted walls of the bedrooms are extensions of the trapezoidal roof-light geometry.

1 The family room and guest suite feature large sliding doors onto the south-facing timber deck. The main living spaces (right) also have direct access to the deck while the bedrooms above have expansive views over the landscape.
2 The central atrium features slate flooring and an elegant stair with a timber balustrade on one side that continues downwards from the first floor landing, and a cantilevered glass balustrade on the other.
3 The view from the first floor reveals open vistas of the main living space, which includes a large fireplace.

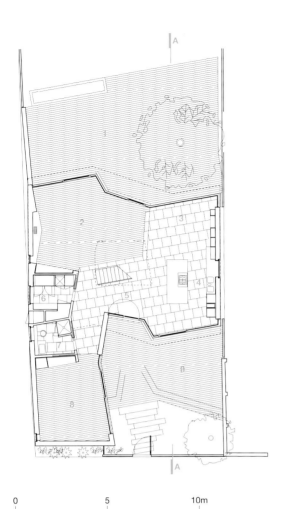

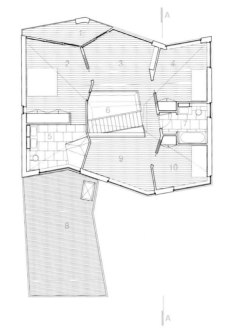

13.01
Ground Floor Plan
1:200
1 Rear deck
2 Living area
3 Dining area
4 Kitchen
5 Entrance
6 Utility room
7 Guest bathroom
8 Guest bedroom /
  family room
9 Front deck

13.02
First Floor Plan
1:200
1 Balcony
2 Master bedroom
3 Family room
4 Bedroom
5 Master bathroom
6 Stair down to
  ground floor
7 Bathroom
8 Roof to guest wing
  on ground floor
9 Study
10 Bedroom

0   5   10m
0   15   30ft

13.03
Section A–A
1:200
1 Garage
2 Tinnocks Lane
3 Guest bedroom /
  family room
4 Front deck
5 Stair
6 Dining area
7 Study
8 Skylight over
  central atrium
9 Family room
10 Rear deck
11 Garden

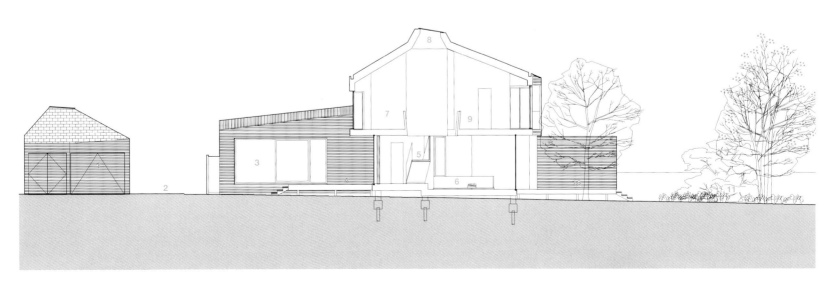

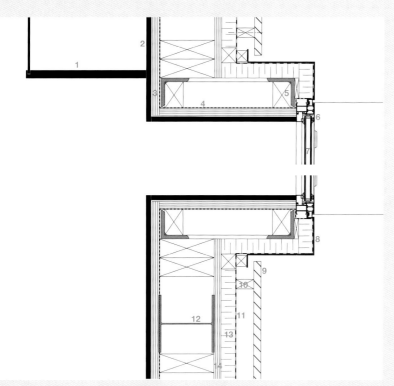

13.04
Kitchen Projecting Window Detail Plan 1:10
1 MDF spray lacquered cupboard carcass
2 600 x 600 mm (23²/₃ x 23²/₃ inch) matt finish limestone tiles
3 Marine plywood
4 Tiles over polythene membrane
5 Timber blocking within 75 x 75 mm (3 x 3 inch) steel angle framing

6 Reynaers fixed window unit
7 30 mm (1¹/₅ inch) glazing unit with 8 mm (³/₁₀ inch) toughened glass outer layer and 16 mm (³/₅ inch) airspace
8 Anodized aluminium flashing
9 19 x 100 mm (³/₄ x 4 inch) hardwood cladding boards with chamfered edges
10 25 x 50 mm (1 x 2 inch) hardwood vertical strapping
11 Breather membrane

12 152 x 152 mm (6 x 6 inch) steel column
13 Wall and ceiling insulation
14 18 mm (7/₁₀ inch) marine plywood

13.05
Typical Window Detail Plan 1:10
1 19 x 100 mm (³/₄ x 4 inch) hardwood cladding board with chamfered edges
2 25 x 50 mm (1 x 2 inch) hardwood vertical strapping
3 Anodized aluminium window surround and sill
4 50 x 150 mm (2 x 6 inch) timber stud
5 MDF spray lacquered cupboard

carcass
6 Dotted line of facade above
7 19 mm (³/₄ inch) MDF covered in oak veneer for window box finish
8 Outward-opening window
9 30 mm (1¹/₅ inch) glazing unit with 8 mm (³/₁₀ inch) toughened glass outer layer and 16 mm (³/₅ inch) airspace
10 Anodized aluminium window surround and sill

11 Breather membrane
12 Wall and ceiling insulation
13 Marine plywood
14 50 x 150 mm (2 x 6 inch) timber stud
15 Vapour barrier
16 25 mm (1 inch) thick double layer of plasterboard
17 12.5 mm (¹/₂ inch) thick single layer of plasterboard
18 50 x 75 mm (2 x 3 inch) timber stud

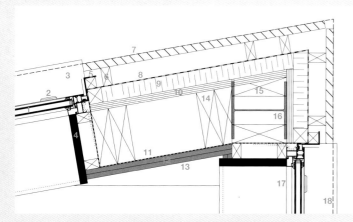

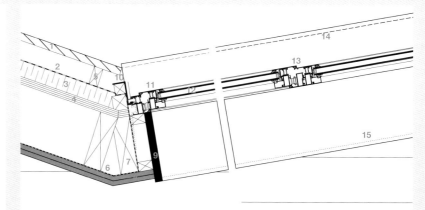

13.06
Wall Junction With Window at North East Corner Detail 1:10
1 30 mm (1¹/₅ inch) glazing unit with 8 mm (³/₁₀ inch) toughened glass outer layer and 16 mm (³/₅ inch) airspace
2 Fixed window
3 Anodized aluminium window surround and sill
4 19 mm (³/₄ inch) MDF covered in oak veneer for window

box finish
5 Anodized aluminium window surround and sill
6 25 x 50 mm (1 x 2 inch) hardwood vertical strapping
7 19 x 100 mm (³/₄ x 4 inch) hardwood cladding board with chamfered edges
8 Breather membrane
9 Wall and ceiling insulation
10 Marine plywood
11 Vapour barrier
12 25 mm (1 inch) thick double layer of

plasterboard
13 Gypsum plaster skim coat
14 50 x 150 mm (2 x 6 inch) timber stud
15 Timber blocking
16 152 x 152 mm (6 x 6 inch) steel column
17 Fixed window
18 Dotted line of facade above

13.07
Wall Junction With Window Next To North East Corner Detail 1:10
1 19 x 100 mm (³/₄ x 4 inch) hardwood cladding board with chamfered edges
2 Breather membrane
3 Wall and ceiling insulation
4 Marine plywood
5 25 x 50 mm (1 x 2 inch) hardwood vertical strapping
6 Vapour barrier

7 50 x 150 mm (2 x 6 inch) timber stud
8 25 mm (1 inch) thick double layer of plasterboard
9 19 mm (³/₄ inch) MDF covered in oak veneer for window box finish
10 Anodized aluminium window surround and sill
11 Outwards-opening window
12 30 mm (1¹/₅ inch) glazing unit with 8 mm (³/₁₀ inch) toughened glass outer layer and

16 mm (³/₅ inch) airspace
13 Transom / changeover
14 Dotted line of facade above
15 Dotted line of steel centre line

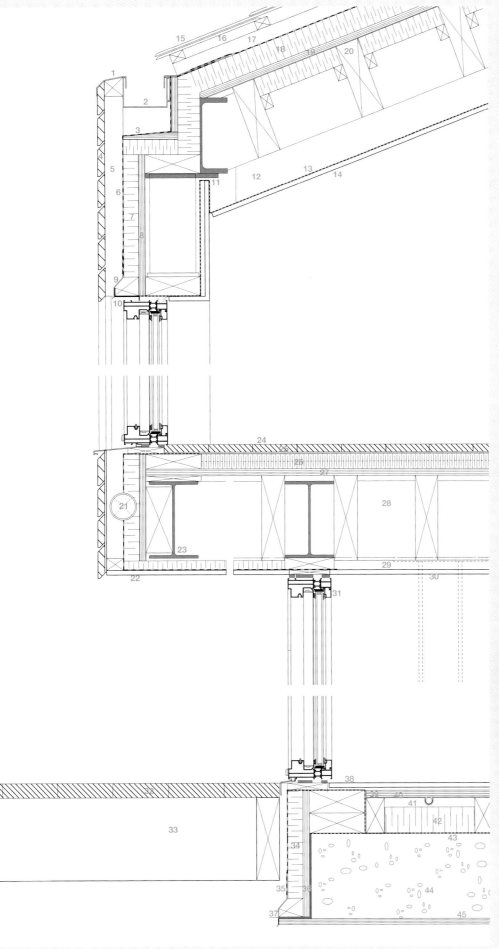

13.08
Sectional Detail at Entrance Window (Ground Floor) and Study Window (First Floor)
1:10

1 Preformed silver anodized aluminium coping to eaves and parapet
2 Box gutter including gutter outlet
3 Plywood sheathing sloped from 10 mm (2/5 inch) to 22 mm (4/5 inch) for drainage purposes
4 19 x 100 mm (3/4 x 4 inch) hardwood cladding boards with chamfered edges
5 25 x 50 mm (1 x 2 inch) hardwood vertical strapping
6 Breather membrane
7 Wall and ceiling insulation
8 Marine plywood
9 Timber cant stripe
10 Monorail sliding window system
11 200 x 75 mm (79/10 x 3 inch) steel beam with 200 x 100 mm (79/10 x 4 inch) plate welded to underside
12 90 x 50 mm (31/2 x 2 inch) battens
13 Vapour barrier
14 12.5 mm (1/2 inch) thick single layer of plasterboard
15 600 x 300 mm (232/3 x 114/5 inch) roof slates
16 38 x 25 mm (11/2 x 1 inch) timber battens
17 38 x 25 mm (11/2 x 1 inch) timber counter battens
18 60 mm (21/3 inch) roof insulation
19 Marine plywood screwed to joists

20 200 x 63 mm (79/10 x 21/2 inch) timber purlins
21 63 mm (21/2 inch) diameter water pipe
22 Single layer of Supalux exterior plasterboard
23 203 x 133 mm (8 x 51/4 inch) steel beam
24 20 x 120 mm (3/4 x 43/4 inch) hardwood flooring
25 Heat emission plate
26 Underfloor heating system
27 Marine plywood
28 225 x 63 mm (84/5 x 21/2 inch) timber joist
29 25 x 50 mm (1 x 2 inch) timber battens
30 12.5 mm (1/2 inch) thick single layer of plasterboard
31 Monorail sliding window system
32 Hardwood external deck board flooring
33 225 x 63 mm (84/5 x 21/2 inch) timber joist
34 Wall and ceiling insulation
35 Breather membrane
36 Marine plywood
37 Metal flashing
38 600 x 600 mm (232/3 x 232/3 inch) limestone floor tiles
39 Marine plywood
40 Heat emission plate
41 Underfloor heating system
42 70 mm (23/4 inch) rigid floor insulation
43 Polythene vapour control barrier
44 225 mm (84/5 inch) thick reinforced concrete slab
45 Exterior grade plywood

Lago Vista Lake House
Lago Vista, Texas, USA

Client
John Huke

Project Team
Thomas Bercy, Calvin Chen

Structural Engineer
Structures, P.E.

Quantity Surveyor
Craig Creager

Lighting Designer
Guenter Recht

Located just 45 minutes from the capital of Texas, the Lago Vista Lake House is submerged into the tranquility of the region's hill country. The structure is located above a small creek, which leads down to the lake below. Commissioned by a highly creative family including a painter, writer and set-designer, the Lago Vista residence programme called for a weekend haven for the artistically inclined family, which also doubles as an inspiring retreat for visiting artists and writers. The concept is a simple shed structure with a large cantilevered roof covering an expansive exterior terrace.

The entry side of the house is expressed as a timber box containing the functional spaces. Having passed through the utilitarian core, the house opens on all sides towards the terrace and creek beyond. The cantilevered structure is further expressed in the foundation in order to convey a sense of levitation. The design creates the feeling of a delicate garden pavilion hovering above the rugged Texas landscape. The structure is a rectangular steel frame with glass enclosures orientated to face the setting sun and the ravine. The glass facade allows uninterrupted vistas over the beautiful landscape of cedar groves and limestone outcrops. The cantilevered roof overhang shades an oversized terrace, creating a generous outdoor space for painting and relaxing. By day the structure is open to the sound of water and the play of light and shadow beneath the trees, while at night its ipe clad timber walls and ceiling are washed with soft light.

1 The 4-metre (14-foot) cantilevered roof protects the oversized terrace, which acts as the main living and relaxation space for the house.
2 The terrace wraps around the pavilion, sitting lightly on the landscape. The timber shell to the rear of the building visually holds the building in place, allowing the expanses of clear glazing that delineate the main spaces to sit lightly underneath the dramatic roof.

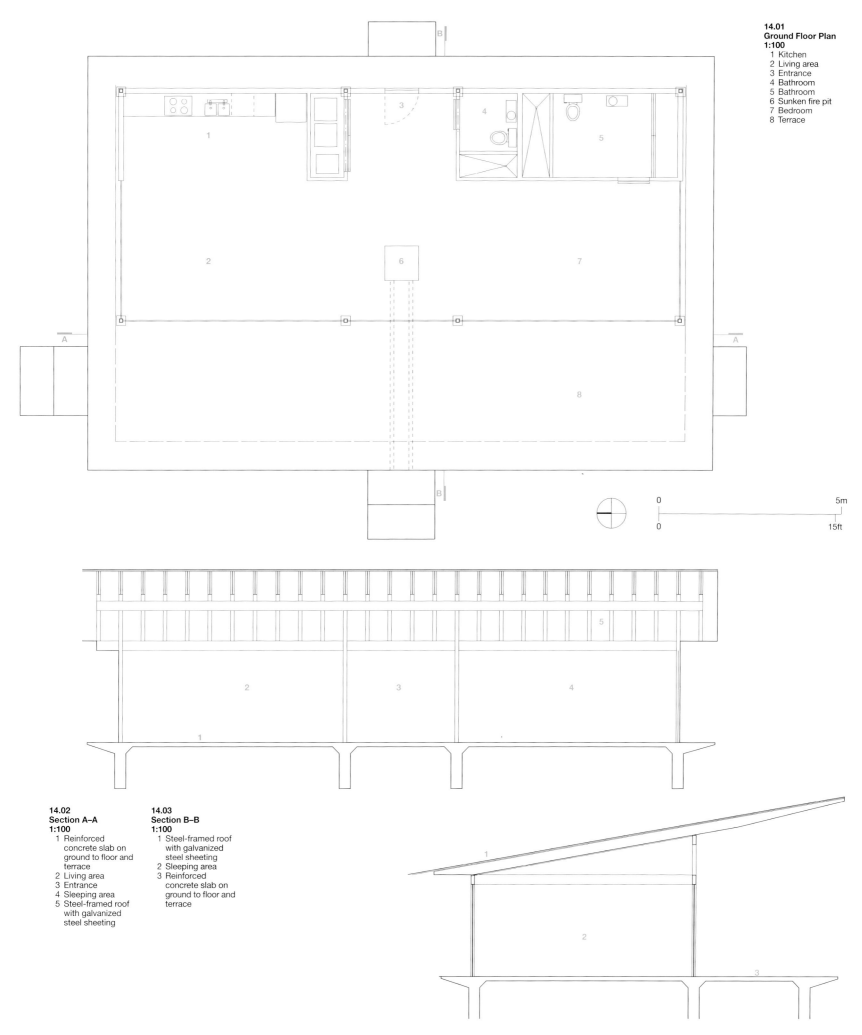

14.01
Ground Floor Plan
1:100
1 Kitchen
2 Living area
3 Entrance
4 Bathroom
5 Bathroom
6 Sunken fire pit
7 Bedroom
8 Terrace

0   5m

0   15ft

14.02
Section A–A
1:100
1 Reinforced
  concrete slab on
  ground to floor and
  terrace
2 Living area
3 Entrance
4 Sleeping area
5 Steel-framed roof
  with galvanized
  steel sheeting

14.03
Section B–B
1:100
1 Steel-framed roof
  with galvanized
  steel sheeting
2 Sleeping area
3 Reinforced
  concrete slab on
  ground to floor and
  terrace

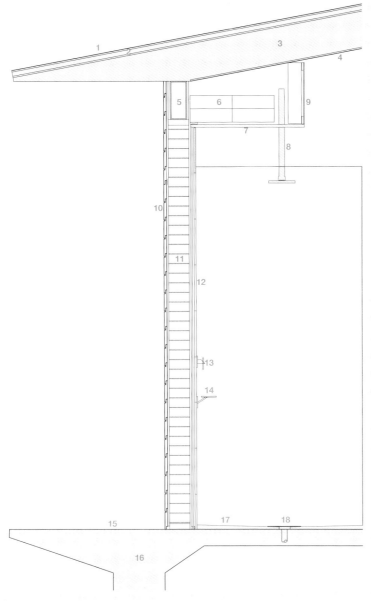

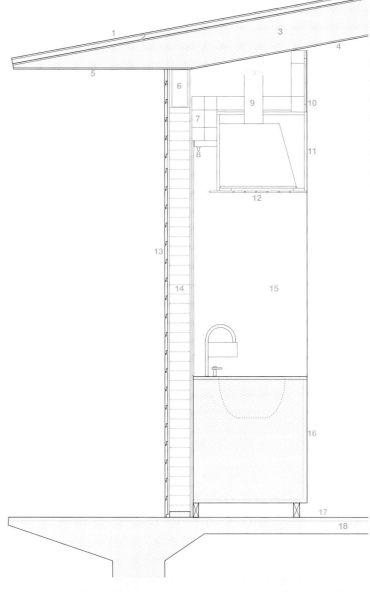

14.04
Detail Section Through Bathroom 1:25
 1 Galvanized metal screw-down roof sheeting
 2 19 mm (3/4 inch) plywood decking over Polyiso insulation
 3 254 x 482 mm (10 x 19 inch) steel beam
 4 25 x 152 mm (1 x 6 inch) ipe ceiling panels
 5 100 x 254 x 6 mm (4 x 10 x 1/4 inch) steel rectangular hollow section
 6 Air conditioning duct
 7 Ipe timber panel
 8 Rain shower
 9 6 mm (1/4 inch) steel fascia panel with

clear powder coat finish
10 Ipe siding
11 Insulation
12 Tiles to shower area
13 Shower valve
14 Soap shelf
15 Self-levelling epoxy floor finish over
16 Reinforced concrete floor slab and footings on grade
17 Floor tiles laid to fall
18 Drain

14.05
Detail Section Through Kitchen 1:25
 1 Galvanized metal screw-down roof sheeting
 2 19 mm (3/4 inch) plywood decking over Polyiso insulation
 3 254 x 482 mm (10 x 19 inch) steel beam
 4 25 x 152 mm (1 x 6 inch) ipe ceiling panels
 5 Steel plate soffit
 6 100 x 254 x 6 mm (4 x 10 x 1/4 inch) steel rectangular hollow section
 7 Air conditioning duct
 8 Concealed fluorescent light fixture
 9 254 mm (10 inch)

diameter duct
10 6 mm (1/4 inch) steel fascia panel with clear powder coat finish
11 Cabinet access door to exhaust hood
12 Ventilation hood with filter
13 Ipe timber external cladding
14 Insulation
15 Steel plate wall finish to kitchen area beyond
16 Kitchen counter
17 Self-levelling epoxy floor finish over concrete slab
18 Reinforced concrete floor slab and footings on grade

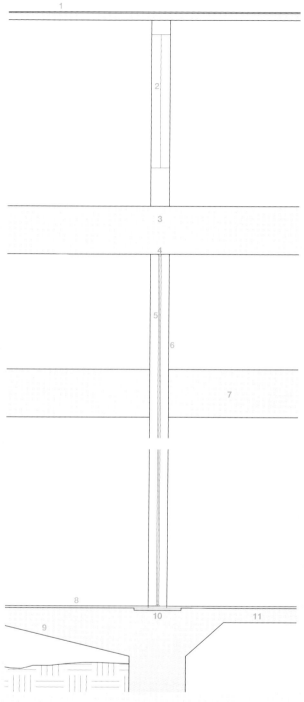

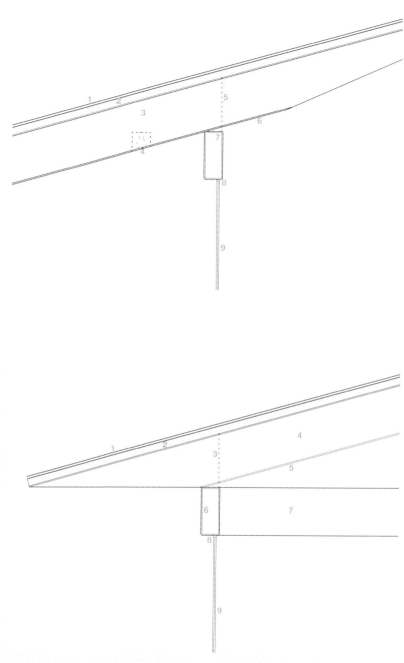

14.06
Detail Section Through External Glazed Wall
1:20
1 Galvanized metal screw-down roof sheeting
2 254 x 482 mm (10 x 19 inch) steel beam tapered at end
3 100 x 254 x 6 mm (4 x 10 x 1/4 inch) steel rectangular hollow section painted black
4 Structural silicone glazing joint
5 Double glazed tinted tempered glass
6 100 x 100 x 6 mm (4 x 4 x 1/4 inch) steel rectangular hollow section painted black
7 100 x 254 x 6 mm

(4 x 10 x 1/4 inch) steel rectangular hollow section painted black
8 Self-levelling epoxy floor finish over concrete slab
9 Tapered concrete cantilevered slab edge
10 254 x 254 x 12 mm (10 x 10 x 1/2 inch) steel plate
11 Reinforced concrete slab on ground

14.07
Detail Section Through Roof Overhang and Glazed Wall 1
1:20
1 Galvanized metal screw-down roof sheeting
2 Steel Vulcraft decking
3 254 x 482 mm (10 x 19 inch) steel beam tapered at end
4 Lighting
5 6 mm (1/4 inch) steel plate shown dotted
6 25 x 152 mm (1 x 6 inch) ipe ceiling panels
7 100 x 254 x 6 mm (4 x 10 x 1/4 inch) steel rectangular hollow section painted black

8 Structural silicone glazing joint
9 Double-glazed tinted tempered glass

14.08
Detail Section Through Roof Overhang and Glazed Wall 1
1:20
1 Galvanized metal screw-down roof sheeting
2 Steel Vulcraft decking
3 6 mm (1/4 inch) steel plate shown dotted
4 254 x 482 mm (10 x 19 inch) steel beam
5 25 x 152 mm (1 x 6 inch) ipe ceiling panels
6 100 x 254 x 6 mm

(4 x 10 x 1/4 inch) steel rectangular hollow section painted black
7 100 x 254 x 6 mm (4 x 10 x 1/4 inch) steel rectangular hollow section painted black
8 Structural silicone glazing joint
9 Double-glazed tinted tempered glass

Beach House
North Caicos, Turks and Caicos
Islands

Project Team
Seth Stein, Andrew Abdulezer,
Richard Vint

Structural Engineer
Atelier 1

Services Engineer
Atelier 10

This luxurious holiday home is located on a deserted beach on North Caicos Island. Each of the three bedrooms, and the main living accommodation, are expressed as individual structures connected by a raised timber walkway. The indigenous dwarf tropical dry forest provides natural screening between the individual pavilions. The plan, whilst adhering to the constraints of the local authorities regarding the distance of buildings from the beach, nevertheless follows a rational grid dictated by the various forms of enclosure as set out in the brief. Various aspects of shelter are provided through a range of enclosure options – mesh screens to maintain air movement, and louvres within sliding or fixed panels to manipulate natural light, ventilation and storm protection. The elimination of glazing as an enclosing element, in conjunction with the shaded perimeter, maximizes openness while eliminating solar gain.

The facade system, which consists of a timber frame module, acts as a filter to the natural environment by adjusting manually to daylight, storm or insect conditions. In the bedroom pavilions, the rear elevation can be opened up completely to unite the shower with the natural vegetation. The bedroom pavilions are arranged with the sleeping area at the centre, gradually opening up towards the beach with a screened sitting area and an open verandah. On the other side of the bedroom, the bathroom occupies one structural bay and includes a semi-enclosed WC and bidet area, cupboards, wardrobes and a niche for hanging rails. The main space features a shower with a curved corrugated steel screen that opens up to the landscape, and a custom-made cantilevered concrete bench with a sculptural stone basin.

1 View of the bedroom pavilions. The open verandahs face the beach and are protected by a timber overhang on the curved roof which culminates in a louvred brise soleil.
2 The living pavilion is elevated above the garage which is approached via a walled driveway
3 View of the living pavilion. The white kitchen is featured against the simple timber finishes used throughout the space.
4 Layers of timber-framed screens and sliding panels protect the bedroom pavilion from the sun, while allowing views of the sand dunes.
5 View of the sleeping space in the bedroom pavilion.

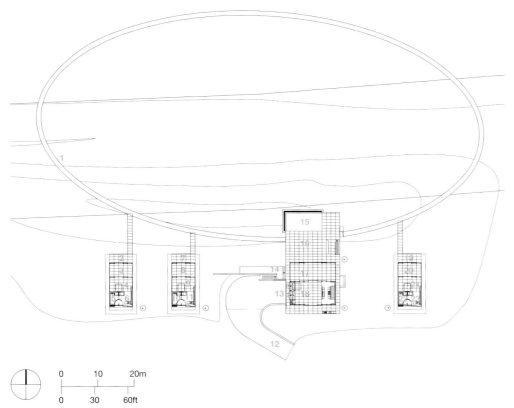

0   10   20m
0   30   60ft

15.01
Ground Floor Plan
1:1000
1 Ramped
  boardwalk to
  beach
2 Open terrace to
  bedroom pavilion
3 Screened terrace
4 Bedroom
5 WC
6 Shower room
7 Open terrace to
  bedroom pavilion
8 Screened terrace
9 Bedroom
10 WC
11 Shower room
12 Driveway
13 Entrance to garage
   and laundry
14 Entrance stair and
   ramp
15 Swimming pool
16 Open terrace to
   living pavilion
17 Screened terrace
18 Kitchen, dining
and living space
19 Open terrace to
   bedroom pavilion
20 Screened terrace
21 Bedroom
22 WC
23 Shower room

15.02
Section A–A
1:100
1 Corrugated metal
  roof on timber
  frame
2 Timber louvred
  between projecting
  beams
3 Stone basin
4 Concrete
  countertop
5 Sliding timber
  framed panel with
adjustable timber
louvres and insect
screen
6 Corrugated metal
  shower enclosure
7 Sliding timber
  framed panel
8 Corrugated metal
  shower enclosure
9 Mirror
10 Bidet
11 Reinforced
   concrete floor slab
12 Timber cladding

15.03
Bedroom Pavilion
Plan
1:100
1 Open terrace
2 Screened terrace
3 Bedroom
4 Cupboard
5 WC
6 Bidet
7 Hot water boiler
8 Wardrobe
9 Corrugated metal
  shower enclosure
10 Shower
11 Hanging rail
12 Stone bench and
   concrete basin

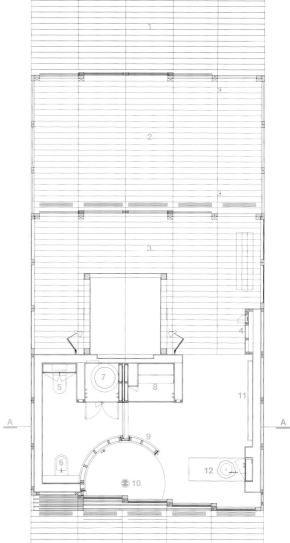

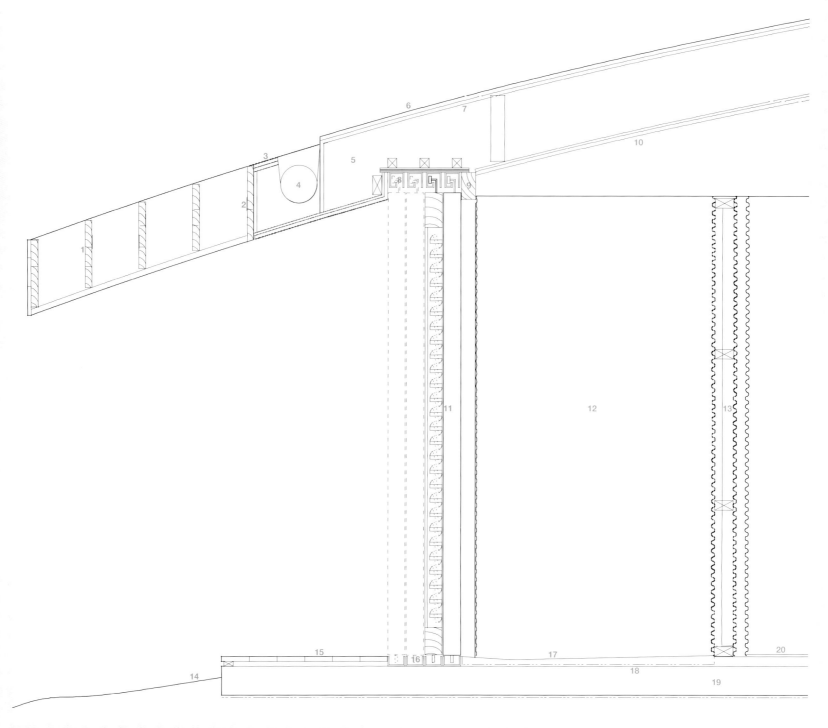

15.04
Bedroom Pavilion
Detail Section 1
1:20
1 Brazilian oak
louvres fixed between
projecting beams
2 Brazilian oak fascia
3 Marine ply
4 Rainwater gutter
5 Insulation
6 Corrugated metal
roof sheeting

7 Marine ply roofing
substrate
8 Recessed tracks
for top hung sliding
panels
9 Brazilian oak block
to match ceiling
cladding
10 Brazilian oak ceiling
lining
11 Sliding timber
framed panel with
adjustable timber

louvres and insect
screen
12 Corrugated metal
cladding to shower
enclosure
13 Timber-framed wall
to shower enclosure
14 Made up ground
level around building
15 Ipe decking
16 Recessed guides
for sliding panels
17 Minimum fall to

deck for effective
drainage
18 Damp proof
membrane
19 Reinforced
concrete membrane
20 Concrete floor
finish

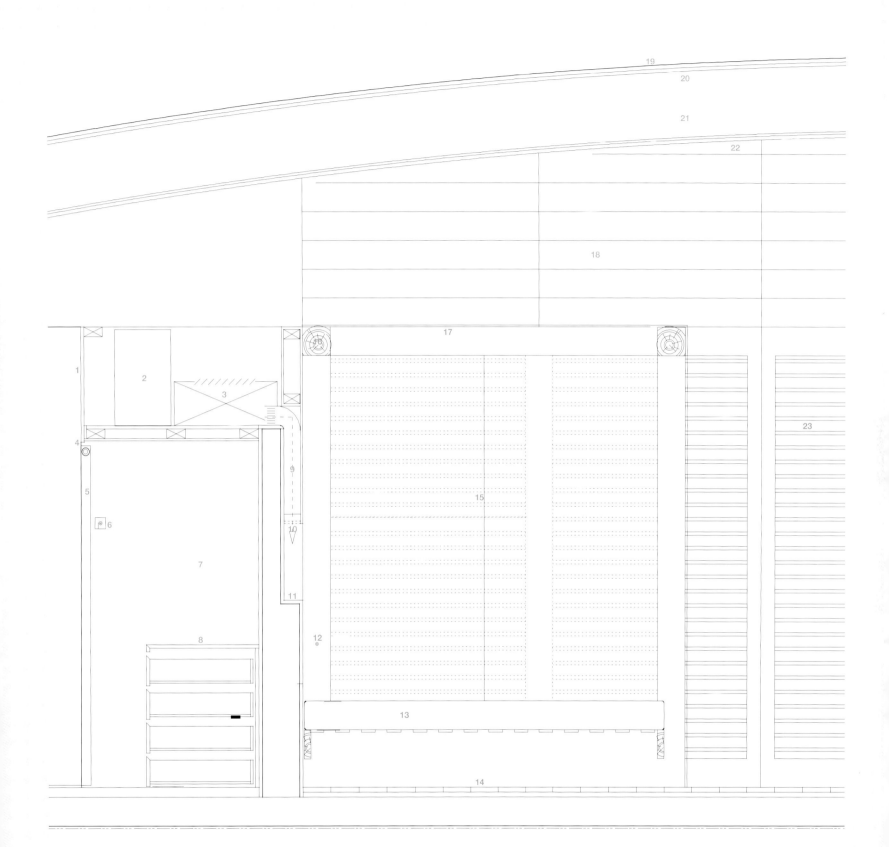

15.05
Bedroom Pavilion
Detail Section 2
1:20
 1 Painted bulkhead
to WC area
 2 Electric boiler
 3 Air conditioning
unit
 4 Finger pull to
cupboard door
 5 Unbleached calico
curtain on track to

cupboard
 6 Switch to WC lights
and extractor fan
 7 Hanging space
 8 Drawers
 9 Air conditioning
duct
 10 Air conditioning
grille
 11 Shelf alcove
 12 Switch to bedside
lamp
 13 Bespoke four

poster bed with insect
screen surround
 14 Brazilian oak floor
 15 Opening to insect
screen
 16 150 x 150 mm (6 x
6 inch) timber battens
to bed frame
 17 Insect screen fixed
in position with Velcro
 18 Brazilian oak
cladding to wall
 19 Corrugated metal

roof cladding
 20 Marine ply roofing
substrate
 21 Insulation
 22 Brazilian oak ceiling
lining
 23 Fixed timber
framed panel with
adjustable timber
louvres

Cedar House
Norfolk, England, UK

Project Team
Anthony Hudson, Dieter Kleiner

Structural Engineer
Alan Conisbee Associates

Quantity Surveyor
Roger Rawlinson Associates

The Cedar House is a prototype for cost-effective, new-build modern housing, designed for a photographer and his family. The brief was for a simple house with two bedrooms and a third room, which could function as both a guest room and office. A separate area was required for a dark room and a larger spacious gallery–studio with separate loading access for large canvases and prints. Situated in the countryside of North Elmham, on the River Wensum, it was important that the building was sensitive to its surroundings and sat comfortably with the local agricultural landscape. The result is a modest rural building, simple in form and evocative of a functional farm building.

A system of prefabricated timber panel floors, walls and roofing, made the building fast to assemble on-site and offered high levels of insulation. In addition, a lightweight roof structure eliminates roof beams, permitting soaring ceilings and seamless open-plan spaces. Large openings, even across corners, were possible without the need for additional structural reinforcement. The final scheme incorporates a cantilevered corner window which frames views onto the river from the living room and a line of glazed doors which fold in completely, extending the living room onto a raised deck. The building has been entirely cloaked in 15,000 untreated cedar shingles, a material which belies the prefabricated system beneath. Fixed to battens over a breathable waste-woodchip building board, cedar was chosen as a more cost effective alternative to weatherboarding. Coupled with the clean lines of the aluminium window surrounds and integrated into a design which cleverly conceals obtrusive rainwater systems, the cedar reads as a dramatic sleek protective cloak, which sits harmoniously with its countryside surroundings.

1 With its walls and roof clad in untreated cedar shingles, the house sits easily in its rural surroundings. Window and door details, including the sliding, folding doors to the living room (left) give the simple building a contemporary twist.
2 The living space opens onto a timber deck via sliding folding timber doors.
3 View of the living room and kitchen. A wood burning stove is incorporated into the kitchen joinery.
4 Clear anodized aluminium window and door surrounds create a transition between the cedar wall shingles and glazed openings.

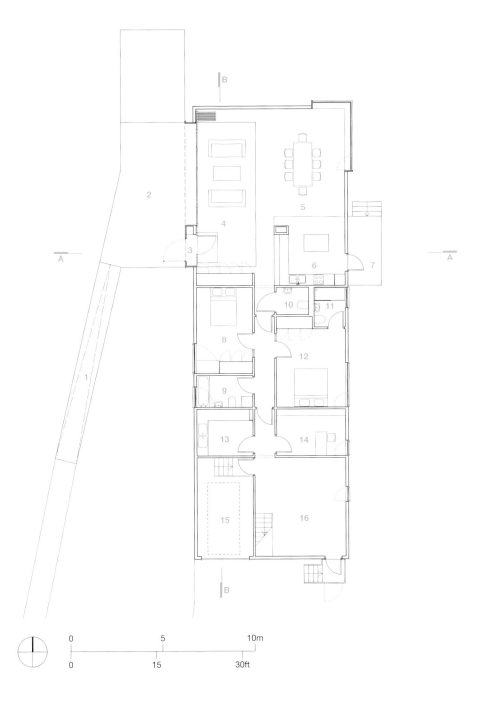

16.01
Ground Floor Plan
1:200
1 Ramp
2 Terrace
3 Entrance
4 Living area
5 Dining area
6 Kitchen
7 Entrance deck
8 Bedroom
9 Bathroom
10 WC
11 Master bathroom
12 Master bedroom
13 Darkroom
14 Office
15 Garage and
   storage with
   mezzanine above
16 Studio

16.02
Section A–A
1:200
1 Terrace
2 Entrance
3 Stacked glass
   doors to terrace
4 Kitchen
5 Kitchen island
6 Corner window
7 Entrance deck

16.03
Section B–B
1:200
1 Mezzanine storage
   to garage
2 Garage
3 Stair up to studio
4 Darkroom
5 Bathroom
6 Bedroom
7 Storage
   cupboards to living
   room
8 Entrance
9 Glass doors to
   terrace
10 Terrace

0   5   10m
0   15   30ft

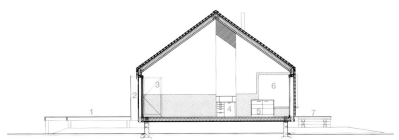

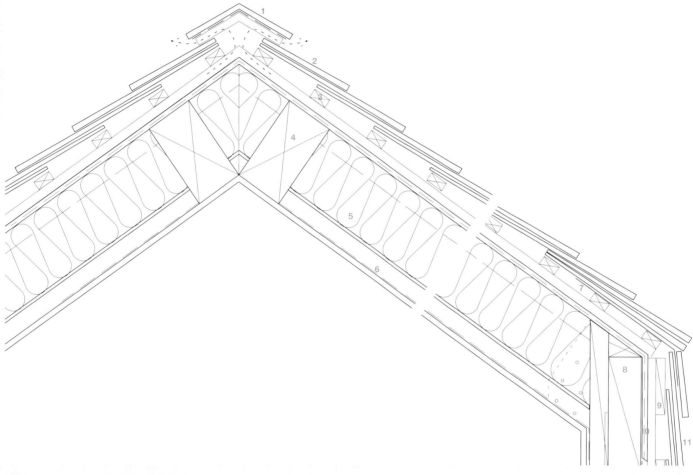

16.04
Roof and Eaves
Detail
1:10
1 Cedar ridge cap
over continuous ridge
ventilator
2 Untreated cedar
roof shingles
3 25 x 50 mm (1 x 2
inch) timber battens
4 Double ridge
beams concealed in
roof thickness
5 Prefabricated roof
cassette comprised of
timber joists at 400
mm (15³/₄ inch)
centres, 9 mm (¹/₃
inch) oriented strand
board, insulation and
15 mm (³/₅ inch)
woodchip breathable
roofing board
6 Vapourcheck
barrier over 12.5 mm
(¹/₂ inch) thick
plasterboard with 2.5
mm (¹/₁₀ inch) skim
coat and paint finish
7 Concealed metal
eaves flashing
8 Parallam edge
beam
9 Treated softwood
eaves board
10 15 mm (³/₅ inch)
taped and sealed
bitroc board
11 Untreated cedar
wall shingles

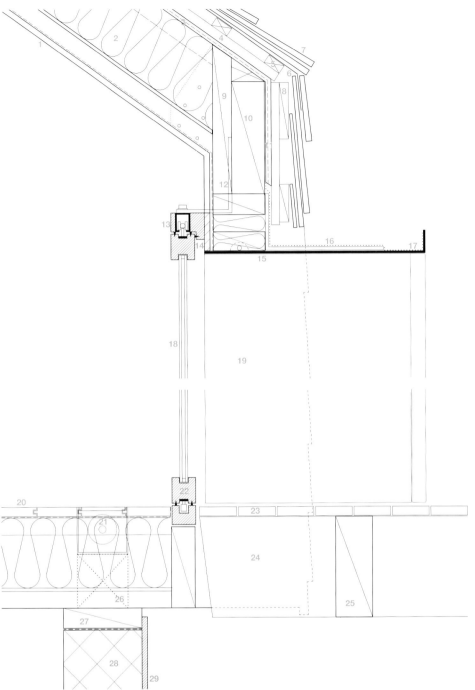

16.05
Sliding Glass Door Detail
1:10

1 Vapourcheck barrier over 12.5 mm (1/2 inch) thick plasterboard with 2.5 mm (1/10 inch) skim coat and paint finish
2 Prefabricated roof cassette comprised of timber joists at 400 mm (153/4 inch) centres, 9 mm (1/3 inch) oriented strand board, insulation and 15 mm (3/5 inch) woodchip breathable roofing board
3 15 mm (3/5 inch) taped and sealed bitroc board
4 25 x 50 mm (1 x 2 inch) soft wood timber battens
5 25 x 50 mm (1 x 2 inch) timber battens
6 Concealed metal eaves flashing
7 Untreated cedar wall shingles
8 Treated softwood eaves board
9 51 x 400 mm (2 x 153/4 inch) end of cassette beam
10 Parallam edge beam
11 15 mm (3/5 inch) taped and sealed bitroc board
12 Steel brackets to support sliding folding doors
13 Sliding folding doors on internal face of wall hung from hidden steel brackets
14 15 mm (3/5 inch) cementitious board to externally exposed areas of internal wall face
15 600 x 60 x 3 mm (232/3 x 21/3 x 1/10 inch) folded metal soffit and opening surround with five factory-cut holes for downlights
16 Two part paint applied gutter membrane with UV protection over brackets, wall and top surface of metal soffit only (not applied to vertical sides)
17 Steel angle gutter / soffit brackets
18 Double-glazed folding sliding doors
19 Galvanized steel clad weather and boil-proof plywood porch enclosure
20 24 mm (9/10 inch) thick tongue and groove floorboards
21 Trench heating
22 Sliding folding doors on internal face of wall hung from hidden steel brackets
23 External timber decking
24 Timber joists
25 Timber joists
26 Floor joists notched for trench heating
27 215 x 53 mm (81/2 x 2 inch) soft wood wall plate
28 225 mm (84/5 inch) blockwork sleeper wall
29 15 mm (3/5 inch) sand cement render

16.06
Window Detail
1:10

1 Vapourcheck barrier over 12.5 mm (1/2 inch) thick plasterboard with 2.5 mm (1/10 inch) skim coat and paint finish
2 Prefabricated roof cassette comprised of timber joists at 400 mm (153/4 inch) centres, 9 mm (1/3 inch) oriented strand board, insulation and 15 mm (3/5 inch) woodchip breathable roofing board
3 15 mm (3/5 inch) taped and sealed bitroc board
4 25 x 50 mm (1 x 2 inch) soft wood timber battens
5 25 x 50 mm (1 x 2 inch) timber battens
6 Concealed metal eaves flashing
7 Untreated cedar wall shingles
8 Treated softwood eaves board
9 51 x 400 mm (2 x 153/4 inch) end of cassette beam
10 Parallam edge beam
11 15 mm (3/5 inch) taped and sealed bitroc board
12 12.5 mm (1/2 inch) taped, jointed and painted plasterboard wall lining over painted MDF linings and skirtings with stop bead at head
13 15 mm (3/5 inch) painted MDF window linings and reveals, butt jointed with 4 x 4 mm (1/6 x 1/6 inch)
14 Damp proof course lapped over angle surrounds at head and under at jambs and under pre-formed sill
15 150 x 150 mm (6 x 6 inch) anodized aluminium angles to form window head and jamb surrounds fixed directly to windows
16 Mill-finished aluminium window frame
17 Double-glazed window unit
18 Location of folding shutters shown dotted
19 Vertical damp proof course lapped under surrounds
20 Double-glazed timber windows with tilt turn operation, trickle vents in head, rebate
14 Damp proof course lapped over angle surrounds at head and under at jambs and under pre-formed sill
21 Timber sill
22 Metal sill flashing concealed between shingles
23 Untreated cedar wall shingles
24 15 mm (3/5 inch) painted MDF wall linings butt jointed with 4 x 4 mm (1/6 x 1/6 inch) rebate
25 Timber floorboards
26 Timber floor joist
27 215 x 53 mm (81/2 x 2 inch) soft wood wall plate
28 225 mm (84/5 inch) blockwork sleeper wall
29 15 mm (3/5 inch) sand cement render

clear matt seal internally and mill-finish aluminium clad externally including sill

Future House
Sydney, New South Wales, Australia

Client
Timber Development Association
(NSW)

Project Team
Stephanie Smith, Ken McBryde, Alex
Phegan, Andreas Traxler, Tine
Fonnesberg, Louise Balle

Structural Design and Prefabrication
Bruce Hutchings Timberbuilt

Main Contractor
Joseph Moser

Innovarchi was selected to design the
timber house for the Year of the Built
Environment House of the Future
exhibition in 2004, held in the
Sydney Opera House Forecourt and
Sydney Olympic Park. The exhibition
was a showcase of six sustainable,
affordable and futuristic housing
designs, each using a different base
material. Innovarchi's timber house
explores the single-family dwelling
and its relationship to the
environment. Instead of the house
having a series of options promoting
ecological sustainability that may
or may not be included by the buyer,
the Future House incorporates
ecological sustainability as part of the
core solution.

The surface has been developed as
a metaphor for a piece of landscape.
It undulates to form internal and
external spaces that blur the
distinction between the natural and
the built environment. The skin
simultaneously becomes roof, wall
and floor, depending on its location.
This skin also acts as a shading
mechanism, a solar collector,
maximizes water catchment and
houses the recycling systems. It is
also the place that people inhabit and
experience those systems as part of
the external environment of the house.
Whilst some typical timber products
are used, the house aims to challenge
traditional thought about how timber
can be employed. It introduces
advances in materials technology
by using compressed wood fibre for
the skin, which represents more
judicial use of renewable resources.

1 The cladding is
natural wood-fibre
compressed panels,
embossed to create a
non-slip surface. The
strip of glazing is also
a fully integrated
dye-based solar
collector. By day it acts
as a skylight, and
landscape feature-
lighting by night.
2 The arching wings of
the compressed wood-
fibre shells describe
the three main spaces
of the interior – the
living spaces, the
bedroom and
bathroom, and the
wet area pod, which
contains the shower
room and WC.
3 LED floor-lighting
provides gentle
ambient light by night.
4 View of the kitchen
where grey water is
collected and recycled.
The internal modular
wall and ceiling linings
are fixed by Velcro,
and are readily
changed to suit the
changing needs of the
inhabitants.

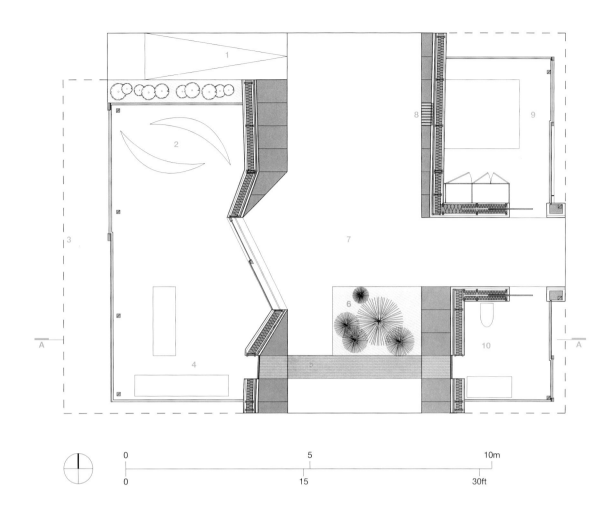

0		5		10m
0		15		30ft

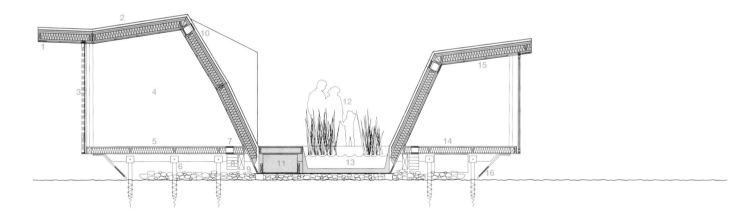

77

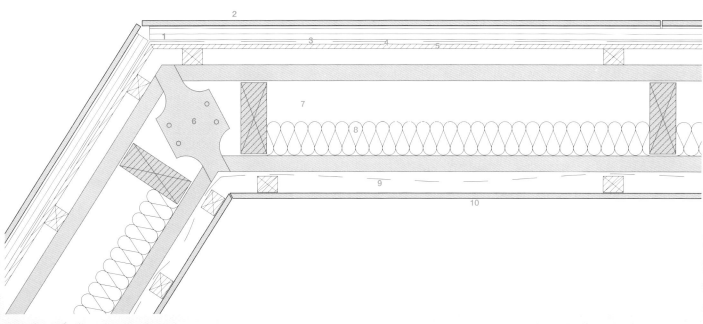

17.03
Typical Wall / Roof Cladding Detail
1:10
1 Velcro joint
2 Compressed wood-fibre cladding
3 Insulated reflective paper foil ventilation duct
4 Waterproof membrane
5 12 mm (1/2 inch) plywood

6 Timber fixing plate
7 Laminated veneer timber beam
8 Foil-backed insulation
9 Damp proof membrane
10 Timber panel wall and ceiling lining

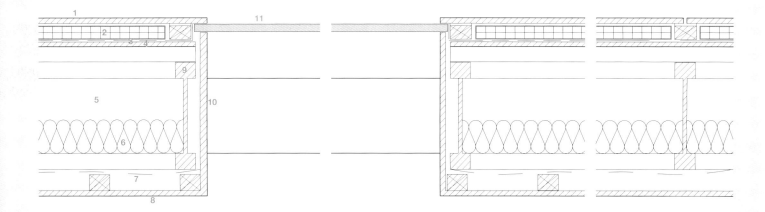

17.04
Wall / Roof Cladding with Solar Panel Detail
1:10
1 Compressed wood-fibre cladding
2 Velcro joint
3 Insulated reflective paper foil ventilation duct
4 Waterproof membrane
5 Laminated veneer

timber beam
6 Foil-backed insulation
7 Damp proof membrane
8 Timber panel wall and ceiling lining
9 Laminated veneer timber beam
10 Compressed wood-fibre reveal to solar panel / window opening
11 Solar titania cells

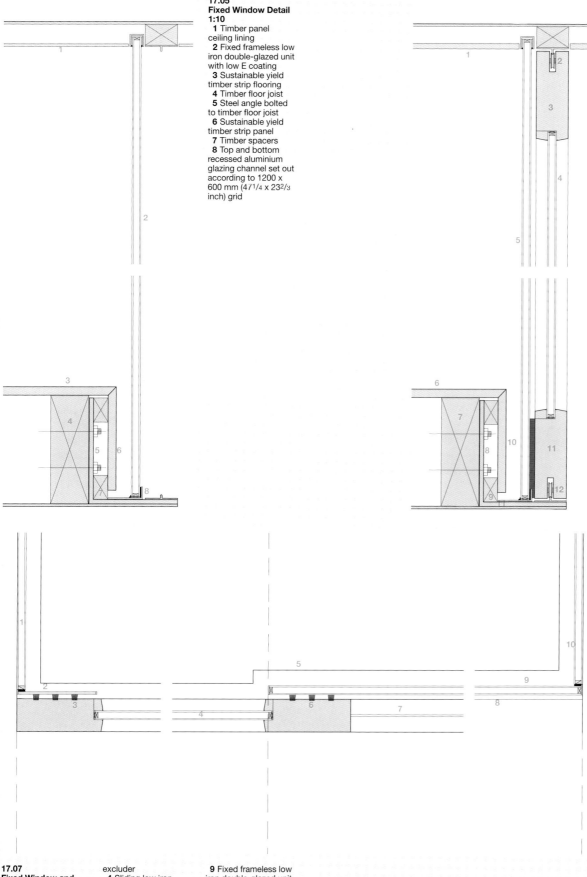

17.05
Fixed Window Detail
1:10
1 Timber panel
ceiling lining
2 Fixed frameless low
iron double-glazed unit
with low E coating
3 Sustainable yield
timber strip flooring
4 Timber floor joist
5 Steel angle bolted
to timber floor joist
6 Sustainable yield
timber strip panel
7 Timber spacers
8 Top and bottom
recessed aluminium
glazing channel set out
according to 1200 x
600 mm (4 $^1/_4$ x 23$^2/_3$
inch) grid

17.06
Fixed Window and
Sliding Door
Sectional Detail
1:10
1 Timber panel
timber ceiling lining
2 Recessed sliding
extruded track for
glazed door
3 Timber door frame
4 Sliding low iron
double glazed unit with
low E coating
5 Fixed frameless low
iron double glazed unit
with low E coating
6 Sustainable yield
timber strip flooring
7 Timber floor joist
8 Steel angle bolted
to timber floor joist
9 Timber spacers
10 Sustainable yield
timber strip panel
11 Timber door frame
12 Recessed sliding
extruded track for
glazed door

17.07
Fixed Window and
Sliding Door Plan
Detail
1:20
1 Fixed frameless low
iron double-glazed unit
with low E coating set
in top and bottom
recessed aluminium
channel
2 Fixed laminated
glass
3 Brush draft

excluder
4 Sliding low iron
double-glazed unit
with low E coating in
timber frame with
recessed extruded
aluminium track
5 Line of floor edge
steps around glass line
6 Brush draft
excluder
7 Sliding door track
8 Damp proof
membrane

9 Fixed frameless low
iron double-glazed unit
with low E coating set
in top and bottom
recessed aluminium
channel
10 Fixed frameless low
iron double-glazed unit
with low E coating set
in top and bottom
recessed aluminium
channel

Cape Schanck House
Cape Schanck, Victoria, Australia

Project Team
Tim Jackson, Jon Clements, Graham
Burrows, Kim Stapleton, George
Fortey, Brett Nixon

Structural Engineer
Adams Consulting Engineers

Main Contractor
BD Projects

Landscape Architect
Site Office Landscape Architects

On the architects' first visit to the site, which features dense coastal heath and ti-tree shrubs, they discovered the remnants of a hollowed-out burnt log. This provided a starting point for an architectural exploration where the form of the log suggested possibilities for the design solution. On approach, the visitor is confronted by an expansive wall which conceals the upper level. The lower level extends from the steep ground plane as a rendered plinth and forms a base much like the surrounding dunes. The entry experience opens to expansive views over the living area, deck and pool. The upper level (conceived as a hollowed-out log) contains the kitchen, dining area, living room, garage and laundry. A secondary upper level (conceived as a branch of the log) contains the study, master bedroom and ensuite. These forms are both finished in spotted gum hardwood cladding, stained black. Cedar windows and cladding with a natural finish are slotted into the exterior.

The lower level contains guest accommodation and conceals functional plant spaces for mechanical systems and pool equipment. The house is orientated to the north-west embracing expansive views. To control passive heating in summer, the western windows are protected by extensive eaves, and motorized external louvres automatically descend once the sun passes through the north axis. Northern glazing is protected by sunshades which limit solar penetration in summer. Further sustainable design considerations include fully automated electrical systems to reduce unnecessary power drain, bore water for garden and pool use and rainwater collection to tanks for all domestic uses.

1 The living room (left) cantilevers out over the landscape, which it overlooks via full-height sliding doors and a balcony. The study and master bedroom (right) are accommodated in another timber box supported on slender steel columns.
2 View of the timber-decked outdoor dining area and pool which are accessed directly from the kitchen and dining area.
3 View from the living room deck. The sloped underside of the cantilevered form continues up to meet the roof plane.
4 The kitchen is designed to read as a black and white element within the predominantly timber interior.
5 The master bedroom enjoys views to both the east and west from large glazed openings. Both windows are protected from unwanted solar gain by external adjustable louvred blinds.

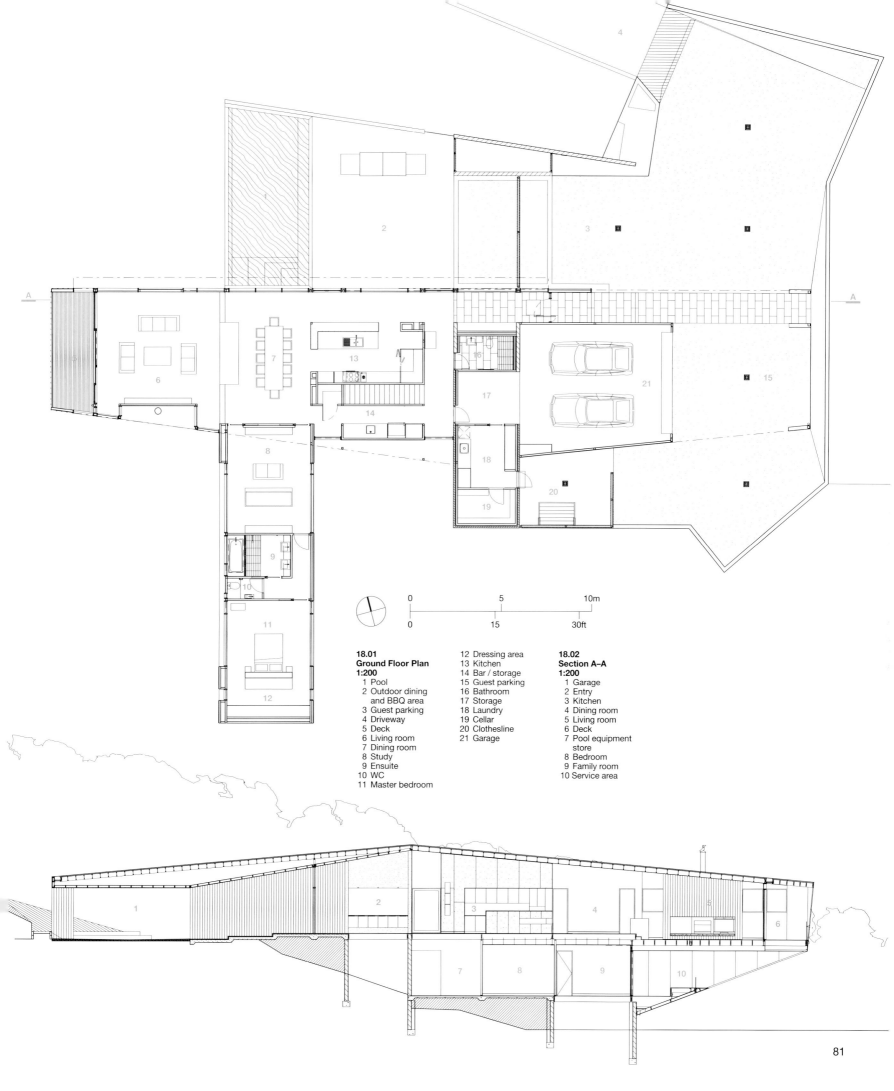

18.01
Ground Floor Plan
1:200
1 Pool
2 Outdoor dining
  and BBQ area
3 Guest parking
4 Driveway
5 Deck
6 Living room
7 Dining room
8 Study
9 Ensuite
10 WC
11 Master bedroom

12 Dressing area
13 Kitchen
14 Bar / storage
15 Guest parking
16 Bathroom
17 Storage
18 Laundry
19 Cellar
20 Clothesline
21 Garage

18.02
Section A–A
1:200
1 Garage
2 Entry
3 Kitchen
4 Dining room
5 Living room
6 Deck
7 Pool equipment
  store
8 Bedroom
9 Family room
10 Service area

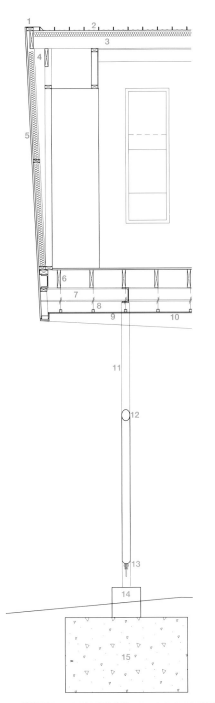

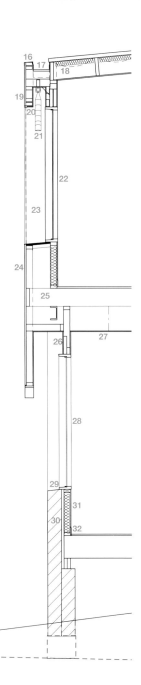

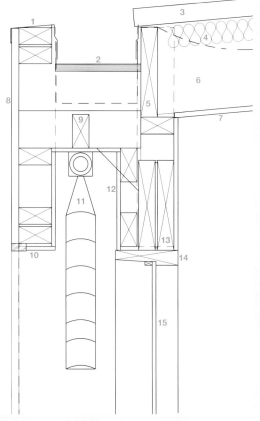

18.04
Box Gutter and
External Blind Detail
1:10
 1 Black Colourbond
sheet metal to wrap
over top chord to form
parapet edge capping
 2 Zincalume box
gutter with minimum
fall of 1:150
 3 Black Colourbond
metal deck roofing
 4 Insulation
 5 Timber beam
 6 Raked timber rafter

 7 10 mm (^{2}/$_5$ inch)
thick plasterboard
ceiling
 8 Timber cladding
with paint finish
 9 Timber blocking for
blind attachment
 10 Compressed fibre
cement sheet lining
with paint finish
 11 Vental external
louvre blind system
 12 Compressed fibre
cement sheet lining
with paint finish
 13 Timber window

head
 14 Cedar window
frame
 15 Clear glazed
window

18.03
Typical Wall Section
Details
1:50
 1 Black Colourbond
sheet metal to wrap
over top chord to form
parapet edge capping
 2 Black Colourbond
metal deck roofing
 3 Timber beam
 4 Timber rafter
 5 Hardwood timber
cladding
 6 Floor beam
 7 Steel beam
 8 Boxed-out soffit
structure
 9 Villaboard soffit
lining with paint finish
 10 Compressed
cement sheet lining
with paint finish

 11 Steel column
 12 Bracing rod
 13 Steel pin
connection
 14 Concrete upstand
to column base plate
fixing
 15 Reinforced
concrete pad footing
 16 Black Colourbond
to wrap over top chord
to form parapet edge
capping
 17 Zincalum box
gutter
 18 Raked timber
rafters
 19 Timber cladding
with paint finish
 20 Compressed fibre
cement lining with
paint finish
 21 External louvre

blind system
 22 Cedar window
 23 Compressed fibre
cement lining to
window surround
 24 Timber cladding
with paint finish
 25 Cantilevered beam
 26 Compressed fibre
cement lining with
paint finish
 27 10 mm (^{2}/$_5$ inch)
thick plasterboard
ceiling
 28 Cedar window
 29 Sloped blockwork
window sill
 30 Blockwork wall with
natural cement render
finish
 31 10 mm (^{2}/$_5$ inch)
thick plasterboard wall
lining

 32 90 x 15 mm (3^1/$_2$ x
^{3}/$_5$ inch) hardwood
skirting board

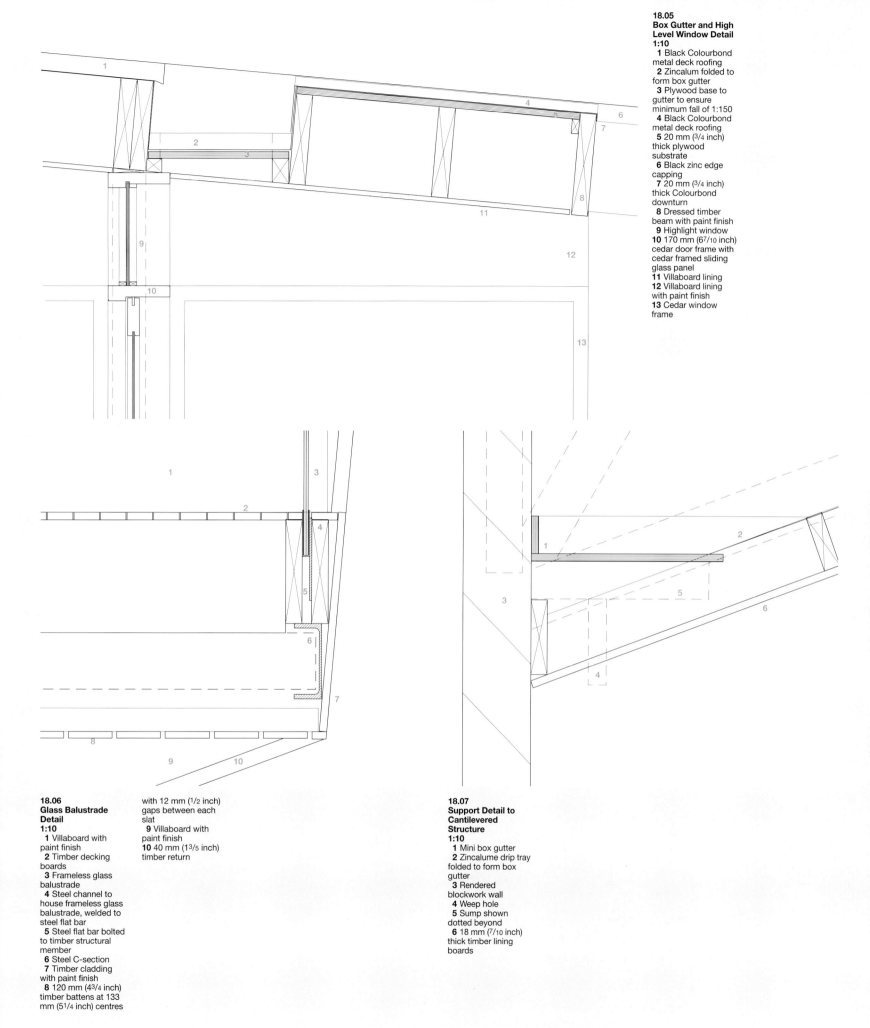

18.05
**Box Gutter and High
Level Window Detail
1:10**
 1 Black Colourbond
metal deck roofing
 2 Zincalum folded to
form box gutter
 3 Plywood base to
gutter to ensure
minimum fall of 1:150
 4 Black Colourbond
metal deck roofing
 5 20 mm ($3/4$ inch)
thick plywood
substrate
 6 Black zinc edge
capping
 7 20 mm ($3/4$ inch)
thick Colourbond
downturn
 8 Dressed timber
beam with paint finish
 9 Highlight window
10 170 mm ($6^7/10$ inch)
cedar door frame with
cedar framed sliding
glass panel
11 Villaboard lining
12 Villaboard lining
with paint finish
13 Cedar window
frame

18.06
**Glass Balustrade
Detail
1:10**
 1 Villaboard with
paint finish
 2 Timber decking
boards
 3 Frameless glass
balustrade
 4 Steel channel to
house frameless glass
balustrade, welded to
steel flat bar
 5 Steel flat bar bolted
to timber structural
member
 6 Steel C-section
 7 Timber cladding
with paint finish
 8 120 mm ($4^3/4$ inch)
timber battens at 133
mm ($5^1/4$ inch) centres

with 12 mm ($1/2$ inch)
gaps between each
slat
 9 Villaboard with
paint finish
10 40 mm ($1^3/5$ inch)
timber return

18.07
**Support Detail to
Cantilevered
Structure
1:10**
 1 Mini box gutter
 2 Zincalume drip tray
folded to form box
gutter
 3 Rendered
blockwork wall
 4 Weep hole
 5 Sump shown
dotted beyond
 6 18 mm ($7/10$ inch)
thick timber lining
boards

Brookes Street House
Brisbane, Queensland, Australia

Project Team
James Russell, Lachlan Nielsen

Structural Engineer
Bligh Tanner Engineers

Main Contractor
James Russell

Nestled between two nineteenth century state heritage-listed buildings, the Brookes Street House is a modern home for a family of four. The site was previously used for car parking, wedged between the listed buildings. Whilst high density development was permitted under the planning scheme, it was decided that a small-scale proposal that enhanced the experience of the heritage-listed buildings was more appropriate. The building is set back from Brookes Street to create a forecourt entry that unites the listed buildings and the house. The new building is a tall narrow structure grafted to the side of the church. Tucked under the house is a small commercial space opening onto the landscaped forecourt with access to the house via a staircase adjacent to the office.

Once through the threshold, one enters a private and secure world. The stairs lead straight up into the heart of the home – a central, open courtyard of green grass bathed in sunlight. The house wraps around three sides of the grass, with the church wall and stained glass windows forming the fourth wall. Living spaces are placed on either side of the courtyard – one a less formal 'play room' and the other with the kitchen and 'grown-up' lounge. Above the living areas are the bedrooms – the children's above the playroom, and the parents' suspended over the kitchen and lounge. A narrow bridge connects the two bedroom wings and overlooks the courtyard. Walls of glass slide away completely at the edges of the living spaces, creating a fluid connection between the grassed and roofed areas. Upper level windows are push-out timber flaps, which also act as eaves for sun and rain protection. Raw industrial materials of concrete and steel for the structure are enriched by the refined timber joinery of the interior.

1 View from the courtyard of the children's playroom and bedrooms above. Light and ventilation to the bedrooms are controlled using adjustable lift-up timber panels.
2 View of the kitchen and living spaces from the courtyard. Access to the bedrooms on the upper level is via a staircase located to one side of the courtyard.
3 The adjacent church with its arched windows and stained glass is an important feature of the house. Here, timber-framed windows frame views of the church's south facade.
4 The master bedroom is located above the kitchen and dining space. Timber is used extensively here in both the revealed structure and joinery elements.

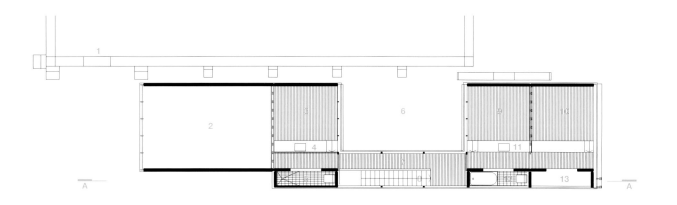

19.01
First Floor Plan
1:200
1 Existing church
2 Void over living
  room below
3 Master bedroom
4 Basin and bench
5 Bathroom
6 Courtyard below
7 Bridge link
8 Stair from ground
  floor below
9 Bedroom
10 Bedroom
11 Basin and bench
12 Bathroom
13 Storage

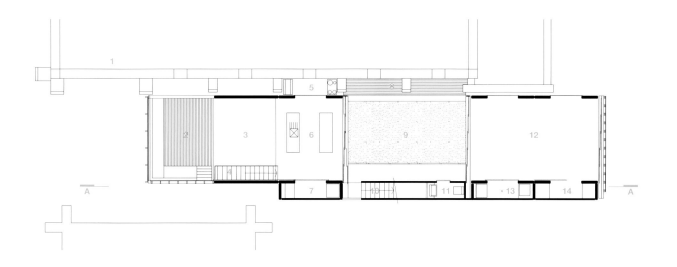

19.02
Ground Floor Plan
1:200
1 Existing church
2 Living area
3 Dining area
4 Stair from office
  below
5 Kitchen
6 Kitchen
7 Pantry
8 Decked courtyard
9 Grassed courtyard
10 Stair to first floor
11 WC
12 Play room
13 Laundry
14 Storage

```
0          5          10m
|----------|----------|
0         15         30ft
```

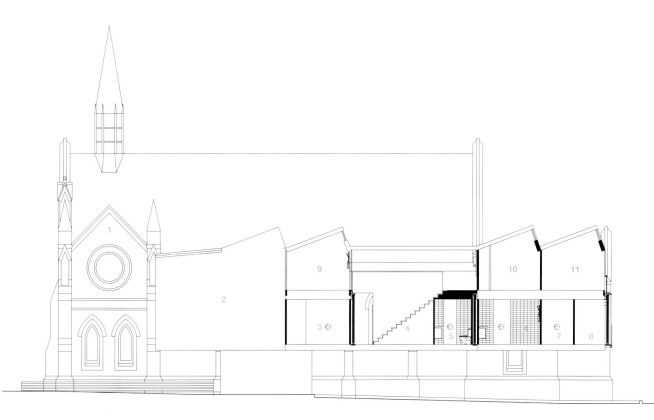

19.03
Section A–A
1:200
1 Existing church
2 Living areas
3 Pantry
4 Courtyard
5 WC
6 Laundry
7 Storage
8 Storage
9 Master bedroom
10 Bedroom
11 Bedroom

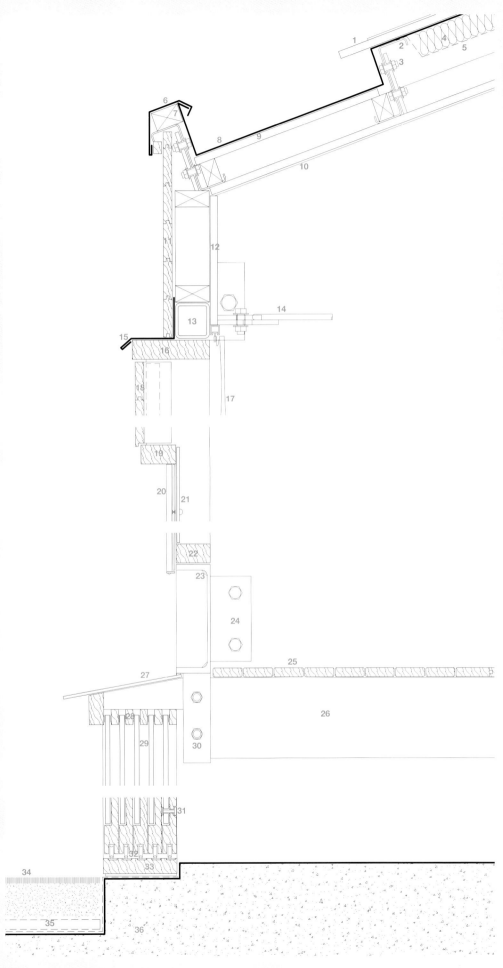

19.04
Roof and Wall Detail Section
1:10
 1 Zincalume Custom Orb roof sheeting
 2 Steel purlin
 3 Bolted connection
 4 Insulation
 5 Sisalation
 6 Zincalume flashing
 7 Timber packing
 8 Zincalume gutter
 9 Zincalume Custom Orb gutter support
10 Pre-finished MDF panel ceiling
11 19 mm (^{3}/4 inch) hardwood tongue and groove cladding
12 Pre-finished MDF panel lining
13 70 mm (2^3/4 inch) steel square hollow section
14 12 mm (^{1}/2 inch) steel tension rod
15 Zincalume flashing
16 140 x 40 mm (5^1/2 x 1^3/5 inch) hardwood head
17 Weatherproof curtain system
18 Hardwood awning window
19 50 x 40 mm (2 x 1^3/5 inch) hardwood sill
20 4 mm (^{1}/6 inch) horizontal coloured glass with lead joining bead
21 6 mm (^{1}/4 inch) toughened glass
22 90 x 40 mm (3^1/2 x 1^3/5 inch) hardwood bottom plate
23 230 mm (9 inch) parallel flange channel
24 Bolted connection to 150 mm (6 inch) concrete wall panel
25 Hardwood shot edge decking
26 170 x 40 mm (6^7/10 x 1^3/5 inch) hardwood joist
27 6 mm (^{1}/4 inch) toughened glass
28 32 x 16 mm (1^1/4 x ^{3}/5 inch) hardwood slats to guide doors
29 10 mm (^{2}/5 inch) glass stacking doors
30 10 mm (^{2}/5 inch) folded steel bracket to take timber joist with bolted connection
31 22 mm (^{4}/5 inch) flush stainless steel patch fitting between door base and toughened glass
32 Heavy duty adjustable brass roller wheels on 190 x 40 mm (7^1/2 x 1^3/5 inch) hardwood door sill with rebated brass tracks screwed at 300 mm (11^4/5 inch) centres
33 Non-compressible timber packer
34 Lawn on washed sand with drainage cell wrapped in geotextile fabric
35 Waterproof membrane system
36 Reinforced concrete floor slab

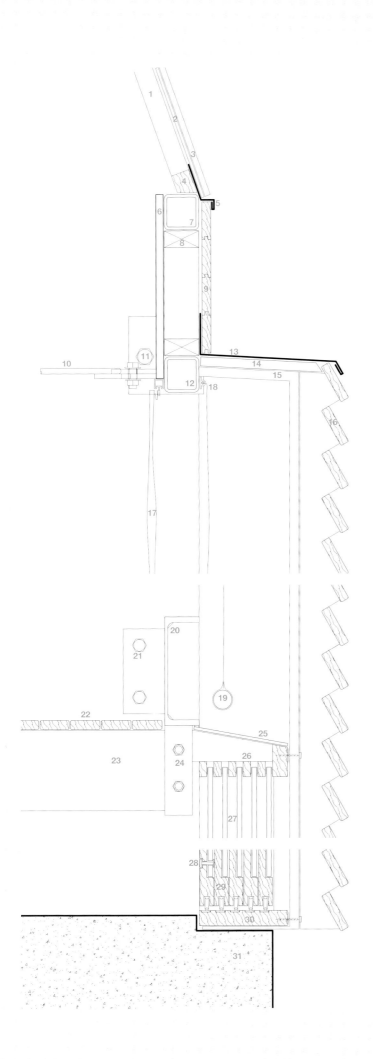

19.05
Wall and Floor Detail
Section
1:10
1 32 x 32 mm (1^1/$_4$ x 1^1/$_4$ inch) hardwood mullions
2 6 mm (^{1}/$_4$ inch) toughened glass
3 32 x 16 mm (1^1/$_4$ x ^{3}/$_5$ inch) hardwood cover strips with 3 mm (^{1}/$_{10}$ inch) glazing tape screwed at 150 mm (6 inch) centres
4 Hardwood sill
5 Zincalume flashing
6 Pre-finished MDF panel ceiling
7 70 mm (2^3/$_4$ inch) steel square hollow section
8 70 x 45 mm (2^3/$_4$ x 1^3/$_4$ inch) timber framing
9 19 mm (^{3}/$_4$ inch) hardwood tongue and groove cladding
10 12 mm (^{1}/$_2$ x inch) diameter steel tension rod
11 Bolted connection to 150 mm (6 inch) concrete wall panel
12 70 mm (2^3/$_4$ inch) steel square hollow section
13 Zincalume flashing
14 25 mm (1 inch) plywood substrate
15 20 mm (^{3}/$_4$ inch) square hollow section frame
16 86 x 19 mm (3^2/$_5$ x ^{3}/$_4$ inch) hardwood slats at 60 degrees on profiled hardwood support
17 Weatherproof curtain system
18 Hardwood cover to square hollow section head
19 Clear vinyl roll down screen with 60 mm (2^1/$_3$ inch) diameter weighted tube base
20 230 mm (9 inch) parallel flange channel
21 Bolted connection to 150 mm (6 inch) concrete wall panel
22 32 x 19 mm (1^1/$_4$ x ^{3}/$_4$ inch) hardwood edge decking
23 170 x 40 mm (6^7/$_{10}$ x 1^3/$_5$ inch) hardwood joist
24 10 mm (^{2}/$_5$ inch) folded steel bracket to take joist
25 6 mm (^{1}/$_4$ inch) toughened glass
26 32 x 16 mm (1^1/$_4$ x ^{3}/$_5$ inch) hardwood slats to guide doors
27 10 mm (^{2}/$_5$ inch) toughened glass stacking doors with felt guide at top
28 22 mm (^{4}/$_5$ inch) flush stainless steel patch fitting between door base and toughened glass
29 Heavy duty adjustable brass roller wheels on 190 x 40 mm (7^1/$_2$ x 1^3/$_5$ inch) hardwood door sill with rebated brass tracks screwed at 300 mm (11^4/$_5$ inch) centres
30 10 mm (^{2}/$_5$ inch) steel bracket to 20 mm (^{3}/$_4$ inch) square hollow section frame
31 Reinforced concrete floor slab

Holly Barn
Reedham, Norfolk, England, UK

Client
Jenny and Alan Rogers

Project Team
Mary Lou Arscott, Simon Knox,
Lucy Thomas

Structural Engineer
Eckersley O'Callaghan

Main Contractor
Willow Builders Ltd

The brief for this project specified a light, airy, contemporary house that could accommodate a large family, and friends who visit frequently. The house had to be in keeping with the surrounding landscape, and use sympathetic local materials. It also had to offer total mobility to one of the clients, who is wheelchair bound. The new two-storey barn has been detailed with a smooth simple timber envelope to generate a clean profile against the skyline. The hidden gutter allows the curved eaves to melt into the roof. Timber boarding on the roof and walls resonates with the traditional local vernacular seen in windmills, boat houses and boat construction in The Norfolk Broads.

Organizationally, this is an upside-down house – four bedrooms, a bathroom and family room are located on the ground floor, with the main living spaces and master bedroom on the first floor, where spectacular views of the surrounding landscape can be fully enjoyed. The top storey is an open-plan barn-like volume, with a curved white ceiling that continues the length of the building. The solid walls that divide the kitchen, living room and master bedroom stop at eaves height, above which are fixed glass panels, so that the ceiling appears as an uninterrupted surface. Externally, timber is the predominant material, with walls clad in alternating strips of wide and narrow Siberian larch ship-lapped boarding. Iroko is used for the louvres to the glazed east and west gables and for the sliding windows and doors. The roof is clad in lapped larch boards. The plan allows for easy manoeuvring space for a wheelchair – wide passages, doorways, and a platform lift which gives access to both floors.

1 The timber building sits comfortably in the Norfolk landscape. Expanses of glazing in fixed and sliding windows, including the glazed gable ends, offer panoramic views in all directions.
2 The plan is arranged so that the living spaces are on the upper level and bedrooms on the ground floor. The entrance (left) opens onto a hallway with the stair and platform lift.
3 On the first floor, a timber-floored corridor runs the length of the building, providing access from the kitchen and dining room to the living room and master bedroom and bathroom beyond.

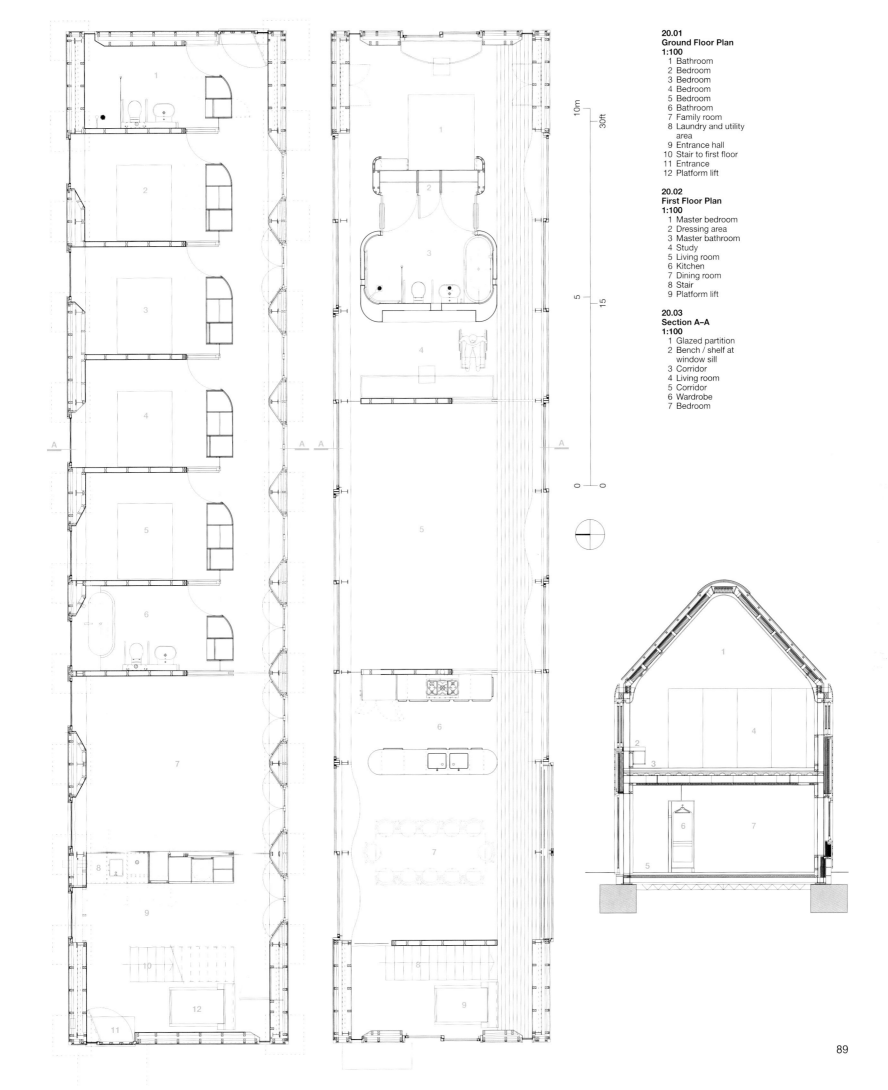

20.01
Ground Floor Plan
1:100
1 Bathroom
2 Bedroom
3 Bedroom
4 Bedroom
5 Bedroom
6 Bathroom
7 Family room
8 Laundry and utility
    area
9 Entrance hall
10 Stair to first floor
11 Entrance
12 Platform lift

20.02
First Floor Plan
1:100
1 Master bedroom
2 Dressing area
3 Master bathroom
4 Study
5 Living room
6 Kitchen
7 Dining room
8 Stair
9 Platform lift

20.03
Section A–A
1:100
1 Glazed partition
2 Bench / shelf at
    window sill
3 Corridor
4 Living room
5 Corridor
6 Wardrobe
7 Bedroom

10m
5
0

30ft
15
0

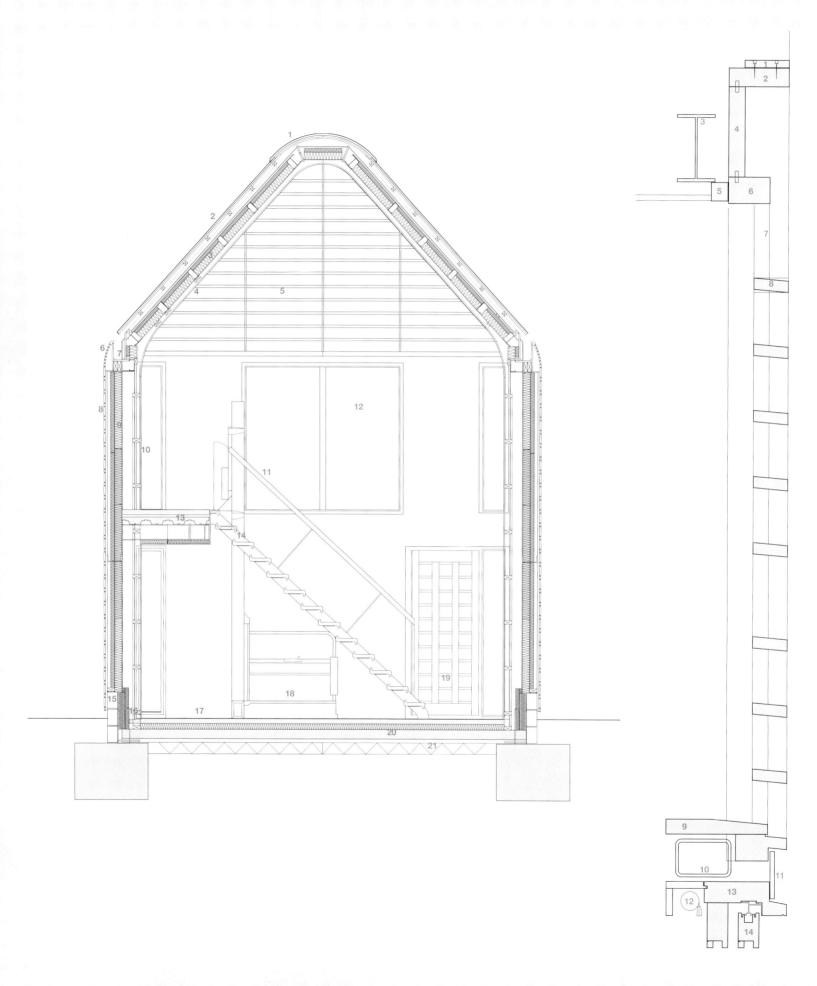

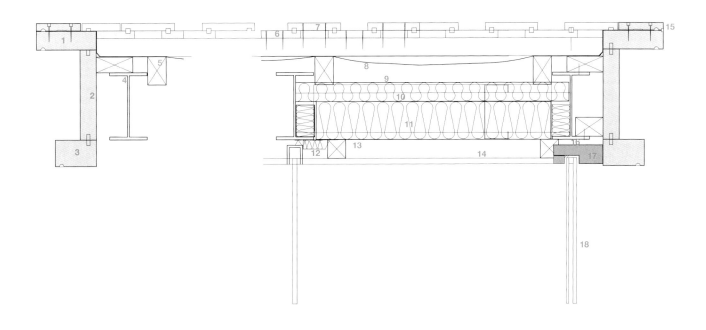

20.04
Detail Section
Through Entrance
1.50
   1 Larch board to roof
   2 Two layers of 150 x
25 mm (6 x 1 inch)
Siberian larch boarding
   3 150 mm (6 inch)
thick insulation
   4 12 mm (1/2 inch)
thick fibrous plaster
ceiling board
   5 Louvre panel to
gable end
   6 Iroko larch tongue
and groove exterior
boarding
   7 Glass reinforced
plastic gutter
   8 Tongue and groove
Siberian larch boards
   9 150 mm (6 inch)
thick insulation
   10 12.5 mm (1/2 inch)
plasterboard
   11 Oak handrail on top
of glass balustrade
   12 Argon-filled clear
double-glazed window
units
   13 100 mm (4 inch)
thick concrete floor
slab on trapezoidal
metal deck
   14 900 mm (352/5 inch)
wide oak treads on
steel stringers
   15 100 mm (4 inch)
thick dense blockwork
   16 12.5 mm (1/2 inch)
thick plasterboard
   17 65 mm (21/2 inch)
thick screed with
underfloor heating
   18 Disabled lift
   19 Iroko front door
beyond
   20 125 mm (5 inch)

thick ground bearing
concrete slab with
damp proof membrane
under
   21 150 mm (6 inch)
hardcore fill

20.05
Louvres to Gable
Ends Detail
1:10
   1 Larch board to roof
   2 Iroko frame
projecting with drip
groove to underside
   3 Universal beam as
verge support
   4 Mirror-clad iroko
board
   5 Iroko sub frame
   6 Iroko frame
   7 Iroko upright
   8 20 x 112 mm (3/4 x
42/5 inch) iroko fin
louvres
   8 Iroko sill
   10 Rectangular box
section
   11 Larch tongue and
groove board
   12 Roller blind
   13 Iroko frame head
   14 Iroko window head

20.06
Larch Cladding Detail
1:10
   1 Iroko frame
   2 Iroko frame
   3 Iroko frame
   4 Universal beam
structural frame
   5 75 x 50 mm (3 x 2
inch) treated soft wood
rafter
   6 144 x 20 mm (52/3 x
3/4 inch) Siberian larch
board with 12 x 6.5
mm (1/2 x 1/4 inch)
water check groove in
each board
   7 144 x 20 mm (52/3 x
3/4 inch) Siberian larch
board with 12 x 6.5
mm (1/2 x 1/4 inch)
water check groove in
each board
   8 48 x 50 mm (19/10 x
2 inch) timber batten
   9 Tyvek moisture
barrier with minimum
sag of 25 mm (1 inch)
at centre span
   10 Insulation
   11 Insulation
   12 Insulation
   13 Proctor Tri-Iso
Super 8 insulation
taped to wall insulation
above
   14 50 x 50 mm (2 x 2
inch) batten screw
fixed to metal purlins
   15 12 mm (1/2 inch) foil
backed plasterboard
with 3 mm (1/10 inch)
skim coat
   16 121 x 20 mm (43/4 x
3/4 inch) Iroko cover
strip screwed and
pelleted over Tyvek
insulation with mastic
bed at centre

   17 Iroko window frame
   18 Argon-filled clear
double-glazed window
units

Lake Tahoe Residence
Lake Tahoe, Nevada, USA

Project Team
David Lake, Billy Johnson, Tenna
Florian, Heather DeGrella

Structural Engineer
Structural-Datum Engineering

Main Contractor
Q&D Construction

Civil Engineer
Gray & Associates

The historic mines of this region, with their simple shed forms on the sloping land, were the inspiration for the design of this family home. The use of exposed concrete, weathered timber and rusted steel, creates a palette of low maintenance, robust materials. The crisp exterior materials give way to warm natural timber, black painted steel and polished concrete floors in the interior. The concept of 'camp' became the design theme for this active family home. The plan evolved into a series of three buildings that loosely form a courtyard, where the garage, workshop and playroom pavilion mimics the slope of the hill and provides a visual screen to the adjacent property.

In the main wing, a private office on the second floor has a crow's nest view from the highest point in the house. On the first floor, bedrooms and bathrooms benefit from views out over the pine-planted landscape. On the ground floor, large rolling glass doors slide away to open the living spaces to the landscape. The glass-enclosed living and dining room, with its balcony for family theatre productions, collects abundant winter sun and cool summer breezes. This space is comprised of two areas of very different character. One is the family living and dining space with generously proportioned furniture and a high timber ceiling. The other is the snug, accessed via three steps leading down from the living room and featuring a low timber-beamed ceiling, a wood burning fireplace and custom built-in lounge seating. The guest accommodation is detached from the main house and can serve as a stand-alone house for a smaller private group.

1 The glazed wall to the family and dining areas is protected by a large timber overhang supported on slender steel columns.
2 The main living and sleeping spaces (centre) are juxtaposed by the kitchen wing (left) and the projecting bedroom wing (right).
3 View of the large family room which is accessed from the kitchen (right) down a short flight of wide steps, and terminates in the privacy of the inglenook sitting area at the far end. Timber panelling is used extensively in the double height space for the walls and ceiling.
4 The inglenook sitting area features a fireplace built into a concrete wall.

21.01
First Floor Plan
1:200
1 Bedroom
2 Bathroom
3 Bathroom
4 Bedroom
5 Storage
6 Stair up from
  ground floor
7 Stair up to second
  floor office
8 Mezzanine
9 Balcony

21.02
Ground Floor Plan
1:200
1 Bedroom
2 Store
3 Sitting area
4 Bathroom
5 Laundry
6 Bathroom
7 Bedroom
8 Storage
9 Stair up to first
  floor
10 Inglenook sitting
   area
11 Family room
12 Family room porch
13 Dining area
14 Entrance porch
15 Washroom
16 Coat cupboard
17 Kitchen
18 Pantry
19 Mud room

21.03
Section A–A
1:200
1 Office
2 Bathroom
3 Bathroom
4 Laundry
5 Inglenook
6 Family room
7 Kitchen beyond

0   5   10m

0   15   30ft

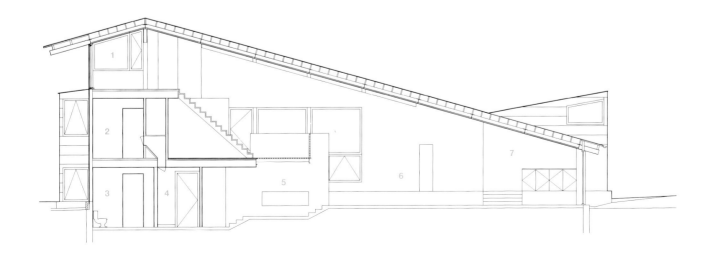

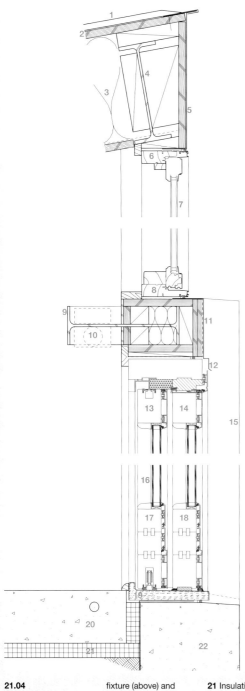

21.04
Sliding Doors to
Kitchen Detail
1:10
 1 Standing seam
Cor-ten metal roof
 2 20 mm (3/4 inch)
plywood deck
 3 Spray foam
insulation
 4 Steel W-section
beam
 5 Standing seam
Cor-ten metal cladding
 6 Metal clad timber
windows
 7 25 mm (1 inch)
thick insulated glass
with low-E coating
 8 Metal clad timber
windows
 9 Exposed steel
W-section lintel
10 Space for light

fixture (above) and
shade (below)
11 Cor-ten metal
cladding
12 Cor-ten metal
flashing
13 Metal clad timber
lift slide doors
14 Metal clad timber
lift slide doors
15 Board formed
concrete wall beyond
16 25 mm (1 inch)
thick insulated glass
with low-E coating
17 Metal clad timber
lift slide doors
18 Metal clad timber
lift slide doors
19 Recessed metal
threshold
20 Finished concrete
topping slab with
radiant heating

21 Insulation board
22 Exposed concrete
floor slab

21.05
Roof Detail at Porch
1:10
 1 Cor-ten metal drip
flashing
 2 Standing seam
Cor-ten metal roof
 3 50 x 150 mm (2 x 6
inch) tongue and
groove decking
 4 190 mm (7 1/2 inch)
Glu-lam beam
 5 Steel channel beam
 6 Steel pipe column
 7 Flat seam Cor-ten
metal cladding
 8 Spray foam
insulation
 9 Spray foam
insulation
10 Steel W-section
beam
11 Fir trim
12 Steel pipe column

13 Anodized
aluminium curtain wall
system
14 25 mm (1 inch)
thick insulated glass
with low-E coating
15 6 mm (1/4 inch)
steel fin plate to
support curtain wall
16 Anodized
aluminium curtain wall
system

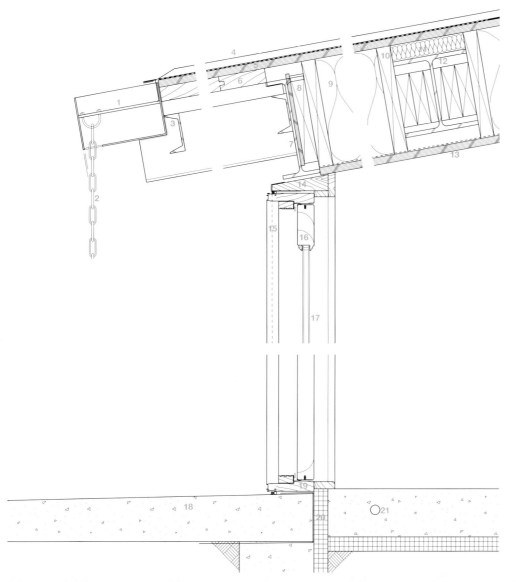

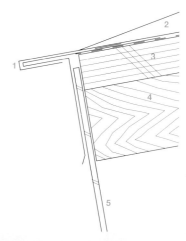

21.06
Roof and Window
Detail at Entry Porch
1:10
 1 Cor-ten steel gutter
 2 Rusted steel rain
chain
 3 Steel channel purlin
 4 Standing seam
Cor-ten metal roof
 5 20 mm (3/4 inch)
plywood deck
 6 50 x 150 mm (2 x 6
inch) tongue and
groove decking
 7 Steel W-section
beam
 8 Timber blocking
 9 Spray foam
insulation
10 Timber joist
11 Spray foam
insulation
12 Steel W-section

beam
13 Finished plywood
ceiling
14 Cor-ten clad timber
blocking
15 Metal clad timber
door
16 Metal clad timber
door
17 25 mm (1 inch)
thick insulated glass
with low-E coating
18 Finished concrete
entry porch slab
19 Metal clad timber
threshold
20 Insulation board
21 Finished concrete
topping slab with
radiant heating

21.07
Roof Detail at Entry
Porch
1:2
 1 Cor-ten metal drip
flashing
 2 Standing seam
Cor-ten metal roof
 3 20 mm (3/4 inch)
plywood deck
 4 50 x 150 mm (2 x 6
inch) tongue and
groove decking
 5 Cor-ten steel gutter

**Cow Stables
Lignières, Switzerland**

Client
Juan Daniel and Cuche Fernand

Project Team
Manuel Bieler, Antoine Robert-
Grandpierre, Laurent Saurer

Structural Engineer
Chabloz et partenaires, GVH

Two farmers, the owners of a large
agricultural estate in the Jura, set in
a landscape of fields, pastures, forests
and mountain valleys, commissioned
Localarchitecture to design a barn for
30 cows. The client wanted a
contemporary building that would
nevertheless fit within the limited
budget allocated by the federal
authorities. Keen to design a building
that would be respectful of traditional
architecture, the architects
conducted a detailed analysis of the
farm typologies in the region. One is
characterized by a roof ridge set
perpendicular to the contour lines;
however this model makes future
enlargement problematic. This layout
was replaced by a typology with a roof
ridge running parallel to the contours,
with end gables designed to facilitate
extension. By combining these
systems, the architects have created
a synthesis of the different traditions,
giving them a contemporary identity.

The stables are arranged over
two floors, with two rows of stalls for
the animals on the ground floor and
storage for winter feed in a mezzanine
loft space above. Both client and
architects share a commitment to
sustainable development, reflected in
close collaboration on the choice and
application of the materials. The
building's structural dimensions were
calculated to take account of locally
available timber, and the construction
details were developed so that the
client could complete the final stages
of the building himself. In addition to
the ecological advantages, the use of
timber made it possible to develop a
load-bearing structure to match the
local tradition of the *ramée* – a large
area of open timber strips that
provides natural ventilation – and
to implement simple details in order
to resolve the complex problem of the
building's geometry.

1 The use of a simple
concrete floor slab and
the gable end of
vertical timber strips
makes future
expansion of the
stables possible.
2 The building is
arranged so that its
length runs parallel to
the existing contours.
The resulting two long
facades are
constructed from
closely spaced timber
columns that allow a
high degree of
ventilation.
3 One of the gable
ends is punctured by
four openings – two on
the ground floor for the
cows and large farming
equipment, one for the
farmers to access the
stalls, and one external
access to the hay loft.
4 The spacing and
positioning of
structural elements
such as the roof joists
and columns are
matched to create a
tight architectural
rhythm that runs
throughout the project.
5 View from the hay
loft, which has
spectacular views
over the countryside.

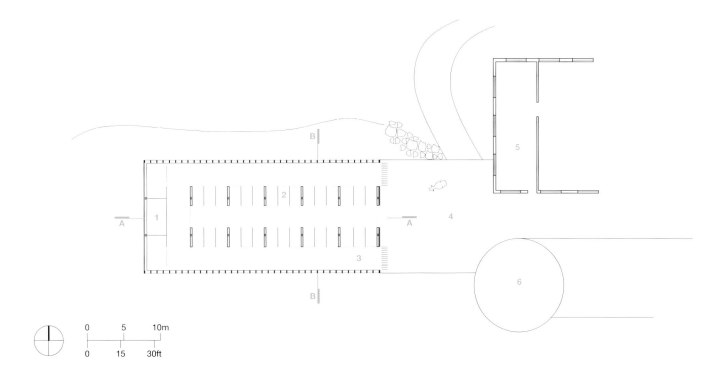

22.01
Floor Plan
1:500
 1 Storage
 2 Cow stalls
 3 Access aisles
 4 Outdoor herding
 area
 5 Existing farm
 building
 6 Turning area

0   5   10m
0   15   30ft

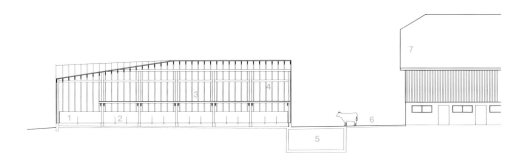

22.02
Section A–A
1:500
 1 Storage
 2 Cow stalls
 3 Hay loft mezzanine
 4 Open timber walls
 5 Manure storage
 tank
 6 Outdoor herding
 area
 7 Existing farm
 building

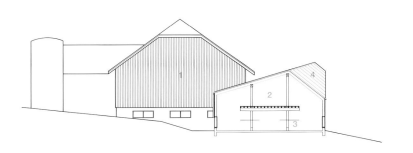

22.03
Section B–B
1:500
 1 Existing farm
 building
 2 Hay loft mezzanine
 3 Cow stalls
 4 Profiled steel sheet
 roofing

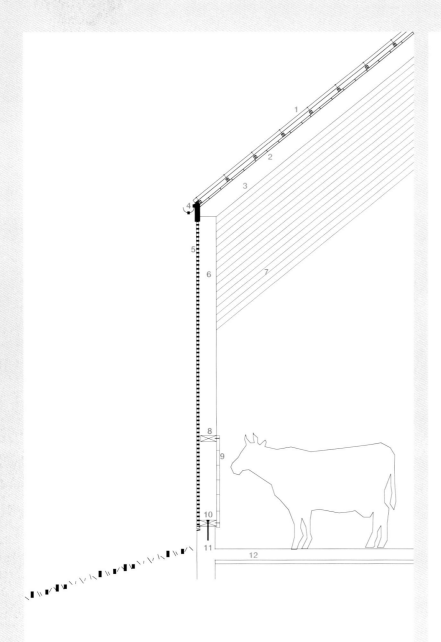

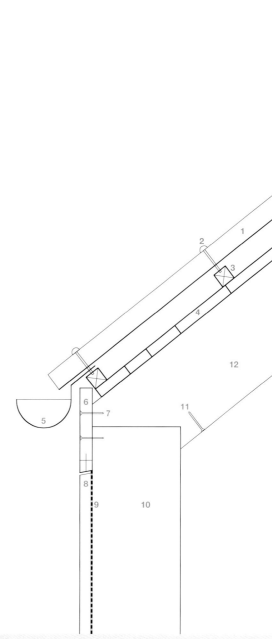

22.04
Typical Wall and Roof
Section Detail
1:50
 1 Profiled steel sheet
roofing
 2 30 mm (1¹⁄₅ inch)
roof board sheeting
 3 203 x 610 mm (8 x
24 inch) solid pine
rafter
 4 Galvanized metal
gutter
 5 Anti-wind mesh
textile
 6 203 x 610 mm (8 x
24 inch) solid pine post
 7 Anti-wind mesh
textile beyond to rear
wall

 8 100 x 610 mm (4 x
24 inch) timber top
plate
 9 100 x 610 mm (4 x
24 inch) interior timber
boarding
10 203 x 609 mm (8 x
24 inch) timber sill
plate
11 Reinforced
concrete foundation
wall
12 150 mm (6 inch)
reinforced concrete
floor slab

22.05
Gutter Section Detail
1:25
 1 Profiled steel sheet
roofing
 2 40 mm (1³⁄₅ inch)
screws
 3 Timber spacers
 4 30 mm (1¹⁄₅ inch)
roof board sheeting
 5 Galvanized metal
gutter
 6 100 x 1118 mm (4 x
44 inch) solid pine
fascia board
 7 60 mm (2¹⁄₃ inch)
Inox screw fasteners
 8 76 x 203 mm (3 x 8
inch) Douglas pine
batten

 9 Anti-wind mesh
textile
10 203 x 609 mm (8 x
24 inch) solid pine post
11 60 mm (2¹⁄₃ inch)
Inox screw fasteners
12 203 x 609 mm (8 x
24 inch) solid pine
rafter

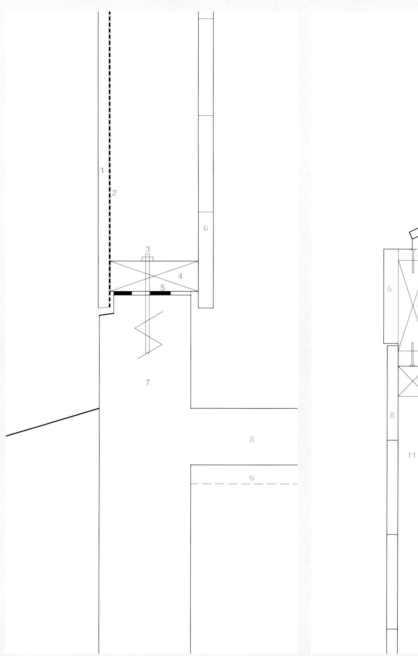

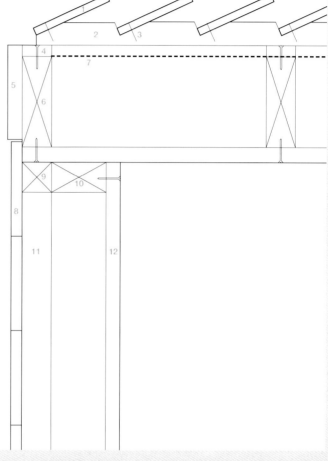

22.06
Foundation and Wall Section Detail
1:25
  1 76 x 203 mm (3 x 8 inch) Douglas pine batten
  2 Ant-wind mesh textile
  3 Anchor bolts
  4 203 x 609 mm (8 x 24 inch) sill plate
  5 Waterproofing membrane
  6 100 x 610 mm (4 x 24 inch) interior timber boarding
  7 Reinforced concrete foundation wall
  8 150 mm (6 inch) reinforced concrete floor slab
  9 Rigid under-slab insulation

22.07
Wall Plan Detail at Corner
1:25
  1 70 x 508 mm (3 x 20 inch) Douglas pine vertical board cladding
  2 Reinforced concrete foundation wall below
  3 60 mm (2$^{1}/_{3}$ inch) Inox screw fasteners
  4 76 x 203 mm (3 x 8 inch) Douglas pine batten
  5 127 x 584 mm (5 x 23 inch) pine vertical fascia
  6 203 x 609 mm (8 x 24 inch) solid pine post
  7 Ant-wind mesh textile
  8 76 x 381 mm (3 x 15 inch) vertical pine board cladding
  9 203 x 203 mm (8 x 8 inch) timber corner framing
  10 381 x 203 mm (15 x 8 inch) timber stud framing
  11 203 x 203 mm (8 x 8 inch) timber sill plate
  12 100 x 381 mm (4 x 15 inch) interior timber boarding

Judenburg West Housing
Judenburg, Austria

Client
Gemeinnützige Wohn-und
Siedlungsgenossenschaft Ennstal

Project Team
Mark Mack, Jeff Alsbrook, Roland
Hagmuller, Ariel Asken

Structural Engineer
Johann Riebenbauer

Main Contractor
Lieb Bau Weiz

Located near the centre of Austria, Judenburg is a small, thirteenth century hill town. As its economy has grown, Judenburg has expanded beyond its historic core, and the area to the north has emerged as a location for low-cost social housing. In Austria, social housing operates on a lease-to-buy system, in which the state subsidizes rents, allowing tenants to buy their apartments after ten years. The system not only creates affordable housing, but establishes an incentive for occupants to invest in their buildings. The city of Judenburg and the state of Styria sponsored a competition, won by Mark Mack, to develop a master plan for 600 units of housing and the infrastructure to support it.

The client, a nonprofit housing provider, hired Mack to design Judenburg West – a four-storey building containing 22 apartments ranging from two to four bedrooms, retail space at ground level and an underground garage. Judenburg West is the first four-storey timber structure in Austria to take advantage of innovative new technology, including panelized construction and prefabricated laminated balconies. For both floors and walls, prefabricated, cloth-laminated panels made from a strong evergreen wood are used – a material (called KHL) that was developed by a Judenburg factory. The walls themselves are sandwiches made of a layer of KHL panels on the inside, untreated larch-wood cladding on the outside, and insulation and an air gap in between. The design provides an open and flexible infrastructure by combining groups of dwellings, public and private open spaces, and pedestrian spaces.

1 The Judenburg West apartment building is part of a masterplan that includes the development of 600 housing units and the infrastructure to support it.

2 The roof of the apartment building takes the form of a lightweight aluminium canopy supported on slender steel columns which are braced back to the building.

3 The balconies, which are attached to the surface of the building, were prefabricated and brought to the site as pre-finished units.
4 Bright colours, a

Mark Mack trademark, are used on the timber panels in the window zone of the facades.

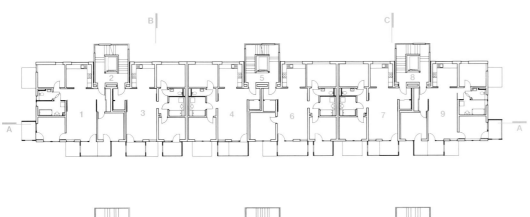

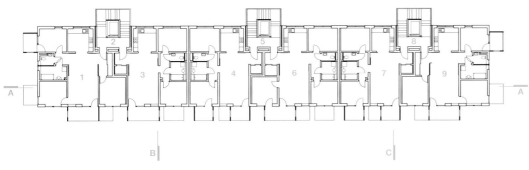

0   5   10m
0   15   30ft

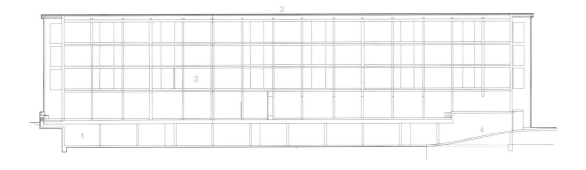

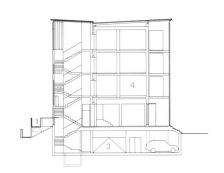

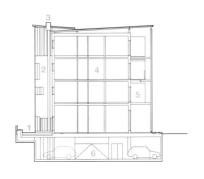

23.01
Third Floor Plan
1:500
1 Three bedroom apartment
2 Stair and elevator core
3 Two bedroom apartment
4 Two bedroom apartment
5 Stair and elevator core
6 Three bedroom apartment
7 Two bedroom apartment
8 Stair and elevator core
9 Three bedroom apartment

23.02
Second Floor Plan
1:500
1 Three bedroom apartment
2 Stair and elevator core
3 Two bedroom apartment
4 Two bedroom apartment
5 Stair and elevator core
6 Three bedroom apartment
7 Two bedroom apartment
8 Stair and elevator core
9 Three bedroom apartment

23.03
Section A–A
1:500
1 Parking garage
2 Apartments
3 Zinc roof
4 Ramp entrance to parking garage

23.04
Section B–B
1:500
1 Entrance
2 Stair core
3 Parking garage
4 Apartments

23.05
Section C–C
1:500
1 Private garden
2 Stair core beyond
3 Ventilation shaft
4 Apartments
5 Balcony
6 Parking garage

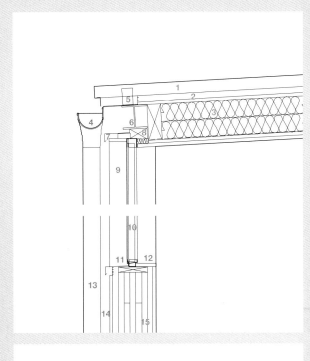

23.06
Roof and Gutter Detail Over Stair
1:20
1 Aluminium sheet roofing
2 Plywood sheeting
3 Insulation
4 Formed metal rainwater gutter
5 Aluminium joining cleat
6 Steel girder
7 Aluminium sheet metal flashing
8 Timber blocking
9 Aluminium sheet metal angle to form window reveal
10 Double glazing window unit
11 Formed aluminium sheet exterior window sill
12 Timber interior window sill
13 Aluminium down pipe
14 Three layered facade plate over ventilated sheeting
15 KLH – cross-laminated solid timber panel

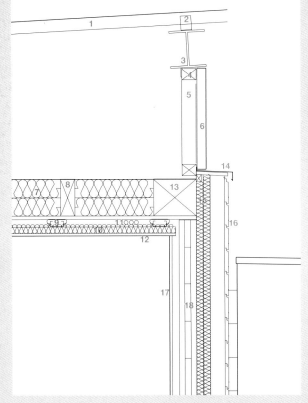

23.07
Main Roof and Exterior Wall Detail
1:20
1 Aluminium sheet roofing
2 Aluminium roof clip
3 Steel beam
4 Timber blocking
5 Framework for perforated plate
6 Perforated plate facade panel
7 200 mm (7⁹/₁₀ inch) insulation
8 Timber rafter
9 Aluminium ceiling clip
10 Soundproof insulation
11 Void for electrical service pipe runs
12 Painted gypsum board ceiling
13 Timber rafter
14 Metal flashing
15 Insulation
16 Horizontal larch wood cladding
17 Painted gypsum board wall lining with air space behind
18 KLH – cross-laminated solid timber panel

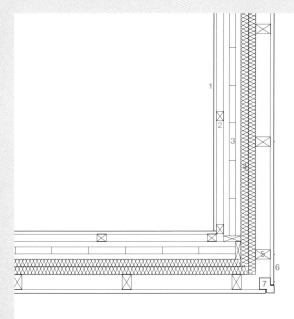

23.08
Corner Wall Plan Detail
1:20
1 Painted gypsum board wall lining with air space behind
2 40 x 50 mm (1⁵/₈ x 2 inch) vertical timber batten
3 KLH – cross-laminated solid timber panel
4 Insulation
5 Timber spacers
6 Horizontal larch wood cladding
7 Corner block

23.09
Wall Between Stair Core and Adjoining Apartments Detail
1:20
1 Painted gypsum board wall lining
2 135 mm (5²/₅ inch) insulation
3 Electrical pipe runs
4 KLH – cross-laminated solid timber panel
5 Soundproof insulation
6 KLH – cross-laminated solid timber panel
7 Timber spacers
8 Painted gypsum board wall lining
9 Painted gypsum board wall lining
10 55 mm (2¹/₁₀ inch) insulation
11 KLH – cross laminated solid timber panel
12 30 mm (1¹/₅ inch) soundproof insulation
13 Timber door jamb
14 Door hinge
15 Timber door
16 Timber door sill

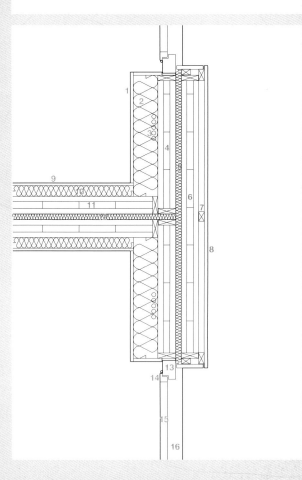

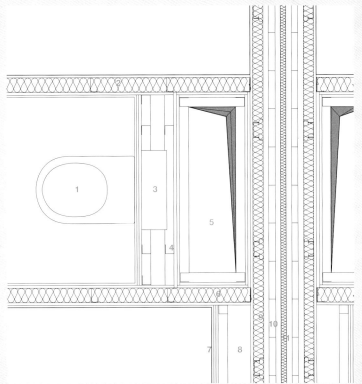

23.10
**Internal Wall /
Bathroom Detail**
1:20
  1 WC
  2 135 mm (5²/₅ inch)
insulation
  3 Cistern to WC
  4 WC mounting
frame
  5 Services void
  6 Internal wall
separating adjoining
apartments
  7 Tiled wall to
bathroom
  8 Services void
  9 Insulation
10 KLH – cross-
laminated solid timber
panel
11 30 mm (1¹/₅ inch)
soundproof insulation

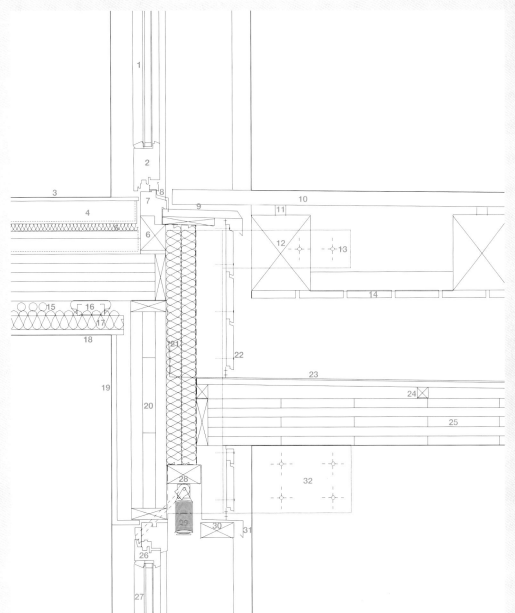

23.11
**Window and Balcony
Detail**
1:10
  1 Double glazed
balcony door
  2 Timber frame to
balcony door
  3 Floating timber
floor
  4 Air space below
timber floor
  5 30 mm (1¹/₅ inch)
soundproof insulation
  6 Timber structure
  7 Timber door sill
  8 Aluminium flashing
to door sill
  9 Aluminium flashing
10 Balcony flooring
11 Timber spacer
12 Timber rafter to
balcony structure
13 Steel bracing
between balcony
structure and load
bearing exterior wall
14 Larch wood soffit
lining to underside of
balcony
15 Electrical pipe run
in ceiling void
16 Aluminium clip for
suspended ceiling
system
17 30 mm (1¹/₅ inch)
soundproof insulation
18 Painted gypsum
board ceiling
19 Painted gypsum
board wall lining
20 95 mm (3³/₄ inch)
KLH – cross-laminated
solid timber panel
21 Insulation
22 Horizontal larch
wood cladding over air
space
23 Tin roofing
24 Timber spacer

25 Balcony roof from
95 mm (3³/₄ inch) KLH
– cross-laminated
solid timber panel
26 Aluminium window
head and frame
27 Double-glazed
window unit
28 Timber support for
sun protection blinds
29 Sun protection
blind in retracted
position
30 Timber cover to sun
protection blind recess
31 Aluminium flashing
32 Steel bracing
between balcony
structure and load
bearing exterior wall

Shopping Roof Apartments
Bohinjska Bistrica, Slovenia

Client
Gradis Skupina G d.d., Ljubljana

Project Team
Rok Oman, Špela Videčnik, Martina
Lipicer, Andrej Gregoric, Meta
Fortuna, Jelka Šolmajer

Structural Engineer
Projecta

Main Contractor
Gradis G group

The initial task from the client was to
build a new shopping mall on the plot
of an existing one. Furthermore, the
new project proposed to use the roof
of the complex for new apartments.
The resulting timber-clad building is
located in Bohinjska Bistrica in the
alpine area of Lake Bohinj with
beautiful views towards the mountains.
The building is organized so that the
apartments open towards mountain
views and the sun at the front, while
the side facade is closed with
windows opening onto balconies that
are cut into the volume. The stepped
form of the building follows the
silhouette of the landscape.

On top of the shopping complex,
the apartments are arranged in a
stepped L-shape, the open side of
which encloses an inner communal
garden on the roof of the shopping
mall. The front and courtyard facade is
constructed in a rhythm of open and
closed timber verticals. Local larch
and slate make reference to traditional
materials used in the area. The
interiors of the apartments include
local materials such as oak parquet
floors and granite-tiled bathrooms.
The structure has been designed so
that the floor plans are as flexible as
possible. The only structural walls
are those that separate the apartment
shell from the rest of the building.
All of the other inner walls are
non-structural and can therefore be
rearranged to suit future requirements.
The structure is comprised of
reinforced concrete columns in the
shopping mall and structural concrete
shear walls in the storage and services
areas. The roof is a combination of flat
and pitched areas that conceal all
services installations such as
chimneys, ventilation and external
air-conditioning.

1 On the north facade,
timber is used
extensively for the
external wall cladding
and the balustrades
which employ spaced
timber verticals to
introduce a varying
rhythm across the
width of the building.
2 The treatment of the
west facade expresses
the climatic conditions.
The building is
protected from
prevailing westerly
winds by alternating
panels of timber and
slate, with balconies
set into the volume.
3 View from an
apartment interior
towards the gravel
covered courtyard on
the roof of the
shopping complex
below.

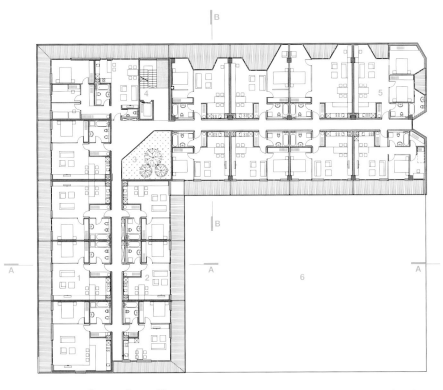

0   5   10m

0   15   30ft

24.01
First Floor Plan
1:500
  1 Large one
    bedroom
    apartment
  2 Medium one
    bedroom
    apartment
  3 Landscaped

courtyard garden
  4 Stair and elevator
    core
  5 Two bedroom
    apartment
  6 Courtyard

24.02
Second Floor Plan
1:500
  1 Two bedroom
    apartment
  2 One bedroom
    apartment
  3 Stair and elevator
    core
  4 Landscaped

courtyard garden
  5 Studio apartment

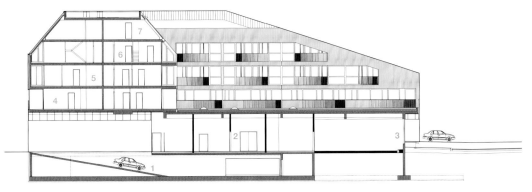

24.03
Section A–A
1:500
  1 Parking garage
    entrance ramp
  2 Entrance to
    shopping mall
  3 Parking garage
    exit
  4 Apartment level
    one
  5 Apartment level
    two
  6 Apartment level
    three
  7 Apartment level
    four

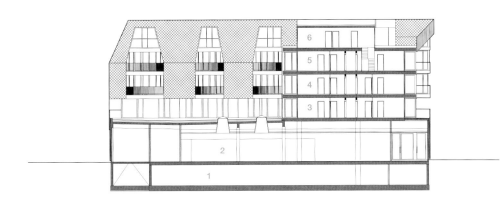

24.04
Section B–B
1:500
  1 Parking garage
  2 Shopping mall
  3 Apartment level
    one
  4 Apartment level
    two
  5 Apartment level
    three
  6 Apartment level
    four

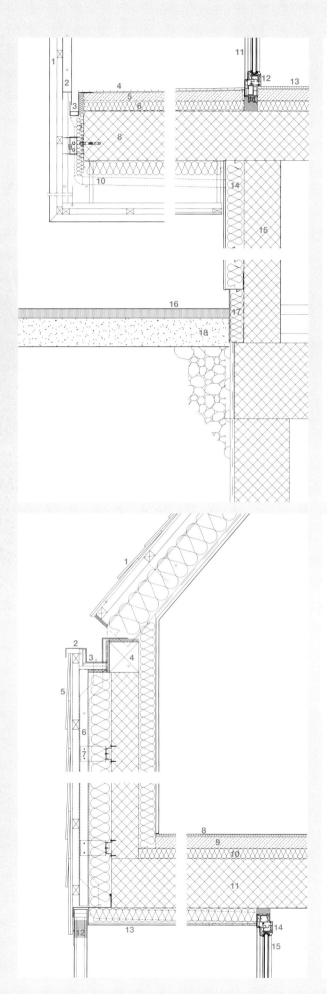

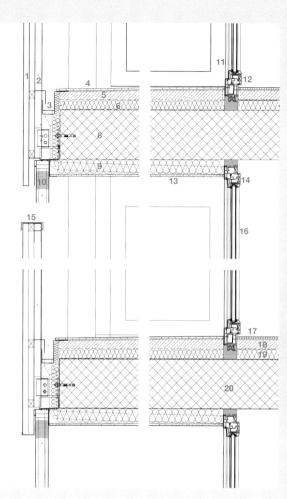

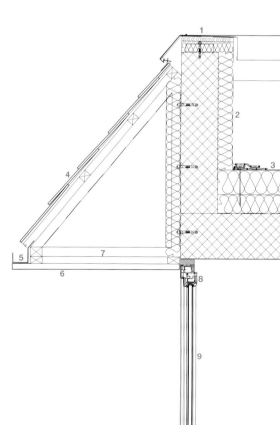

24.05
Facade and Balcony
Section Detail 1
1:20
 1 50 mm (2 inch) timber vertical to balustrade
 2 Steel balustrade structure
 3 Rainwater gutter
 4 10 mm (²/5 inch) stone tiles to balcony glue fixed to cement screed
 5 Cement screed laid to fall to gutter
 6 Thermal insulation
 7 Thermal insulation
 8 Reinforced concrete floor slab
 9 Steel profile with bolt fixing between concrete slab and steel balcony structure
 10 Rainwater outflow pipe
 11 Double glazed sliding balcony door
 12 Steel door frame
 13 10 mm (²/5 inch) oak parquet floor
 14 Thermal insulation
 15 Reinforced concrete wall
 16 Stone tiles
 17 Thermal insulation
 18 Reinforced concrete floor slab

24.06
Facade and Balcony
Section Detail 2
1:20
 1 50 mm (2 inch) timber vertical to balustrade
 2 Steel balustrade structure
 3 Rainwater gutter
 4 10 mm (²/5 inch) stone tiles to balcony glue fixed to cement screed
 5 Cement screed laid to fall to gutter
 6 Thermal insulation
 7 Steel profile with bolt fixing between concrete slab and steel balcony structure
 8 Reinforced concrete floor slab
 9 Thermal insulation
 10 Standard PVC window frame with double glazing and cavity for external blinds
 11 Double-glazed sliding balcony door
 12 Steel door frame
 13 Painted plaster soffit lining
 14 Steel door frame
 15 Sheet metal cover to top of balustrade
 16 Double glazed sliding balcony door
 17 10 mm (²/5 inch) oak parquet floor glued to cement screed layer
 18 Cement screed over polyurethane sheeting
 19 55 mm (2¹/6 inch) sound insulation
 20 260 mm (10¹/4 inch) reinforced concrete slab

24.07
Roof and Facade
Detail 1
1:20
 1 400 x 400 mm (15³/4 x 15³/4 inch) cement composite roof tiles on timber structure with 55 mm (2¹/6 inch) ventilated cavity, rainproof foil, thermal insulation, vapour barrier and fire resistant painted plasterboard lining
 2 Steel parapet capping
 3 Heated gutter
 4 Timber beam
 5 Facade construction from 400 x 400 mm (15³/4 x 15³/4 inch) cement composite tiles on 40 mm (1³/5 inch) timber structure, rainproof foil, thermal insulation, reinforced concrete structure and painted plasterboard interior lining
 6 Vertical rainwater outlet
 7 Steel profile with bolt fixing between concrete slab and external cladding
 8 10 mm (²/5 inch) stone tiles to balcony glue fixed to cement screed
 9 Cement screed laid to fall to gutter
 10 Thermal insulation
 11 260 mm (10¹/4 inch) reinforced composite slab
 12 Standard PVC window frame with double glazing and cavity for external blinds
 13 Painted plaster soffit lining
 14 Steel door frame
 15 Double glazed sliding balcony door

24.08
Roof and Facade
Detail 2
1:20
 1 Steel capping to roof parapet
 2 Roof upstand comprised of 80 mm (3¹/8 inch) thermal insulation, 200 mm (7⁹/10 inch) reinforced concrete wall, 80 mm (3¹/8 inch) thermal insulation and rainproof foil
 3 Flat roof construction from hydro-insulation, 200 mm (7⁹/10 inch) thermal insulation, vapour barrier and 240 mm (9¹/2 inch) reinforced concrete slab
 4 130 x 130 mm (5¹/8 x 5¹/8 inch) cement composite sheets on timber structure with polyurethane sheet lining
 5 Steel rainwater gutter
 6 Soffit lining from 30 x 40 mm (1¹/5 x 1³/5 inch) timber horizontals
 7 Steel soffit structure
 8 Steel window frame
 9 Double-glazed sliding balcony door

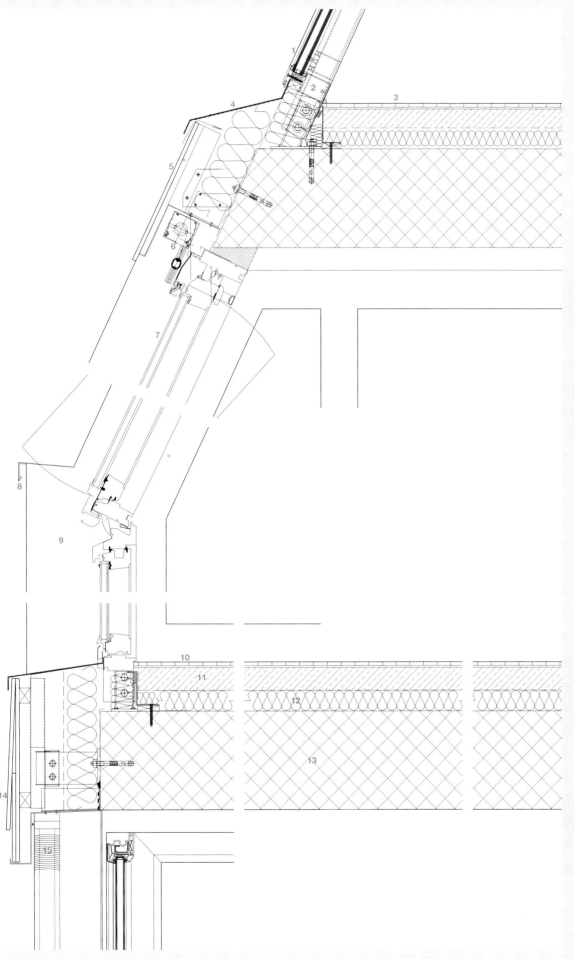

24.09
Skylight and Floor
Detail
1:10

1 Roof window
2 Aluminium-framed roof window
3 Floor construction from 10 mm (^{2}/$_5$ inch) oak parquet floor glued to 50 mm (2 inch) cement screed over polyurethane sheeting, 55 mm (2^1/$_{10}$ inch) sound insulation and 260 mm (10^1/$_4$ inch) reinforced concrete slab
4 Metal sheet capping
5 Facade construction from 400 x 400 mm (15^3/$_4$ x 15^3/$_4$ inch) cement composite tiles on steel profile fixed in reinforced concrete slab over ventilated cavity, hydro-insulation foil and 100 mm (4 inch) thermal insulation
6 External blind shading system
7 Roof window
8 Metal drip profile
9 Sheet metal wall lining
10 10 mm (^{2}/$_5$ inch) oak parquet floor glued to cement screed layer
11 Cement screed over polyurethane sheeting
12 55 mm (2^1/$_{10}$ inch) sound insulation
13 260 mm (10^1/$_4$ inch) reinforced concrete slab
14 130 x 130 mm (5^1/$_{10}$ x 5^1/$_{10}$ inch) cement composite sheets on timber structure with polyurethane sheet lining
15 Standard PVC window frame with double glazing and cavity for external blinds

Light-Catcher
Soest, Utrecht, The Netherlands

Client
Steendelaar-Mastenbroek family

Project Team
Theo Rooijakkers, Paddy Tomesen

Structural Engineer
Ingenieursbureau Boorsma

Main Contractor
Bouwonderneming T.J. Van de Belt

The Kerkebuurt (church neighbourhood) in Soest is a small historical town centre that, in its entirety, has been given protected rural site status. One of the most characteristic buildings in the area is the former Old Men and Women's House, built in 1782. The owner wanted to increase the size of the house, but all suggestions were vetoed by the town's heritage organization. Therefore it was decided to build a freestanding garden pavilion on the site of two former barns. It contains additional storage space and can be used as a guest house or workshop, complete with a large, partly covered, terrace.

The pavilion is a two-storey building with a basement and ground floor. In the basement, a poured concrete container was lined with timber, which when cured retained the grained texture. The superstructure is constructed entirely from timber, to which 15 load-bearing larch columns rise in a tight rhythm. The lightness of the garden pavilion, with its open-framed construction and extensive use of glass, is underlined by the difference in level between the garden and the ground floor. A strip of glass between the basement and ground floor allows visual contact with the outside world. The pavilion opens up to the garden: both the southern and eastern facades are fully glazed with larch brise-soleil protecting the interior from solar gain. Six moveable larch screens are placed on the outside of the glass – these can be manoeuvred to create various conditions of openness and privacy. A rigid core at the centre of the pavilion links the two storeys and contains ventilation, heating and other services.

1 Timber is employed extensively both inside and out. Sliding timber screens create opportunities to reveal or conceal the interior, while a terrace that wraps two sides of the building opens the interior up to the landscape.
2 The timber structure sits lightly in the historic town centre. The Light-Catcher is an addition to the gabled roofed Old Men and Women's House (left).

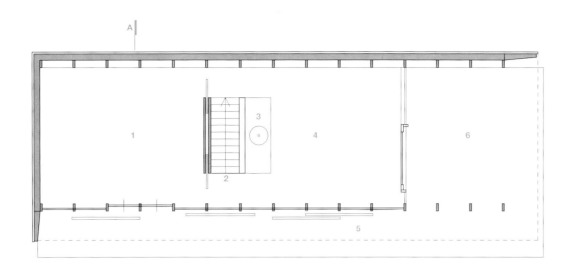

25.01
Ground Floor Plan
1:100
1 Storage
2 Stair up from basement
3 Kitchenette
4 Studio
5 Deck
6 Terrace

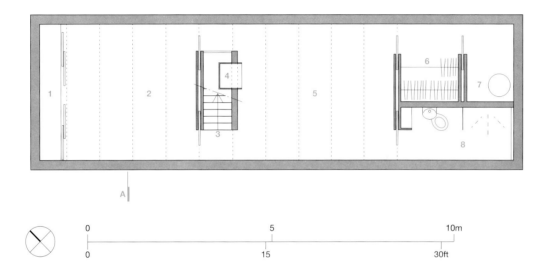

25.02
Basement Floor Plan
1:100
1 Cupboard
2 Storage
3 Stair up to ground floor
4 Niche
5 Room
6 Cloakroom
7 Services
8 Bathroom

0   5   10m

0   15   30ft

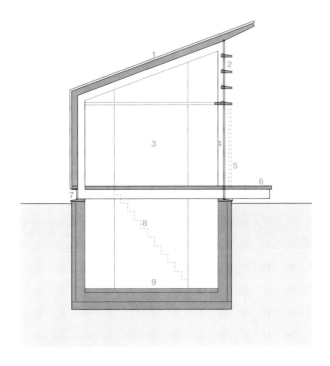

25.03
Section A–A
1:100
1 Larch ship-lapped boarding roof
2 Larch brise soleil
3 Storeroom
4 Glass facade
5 Moveable timber screen shown dotted
6 Deck
7 Glazed window
8 Stair shown dotted
9 Basement storage
10 Concrete basement structure

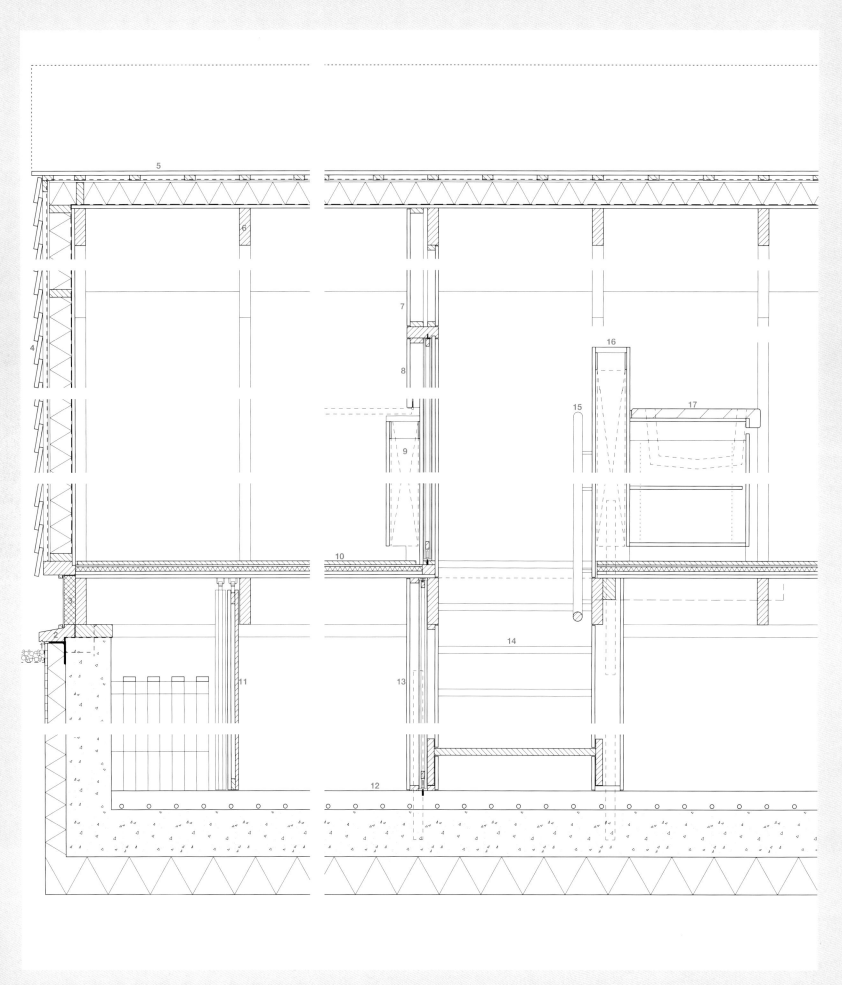

25.04
Longitudinal Section Detail
1:20

1 15 mm (^{3}/$_5$ inch) fibre cement cladding over 100 mm (4 inch) extruded polystyrene insulation over 250 mm (9^4/$_5$ inch) exposed concrete wall
2 Larch sill
3 18 mm (^{7}/$_{10}$ inch) larch veneered plywood over 60 mm (2^1/$_3$ inch) extruded polystyrene insulation
4 19 x 145 mm (^{3}/$_4$ x 5^7/$_{10}$ inch) sawn larch shiplap boarding with acrylic-latex paint finish over 27 x 50 mm (1 x 2 inch) impregnated battens with moisture diffusing membrane, 10 mm (^{2}/$_5$ inch) oriented strand board, 121 mm (4^3/$_4$ inch) mineral wool thermal insulation, vapour barrier and 18 mm (^{7}/$_{10}$ inch) larch-veneered plywood lining
5 19 x 145 mm (^{3}/$_4$ x 5^7/$_{10}$ inch) sawn larch shiplap boarding with acrylic-latex paint finish over 27 x 50 mm (1 x 2 inch) impregnated battens with moisture diffusing membrane, 10 mm (^{2}/$_5$ inch) oriented strand board, 121 mm (4^3/$_4$ inch) mineral wool thermal insulation, vapour barrier and 18 mm (^{7}/$_{10}$ inch) larch-veneered plywood lining
6 59 x 196 mm (2^1/$_3$ x 7^7/$_{10}$ inch) larch rafters
7 Larch wall lining
8 Folding work table suspended from hinged joint secured with three nuts and larch batten
9 Two 700 x 900 x 150 mm (27^3/$_5$ x 35^2/$_5$ x 6 inch) convector heaters with built-in wall switch
10 20 mm (^{3}/$_4$ inch) larch strip flooring adhesive fixed to 10 mm (^{2}/$_5$ inch) plywood over 24 mm (9/$_{10}$ inch) mineral wool insulation, 2 x 18 mm (^{1}/$_{10}$ x ^{7}/$_{10}$ inch) plywood and 59 x 246 mm (2^1/$_3$ x 9^2/$_3$ inch) larch floor beams
11 Larch-clad sliding cupboard doors
12 Underfloor heating system embedded in reinforced concrete floor slab finished with cement topping and protective coating, insulated with 200 mm (7^9/$_{10}$ inch) extruded polystyrene
13 Sliding door with guidance profile sliding door armour
14 Larch stair treads
15 Larch circular section balustrade
16 Larch grating to service duct
17 Timber kitchen unit with concrete worktop

25.05
Cross Section Detail Through Eaves and External Wall
1:20

1 19 x 145 mm (^{3}/$_4$ x 5^7/$_{10}$ inch) sawn larch shiplap boarding with acrylic-latex paint finish over 27 x 50 mm (1 x 2 inch) impregnated battens with moisture diffusing membrane, 10 mm (^{2}/$_5$ inch) oriented strand board, 121 mm (4^3/$_4$ inch) mineral wool thermal insulation, vapour barrier and 18 mm (^{7}/$_{10}$ inch) larch-veneered plywood lining
2 Larch capping
3 18 mm (^{7}/$_{10}$ inch) larch-veneered plywood soffit lining
4 Fixed glazing
5 90 x 296 mm (3^1/$_2$ x 11^2/$_3$ inch) larch louvres
6 59 x 296 mm (2^1/$_3$ x 11^2/$_3$ inch) larch column
7 Double glazing with 8 mm (3/$_{10}$ inch) safety glass and 15 mm (3/$_5$ inch) cavity
8 Larch sliding shutter constructed from 18 x 59 mm (^{7}/$_{10}$ x 2^1/$_3$ inch) larch strips on 22 x 58 mm (4/$_5$ x 2^1/$_3$ inch) bearers
9 20 mm (^{3}/$_4$ inch) larch strip flooring adhesive fixed to 10 mm (^{2}/$_5$ inch) plywood over 24 mm (9/$_{10}$ inch) mineral wool insulation, 2 x 18 mm (^{1}/$_{10}$ x ^{7}/$_{10}$ inch) plywood and 59 x 246 mm (2^1/$_3$ x 9^2/$_3$ inch) larch floor beams
10 Double glazing with 8 mm (3/$_{10}$ inch) safety glass and 15 mm (3/$_5$ inch) cavity
11 Reinforced concrete basement structure
12 Larch sill
13 15 mm (3/$_5$ inch) fibre cement cladding over 100 mm (4 inch) extruded polystyrene insulation over 250 mm (9^4/$_5$ inch) exposed concrete wall
14 Treated larch decking boards
15 Larch bearer
16 Adjustable steel support
17 Reinforced concrete footing

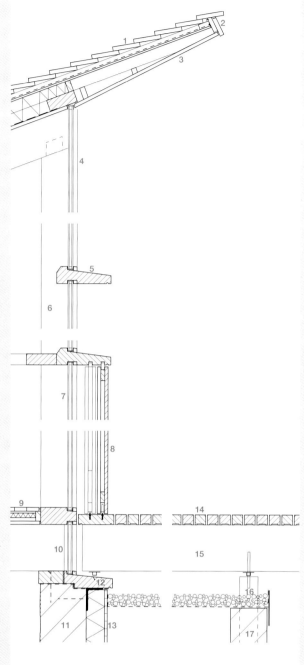

**Maison Goulet
Sainte-Marguerite-du-Lac-Masson,
Québec, Canada**

Client
Marlène Goulet

Project Team
Mario Saia, Marc Pape, Nadia Meratla

Landscape Architect
Claude Cormier Architectes-
Paysagistes

Main Contractor
Michel Riopelle

Maison Goulet is situated 60 miles (96 kilometres) north of the city near the village of Sainte Marguerite-du-Lac-Masson, and is surrounded by thick forest and countless small lakes. The owners purchased an 80 acre (32 hectare) plot of land on a ridge overlooking Lake Grenier. Existing buildings on the site, including a rustic cottage with small additions, were kept for use by the client's children and grandchildren in summer, but when the couple decided to create a year-round retreat, they wanted to create a comfortable contemporary house without encroaching on the fragile lakeside environment.

A long narrow plateau towards the top of the property away from the lake became the site for the new house, placed below two rock faces. The two-storey house consists of a ground floor with screened terraces at either end, with a kitchen and double-height living and dining area in between. On the first floor, two bedrooms and a bathroom are located above the kitchen at one end, with a studio and office at the other end, separated by the void over the living room below. Two chimney stacks anchor the steel-reinforced timber-framed structure to the site. A basement level, constructed from field stones, contains a mud room and workshop. On the exterior, zinc cladding is interrupted for large expanses of timber-framed windows and doors that open the interior up to the wooded landscape. The interior is lined entirely in horizontal fir-faced plywood panels. These timber panels, used without mouldings or framework of any kind, are used for all walls and ceilings, lending a natural warmth to the interior spaces.

1 At the south-east end of the house, a small terrace opens off the kitchen. All of the openings, including doors, windows and the terrace framing are constructed from Douglas fir timber.
2 The central living space occupies the full height of the building. Beyond, a screened terrace is defined by a rustic stone wall complete with fireplace.
3 Two symmetrical staircases provide access to the first floor bedrooms and studio, while clearly demarcating the open family zone below from the private spaces above. The staircase is braced between the almost opaque northern exterior wall and the timber-framed interior wall.

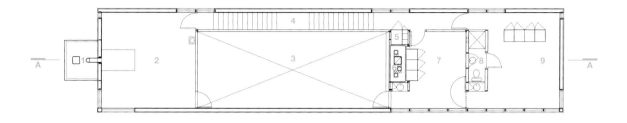

26.01
First Floor Plan
1:200
  1 Chimney
  2 Studio
  3 Void over living room
  4 Stair up from ground floor
  5 Storage
  6 Chimney
  7 Bedroom
  8 Bathroom
  9 Master bedroom

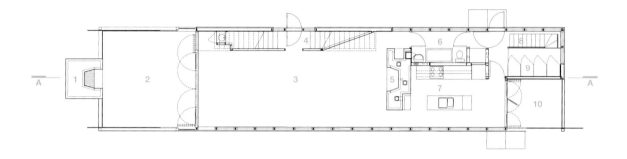

26.02
Ground Floor Plan
1:200
  1 Fireplace
  2 Screened terrace
  3 Living room
  4 Stair to first floor
  5 Fireplace
  6 Bathroom
  7 Kitchen
  8 Stair to basement
  9 Cloakroom
  10 Screened terrace

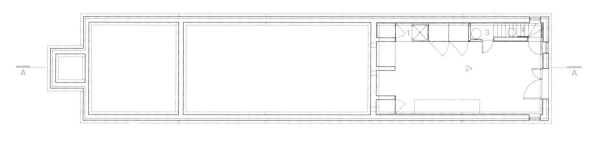

26.03
Basement Floor Plan
1:200
  1 Shower
  2 Studio
  3 Hot water storage
  4 Stair to first floor

0   5   10m
0   15   30ft

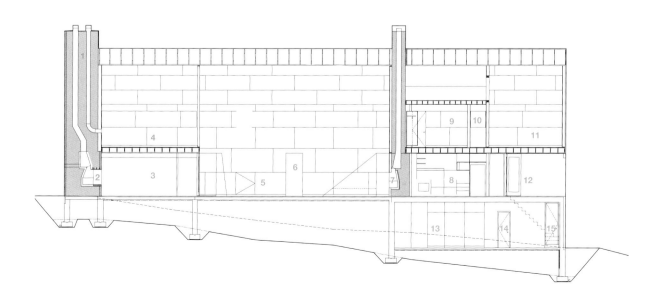

26.04
Section A–A
1:200
  1 Chimney stack
  2 Fireplace
  3 Screened terrace
  4 Studio
  5 Living room
  6 Stair to first floor
  7 Fireplace
  8 Kitchen
  9 Bedroom
  10 Bathroom
  11 Master bedroom
  12 Screened terrace
  13 Mud room
  14 Hot water storage cupboard
  15 Stair to ground floor

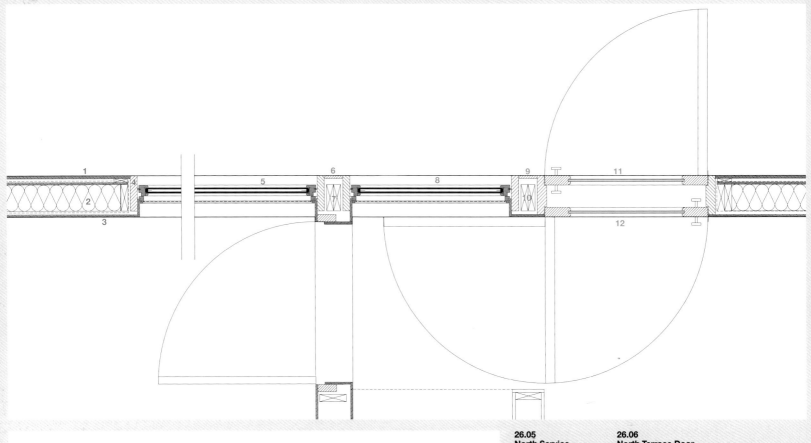

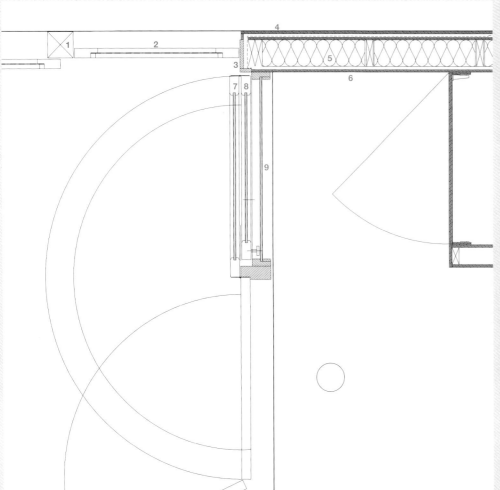

26.05
North Service Entrance and Window Plan Detail
1:20
1 Zinc cladding over air barrier, plywood interior backing and furring channels
2 152 mm (6 inch) insulation
3 Fir-faced plywood interior lining
4 Steel-reinforced timber frame
5 Timber-framed window
6 Timber fascia
7 Steel-reinforced timber frame
8 Timber-framed window
9 Timber fascia
10 Steel-reinforced timber frame
11 Screened timber-framed door
12 Glazed timber-framed door

26.06
North Terrace Door Plan Detail
1:20
1 Fir column
2 Timber frame for screen panel
3 Timber window reveal
4 Zinc cladding over air barrier, plywood interior backing and furring channels
5 152 mm (6 inch) insulation
6 Fir-faced plywood interior lining
7 Glazed timber-framed door folded flat against fixed window in open position
8 Screened timber-framed door folded flat against fixed window in open position
9 Clear glazed fixed window

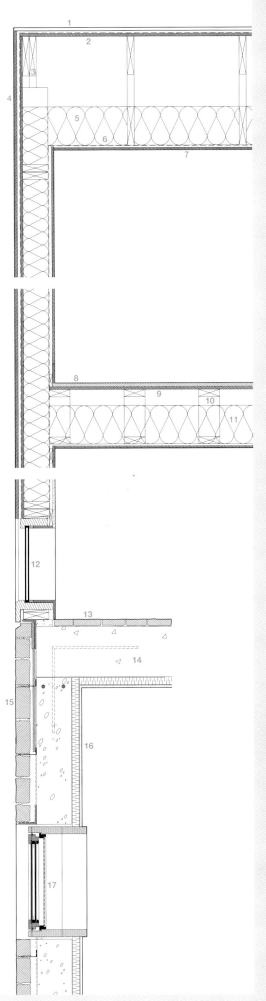

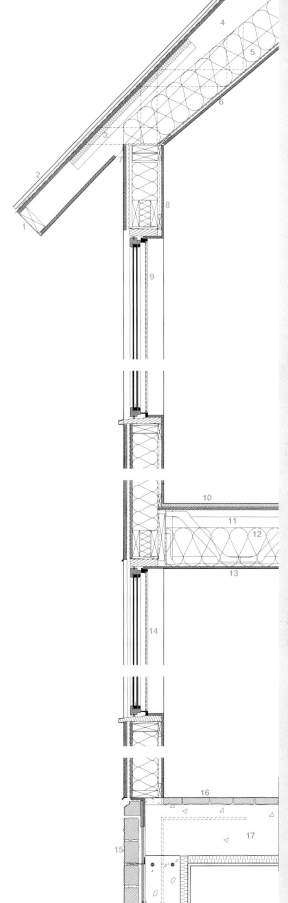

26.07
Typical Wall Section 1
1:20
1 Galvanized steel roof sheeting over blue skin membrane
2 Plywood roofing substrate
3 Double timber roof framing
4 Zinc cladding over air barrier, plywood interior backing and furring channels
5 150 mm (6 inch) insulation
6 Vapour barrier and furring channel
7 Fir-faced plywood ceiling lining
8 Maple wood floor
9 Plywood flooring substrate
10 Timber truss
11 Acoustic insulation
12 Timber-framed window
13 Flagstone flooring
14 Reinforced concrete floor slab
15 Field stone external wall
16 Gypsum board lining over metal furring and polystyrene insulation
17 Double-glazed window unit

26.08
Typical Wall Section 2
1:20
1 Galvanized steel eaves capping
2 Galvanized steel roof sheeting over blue skin membrane and plywood substrate
3 Air deflector
4 Timber A-frame truss
5 Insulation
6 Fir-faced plywood ceiling lining on furring channel and vapour barrier
7 Screened air intake
8 Fir-faced plywood wall lining on furring channel and vapour barrier
9 Double-glazed timber-framed window
10 Maple wood floor over plywood substrate
11 Timber truss
12 Acoustic insulation
13 Fir-faced plywood ceiling lining on furring channels
14 Double-glazed timber-framed window
15 Field stone external wall
16 Flagstone flooring
17 Reinforced concrete floor slab

Lakeside House
Çanakkale, Marmara, Turkey

Client
Filip Amram

Project Team
Ufuk Buluttekin, Nilay Arslan,
Muharrem Caglan

Structural Engineer
Mustafa Sikman

Services Engineer
GMD Engineering

Situated in the untouched landscape of the Kaz Mountains, this house sits close to the shore of an artificial lake and has been designed to respect the fragile mountain environment without damaging the ecological balance. All the structural components were constructed with a small budget and within a short five week period after well-planned preliminary work. During this preliminary research process, various manufacturers were consulted to arrive at a construction process that would result in the least disturbance to the site and the shortest on-site construction period.

The resulting house features 100 square metres (1,076 square feet) of enclosed interior space and 70 square metres (753 square feet) of open space. The interior is arranged simply along the length of the rectangular plan as a central living and dining space with bedroom and en suite bathroom at either end. One long facade and the two shorter ones are clad in timber boards and interrupted only by the centrally placed entrance and small windows for the two bathrooms. The other long facade, however, enjoys views out across the landscape via full height sliding glass panels. A spacious timber deck wraps around one corner of the house, featuring an outdoor shower and retractable cloth sunshades to protect the deck and the interior from the hot summer sun. The timber framed and clad house is elevated above the site on braced steel columns which add to the perceived lightness of the structure as well as minimizing the impact of the building on the sensitive site.

1 All of the interior spaces enjoy views towards the lake through the expansive sliding glass doors which also give access to the large timber deck.

2 On the rear facade, the timber cladding is broken only by a horizontal slot window that illuminates the kitchen, and the entrance, which is accessed by a short

flight of timber stairs.
3 View of the kitchen and dining area. The predominantly white interior features accents of dark wood in the kitchen cabinetry and furniture.

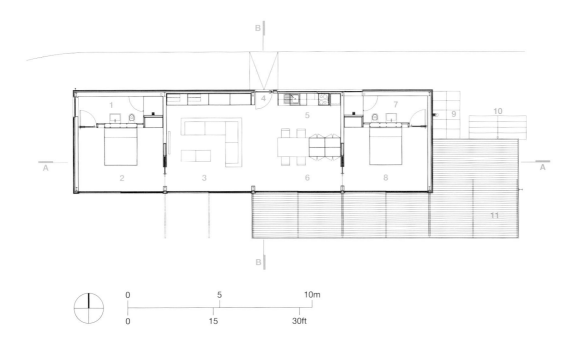

27.01
Ground Floor Plan
1:200
1 Bathroom
2 Bedroom
3 Living area
4 Entrance
5 Kitchen
6 Dining area
7 Bathroom
8 Bedroom
9 Outdoor shower
10 Stair to deck
11 Deck

0   5   10m

0   15   30ft

27.02
Section A–A
1:200
1 Door to bathroom
2 Bedroom
3 Wardrobe
4 Storage to living room
5 Entrance
6 Kitchen
7 Wardrobe
8 Bedroom
9 Door to bathroom
10 Deck

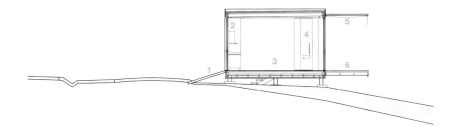

27.03
Section B–B
1:200
1 Entrance stair
2 Kitchen
3 Living and dining area
4 Door to bedroom
5 Sunshade canopy
6 Deck

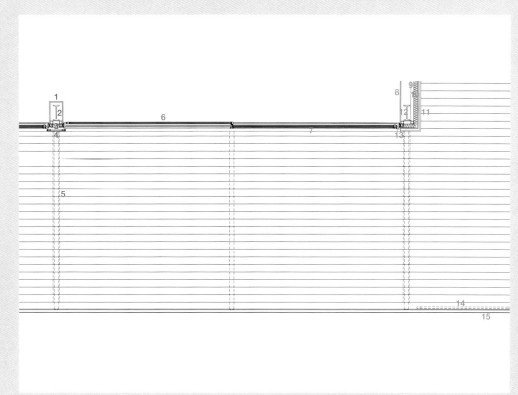

27.04
Facade Detail Plan
1:50
1 Gypsum board interior lining with painted finish
2 Universal steel column
3 Insulation
4 Aluminium composite panel
5 60 mm (2¹/₃ inch) diameter circular steel section for sunshade frame over, shown dotted
6 Insulated aluminium framed sliding glass door
7 Aluminium-framed insect screen
8 Gypsum board interior lining with painted finish
9 Steel channel
10 Heat insulation and waterproof membrane
11 Timber facing on timber sub frame
12 Universal steel column
13 Timber bead
14 20 mm (³/₄ inch) diameter steel bracing under deck shown dotted
15 4 mm (¹/₆ inch) stainless steel profile to deck edge

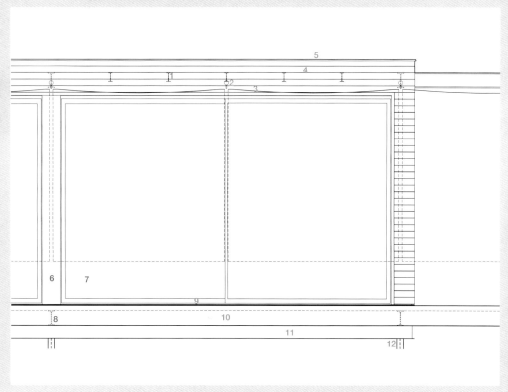

27.05
Facade Detail
1:50
1 Universal steel column
2 60 mm (2¹/₃ inch) diameter circular steel section for sunshade frame
3 Fabric sunshade
4 Timber cladding
5 4 mm (¹/₆ inch) stainless steel profile capping
6 Aluminium composite panel
7 Insulated aluminium-framed sliding glass door
8 Universal steel column
9 4 mm (¹/₆ inch) stainless steel profile to deck edge
10 Timber bearer to deck
11 Steel beam to deck support
12 Steel column

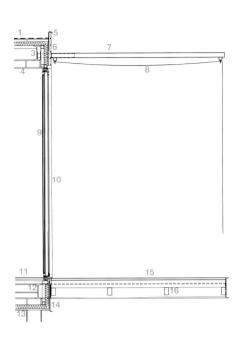

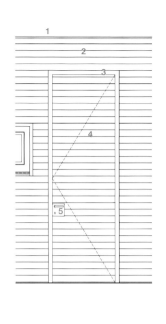

27.06
Facade Section Detail
1:50
1 Mineral waterproof membrane over oriented strand board and timber sub frame
2 Insulation
3 Universal steel beam
4 Gypsum board ceiling lining with painted finish
5 4 mm (1/6 inch) stainless steel profile capping
6 Timber board cladding
7 60 mm (2 1/3 inch) diameter circular steel section for sunshade frame
8 Natural canvas sunshade
9 Insulated aluminium-framed sliding glass door
10 Aluminium-framed insect screen
11 Timber floorboards
12 Universal steel beam
13 Insulation over timber board cladding
14 Aluminium cover panel
15 Timber boards to deck
16 Rectangular steel hollow section joist

27.07
Entrance Door Section Detail
1:50
1 4 mm (1/6 inch) stainless steel profile capping
2 Timber board cladding
3 Mineral waterproof membrane over oriented strand board and timber sub frame
4 Insulation
5 Universal steel beam
6 Gypsum board ceiling lining with painted finish
7 Tongue and groove panelled timber door
8 Aluminium cover panel
9 Timber floorboards
10 Universal steel beam
11 Insulation over timber board cladding
12 Steel column
13 Reinforced concrete footing

27.08
Entrance Door Elevation Detail
1:50
1 4 mm (1/6 inch) stainless steel profile capping
2 Timber board cladding
3 Timber door frame
4 Tongue and groove panelled timber door
5 Stainless steel lock plate and door handle

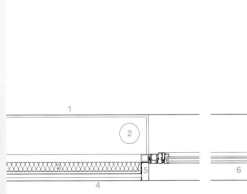
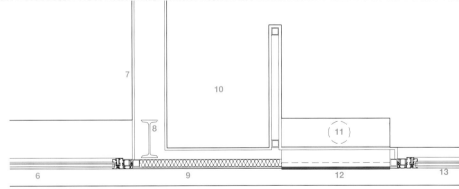
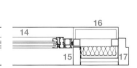

27.09
Rear Facade Plan Detail
1:20
1 Waterproof plasterboard with paint finish to bathroom
2 Concealed downpipe for roof drainage
3 Insulation
4 Timber cladding
5 Timber window reveal
6 Insulated aluminium-framed window
7 Waterproof plasterboard with paint finish to bathroom
8 Universal steel column
9 Painted fibre cement sheet cladding
10 Fridge recess
11 Extractor fan and vent over hob
12 Aluminium composite sheeting
13 Insulated aluminium-framed window
14 Timber window sill
15 Timber window reveal
16 Gypsum board interior lining with painted finish
17 Timber door frame

Pencalenick House
Polruan, Cornwall, England, UK

Project Team
Seth Stein, Andrew Abdulezer, Samina
Choudhry

Structural Engineer
Barry Honeysett Engineering

Main Contractor
John Gower Designs, Clive Ralphs
Heating and Plumbing

Landscape Architect
Topia Landscapes

The brief was for a holiday home for
the client and his family on a site
overlooking the picturesque Fowey
estuary. The building was to respond
to the site's topography, aspect and
environment in a sensitive yet
thoroughly contemporary manner. The
response to the brief led to a curved
plan that followed the site contours
and was embedded into the steeply
sloping hillside. A turfed roof
continues into the landscape whilst
the perimeter indicates the structural
form beneath. A line of glazing set at
the same level as the grass denotes
the internal circulation spine which
links the various living spaces, and the
retaining wall against the hill. From
the water the long volume is clearly
book-ended into the hill by means of
Cornish slate retaining walls that also
facilitate changes in level within the
building and the landscape beyond.

The choice of materials includes
cedar external cladding, Cornish slate,
salvaged elm used for internal floors
and joinery, and sandblasted glass for
the gallery, the overall effect of which
creates a building which sits very
comfortably with the surrounding
woodland. The site was delineated
via a new earth retaining concrete
structure creating a shelf upon which
to construct the glu-laminated timber
frame structure of the house. The
green roof, seeded with a bespoke
mixture of local grasses, is supported
off the timber structure in a 900-
millimetre (three-foot) thick roof
cassette that both insulates the
building below and conceals its form
from higher elevations.

1 The house is
arranged with living
spaces on the lower
level. Upstairs, the
bedrooms and
bathrooms are
arranged on one side
of a void over the living
spaces, with an office
and TV room on the
other side of a glass
bridge.
2 Timber is used
extensively throughout
the building. Here, the
soffit lining, balustrade,
window frames and
solid louvre panels are
constructed from
untreated timber.
3 A glass bridge with
translucent glass
balustrade connects
both sides of the upper
level. Bookcases,
which line the resulting
double-height space,
are lit from above by
a skylight.
4 In the living and
dining room, a stone
fireplace surround
anchors the space,
while double glazing
opens up the interior to
views of the estuary,
bringing in abundant
natural light.

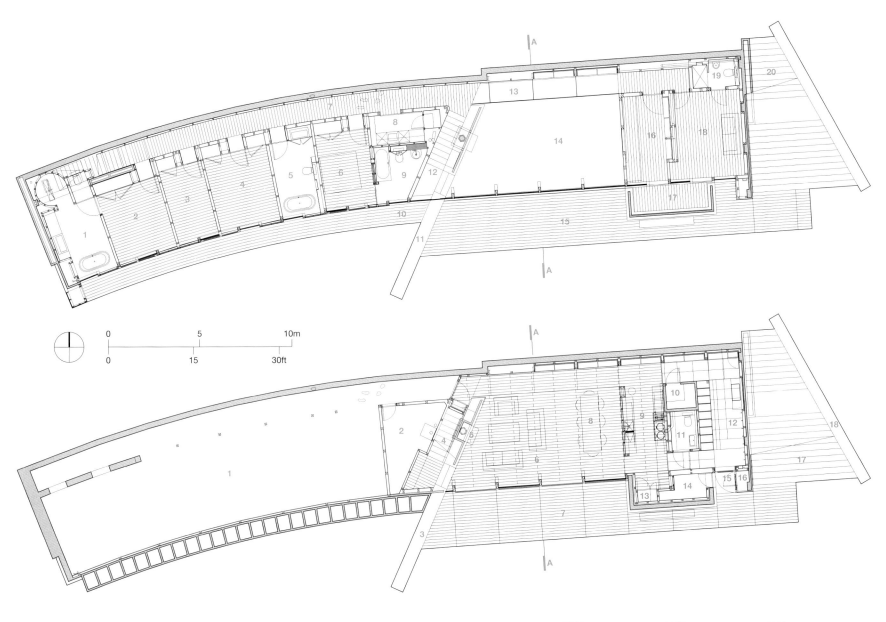

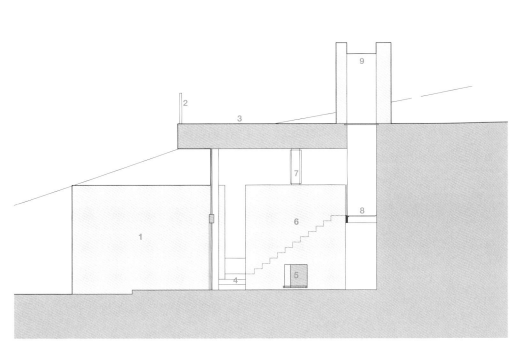

28.01	28.02	28.03
First Floor Plan	**Ground Floor Plan**	**Section A–A**
1:200	**1:200**	**1:200**
1 Master bathroom	1 Under building area	1 Stone retaining wall
2 Master bedroom	2 Boiler room	2 Balustrade to grassed roof
3 Bedroom	3 Stone retaining wall	3 Grassed roof
4 Bedroom	4 Stair to first floor	4 Stair to first floor
5 Bathroom	5 Fireplace	5 Wood burning stove
6 Bedroom	6 Living room	6 Stone retaining wall
7 Corridor	7 Terrace	7 Chimney flue
8 Utility room	8 Dining room	8 Glass bridge
9 Bathroom	9 Kitchen	9 Skylight
10 Terrace	10 Pantry	
11 Stone retaining wall	11 WC	
12 Stair from ground floor	12 Mud room	
13 Glass bridge	13 Fridge	
14 Void over living and dining areas below	14 Storage	
15 Terrace below	15 Entrance	
16 Office	16 Bin store	
17 Terrace	17 Entrance deck	
18 TV room	18 Stone retaining wall	
19 WC and shower		
20 Entrance deck below		

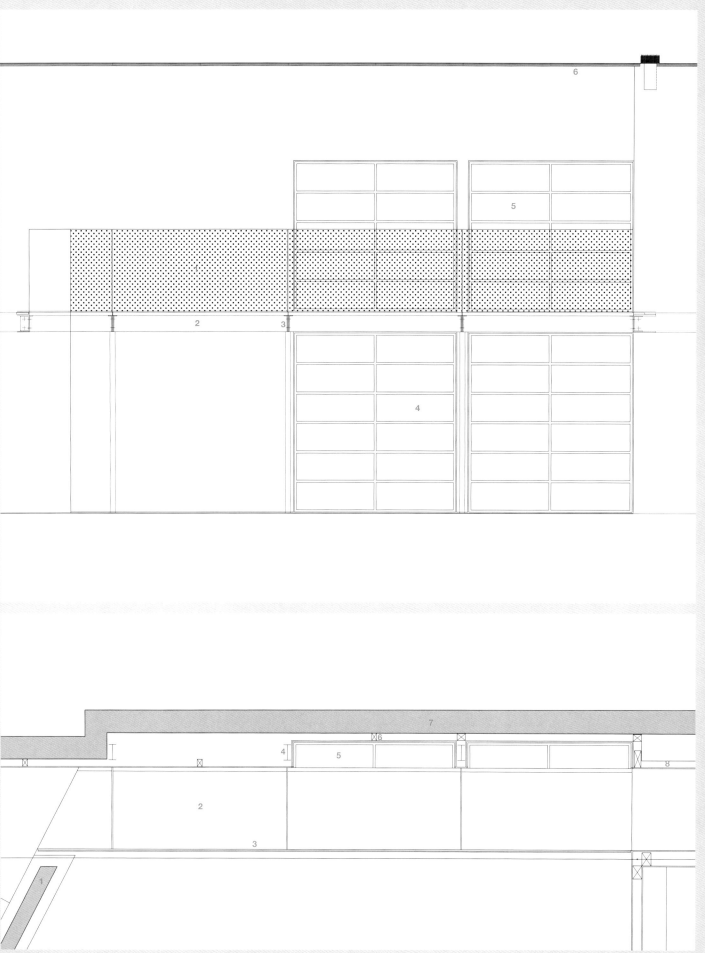

 1 Translucent glass balustrade
 2 Painted steel frame to deck structure
 3 Painted steel frame to deck structure
 4 Timber bookshelves to library
 5 Timber bookshelves to library
 6 Glazed skylight

28.05
Glass Bridge Plan Detail
1:50
 1 Slate fireplace wall
 2 Translucent glass floor
 3 Translucent glass balustrade
 4 Steel structural column
 5 Timber bookshelves to library
 6 Timber stud frame
 7 Retaining structural wall
 8 Timber stud wall

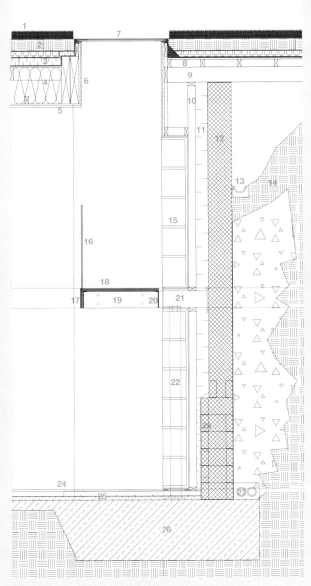

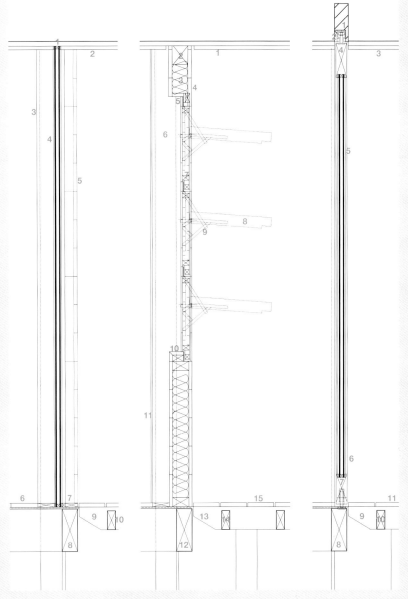

28.06
Glass Bridge Section Detail
1:50
1 Grass roof
2 Lightweight soil
3 Rigid thermal insulation
4 Timber roof structure
5 Plasterboard ceiling
6 Plasterboard reveal to skylight
7 Glazed skylight
8 Timber joists
9 Timber joists
10 Timber wall stud
11 Rigid thermal insulation
12 Structural retaining wall
13 French drain
14 Soil backfill
15 Timber bookshelves to library
16 Translucent glass

balustrade
17 Painted steel framed deck structure
18 Translucent glass floor
19 Painted steel framed deck structure
20 Painted steel framed deck structure
21 Cantilevered steel fin
22 Timber bookshelves to library
23 Structural retaining wall
24 Elm floorboards
25 Under floor heating on rigid insulation
26 Cast in-situ reinforced concrete foundation
27 Land drain

28.07
Facade System – Fixed Glass Panel Detail
1:20
1 Fixed glazing channel
2 Cedar soffit lining
3 Painted plasterboard wall
4 Fixed double glazed unit
5 External cedar panelling
6 Elm floor boards
7 Fixed glazing channel
8 Timber structure
9 External timber deck structure
10 External timber deck structure

28.08
Facade System – Timber Louvre Detail
1:20
1 Cedar soffit lining
2 Timber header
3 Rigid insulation
4 External cedar cladding
5 Timber window reveal
6 Cedar clad post
7 Insulated louvre panel (closed)
8 Insulated louvre panel (open)
9 Louvre mechanism
10 Cedar sill
11 Painted plasterboard wall
12 Timber structure
13 External timber deck structure
14 External timber deck structure
15 Cedar deck

28.09
Facade System – Sliding Glass Panel Detail
1:20
1 Timber support for sliding door operation gear
2 Sliding door operation gear
3 Cedar soffit lining
4 Cedar window frame
5 Double glazed unit
6 Double glazed unit
7 Cedar window frame
8 Timber structure
9 External timber deck structure
10 External timber deck structure
11 Cedar deck

Bangalay House
Upper Kangaroo Valley, New South Wales, Australia

Client
Alastair & Molly Stevenson

Project Team
Peter Stutchbury, Phoebe Pape,
Marika Jarv

Structural Engineer
Prof. Max Irvine

Main Contractor
Tony Lake Constructions

The Bangalay House is located on a site that was once part of the Budderoo National Park on the south coast of New South Wales. The brief required a place for entertaining, eating, sleeping and a study from which to run an olive plantation business. In response, the house is designed as an elegant shed, orientated towards the north to make the most of passive solar gain. The building's uncomplicated circulation runs off a long central corridor. A simple skillion roof rises towards the east where the living areas are located, allowing a greater sense of space and light. The bedrooms are positioned on the western side, as the roof gently lowers to provide containment and security, but then lifts up as a gesture to the view that lies beyond.

The heart of the house is a large sheltered courtyard which serves as mediator between the public and private. To the south, robust concrete block bays for thermal mass accommodate service areas such as washing and storage. Large timber-framed sliding glass doors surround the house, allowing the building to open and close and frame the landscape. A large cantilevered verandah roof hangs above these openings, providing uninterrupted shelter. The building's simple palette consists of timber, plywood, steel and concrete. Timber and plywood are used extensively to soften the austerity of the other materials. The main structure consists of a series of recycled hardwood portal frames. The double beam structure allows enough inherent strength to cantilever verandah trusses, while also providing a cavity for services.

1 View of the north facade where the central covered courtyard and BBQ area overlook an existing dam that has been integrated into the landscape.
2 To the east, the living area opens up to a covered verandah. Above, high level glazing brings natural light into the house.
3 View of the courtyard with the kitchen to the left and the bedrooms to the right. The timber structure, including the double beam system, is left exposed.
4 Sliding glass panels above the kitchen countertops slide away to connect the living spaces to the courtyard dining area.

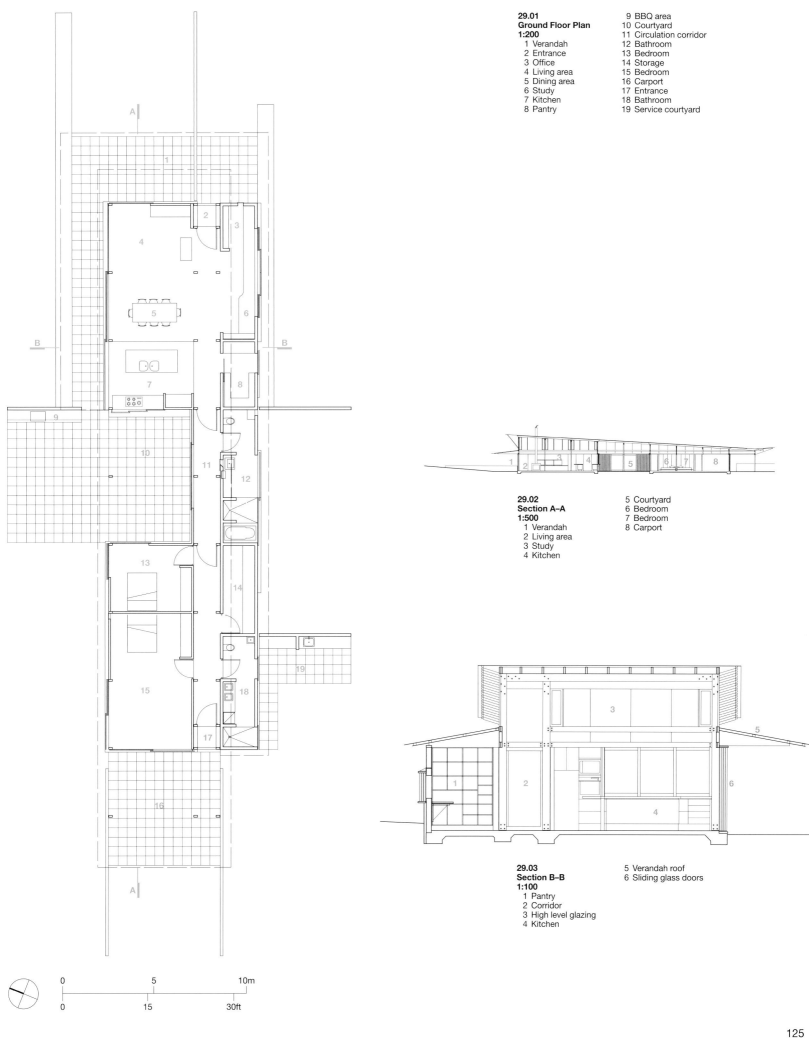

29.01
Ground Floor Plan
1:200
1 Verandah
2 Entrance
3 Office
4 Living area
5 Dining area
6 Study
7 Kitchen
8 Pantry
9 BBQ area
10 Courtyard
11 Circulation corridor
12 Bathroom
13 Bedroom
14 Storage
15 Bedroom
16 Carport
17 Entrance
18 Bathroom
19 Service courtyard

29.02
Section A–A
1:500
1 Verandah
2 Living area
3 Study
4 Kitchen
5 Courtyard
6 Bedroom
7 Bedroom
8 Carport

29.03
Section B–B
1:100
1 Pantry
2 Corridor
3 High level glazing
4 Kitchen
5 Verandah roof
6 Sliding glass doors

0   5   10m

0   15   30ft

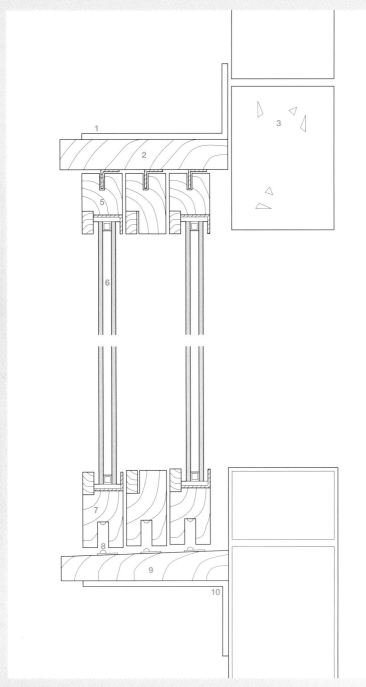

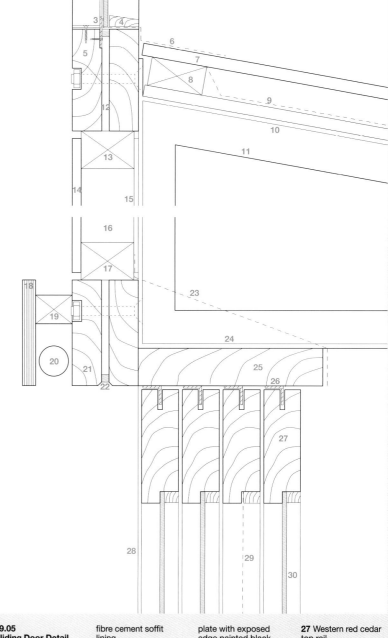

29.04
Timber Sliding
Window Detail
1:5
1 Copper flashing
2 140 x 40 mm (5¹/₂ x
13/5 inch) hardwood
timber head
3 Concrete lintel
4 25 x 25 x 3 mm (1 x
1 x ¹/₁₀ inch) brass
angle
5 70 x 40 mm (2³/₄ x
1¹/₂ inch) western red
cedar top rail
6 Double glazing unit
7 90 x 40 mm (3¹/₂ x
13/5 inch) western red
cedar top rail
8 Roller system on
bronze runner track
9 140 x 40 mm (5¹/₂ x
13/5 inch) hardwood
sill with cut slope
10 100 x 75 x 8 mm (4
x 3 x ³/₁₀ inch)
galvanized angle with
gusset

29.05
Sliding Door Detail
1:5
1 40 x 40 x 3 mm
(13/5 x 13/5 x ¹/₁₀ inch)
aluminium T-section
glazing bar and base
plate powder-coated
black
2 Fixed glazing panel
3 40 x 3 mm (13/5 x
¹/₁₀ inch) aluminium
flat bar powder-coated
black, saw cut and
fixed into beam
4 Timber beading
5 Two 135 x 40 mm
(5¹/₃ x 13/5 inch)
hardwood beams
bolted together
6 Flashing
7 Colourbond
Custom Orb roofing
8 70 x 38 mm (2³/₄ x
1¹/₂ inch) timber fixing
battens
9 Sisalation
10 15 mm (³/₅ inch)

fibre cement soffit
lining
11 50 x 50 x 6 mm (2 x
2 x ¹/₄ inch) T-section
galvanized and
painted steel gussets
12 10 mm (²/₅ inch)
fixing plate between
beams
13 Timber top plate
with exposed edge
painted black
14 12 mm (¹/₂ inch)
hoop pine plywood
inserts between
beams to inside with
10 mm (²/₅ inch)
shadowline to
junctions
15 6 mm (¹/₄ inch) fibre
cement inserts
between beams to
outside with 10 mm
(²/₅ inch) shadowline
to junctions
16 Timber studs at
gusset centres
17 Timber bottom

plate with exposed
edge painted black
18 18 mm (⁷/₁₀ inch)
hoop pine veneer
plywood pelmet
between posts to
conceal blinds
19 50 x 38 mm (2 x
1¹/₂ inch) continuous
timber spacer to seal
pelmet
20 Roller blind system
21 Two 140 x 40 mm
(5¹/₂ x 13/5 inch)
hardwood beams
bolted together
22 Sikaflex
23 Copper flashing
24 Window head
bolted through to
gusset bottom flange
25 250 x 50 mm (9⁴/₅ x
2 inch) hardwood door
head
26 25 x 25 x 3 mm (1 x
1 x ¹/₁₀ inch)
aluminium angle head
guide

27 Western red cedar
top rail
28 Two 200 x 45 mm
(7⁹/₁₀ x 1³/₄ inch)
hardwood portal posts
bolted together
29 Flyscreen mesh
30 Clear glazing to
sliding door

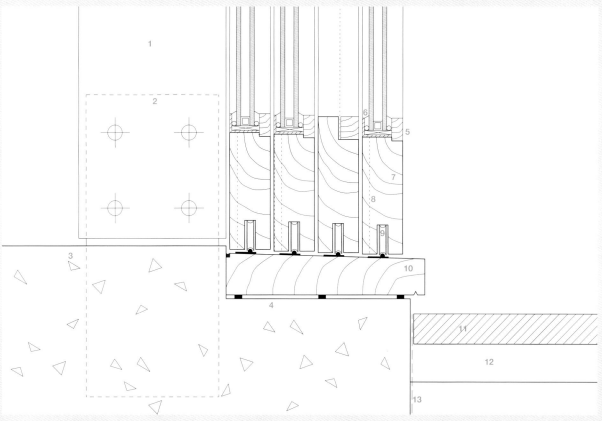

29.06
Door Section Detail
1:5
  1 Two 200 x 45 mm
(7⁹/₁₀ x 1³/₄ inch)
hardwood portal posts
bolted together
  2 10 mm (²/₅ inch)
galvanized steel plate
stirrups shown dotted
  3 Reinforced
concrete slab with
polished and waxed
finish
  4 70 mm (2³/₄ inch)
setdown in slab for sill
  5 Timber beading
  6 40 x 25 x 3 mm
(1³/₅ x 1 x ¹/₁₀ inch)
aluminium angle fixed
to bottom rail
  7 155 x 55 mm (6¹/₁₀
x 2¹/₁₀ inch) rebated
Western red cedar
bottom rail
  8 Henderson flush
door locks shown
dotted
  9 Sheave block
  10 Hardwood sill on
packers with Sikaflex
edge to angle
  11 Stone pavers
  12 50 mm (2 inch)
sand bed on
compacted fill
  13 Waterproof
membrane

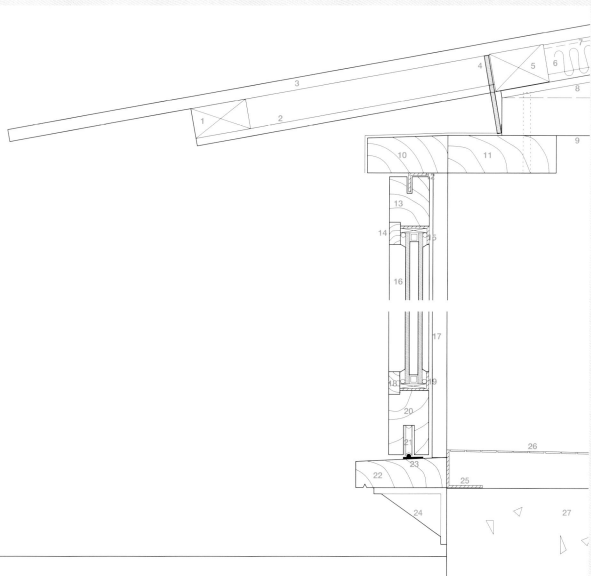

29.07
Roof Section and
Door Section Detail
1:5
  1 75 x 40 mm (3 x
1³/₅ inch) hardwood
roof stiffening beam
  2 50 x 10 mm (2 x ²/₅
inch) galvanized steel
bar at gusset centres
to support roof
stiffening batten
  3 Colourbond
Custom Orb roofing at
10 degree slope
  4 8 gauge stainless
steel screws to fix 6
mm (¹/₄ inch) acrylic
inserts to face of
batten
  5 75 x 50 mm (3 x 2
inch) roof batten
  6 Insulation
  7 Sisalation
  8 15 mm (³/₅ inch)
hoop pine plywood
ceiling lining fixed to
gussets
  9 Timber-framed and
plywood-clad gusset
  10 110 x 50 mm (4¹/₃ x
2 inch) sloped
hardwood continuous
head
  11 150 x 50 mm (6 x 2
inch) hardwood head
between blockwork
walls supported with
galvanized steel rod,
bolted through to
gusset above
  12 25 x 25 x 3 mm (1 x
1 x ¹/₁₀ inch)
aluminium angle head
guide
  13 66 x 55 mm (2³/₅ x
2¹/₆ inch) rebated
Western red cedar top
rail
  14 Timber beading
  15 40 x 25 x 3 mm
(1³/₅ x 1 x ¹/₁₀ inch)
aluminium angle fixed
to top rail
  16 Double glazing unit
  17 25 x 40 mm (1 x
1³/₅ inch) hardwood
batten fixed to
blockwork wall
  18 Timber beading
  19 40 x 25 x 3 mm
(1³/₅ x 1 x ¹/₁₀ inch)

aluminium angle fixed
to bottom rail
  20 85 x 55 mm (3¹/₃ x
2¹/₆ inch) rebated
Western red cedar
bottom rail
  21 Sheave block
  22 125 x 50 mm (5 x 2
inch) sloped hardwood
sill with Sikaflex edge
to angle
  23 Bronze runner
  24 100 x 75 x 8 mm (4
x 3 x ³/₁₀ inch)
galvanized steel
unequal angle with 4
mm (¹/₆ inch) gusset
sill support
  25 50 x 50 x 3 mm (2 x
2 x ¹/₁₀ inch)
aluminium angle to the
edge
  26 Mosaic tiles on
screed laid to fall to
waste
  27 Reinforced
concrete slab and
footings

Sunset Cabin
Lake Simcoe, Ontario, Canada

Project Team
Michael Taylor, Michael Lafreniere

Landscape Architect
GROW

Main Contractor
The Brothers Dressler / Yaan Poldaas

The clients for the Sunset Cabin entertain up to 15 overnight visitors at a time during the summer at the family cottage on Lake Simcoe, to which they have been coming for the past 25 years. During the summer, they move to the cottage full time and requested a new private retreat in a separate sleeping cabin for their personal use where they would be able to lie in bed and watch the sunset. All components are built-in, including the bed and a wall of storage cabinets on either side. The floor of the cabin extends outside towards the lake to become a deck with access to an outdoor shower enclosed by a cedar screen. Cedar is used for window frames, doors and cladding. The timber is untreated, gradually turning silver and blending into the landscape. All interior surfaces are birch veneer plywood panels – floors, back wall, ceiling and storage, so no repainting is required.

The cabin was first constructed in a car park in Toronto over a period of four weeks by a group of furniture craftsmen. This allowed for details to be worked out precisely and all the components to be prefabricated. These were numbered, disassembled and reconstructed on-site in just ten days. Three walls of the cabin are floor to ceiling glass, wrapped by an exterior horizontal cedar screen on two sides for privacy and sun shading. A large cut-out in the screen is carefully located to provide spectacular views of the setting sun from the bed. Gaps between the individual members of the screen increase arbitrarily as the cabin gets closer to the lake. The gaps frame snapshots of random, seemingly abstract compositions of vegetation, lake and sky. As the sun sets, the varied openings within the screen filter the light into shifting patterns on the interior surfaces. At night, the effect is reversed and the cabin glows like a lantern.

1 View of the south facade. Beyond the cedar screen, the chimney for the wood-burning stove is visible. The timber-clad volume to the north contains the WC with the open shower on the deck beyond.
2 The western facade introduces panels of unscreened glazing which are placed opposite the bed so that the occupants can enjoy views over the lake.
3 The bedroom contains abundant built-in storage fabricated from veneered plywood. The veneered plywood continues in the floor, and ceiling, while the windows, door frames, and the rhythmic screen are all solid cedar.
4 To the west, the cedar screen is placed close to the full-height glazing to protect it from solar gain and glare.

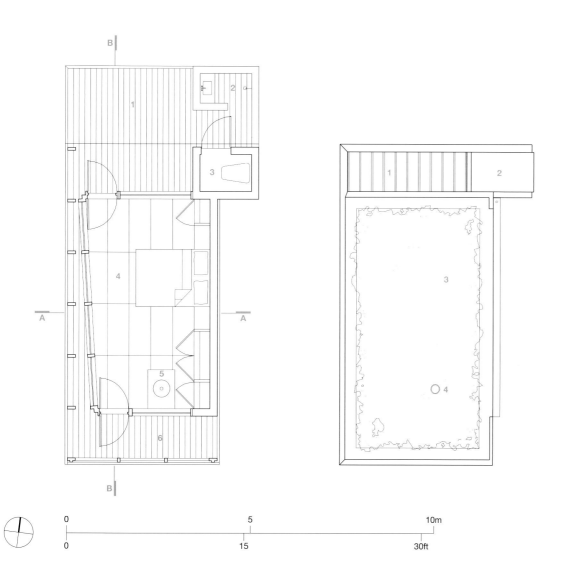

0   5   10m

0   15   30ft

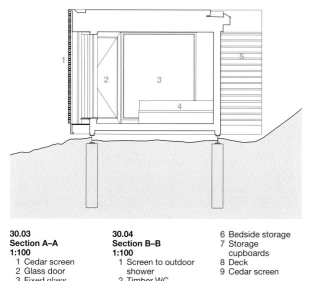

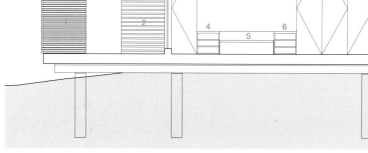

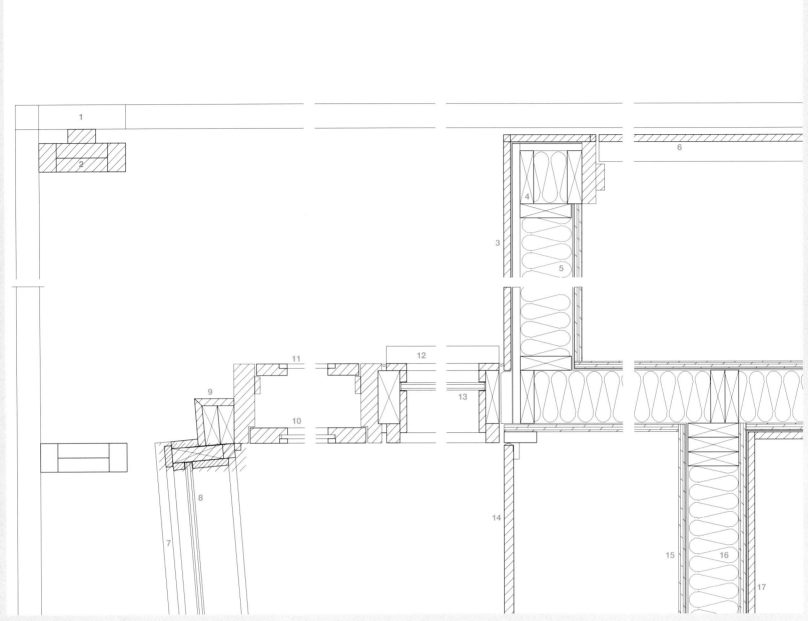

**30.05
External Wall Plan
Detail
1:10**
1 Cedar screen
2 Built-up cedar post
3 Cedar siding to WC
enclosure
4 Timber stud frame
5 Wall insulation
6 19 mm (3/4 inch)
cedar siding on cedar
door
7 Cedar sill below
8 25 mm (1 inch)
thermal glass unit in
built-up cedar frame
9 19 mm (3/4 inch)
cedar trim
10 44 mm (13/4 inch)
insulated glass door in
cedar frame

11 6 mm (1/4 inch)
screen door in cedar
frame
12 Cedar sill below
13 25 mm (1 inch)
thermal glass unit in
built-up cedar frame
14 25 mm (1 inch)
birch veneer plywood
door on pivot hinges
15 19 mm (3/4 inch)
cedar siding
16 Wall insulation
17 19 mm (3/4 inch)
cedar siding

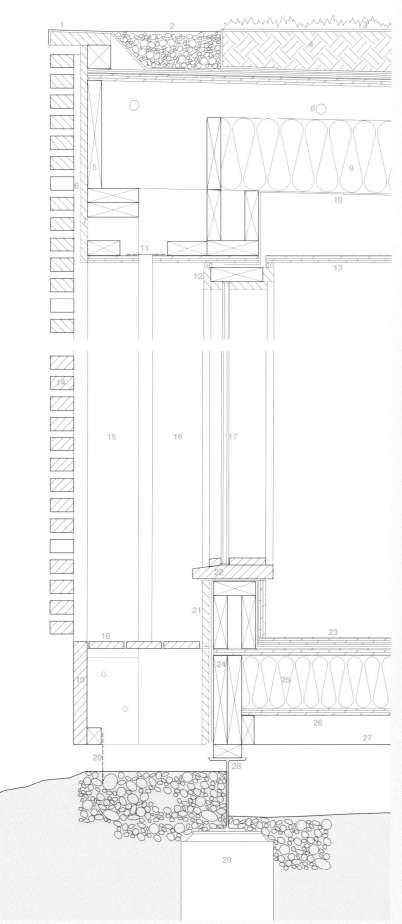

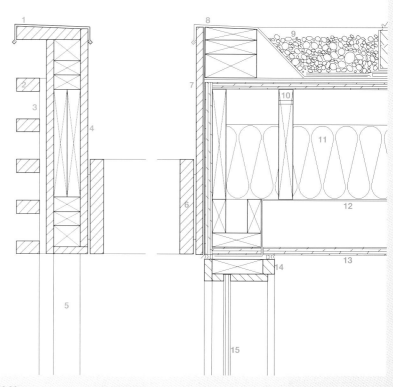

30.06
Wall Section Detail at Roof and Floor
1:10
 1 Metal flashing
 2 River stones to roof drainage system
 3 Green roof of sedums and herbs
 4 Green roof growing medium
 5 50 x 305 mm (2 x 12 inch) joists at 405 mm (16 inch) centres
 6 19 x 76 mm (3/4 x 3 inch) wide cedar spacers
 7 19 mm (3/4 inch) wide cedar fascia
 8 Ventilation holes in joists
 9 Batt insulation
 10 Vapour barrier
 11 Continuous screen vent
 12 Cedar window frame
 13 19 mm (3/4 inch) wide birch veneer plywood ceiling panels
 14 63 x 35 mm (2 1/2 x 1 3/8 inch) cedar screen
 15 Cedar post beyond
 16 Open space between glazing and cedar screen
 17 25 mm (1 inch) thermal glass unit in built-up cedar frame
 18 19 mm (3/4 inch) wide cedar decking
 19 38 mm (1 1/2 inch) cedar fascia at deck edge
 20 Recessed insect screen
 21 19 mm (3/4 inch) cedar fascia
 22 Cedar window sill
 23 19 mm (3/4 inch) wide birch veneer plywood flooring
 24 Pressure treated timber floor joists
 25 Floor insulation
 26 19 mm (3/4 inch)

pressure treated plywood
 27 Floor joist
 28 Steel beam
 29 Reinforced concrete caisson

30.07
Wall Section Detail Through Open Trellis
1:10
 1 Metal flashing
 2 63 x 35 mm (2 1/2 x 1 3/8 inch) cedar screen on 19 mm (3/4 inch) wide cedar spacers
 3 19 mm (3/4 inch) wide cedar fascia
 4 19 mm (3/4 inch) wide cedar fascia
 5 Cedar post beyond
 6 38 x 241 mm (1 1/2 x 9 1/2 inch) cedar trellis on 12 mm (1/2 inch) spacers
 7 19 mm (3/4 inch) wide cedar fascia
 8 Metal flashing
 9 River stones to roof drainage system
 10 50 x 304 mm (2 x 12 inch) joists
 11 Batt insulation
 12 Vapour barrier
 13 19 mm (3/4 inch) wide birch veneer plywood ceiling panels
 14 Cedar window frame
 15 25 mm (1 inch) thermal glass unit in built-up cedar frame

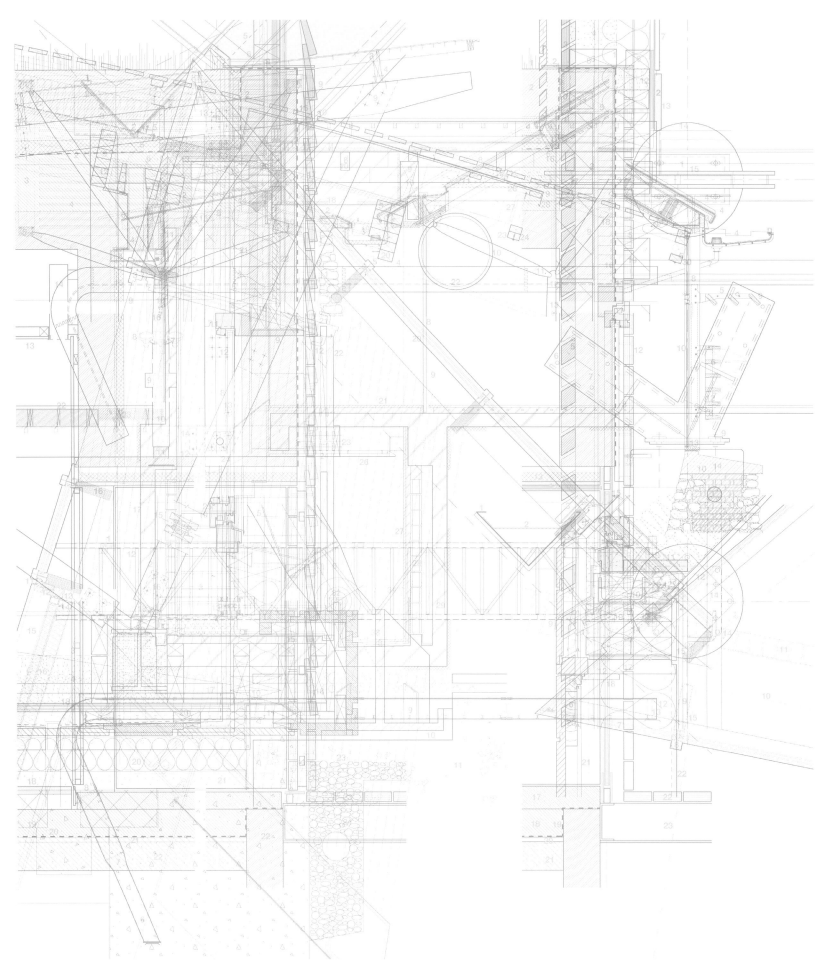

132

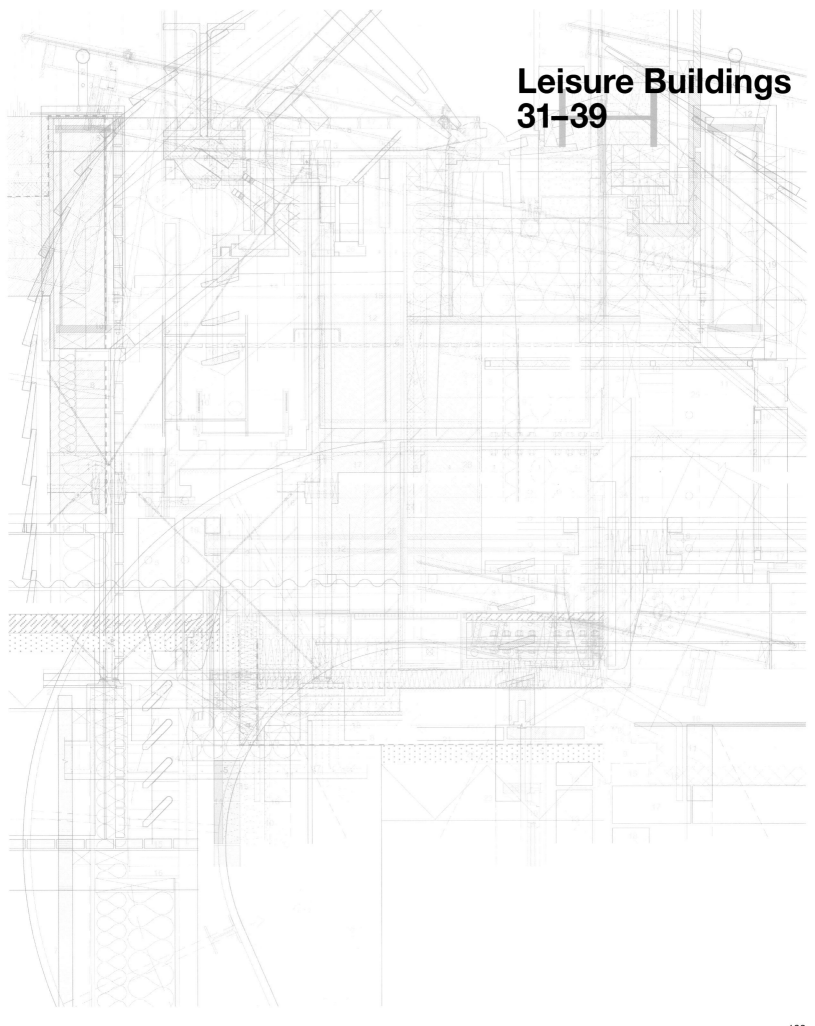

Leisure Buildings
31–39

**WWT Welney Visitor Centre
and Footbridge
Cambridgeshire, England, UK**

Client
The Wildfowl and Wetlands Trust

Project Team
Paul Appleton, Robin Gray, Robin
Williams, Mike Durran

Structural and Services Engineer
Arup

Quantity Surveyor
Davis Langdon LLP

The primary aim of this project was
to improve the accessibility of the
wetlands for the centre's growing
number of visitors and expanding
education programme. The new visitor
centre and footbridge provide a new
connection to an existing observatory
and hide and houses exhibition space,
education areas, offices, a shop, cafe
and associated external spaces. The
design was influenced by the local
barn vernacular and the strong
linearity of the Fenland context.
Internal spaces are collected around
the route from the entrance to the
bridge, in a single barn-like volume.
The outer timber skin gives way to
allow both physical and visual
connections to the surroundings. The
untreated Siberian larch cladding is
used in three ways: as the primary
skin in feather-edged boarding, rising
unbroken from ground to roof ridge;
tongue and groove boarding where
the primary skin is cut back; and
trapezoidal battens to give a lighter,
screen-like quality to the gable ends.

The fully sustainable Siberian
larch envelope acts as a rain screen
and breathable skin, with a ventilated
cavity and breather membrane
behind. The use of overlapping
boarding allows the cladding to fold
over from the facades onto the roof.
This innovative system afforded the
removal of traditional eaves and
gutters, allowing rainwater to be
collected and fed into adjacent reed
beds for filtering and re-use. The
primary structure is formed from
Glu-lam timber frames of common
spruce which work in conjunction with
the first floor plate, formed from a ply
deck and timber I-sections, providing
lateral resistance to the high wind
loadings of the Fenlands.

1 The external timber
cladding was devel-
oped in conjunction
with TRADA, the
Timber Research and
Development
Association, enabling
the Siberian larch
boards to travel
seamlessly from the
walls to the roof over
curved battens.
2 Large panes of
clear glazing bring
abundant natural light
into the building.
Where the glazing is
fixed, panels of
adjustable louvres
allow for ventilation.
3 View of the first floor
where the Glu-lam
softwood structure is
left exposed.

31.01
Ground Floor Plan
1:200
1 Entrance lobby
2 Store
3 Elevator
4 Main stair
5 Entrance foyer
6 Reception
7 Male WC
8 Disabled WC
9 Cleaners' store
10 Female WC
11 Exhibition space
12 Store
13 Education office
14 Education space
15 Staff room
16 Reserve office
17 Plant room
18 External covered
   space
19 Stair
20 Elevator

0		5		10m

0	15		30ft

31.02
First Floor Plan
1:200
1 Shop
2 Elevator
3 Main stair
4 Void over foyer
5 Male WC
6 Disabled WC
7 Store
8 Female WC
9 Store
10 Kitchen
11 Servery
12 Meeting room /
   cafe space
13 Cafe space
14 General office
15 Footbridge above
16 Stair to bridge
   terrace
17 Elevator lobby
18 Elevator
19 External cafe
   space

31.03
Section A–A
1:200
1 Cycle stands
2 New footbridge
3 Entrance lobby
4 Entrance foyer /
   reception
5 Shop
6 Corridor
7 Void over
   reception
8 Roof light
9 Large window

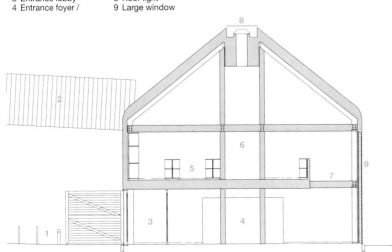

31.04
Section B–B
1:200
1 New footbridge
2 Roof light
3 Window to bridge
   terrace
4 Cafe space
5 Exhibition space
6 Corridor
7 Education space

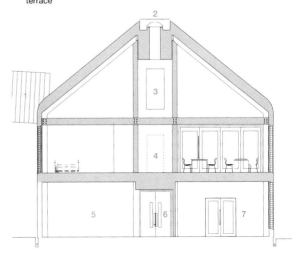

135

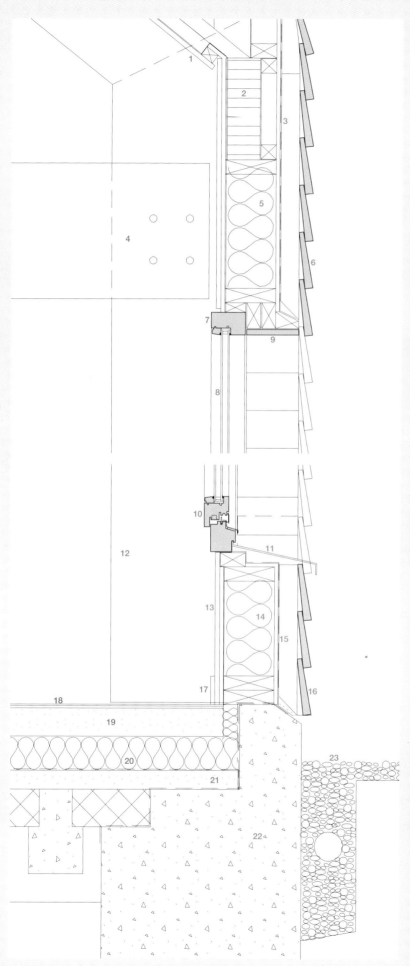

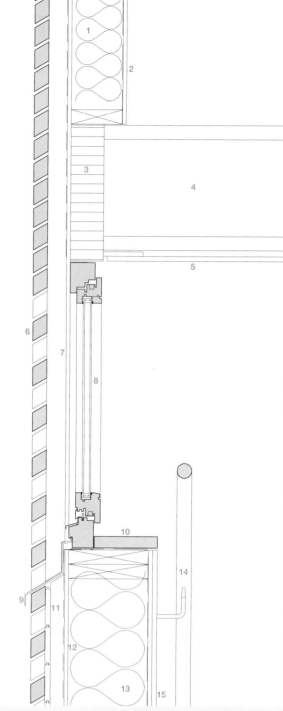

31.05
Typical Window Head and Base Detail
1:10
1 Plasterboard lining on vapour barrier
2 Glue-laminated softwood structural frame
3 Ventilated cavity and breather membrane
4 Glue-laminated softwood structural frame
5 Recycled paper insulation
6 Untreated Siberian larch, 150 mm (6 inch) wide horizontal feather edge boards with fine sawn finish
7 Hardwood timber window frame
8 Double-glazed safety glass window
9 Untreated Siberian larch soffit board
10 Hardwood timber window frame with clear double-glazed safety glass
11 Galvanized mild steel sill with flashing trims
12 Glue-laminated softwood structural column
13 Plasterboard lining on vapour barrier
14 Recycled paper insulation
15 Breather membrane fixed to bitumen impregnated sheathing board
16 Untreated Siberian larch, 150 mm (6 inch) wide horizontal feather edge boards with fine sawn finish
17 White-painted timber skirting board
18 Hardwood timber floorboards
19 Concrete screed
20 Insulation
21 Concrete screed over reinforced concrete floor slab
22 Fairfaced reinforced concrete upstand chamfered to allow moisture to drain out
23 French drain collection rainwater run-off

31.06
Screened Window Detail
1:10
1 Recycled paper insulation
2 Oriented Strand Board (OSB) lining on vapour barrier
3 Glue-laminated softwood structural beam
4 Timber I-section joist
5 Plasterboard lining to soffit
6 Untreated Siberian larch 50 x 38 mm (2 x 1¹/₂ inch) profiled horizontal battens with fine sawn finish installed with alternate battens omitted in front of window
7 Untreated Siberian larch vertical battens with fine sawn finish where visible in front of window
8 Hardwood timber window frames with clear double-glazed safety glass
9 Galvanized mild steel sill
10 Hardwood timber sill
11 Untreated Siberian larch 100 mm (4 inch) wide tongue and grooved boards on vertical support battens
12 Breather membrane on bitumen impregnated sheathing board
13 Recycled paper insulation
14 Hardwood timber handrail to stair
15 Plasterboard lining on vapour barrier

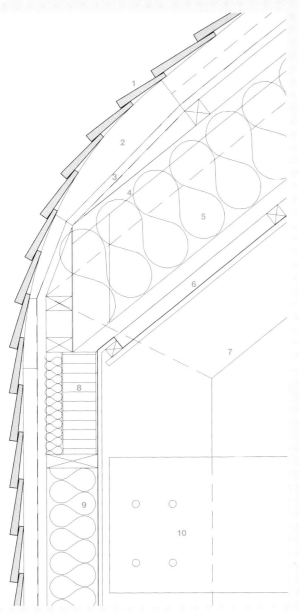

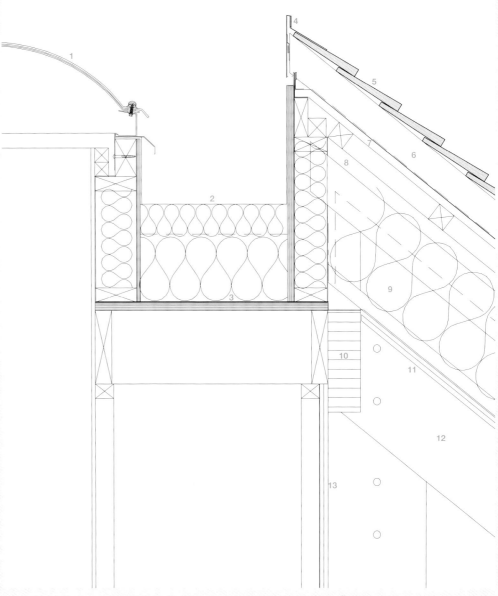

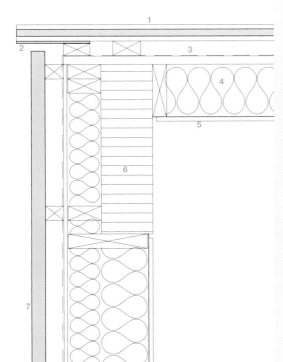

31.07
Eaves Detail
1:10
  1 Untreated Siberian larch 200 mm ($7^9/10$ inch) wide horizontal feather edge boards with fine sawn finish
  2 Vertical treated softwood battens shaped to form the radius of the roof edge with a ventilated cavity between battens
  3 Breather membrane on roof sheathing board supported on horizontal battens
  4 Timber I-section rafters at 600 mm ($23^2/3$ inch) centres
  5 Recycled paper insulation to fill cavity
  6 Plasterboard lining on vapour barrier
  7 Glue-laminated softwood structural frame
  8 Glue-laminated softwood structural frame
  9 Recycled paper insulation
  10 Glue-laminated softwood structural frame

31.08
Ridge Detail
1:10
  1 Polycarbonate thermo-formed dome
  2 High performance polymeric roof membrane fixed to rigid insulation layer laid to fall
  3 Single layer of 18 mm ($7/10$ inch) weather and boil proof (WBP) plywood fixed to softwood timber battens forming the carcass of the recessed roof with vapour control layer on top
  4 Galvanized mild steel ridge flashing
  5 Untreated Siberian larch 200 mm ($7^9/10$ inch) wide horizontal feather edge boards with fine sawn finish
  6 Vertical treated softwood battens with ventilated cavity between
  7 Breather membrane on roof sheathing board
  8 Timber I-section rafters at 600 mm ($23^2/3$ inch) centres
  9 Recycled paper insulation to fill cavity
  10 Glue-laminated softwood structural frame

11 Plasterboard lining on vapour barrier
12 Glue-laminated structural frame
13 Plasterboard lining on timber stud frame

31.09
External Wall Corner Plan Detail
1:10
  1 Untreated Siberian larch 150 mm (6 inch) wide horizontal feather edge boards with fine sawn finish
  2 Galvanized mild steel edge trim
  3 Breather membrane fixed to a bitumen impregnated sheathing board
  4 Recycled paper insulation
  5 Plasterboard lining on vapour barrier
  6 Glue-laminated softwood structural column
  7 Untreated Siberian larch 50 x 38 mm (2 x $1^1/2$ inch) profiled horizontal battens with fine sawn finish

António Portugal & Manuel Reis, Architects

Brufe Restaurant
Brufe, Terras de Bouro, Portugal

Client
Turisbrufe, Sociedade de Gestão
Turística de Brufe

Project Team
António Portugal, Manuel Reis, Paulo
Freitas

Structural Engineer
Salvador e Oliveira Almeida

This understated and elegant restaurant stands on a sloping site that descends towards the Homem River, near the small village of Brufe, in Portugal's rugged far north. Its long, low slung volume echoes the forms of the granite terraces on which it is poised, with the roof continuing the natural platform of rock. Much of its bulk is excavated into the hillside, so that the roof becomes part of the terrain – a grass-covered plateau. The main entrance is located in the platform below, with service areas pushed against the hillside and public spaces placed to take advantage of the wide open landscape. From the vantage point of the entrance, diners descend external stairs cut into the hill to another terrace thrusting out from the box of the restaurant.

Dining takes place in a large, airy room illuminated by long picture windows, while the cooking and serving is kept out of sight in the buried rear of the building. The orientation and location searches for an intimate relation with the context, as well as the choice of materials: granite walls and timber for the non-glazed part of the main elevation, which continues the horizontal plane of the exterior deck. Rough horizontal planks of timber are employed to clad both lower terrace and box, giving it a rustic, barn-like character that echoes the vernacular architecture of the surrounding farm buildings. The building relates to its setting, deferring to the landscape but celebrating it. The simple materials are combined with a restrained architectural language to achieve powerful effects.

1 To make up the difference in height between the upper and lower parts of the site, the restaurant sits on a built-up wall of rough stone boulders.
2 The west facade is clad in bans of untreated timber that will weather to a silvery grey over time.
3 The long band of glazing that opens up the dining room to the view is set back to protect it from the weather and shade it from the western sun.
4 The main entrance is formed from a bay of glazing flush with the external face of the building.
5 At night, the interior of the dining room glows. A large wall of timber joinery divides the waiting area from the dining room, as well as housing the fireplace.

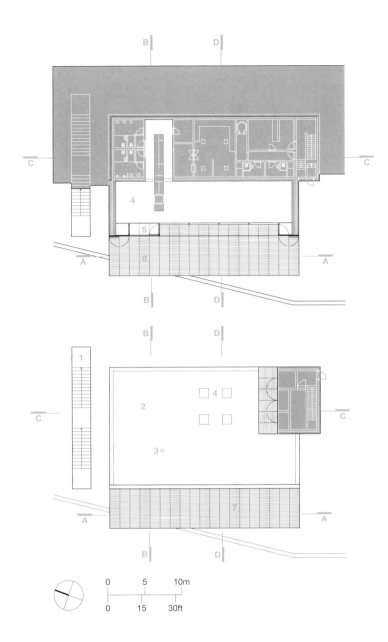

32.01
Lower Floor Plan
1:500
1 External stair
2 Female WC
3 Male WC
4 Waiting area
5 Entrance
6 Terrace
7 Storage unit and
   fireplace
8 Pantry
9 Kitchen servery
10 Kitchen
11 Storage
12 Staff WC
13 Staff WC
14 Service entrance
   and stair

32.02
Roof Plan
1:500
1 External stair
2 Grass roof
3 Chimney
4 Skylights over
   kitchen
5 Service
   installations
6 Service entrance
7 Terrace below

32.03
Section A–A
1:500
1 External stair
2 Stone cladding to
   exterior entrance
   area
3 Entrance
4 Upper service
   entrance
5 Lower service
   entrance

32.04
Section B–B
1:500
1 Services
2 Storage unit
3 Fireplace
4 Entrance
5 Terrace

32.05
Section C–C
1:500
1 External stair
2 Male WC
3 Kitchen servery
4 Kitchen
5 Storage
6 Services
7 Service stair

32.06
Section D–D
1:500
1 Service entry
2 Kitchen
3 Dining room
4 Entrance
5 Terrace

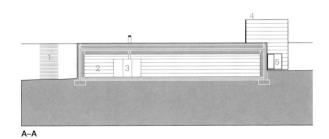

A–A

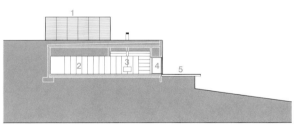

B–B

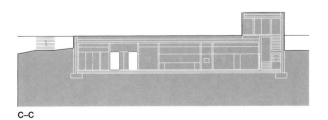

C–C

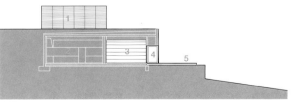

D–D

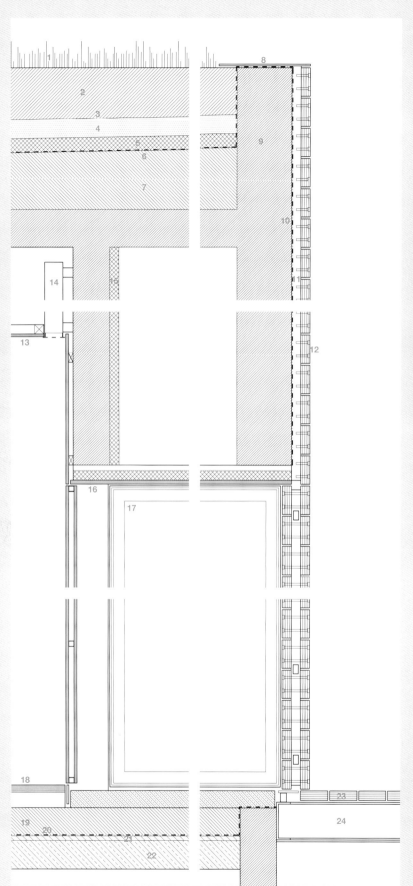

32.07
Detail Section Through Facade and Entrance 1
1:20
1 Grass roof
2 Top soil
3 Geotextile cloth
4 100 mm (4 inch) lightweight expanded clay aggregate
5 50 mm (2 inch) extruded polystyrene insulation
6 Polyester reinforced synthetic waterproof sheeting
7 Lightweight expanded clay aggregate
8 500 x 10 mm (197/10 x 2/5 inch) Corten steel sheet capping
9 Reinforced concrete wall structure
10 Waterproof bituminous emulsion to concrete surface
11 Steel substructure for fixing timber battens
12 External cladding from solid timber slats
13 Veneered plywood ceiling
14 Downlight fixture
15 50 mm (2 inch) extruded polystyrene insulation
16 Veneered plywood ceiling
17 Double-glazed entrance door
18 Solid timber suspended flooring
19 Concrete floor structure embedded with electro-welded mesh
20 Damp proof membrane
21 Regularization layer
22 Gravel bed
23 Solid timber decking to terrace
24 Steel beams to terrace structure

32.08
Detail Section Through Facade and Entrance 2
1:20
1 Grass roof
2 Top soil
3 Geotextile cloth
4 100 mm (4 inch) lightweight expanded clay aggregate
5 50 mm (2 inch) extruded polystyrene insulation
6 Polyester reinforced synthetic waterproof sheeting
7 Lightweight expanded clay aggregate
8 500 x 10 mm (197/10 x 2/5 inch) Corten steel sheet capping
9 Lightweight reinforced concrete wall structure
10 Waterproof bituminous emulsion to concrete surface
11 Steel substructure for fixing timber battens
12 External cladding from solid timber slats
13 50 mm (2 inch) extruded polystyrene insulation
14 Veneered plywood ceiling
15 10 mm (2/5 inch) steel flat door frame
16 Clear double-glazed door
17 Polished concrete floor
18 Concrete floor structure embedded with electro-welded mesh
19 Damp proof membrane
20 Regularization layer
21 Gravel bed
22 Solid timber decking to terrace
23 Steel beams to terrace structure

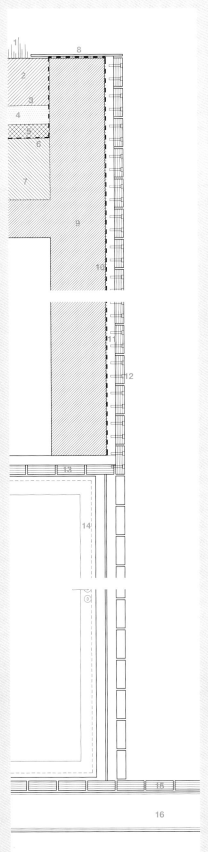

32.09
Detail Section
Through Facade
1:20
 1 Grass roof
 2 Top soil
 3 Geotextile cloth
 4 100 mm (4 inch)
lightweight expanded
clay aggregate
 5 50 mm (2 inch)
extruded polystyrene
insulation
 6 Polyester reinforced
synthetic waterproof
sheeting
 7 Lightweight
expanded clay
aggregate
 8 500 x 10 mm
(19^7/$_{10}$ x ^{2}/$_5$ inch)
Corten steel sheet
capping
 9 Lightweight
reinforced concrete
wall structure
 10 Waterproof
bituminous emulsion
to concrete surface
 11 Steel substructure
for fixing timber
battens
 12 External cladding
from solid timber slats
 13 Solid timber slats to
soffit lining
 14 Double-glazed
entrance door
 15 Solid timber
decking to terrace
 16 Steel beams to
terrace structure

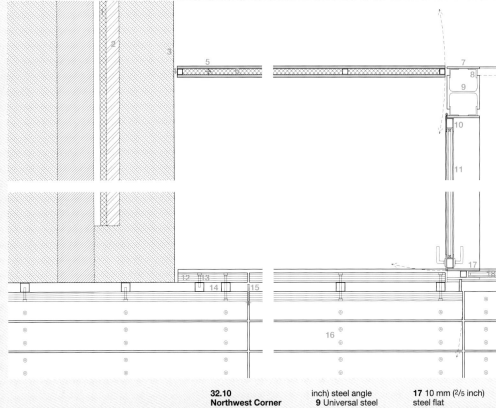

32.10
Northwest Corner
Facade Plan Detail
1:20
 1 Extruded
polystyrene insulation
 2 Brick
 3 Granite wall
 4 30 x 30 mm (1^1/$_5$ x
1^1/$_5$ inch) steel section
 5 Veneered plywood
 6 Extruded
polystyrene insulation
 7 10 mm (^{2}/$_5$ inch)
steel flat
 8 50 x 50 mm (2 x 2
inch) steel angle
 9 Universal steel
column
 10 50 x 35 mm (2 x
1^3/$_8$ inch) steel section
 11 Clear double
glazing
 12 Solid timber slats
 13 Screw fixing
between timber slats
and steel substructure
 14 50 x 50 mm (2 x 2
inch) steel section
 15 Steel hinge
 16 Timber decking to
terrace
 17 10 mm (^{2}/$_5$ inch)
steel flat
 18 Clear double
glazing

Anglesey Abbey Visitor Centre
Cambridge, England, UK

Client
The National Trust

Structural Engineer
Scott Wilson

Services Consultant
Max Fordham

Quantity Surveyor
Davis Langdon

The Anglesey Abbey House and Gardens estate comprises 40 hectares (100 acres) of garden and parkland. In 1976 The National Trust commissioned the first permanent visitor centre, providing a cafe, shop and information point. The original building comprised a beautifully simple 'Miesian' pavilion with expressed structural framing, timber cladding, and full-height glazed screens and sliding panels serving as a gateway directing visitors into the gardens. The new building takes its lead from the old pavilion, conceived as a series of interconnecting pitched steel frames that form vistas out towards the garden. Between these aisles the building is linked by a shallow vaulted reception area that signals, with a wider structural bay and change in elevation form, the entry and exit points to the building.

To one side of the entrance, and visually connected to the garden, are the restaurant, toilets, commercial kitchen and subsidiary spaces. On the other side of the lobby are the multi-purpose education room, shop and office spaces. The structural grid is subtly reflected through to the external cladding, where vertical members are introduced to express the grid. Subsequent subdivisions of all the cedar elements derive from a module associated with the main cladding board width. Cedar brise soleils in the upper sections of the gable ends prevent unwanted external solar reflection from the glass and unnecessary solar gain, whilst ensuring high daylight levels and filtered dappled light are let in. A simple palette of modern materials – predominantly mill-finished aluminium and untreated cedar – will weather naturally over time, settling into hues of soft silvery greys.

1 View of the east facade where the glazed entrance space that links the two wings opens onto the gardens on the other side of the building.
2 On the west facade the restaurant (left) has large expanses of glazing to bring light and views of the gardens into the building.
3 Solid cedar planks clad the lower part of the building while the upper gable features cedar louvres over clear glazing. The roof is clad in galvanized corrugated sheeting.
4 The elegant pitched roofs include large overhangs which protect the interior from the weather and are lined with cedar planks.

0   5   10m

0   15   30ft

33.01
Ground Floor Plan
1:500
1 Education room
2 Furniture store
3 Plant room
4 Staff rest room
5 Cashier's office
6 Goods entrance
7 Retail manager's office
8 Staff WC
9 Servery
10 Visitor services

manager
11 Retail storage area
12 Stationery store
13 Shop
14 Entrance
15 Recruitment area
16 Reception area
17 Entrance
18 Restaurant
19 Restaurant terrace
20 Servery
21 Till
22 Bar seating
23 Parents WC

24 Male WC
25 Cleaners' cupboard
26 Disabled WC
27 Female WC
28 Staff WC
29 Staff rest room
30 Staff shower
31 Male and female changing area
32 Dishwashing area
33 Kitchen
34 Dry store
35 Cleaners'

cupboard
36 Freezer and cold room
37 Services entrance
38 Service entrance and lobby
39 Dry goods store
40 Catering manager's office

33.02
Section A–A
1:500
1 Restaurant
2 Entrance lobby
3 Ancillary spaces lobby
4 Cashier's office

33.03
Section B–B
1:500
1 Dishwashing area
2 Kitchen
3 Cleaners' cupboard
4 Entrance lobby
5 Shop

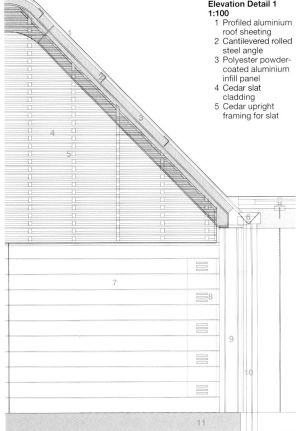

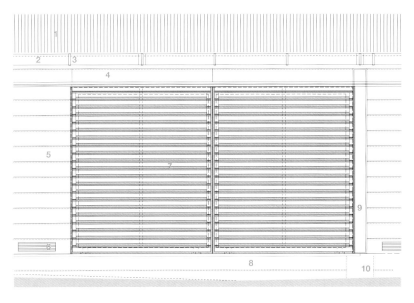

33.04
Elevation Detail 1
1:100
1 Profiled aluminium roof sheeting
2 Cantilevered rolled steel angle
3 Polyester powder-coated aluminium infill panel
4 Cedar slat cladding
5 Cedar upright framing for slat

cladding
6 Mill-finished aluminium gutter
7 Cedar board cladding
8 Ventilation slots routed from timber cladding
9 Cedar board cladding
10 Mill-finished aluminium rain water pipe
11 Blockwork plinth

33.05
Elevation Detail 2
1:100
1 Profiled aluminium roof sheeting
2 Mill-finished aluminium gutter
3 Mill-finished aluminium gutter bracket
4 Cedar board cladding
5 Cedar board cladding

6 Ventilation slots routed from timber cladding for sub-floor ventilation
7 Sliding cedar shutters
8 Blockwork plinth
9 Cedar board cladding
10 In-situ concrete plinth

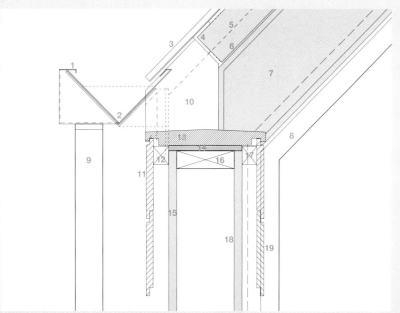

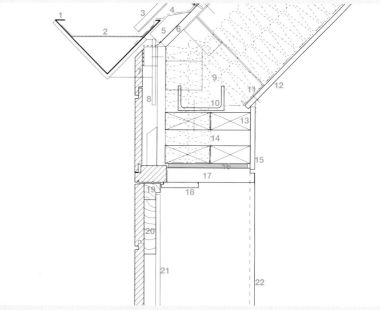

33.06
Roof, Gutter and
External Wall Detail 1
1:10
 1 Lipped aluminium
to form gutter edge
 2 Mill-finished
aluminium gutter
 3 Corrugated
mill-finished aluminium
 4 Shaped
cantilevered rolled
steel section
 5 Mill-finished
aluminium flashing
 6 Mill-finished
aluminium gutter
 7 Polyester powder-
coated aluminium
insulated panel
 8 Polyester powder-
coated aluminium
curtain walling system
 9 Mill-finished
aluminium down pipe
10 Untreated cedar
cladding
11 Untreated cedar
cladding
12 Treated softwood
framing
13 Cedar capping
14 Plywood
15 Bitumen
impregnated
fibreboard
16 Treated softwood
framing
17 Treated softwood
framing
18 Bitumen
impregnated
fibreboard
19 Untreated cedar
cladding

33.07
Wall, Floor and
Foundation Detail
1:10
 1 Untreated cedar
cladding
 2 Insect mesh
 3 Bitumen
impregnated
fibreboard
 4 Insulation
 5 Treated softwood
framing
 6 Treated softwood
framing
 7 Painted
plasterboard interior
lining
 8 Untreated cedar
louvres
 9 Air brick
10 Insulation
11 Timber skirting
12 Timber floorboards
13 Vapour control
barrier
14 Gravel margin
15 Fair face blockwork
plinth
16 Periscopic floor
vent
17 Vertical damp
proof course

33.08
Wall and Window
Plan Detail
1:10
 1 Painted
plasterboard interior
wall lining
 2 Treated softwood
framing
 3 Services void
 4 Insulation with
vapour control barrier
 5 MDF lining
 6 Treated softwood
framing
 7 Untreated cedar
external cladding
 8 Untreated cedar
external cladding
 9 Polyester powder-
coated aluminium
curtain walling frame
(interior)
10 Double-glazed
window unit
11 Polyester
powder-coated
aluminium curtain
walling frame (exterior)
12 Untreated cedar
external cladding
13 MDF lining

33.09
Roof, Gutter and
External Wall Detail 2
1:10
 1 Mill-finished
aluminium gutter
 2 Internal support
strap to gutter
 3 Corrugated
mill-finished aluminium
roof sheeting
 4 Breather membrane
 5 Treated softwood
framing
 6 Structural plywood
 7 Untreated cedar
cladding
 8 Mill-finished
aluminium gutter
bracket
 9 Insulation
10 Structural
steelwork
11 Mild steel purlin
12 Painted
plasterboard interior
wall lining
13 Treated softwood
framing
14 Vapour control
barrier
15 Painted
plasterboard interior
wall lining
16 Bitumen
impregnated
fibreboard
17 Cedar reveal
18 Timber corner stop
19 Timber corner bead
20 Timber framing
21 Painted
plasterboard interior
wall lining
22 Cedar reveal

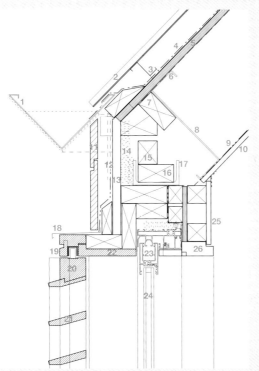

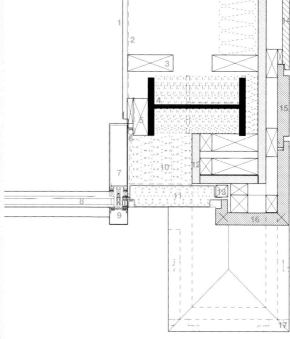

33.10
Roof and Louvred Wall Detail
1:10
1 Mill-finished aluminium gutter
2 Corrugated mill-finished aluminium sheet roofing
3 Roof sheet carrier rail
4 Mill-finished aluminium flashing
5 Structural plywood
6 Plywood fixing system
7 Treated softwood framing
8 Mild steel purlin
9 Vapour control barrier
10 Painted plasterboard ceiling lining
11 Untreated cedar cladding
12 Vapour control barrier
13 Bitumen impregnated fibreboard
14 Insulation
15 Treated softwood framing
16 Treated softwood framing
17 Steel U-section
18 Mill-finished aluminium flashing
19 Cedar trim
20 Frame to untreated cedar sliding shutter
21 Untreated cedar slats to sliding shutter
22 Cedar trim
23 Polyester powder-coated aluminium sliding door frame
24 Double-glazed window unit
25 Painted plasterboard wall lining
26 MDF lining

33.11
Wall and Glazing Plan Detail
1:10
1 Painted plasterboard wall lining
2 Vapour control barrier
3 Treated softwood framing
4 Universal steel column
5 Treated softwood framing
6 Silicone sealant
7 Polyester powder-coated aluminium window frame (Interior)
8 Double-glazed window unit
9 Polyester powder-coated aluminium window frame (exterior)
10 Insulation
11 Polyester powder-coated insulated aluminium wall panel
12 Bitumen impregnated fibreboard
13 Timber fillet piece
14 Untreated cedar external cladding
15 Untreated cedar external cladding
16 Untreated cedar external cladding
17 Cedar capping over external wall below

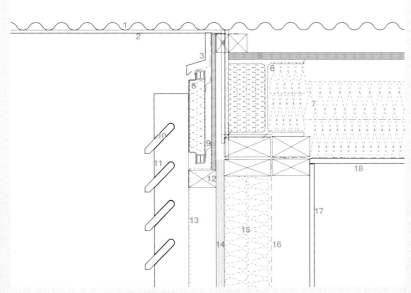

33.12
Roof and Louvred Wall Detail
1:10
1 Corrugated mill-finished aluminium sheet roofing
2 Shaped cantilevered rolled steel angle
3 Mill-finished aluminium flashing
4 Treated softwood framing
5 Structural plywood
6 Universal steel beam
7 Insulation
8 Polyester powder-coated aluminium insulated panel
9 Steel bracket
10 Untreated cedar slats
11 Cedar stud
12 Treated softwood framing
13 Insect mesh
14 Bitumen impregnated fibreboard
15 Insulation
16 Vapour control barrier
17 Painted plasterboard wall lining
18 Painted plasterboard ceiling lining

33.13
Louvred Wall and Floor Detail
1:10
1 Untreated cedar slats
2 Untreated cedar sliding shutter frame
3 Proprietary sliding cedar shutter gear
4 Southern yellow pine decking board
5 Mild steel support angle
6 Double-glazed sliding door system
7 Polyester powder-coated aluminium sliding door frame system
8 Polyester powder-coated aluminium sliding door frame system
9 Timber packer
10 Large format ceramic floor tiles
11 Cement screed with integrated heating
12 Top course of blockwork plinth
13 External leaf of fair face blockwork plinth
14 Damp proof course
15 Flooring grade insulation
16 Beam and block flooring
17 Internal leaf of fair face blockwork plinth

**Prairie Ridge Ecostation for Wildlife
and Learning
Raleigh, North Carolina, USA**

Client
North Carolina Museum of Natural
Sciences

Project Team
Frank Harmon, Sarah Queen,
Lee Queen

Structural Engineer
Tim Martin PE

Main Contractor
Buildsense

This project, an outpost of the North
Carolina Museum of Natural Sciences,
is used for field classes and research
in an open-air classroom, completely
ensconced in nature in order to foster
a hands-on appreciation of the state's
natural resources and diversity. The
goal of the project is to focus on a
disappearing part of the state's
environment – the piedmont prairie –
and to demonstrate how architecture
can enhance the natural environment.
Through its design and construction,
the classroom exemplifies
environmental stewardship and
sustainability practices. The building
is connected to nature through its
siting and orientation, selection of
materials, and other principles of
sustainability. These factors directly
informed the architectural expression
through the use of deep overhangs,
air flow underneath and through the
building, and natural lighting. The
architect's knowledge of vernacular
buildings directly influenced the design.
Traditional buildings made the most of
openings to catch prevailing breezes,
roof overhangs for shade, and
porches for cool indoor-outdoor areas.
All of these strategies were employed
in the design of this building.

Local materials are used to reduce
transportation and to promote
responsible use of local forests. The
framing is of parallel-strand timbers
and southern yellow pine lumber, and
the envelope is Atlantic white cedar,
native to the state. All of the timber is
unfinished and will weather gracefully
under the roof overhangs. The timber
siding is used as a rain screen, open
to the air on all four sides. The building
is also raised above the ground so
that all joints are open to the air.

1 The classroom is
poised above the site
to provide views of the
major ecological
zones. The building is
located on the fringe of
the forest to minimize
disturbance to trees.

2 The siting strategy
was to have almost
zero impact on the site
so that the building will
serve as a model for
sustainable open
space and bio-
diversity in the region.

3 Architectural
strategies, including
large roof overhangs,
covered verandahs
and large openings,
create a comfortable
classroom environment
that requires no

mechanical heating or
cooling systems.
4 Timber is used
extensively in the
building, for the
structure, cladding,
decks and flooring. It
has been left to

weather naturally,
which will lend a silvery
patina to the building
in time.

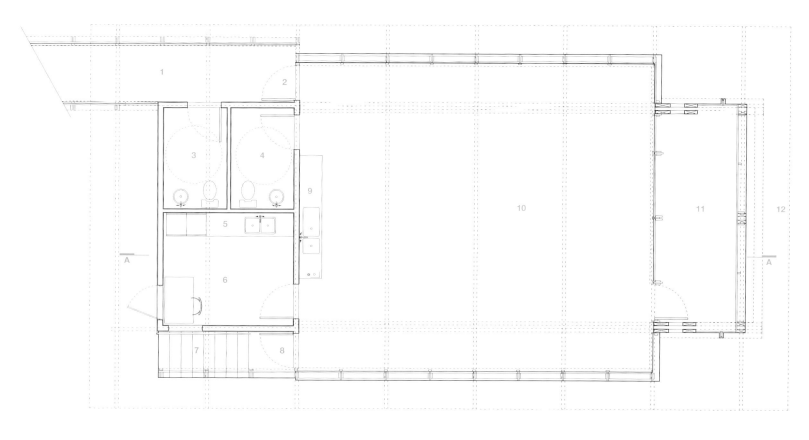

34.01
Floor Plan
1:100
1 Bridge
2 Entrance
3 WC
4 WC
5 Staff workspace
6 Office
7 External stair
8 Exit
9 Classroom
  workspace
10 Classroom
11 Balcony
12 Line of roof
  overhang over

34.02
Section A–A
1:100
1 Corrugated metal
  roof
2 Exposed timber
  beam
3 Plywood interior
  lining to external
wall
4 Timber decking
  over timber floor
  joists
5 Timber beam
6 Concrete block
  wall
7 Concrete footing
8 Metal hog wire
fencing
9 Insect screen
10 Timber column
  and screen
  architravea
11 Galvanized steel
  base plate on
  concrete
  foundation
12 Timber support
  structure
13 Timber balustrade
  to balcony

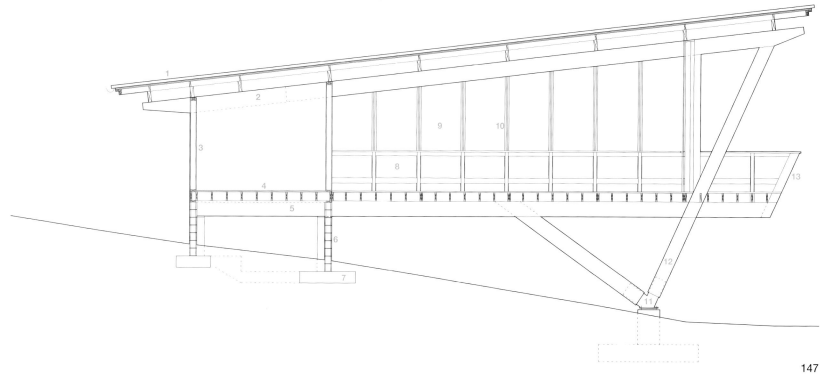

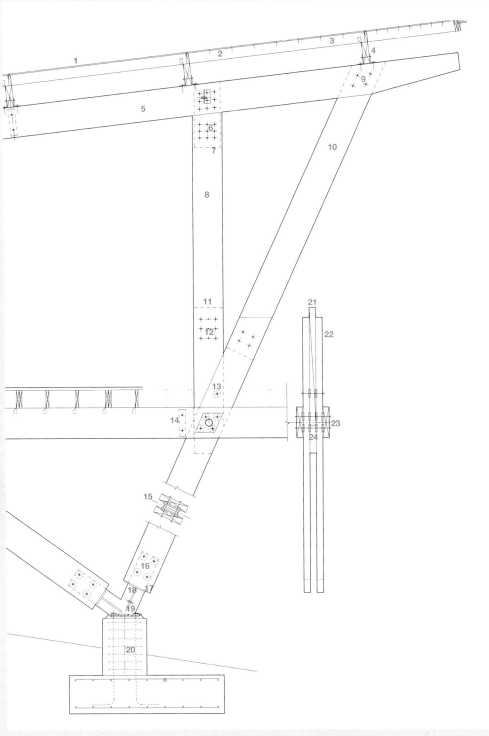

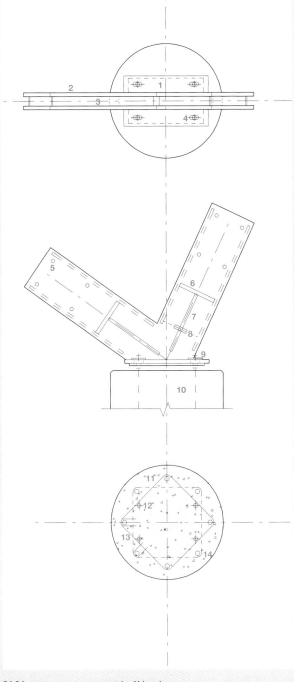

34.03
Typical Section
Through Roof,
Balcony and
Foundation Detail 1
1:50
1 Corrugated roof
sheeting on 19 mm (3/4
inch) plywood
sheathing
2 Nail fixings at 152
mm (6 inch) centres
within 1,220 mm (4
feet) of roof edge
3 50 x 150 mm (2 x 6
inch) timber purlins at
406 mm (16 inch)
centres
4 Timber joists bolted
to beam below with
galvanized angles
5 Timber girder with

full contact between
girder and column
below
6 15 mm (3/5 inch)
diameter through bolts
7 Splice block
8 Timber column
9 15 mm (3/5 inch)
diameter through bolts
10 Diagonal timber
column
11 Vertical splice block
continued through
connection
12 15 mm (3/5 inch)
diameter through bolts
13 19 mm (3/4 inch)
diameter through bolt
with shear plates
14 Solid timber
blocking, one on each
side of discontinued

girder centre member
with 19 mm (3/4 inch)
diameter through bolts
15 19 mm (3/4 inch)
diameter through bolt
with shear plate either
side of bracket (shown
in section)
16 19 mm (3/4 inch)
diameter through bolt
with shear plate either
side of bracket (shown
in elevation)
17 Steel bracket
shown dotted
18 Full contact
between timber end
grain and plate shelf
19 Washers to slip
critical, steel bearing
plates on non-shrink
grout bed

20 610 mm (24 inch)
diameter reinforced
concrete pier on
footing over
compacted gravel
backfill or undisturbed
soil suitable for
bearing load
21 Vertical splice block
beyond
22 Top of diagonal
column
23 Floor girder with 19
mm (3/4 inch) diameter
through bolts
24 100 mm (4 inch)
diameter shear plate
connector

34.04
Column Base Fitting
and Pier Detail
1:20
1 Slip critical steel
bearing plate with
standard size holes
2 12 mm (1/2 inch)
thick steel web plate
3 15 mm (3/5 inch)
steel flange
4 Bearing plate below
with slotted holes for
field adjustment of
columns
5 19 mm (3/4 inch)
diameter hole
6 Column bearing
plate
7 Steel plate with
right and left hand
configurations to

receive X-bracing
clevis
8 19 mm (3/4 inch)
diameter hole to
receive clevis pin
9 Washers to steel
connection plate on
non-shrink grout bed
10 610 mm (24 inch)
diameter reinforced
concrete pier
11 610 mm (24 inch)
diameter reinforced
concrete pier
12 22 mm (4/5 inch)
diameter anchor bolt
13 Vertically staggered
square tie at 100 mm
(4 inch) centres
14 Vertical reinforcing
bar

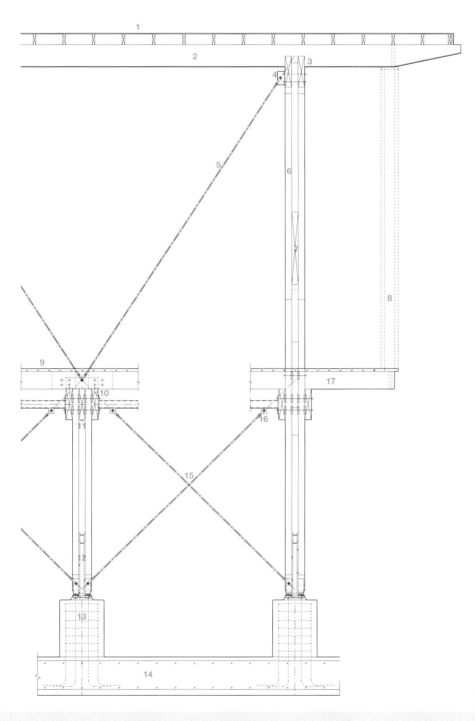

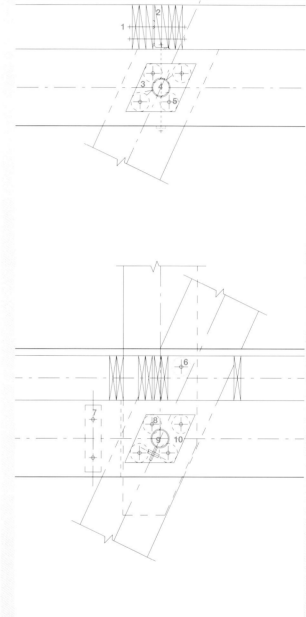

34.05
Typical Section Through Roof, Balcony and Foundation Detail 2
1:50
1 Corrugated roof sheeting on 19 mm (3/4 inch) plywood sheathing
2 Timber beam at 203 mm (8 inch) centres
3 Double timber girder
4 Clip angle
5 15 mm (3/5 inch) diameter tension rod with clevis, lock nut and 19 mm (3/4 inch) diameter pin at each end

6 Double timber vertical column
7 Diagonal timber column
8 50 x 253 mm (2 x 10 inch), with 50 x 152 mm (2 x 6 inch) each side, screen post at 1,220 mm (4 foot) centres
9 Timber floorboards
10 12 x 100 mm (1/2 x 4 inch) lag screw in horizontal leg of angle
11 12 mm (1/2 inch) diameter through bolt with bearing plate
12 Steel fitting bracket to angled column assembly
13 610 mm (24 inch) diameter reinforced

concrete pier
14 Reinforced concrete footing
15 Clamp to tension rods
16 19 mm (3/4 inch) diameter clevis pin and lock nut at shear tab of pipe strut
17 Cantilevered floor joist

34.06
Typical Floor Details
1:20
1 12 mm (1/2 inch) diameter through bolts each side of joist splice
2 Clip angle between joists to receive clevis from above
3 12 mm (1/2 inch) thick plate at each end of 89 mm (31/2 inch) standard pipe strut
4 89 mm (31/2 inch) standard pipe strut
5 19 mm (3/4 inch) diameter through bolt with shear plate beyond
6 19 mm (3/4 inch) diameter through bolt

with shear plates
7 89 x 89 x 355 mm (31/2 x 31/2 x 14 inch) blocking, one on each side of discontinued girder centre member with 19 mm (3/4 inch) diameter through bolt
8 19 mm (3/4 inch) diameter through bolt with shear plate beyond
9 89 mm (31/2 inch) standard pipe strut with shear tab to receive clevis from below
10 12 mm (1/2 inch) thick plate at each end of 89 mm (31/2 inch) standard pipe strut

The Savill Building
Surrey, England, UK

Client
The Crown Estate

Project Team
Glenn Howells, Matthew McGrory,
Jamie Webb, Reinhold Schmaderer

Structural Engineer
Engineers HRW, Buro Happold

Main Contractor
Verry Construction

The building is a new visitor facility for
the existing Savill Garden. It houses
a new shop with greenhouse and
nursery, restaurant, lecture rooms,
toilets, reception and ticketing
facilities. Remodelling of the existing
car park was also carried out to blend
seamlessly with the building and
garden. The brief was to provide a
new building to replace the existing
facilities, and hence improve the
profile of the centre and increase
visitor numbers to the gardens. The
form of the building is in response to
its surroundings – the natural form of
the curving grid shell roof is
subservient to the mature trees but
high enough to give the building
presence. The grid shell is set to lie
just above the level of the established
rhododendrons, which form an
important part of the entrance
elevation and maintain the established
identity of Rhododendron Drive. The
ancillary services have been located
within a gradually sloping structure,
which has a vegetated roof to further
lessen the impact of the building.

Internally, the roof's organic form
creates dynamic spaces for the
general public to enjoy while unifying
the building's various functions in a
single space. The roof form is derived
from a combination of intuitive design
aesthetics and complex engineering
to ensure structural integrity.
Combining contemporary engineering
with traditional craft skills, the
bespoke gridshell roof is made from
larch sourced from FSC plantations in
Windsor Forest on The Crown Estate
and clad with green oak. On the north
side of the building, the roof is raised
up with full-height glazing, giving
virtually unobstructed views across
the gardens from within the building.

1 The gridshell roof,
a specialized form of
timber construction,
consists of four layers
of timber which are
manipulated into a
double curved shell
form.

2 On the east side of
the building, the roof is
raised up with
full-height glazing,
giving virtually
unobstructed views
across the gardens
from within the

building.
3 For practical site
jointing, the larch
laths in the roof are
connected directly to
the steel edge with
fingers of Kerto LVL
(laminated veneered

lumber), which are
bolted between the
laths and support
ledges on the steel
tube.

35.01
Ground Floor Plan
1:1000
 1 Garden shop
 2 Garden entrance
 3 Restaurant terrace
 4 Service yard
 5 Plant store
 6 Greenhouse
 7 Shop
 8 Store room
 9 Server room
10 Office
11 Office
12 Retail staff WC
13 Female WC
14 Male WC
15 Ticketing and shop
   checkout pod
16 Main entrance
17 Display pod
18 Restaurant
19 Servery
20 Restaurant staff
   station
21 Seminar room
22 Kitchen
23 Staff rooms
24 Restaurant change
   and WC area
25 Plant room
26 Restaurant stores
27 Bin store

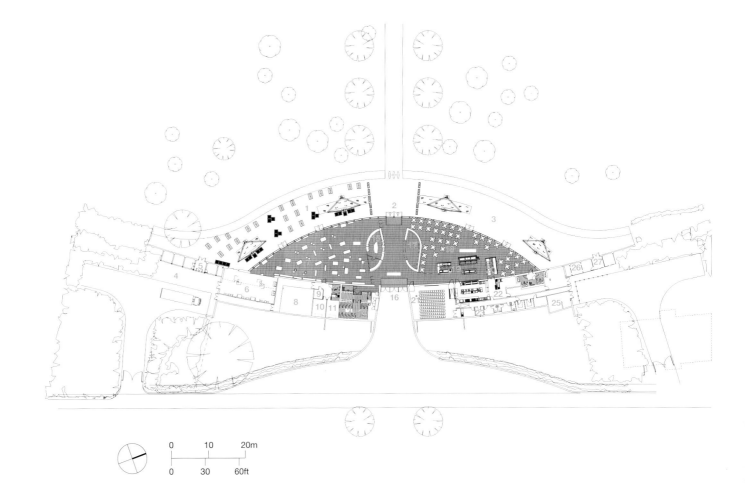

0   10   20m

0   30   60ft

35.02
Entrance Elevation
1:1000
 1 Service gates
 2 Rhododendrons
 3 Clerestory glazing
 4 Gridshell roof
 5 Entrance
 6 Earth structure
 7 Rhododendrons
 8 Service gates

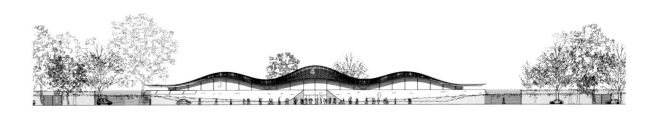

35.03
Garden Elevation
1:1000
 1 Rhododendrons
 2 Brick wall
 3 Glazing to
   restaurant
 4 Gridshell roof
 5 Glazing to shop
 6 Brick wall
 7 Rhododendrons

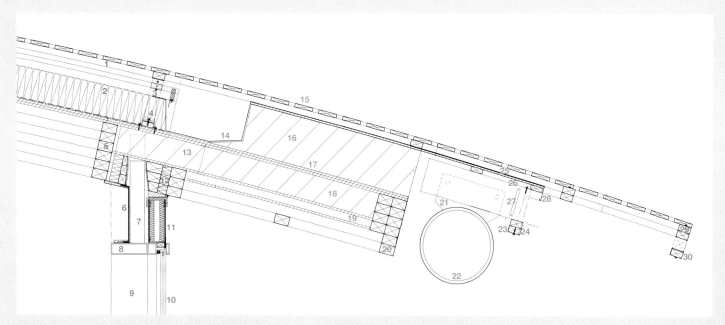

35.04
Typical Roof and Clerestory Glazing Section Detail
1:20
1 75 x 35 mm (3 x 1³/₈ inch) oak support bearer
2 Thermal insulation
3 Metal upstand and support to rainscreen
4 Bolted fixing to gridshell roof
5 Timber blocking out and glazing support
zone
6 Metal flashing fixed at top and bottom to allow for movement
7 Steel spigot
8 Steel and aluminium window head transom
9 Steel and aluminium mullion
10 Double glazing unit
11 Specialist head detail formed from EPDM membrane bonded to carrier and
glazed into glazing system
12 Thermal insulation
13 Timber blocking and laminated timber zone with voids filled with foil-faced rockwool insulation quilts to maintain thermal continuity
14 Preformed metal gutter
15 20 x 100 mm (³/₄ x 4 inch) oak rainscreen boards at 135 mm
(5¹/₃ inch) centres
16 Gutter framing zone
17 Double layer plywood diaphragm
18 Timber gridshell roof
19 Laminated timber blocking
20 Perimeter blocking
21 Steel connector plate
22 Steel hollow circular section steel edge beam
23 Anti-roosting bird
wire
24 35 x 65 mm (1³/₈ x 2¹/₂ inch) oak batten
25 75 x 35 mm (3 x 1³/₈ inch) oak support bearer
26 Bolt connection
27 Anti-roosting bird wire
28 Stainless steel drip edge to roof membrane
29 35 x 65 mm (1³/₈ x 2¹/₂ inch) oak batten to match rainscreen
and designed to follow outline of edge beam in facets
30 Two 35 x 65 mm (1³/₈ x 2¹/₂ inch) oak batten in continuous sandwich construction with mid-span blocking

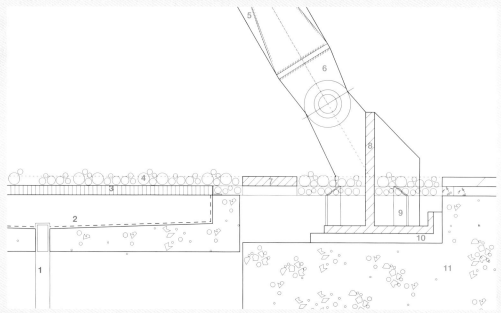

35.05
Steel Prop Base Detail
1:20
1 Yard gulley and underground drainage
2 Tanking to gulley laid to fall
3 Steel grille to receive pebble infill
4 Pebble infill to rainwater collection gulley
5 Steel support prop
6 Steel pin connector
7 Paving
8 Steel base plate
9 Steel base plate
10 Epoxy levelling grout
11 Reinforced concrete foundation

35.06
Corner Glazing Detail
1:20
1 Flashing
2 Transom below
3 Trim on transom below
4 Metal coverplate
5 Mastic joint
6 Stainless steel tie rod
7 Double glazing unit
8 Aluminium glazing capping
9 Metal and
aluminium mullion
10 Line of lighting trough shown dotted
11 Brick on end coping

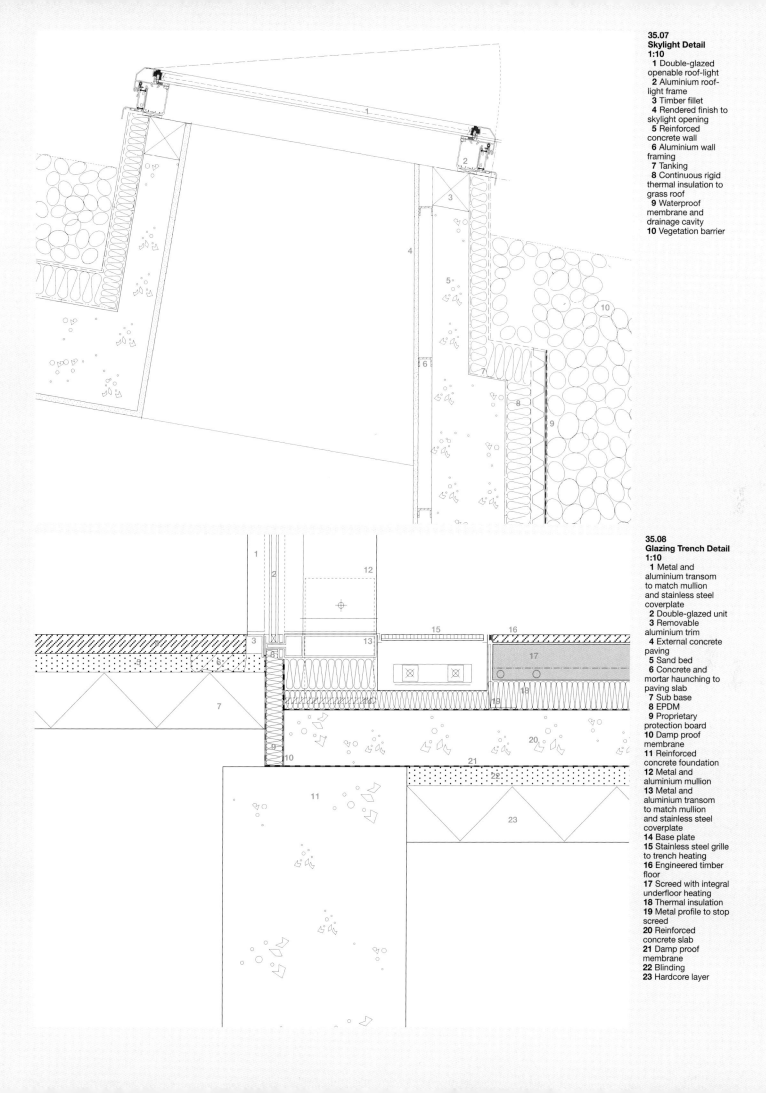

35.07
Skylight Detail
1:10
1 Double-glazed openable roof-light
2 Aluminium roof-light frame
3 Timber fillet
4 Rendered finish to skylight opening
5 Reinforced concrete wall
6 Aluminium wall framing
7 Tanking
8 Continuous rigid thermal insulation to grass roof
9 Waterproof membrane and drainage cavity
10 Vegetation barrier

35.08
Glazing Trench Detail
1:10
1 Metal and aluminium transom to match mullion and stainless steel coverplate
2 Double-glazed unit
3 Removable aluminium trim
4 External concrete paving
5 Sand bed
6 Concrete and mortar haunching to paving slab
7 Sub base
8 EPDM
9 Proprietary protection board
10 Damp proof membrane
11 Reinforced concrete foundation
12 Metal and aluminium mullion
13 Metal and aluminium transom to match mullion and stainless steel coverplate
14 Base plate
15 Stainless steel grille to trench heating
16 Engineered timber floor
17 Screed with integral underfloor heating
18 Thermal insulation
19 Metal profile to stop screed
20 Reinforced concrete slab
21 Damp proof membrane
22 Blinding
23 Hardcore layer

Norwich Cathedral Refectory
Norwich, Norfolk, England, UK

Client
The Dean and Chapter of Norwich
Cathedral

Project Team
Michael Hopkins, Andrew Barnett,
Mike Taylor, Sophy Twohig, Gary
Collins, Emma Frater, Aikari Paing,
Amy Napier

Structural Engineer
Buro Happold

Main Contractor
RG Carter, Norwich

The new refectory for the Norwich
Cathedral Visitor Centre is influenced
by an architectural language that
celebrates the meeting of old and new
with materials chosen to fit with the
existing fabric of the medieval cloister,
whilst being expressly modern in their
use. Instead of isolating the new
facilities and avoiding the complexities
of working within the existing building
fragments, this competition-winning
proposal had a head-on approach to
integration. By fully engaging with the
existing structure, the design not only
provides new, much needed facilities
including a restaurant, toilets, disabled
access and library extension, but also
addresses the resolution of the whole
precinct of buildings, restoring the
cloister and rationalizing accessibility.

The refectory is situated on the
original site of the monastery refectory
and rises up from original stone
boundary walls to reveal itself as a
free-standing, single-storey timber
box. The main material for the new
structure is English oak, which is used
in an unmistakably modern manner.
Oak was chosen as it has traditionally
been used in ecclesiastical settings as
well as being exceptionally strong,
enabling the complex engineering for
the cantilevered roof to work. Other
materials have been chosen to further
emphasize the meeting of old and
new – for instance, frameless glass
expresses the new structure whilst
minimizing the impact on the original
building, while the new cast-lead roof
cantilevers elegantly towards the
cloister wall, avoiding loading on the
fabric through the use of English oak
columns and finger props, flitched
with stainless steel.

1 The main entrance
(right) stands at a
break in the historic
stone wall which
denotes the original
refectory structure.
2 Timber-framed
glazing is built up from
the top of the original
stone wall to create
a weatherproof
envelope, but leaving
the stone wall virtually
untouched. On the first
floor the inside face of
the wall forms part
of the double-height
view from the
refectory, which
includes the elegant
timber roof structure.
3 English oak has
been used extensively
throughout the building
including these robust
sun louvres on the
south facade.
4 View of the refectory
where the oak ceiling is
supported on tapered
oak props and columns.

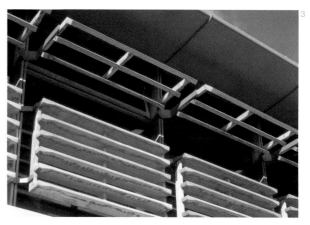

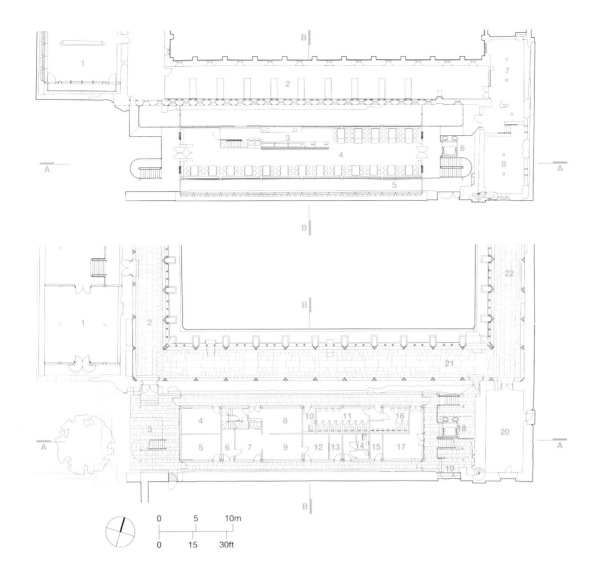

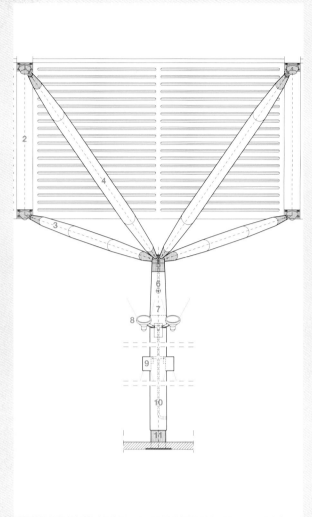

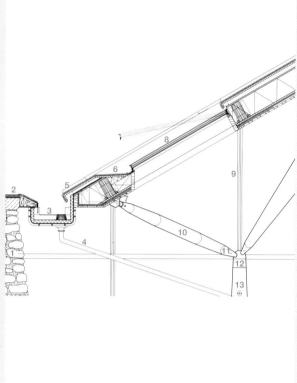

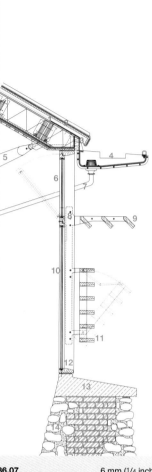

36.05
Oak Ceiling and Structure Elevation Detail
1:50
1 Satin stainless steel connection element
2 Satin stainless steel connection element
3 Laminated English oak finger prop
4 Laminated English oak finger prop
5 Stainless steel column top connection
6 Internal connection between steel column top and timber column
7 Laminated English oak column
8 Uplighter
9 Downlighter
10 Electrical conduit
11 Bead-blasted stainless steel skirting collar

36.06
Roof, Gutter and Skylight Detail
1:50
1 Existing medieval stone wall
2 Roof construction from lead sheets, solid core timber lead rails, building paper, 16 mm ($3/5$ inch) plywood boarding, 30 mm ($1^1/5$ inch) air gap, 18 mm ($7/10$ inch) structural plywood boarding, steel back to back double C-section steels, acoustic insulation, vapour barrier and 20 mm ($3/4$ inch) solid oak plywood boarding ceiling lining on 50 x 30 mm (2 x $1^1/5$ inch) battens
3 Gutter to south cloister and refectory roof from membrane gutter lining, high density rigid thermal insulation and grey-painted gutter in 6 mm ($1/4$ inch) galvanized steel
4 Brushed stainless steel 50 mm (2 inch) syphonic down pipe
5 Insect mesh
6 Timber purlin fixed to the main joists with 264 x 50 mm ($10^2/5$ x 2 inch) metal gusset plates
7 Stainless steel bosse connection
8 Paint-finished openable extruded aluminium-framed rooflight
9 Line of clear glazing beyond
10 Laminated English oak finger prop
11 Satin stainless steel connection element
12 Stainless steel column top connection
13 Laminated English oak column

36.07
Louvre and Glazing Detail to South Facade
1:50
1 Timber purlin fixed to the main joists with 264 x 50 mm ($10^2/5$ x 2 inch) metal gusset plates
2 Roof construction from lead sheets, solid core timber lead rails, building paper, 16 mm ($3/5$ inch) plywood boarding, 30 mm ($1^1/5$ inch) air gap, 18 mm ($7/10$ inch) structural plywood boarding, steel back to back double C-section steels, acoustic insulation, vapour barrier and 20 mm ($3/4$ inch) solid oak plywood boarding ceiling lining on 50 x 30 mm (2 x $1^1/5$ inch) battens
3 Insect mesh
4 Gutter to south cloister and refectory roof from membrane gutter lining, high density rigid thermal insulation and grey-painted gutter in 6 mm ($1/4$ inch) galvanized steel
5 Laminated English oak finger prop
6 Opening fan light for ventilation constructed from solid English oak frame with automatic actuator and 25 mm (1 inch) double-glazed unit
7 Brushed stainless steel syphonic down pipe
8 Continuous galvanized steel support brackets for solid English oak louvres
9 Solid English oak louvres
10 Fixed window constructed from solid English oak frame and 25 mm (1 inch) double-glazed unit
11 Solid English oak louvre blade
12 English oak window sill
13 Clipsham limestone sill
14 Existing medieval stone wall

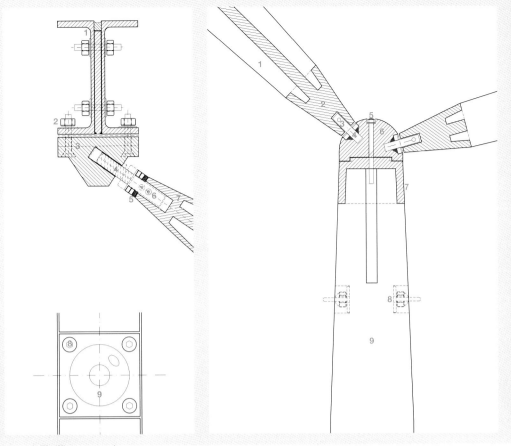

36.08
Ceiling Strut
Connection
1:10
1 Steel back to back
double C-section
steels to roof structure
2 Countersunk bolts
fixing through stainless
steel bosse connection
to roof structure above
3 Satin stainless steel
connection bosse with
threaded hole for pin
connection
4 Threaded stainless
steel pin through end
cap
5 Plastic separation
washer
6 Threaded dowel
7 Stainless steel end
cap with threaded hole
for stainless steel pin
8 Countersunk bolts
fixing through stainless
steel bosse connection
to roof structure above
9 Satin stainless steel
connection bosse with
threaded hole for pin
connection

36.09
Timber Column and
Prop Connection
Detail
1:10
1 Laminated English
oak finger prop
2 Stainless steel end
cap connection
3 Threaded dowel
4 Stainless steel
dowel
5 Stainless steel bolt
6 Satin stainless steel
column top connection
7 Column top
connection collar
8 Downlighter
9 Laminated English
oak column

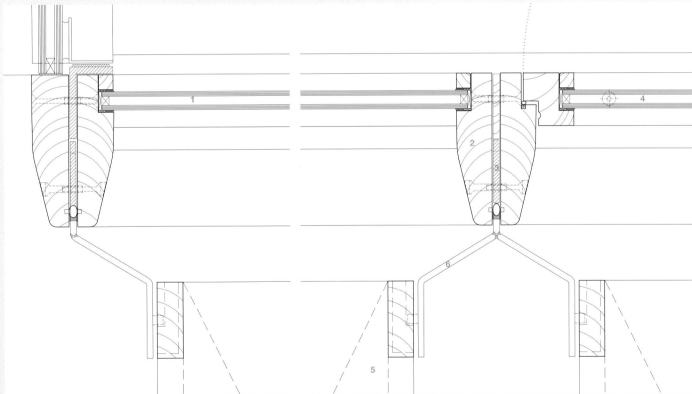

36.10
South Facade
Horizontal Section
Detail
1:5
1 Fixed window
constructed from solid
English oak frame and
25 mm (1 inch) double-
glazed unit
2 Solid English oak
vertical with
galvanized and
painted mild steel
flitch, and louvered
bracket
3 Continuous

galvanized steel
support brackets for
solid English oak
louvres
4 Opening fan light
for ventilation
constructed from solid
English oak frame with
automatic actuator
and 25 mm (1 inch)
double-glazed unit
5 Solid English oak
louvre blade
6 Galvanized steel
support brackets for
solid English oak
louvres

Onsen Hotel
Ginzan, Onsen, Japan

Client
Atsushi Fuji

Project Team
Kengo Kuma, Makoto Shirahama,
Sayaka Mizuno

Structural Engineer
K. Nakata and Associates

Main Contractor
Aiwa Construction

The four-storey Onsen (meaning 'hot spring') Hotel stands at the bottom of a valley in a snowy region of northern Japan. Ginzan is renowned for its abundant hot springs, which were discovered in the seventeenth century. Ginzan was severely damaged by a flood in 1913, but recovered with the construction of three- to four-storey buildings that featured the distinctive design traits of the Taisho period in Japan. Despite the popularity of the area, the number of hotels has not increased, due to the limited amount of land available for building. Given the lack of space, the architects undertook a large-scale refurbishment of the existing Onsen Hotel, rather than construct an entirely new building, which would have abandoned the traditional idea of the three-storey wooden house.

Instead, they preserved the existing structure, removing the concrete elements that had been added when the hotel was enlarged. One of the major undertakings was the checking of every single part of the timber structure to replace any worn pieces with new wood in order to increase the building's earthquake resistance. The existing facade was renovated utilizing timber from the original 100-year-old hotel while the interior space was reorganized by adding an atrium. The atrium is surrounded by a delicate screen made from four millimetre (one tenth of an inch) wide slits of bamboo. An almost-transparent stained glass called Dalle de Verre, first used in the Middle Ages, fits into the opening which faces the exterior space. These bamboo screens, neither transparent nor opaque, provide a soft light and shade to the interior, creating a space to heal and relax, complementing the effects of bathing in the Onsen.

1 The entrance to the hotel is via a small bridge then a path that crosses ponds that flank the entrance. Clear glazing to the entry lobby gives way elsewhere in the building to windows screened by fine bamboo brise soleil.
2 The bamboo screens, known as *sumushiko*, are used to screen all of the glazing and are also adapted to other elements of the building including the gable ends, and in a larger format to the entrance facade.
3 Bedrooms for guests are treated as calming, restorative spaces. Existing timber structure becomes a feature, contrasted with new timber floors and built-in furniture, and white walls.
4 The private bathing areas have been transformed into contemporary havens of understated luxury. Here, bamboo screens on all of the surfaces create a linear texture of light and shade.

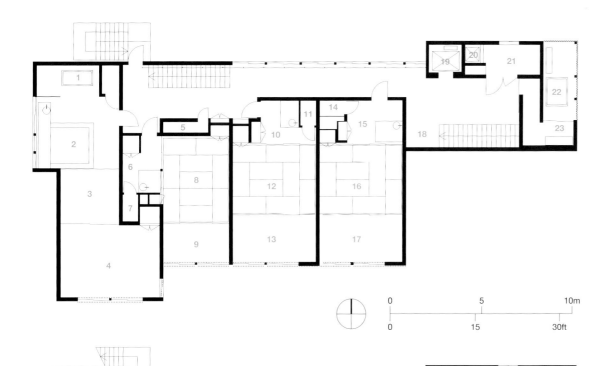

37.01
Second Floor Plan
1:200
1 Private bathing area
2 Bed / sleeping area
3 Living area
4 Dining area
5 Storage
6 Stone washroom
7 WC
8 Tatami room
9 Living area
10 Stone washroom
11 WC
12 Tatami room
13 Living area
14 WC
15 Stone washroom
16 Tatami room
17 Living area
18 Stair landing
19 Elevator
20 Dumb waiter
21 Pantry
22 Stone washroom
23 Living area

37.02
First Floor Plan
1:200
1 Private bathing area
2 Stone washroom
3 Bed / sleeping area
4 Dining area
5 Tatami room
6 Stone washroom
7 WC
8 Tatami room
9 Living area
10 Stone washroom
11 WC
12 Tatami room
13 Living area
14 Void over entrance hall below
15 Stair landing
16 Elevator
17 Dumb waiter
18 Pantry
19 Stone washroom
20 WC
21 Tatami room
22 Living area

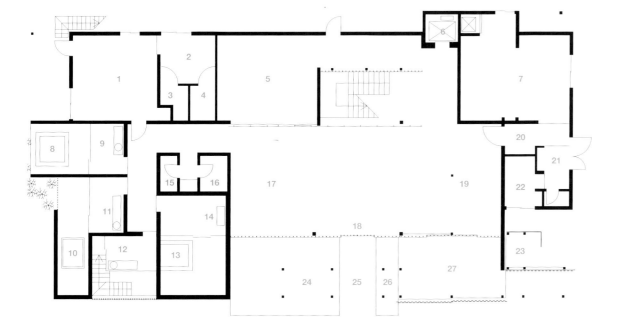

37.03
Ground Floor Plan
1:200
1 Staff room
2 Staff bathroom
3 WC
4 WC
5 Offices
6 Elevator
7 Kitchen
8 Hot spring bath
9 Dressing area
10 Hot spring bath
11 Dressing area
12 Dressing area
13 Hot spring bath
14 Dressing area
15 WC
16 WC
17 Lounge area
18 Entrance
19 Lounge area
20 Pantry
21 Staff entrance
22 Staff rest room
23 Gas cylinder storage
24 Water pond
25 Entrance path
26 Water pond
27 Cafe

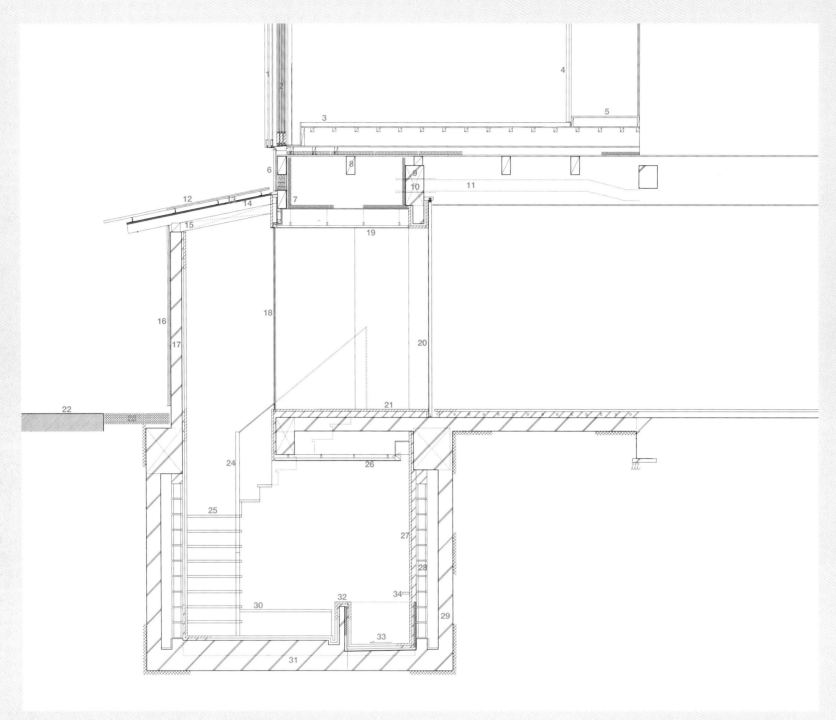

37.04
Detail Building
Section 1
1:50

1 12 x 40 mm ($\frac{1}{2}$ x 1$\frac{3}{5}$ inch) elm timber lattice door screen elements at 100 mm (4 inch) centres
2 Elm timber door
3 Hemless tatami floor
4 Elm timber lattice interior door
5 Timber floor slats for drainage
6 Mortar-coated elm timber lattice spandrel panel
7 Insulation
8 Timber beam
9 Concrete beam
10 Sleeve hole for ventilation
11 Exhaust duct
12 30 x 100 mm (1$\frac{1}{5}$

x 4 inch) elm canopy elements at 200 mm (7 $\frac{9}{10}$ inch) centres
13 Coated glass to prevent glare
14 Timber rafter
15 Ventilation slit
16 Elm timber *Yamato* (Japanese) style exterior cladding
17 Concrete wall
18 Float glass interior screen
19 Bamboo ceiling lining
20 Interior sliding door from elm timber veneer
21 Timber floorboards
22 Stone footpath
23 Broken rock edging between path and building
24 Stainless steel handrail and balustrade

25 Open timber stair treads
26 Bamboo ceiling lining
27 Timber wall lining
28 Waterproof double wall of concrete block
29 Concrete retaining foundation wall
30 Raised washroom floor
31 Pressure resisting board embedded in concrete foundation
32 Timber bath surround
33 Sloped timber bottom to bathtub
34 Acrylic bath spout

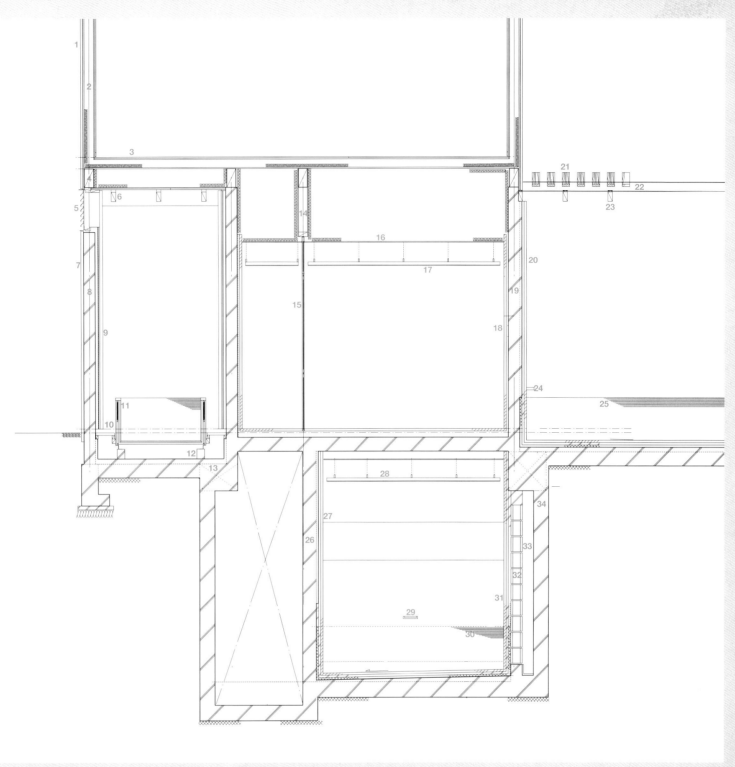

37.05
Detail Building
Section 2
1:50

1 Mortar-sprayed coating to external wall
2 External timber wall
3 Elm timber flooring
4 Timber beam
5 Waterproof boarding fascia
6 Timber rafter
7 Mortar-sprayed coating to external concrete wall
8 Exterior concrete wall
9 12 x 40 mm ($^1/_2$ x $1^3/_5$ inch) Japanese cypress wall lattice
10 12 x 40 mm ($^1/_2$ x $1^3/_5$ inch) Japanese cypress floor lattice
11 Japanese cypress bathtub

12 Concrete bathtub foundation
13 Concrete beam
14 Timber internal partition
15 Float glass
16 High pressure wood wool cement board for sound insulation
17 Bamboo ceiling lining
18 Timber wall lining
19 Concrete partition wall
20 Chinese black granite wall cladding
21 30 x 100 mm ($1^1/_5$ x 4 inch) elm timber lattice elements at 200 mm (8 inch) centres
22 Timber joist
23 Timber window frame
24 Acrylic bathtub spout

25 Chinese black granite bathtub
26 Concrete partition wall
27 Timber wall lining
28 Bamboo ceiling lining
29 Acrylic bathtub spout
30 Timber bathtub
31 Timber wall lining
32 Waterproof double wall of concrete block
33 Waterproof wall cavity
34 Concrete retaining foundation wall

Avenham Park Pavilion
Preston, Lancashire, England, UK

Client
Preston City Council

Project Team
Ian McChesney, Michael Westthorpe,
Pola Fitzgerald

Structural Engineer
Atelier One

Landscape Architect
Fenella Griffin + Edward Hutchison

This project was won by the McChesney Architects through an RIBA competition. It forms the centrepiece in a Heritage Lottery Funded scheme to restore the landscape, buildings and artifacts in two adjacent green spaces, namely Avenham and Miller Parks. Edward Milner, the noted English landscape gardener, originally designed the two parks in the 1860s. Avenham Park is laid out over a distinct hill that drops away towards the River Ribble. The building is sited at the foot of the incline, benefiting from a panoramic view of the park and city of Preston to the north. It is significantly overlooked from the park entrance and so the roof design is a key factor in the design.

The building comprises a cafe, toilet facilities, ranger's base, external performance space and a multi-function space that doubles as a classroom. It is set upon a new 1.6-metre (5-foot) high landform that protects it from flood waters. The crescent-shaped plan is a response to the site and the key functions of external performance space and external cafe. To the north, the building encloses a natural auditorium; to the south, the building fans out to create an external cafe area. The building is constructed from blockwork walls and a timber roof clad in zinc sheet. The roof is built up from a combination of Glu-lam beams at each roof overlap, timber joists and plywood sheathing. The sheathing makes the whole structure work together as a stressed skin making it very robust. The curtain wall to the north is a combination of structural timber sections and a proprietary aluminium glazing system. All windows and doors are bespoke units manufactured from Douglas fir.

1 The north facade features extensive full-height timber-framed glazing to benefit from expansive views across the park.
2 The timber roof is comprised of six inclined planes with zinc sheeting to the upper surface and plywood lining to the soffit. The timber window framing is contrasted with dark aluminium glazing sections that follow the line of the roof panels.
3 View of the cafe terrace. The large sheltering roof overhang allows the terrace to be used year round.
4 The multi-function room features black painted steel trusses to create an open floor plan.

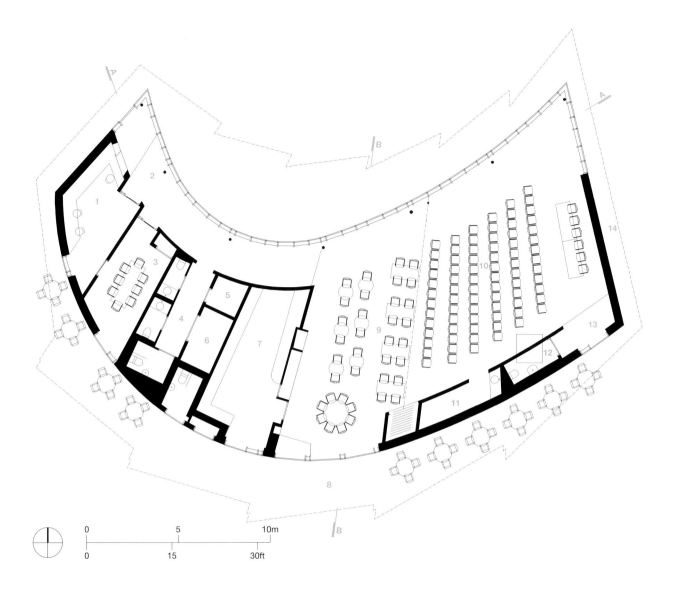

0		5		10m
0	15		30ft	

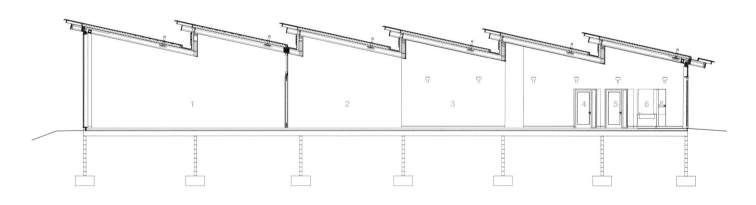

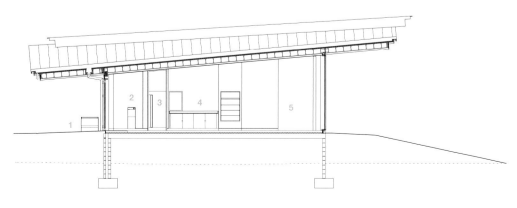

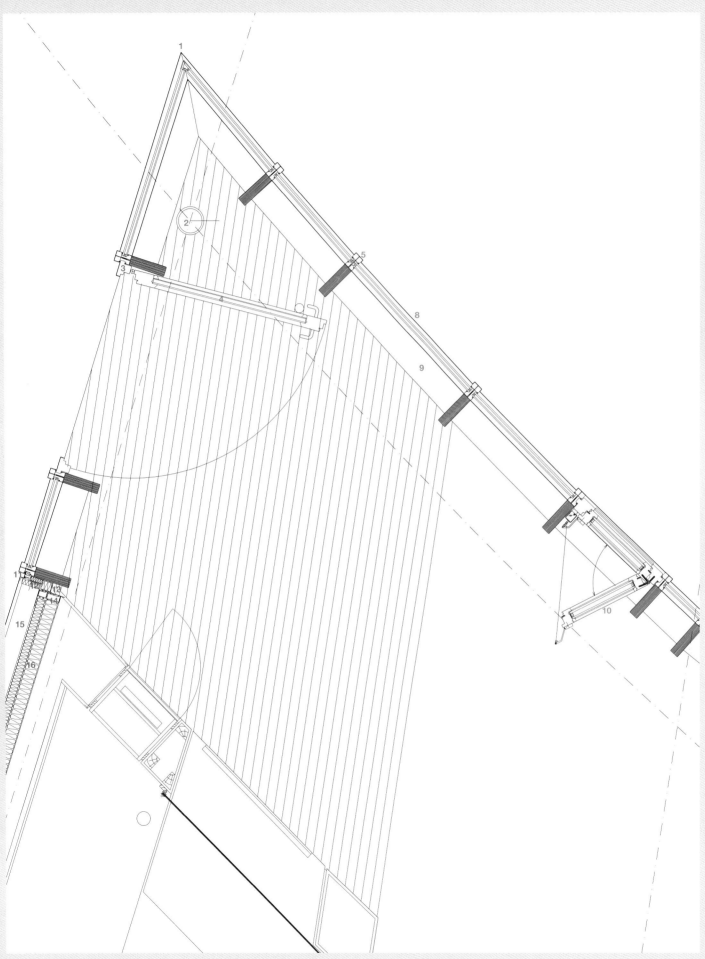

38.04
North-West Corner
Glazing Plan Detail
1:20
  1 Silicone joint with aluminium sheet cap
  2 Circular steel column
  3 Timber door frame
  4 Glazed door with timber frame
  5 Douglas fir mullion cap
  6 Aluminium curtain wall section
  7 Kerto (dimensionally stable laminated veneered timber) mullion
  8 Aluminium transom cap
  9 Kerto (dimensionally stable laminated veneered timber) transom
  10 Douglas fir framed glazed opening vent
  11 Corner bead
  12 Vertical damp proof course
  13 Soft wood block
  14 Proprietary cavity closer
  15 Dense blockwork
  16 Mineral wool insulation

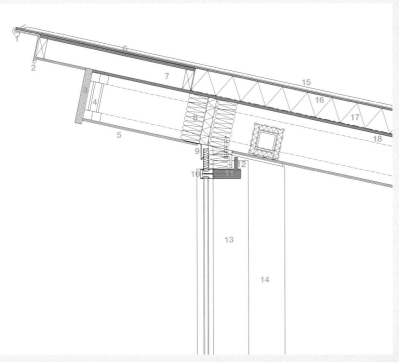

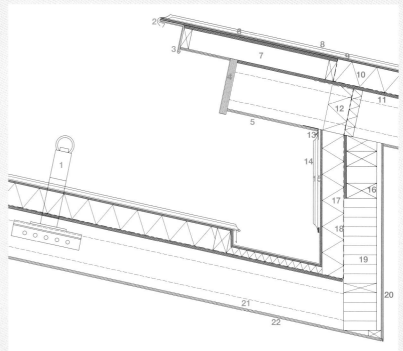

38.05
Curtain Wall to Soffit and Roof Edge Detail
1:20
1 Galvanized metal plate to support roof edge
2 Zinc fascia
3 35 mm (1³/8 inch) Kerto (dimensionally stable laminated veneered timber) fascia
4 250 mm (9⁴/5 inch)

timber I-joists at 400 mm (15³/4 inch) centres
5 Spruce plywood soffit lining
6 Spruce plywood
7 Timber outrigger framing
8 Mineral wool insulation
9 Aluminium flashing
10 Aluminium curtain wall section
11 Kerto ply transom

12 Steel support bracket
13 Kerto ply mullion
14 Circular steel column
15 Zinc standing seam roof sheet
16 Vapour barrier structured underlay
17 120 mm (4³/4 inch) insulated decking panel
18 Vapour barrier on separation layer

38.06
Roof Plate Overlap Detail
1:20
1 'Mansafe' fall protection post
2 Galvanized metal plate to support roof edge
3 Zinc fascia
4 35 mm (1³/8 inch) Kerto (dimensionally stable laminated veneered timber)

fascia
5 Spruce plywood soffit lining
6 Spruce plywood
7 Timber outrigger framing
8 Zinc standing seam roof sheet
9 Vapour barrier structured underlay
10 120 mm (4³/4 inch) insulated decking panel
11 Vapour barrier on

separation layer
12 120 mm (4³/4 inch) insulated decking panel
13 Zinc flashing
14 Vertical zinc standing seam panel
15 Vapour barrier structured underlay
16 Timber framing
17 120 mm (4³/4 inch) insulated decking panel
18 Vapour barrier on

separation layer
19 700 x 180 mm (27³/5 x 7¹/10 inch) Glu-lam beam
20 Spruce plywood lining
21 250 mm (9⁴/5 inch) timber I-joists at 400 mm (15³/4 inch) centres
22 Spruce plywood ceiling lining

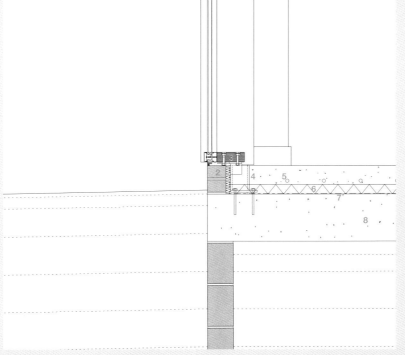

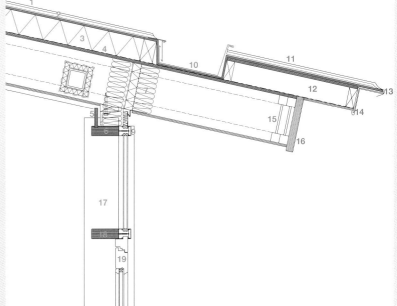

38.07
Curtain Wall to Slab Detail
1:20
1 Aluminium curtain wall section
2 Blue brick
3 Kerto (dimensionally stable laminated veneered timber) transom
4 Steel support bracket
5 Concrete screed

with under floor heating pipes
6 50 mm (2 inch) rigid foam insulation
7 Damp proof membrane
8 Reinforced concrete floor slab

38.08
Gutter, Eaves and Glazed Wall Detail
1:20
1 Zinc standing seam roof sheeting
2 Vapour barrier structured underlay
3 120 mm (4³/4 inch) insulated decking panel
4 Vapour barrier on separation layer
5 Steel support

barrier
6 Kerto (dimensionally stable laminated veneered timber) transom
7 Mineral wool insulation
8 Aluminium flashing
9 Aluminium curtain wall section
10 Zinc lined concealed rainwater gutter
11 Spruce plywood

12 Timber outrigger framing
13 Galvanized metal plate to support roof edge
14 Zinc fascia
15 250 mm (9⁴/5 inch) timber I-joists at 400 mm (15³/4 inch) centres
16 35 mm (1³/8 inch) Kerto (dimensionally stable laminated veneered timber)

fascia
17 Kerto ply mullion
18 Kerto ply transom
19 Glazed timber door and frame

Aurland Lookout
Aurland, Norway

Client
Norwegian Transport Department

Project Team
Todd Saunders, Tommie Wilhelmsen

Structural Engineer
Node AS, Bergen

Main Contractor
Veidekke AS, Sogndal

The site for the Aurland Lookout is close to the small town of Sogn og Fjordane, one of the larger fjords on the west coast of Norway. 'Nature first and architecture second' is the guiding principle for the design. It was immediately apparent that the buildings should encroach on the pristine mountain landscape as little as possible. The design takes the form of an expressive bridge-like structure, launched from the side of the mountain and terminating in a plunging downward curve. While minimal in form and execution, the drama of the geometry complements the steep mountain landscape while conserving its surroundings – for example, all of the pine trees on the site were retained throughout the construction process. The design includes a small parking area for two buses and ten cars, located further up the road away from the lookout to maintain the purity of the place.

The structure takes the form of a diving board, constructed using load-bearing galvanized steel covered with environmental pressure-treated pine. The load-bearing system is two parallel frames of rectangular sections with a criss-cross framework for the floor sitting between them. The walking platform is constructed from massive planks of timber, laid to create a small fall to either side for drainage. The balustrade is clad in laminated timber while the underside is clad in open timber slats. To make the experience even more dramatic the architecture creates the experience of leaving the mountainside and walking out into the air where the timber-clad platform terminates only in a tilted sheet of frameless glass, while the ground plane and balustrades continue on in a plunge towards the Aurland Fjord.

1 The dramatic form of the lookout intensifies the experience of viewing the sublime mountain and fjord scenery.
2 Timber cladding is used for the walking surface as well as the balustrades and the underside. The galvanized steel structure, only visible at the end of the lookout, blends into the forest, further contributing to the illusion that the bridge is floating above the fjord.
3 The walkway terminates in a frameless panel of glass, contributing to the already vertiginous experience of appreciating the spectacular view.

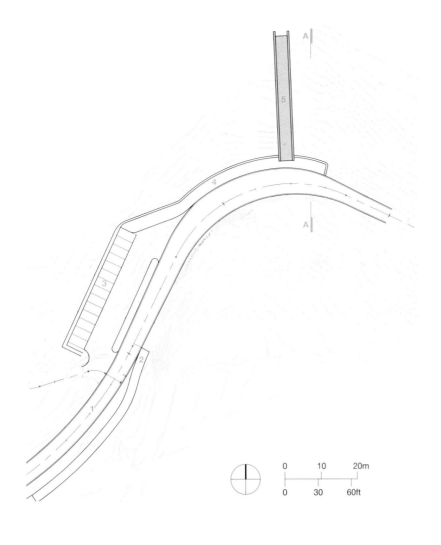

39.01
Site Plan
1:1000
1 Approach road
2 Footpath
3 Car park
4 Footpath
5 Lookout

0   10   20m
0   30   60ft

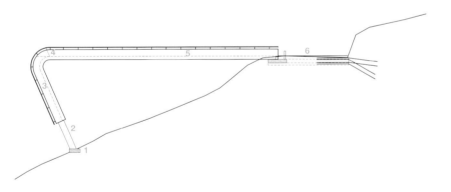

39.02
Section A–A
1:500
1 Concrete footing
2 Steel frame
3 Timber-clad
  balustrade return
4 Glass balustrade
5 Timber platform
6 Approach road
  and footpath

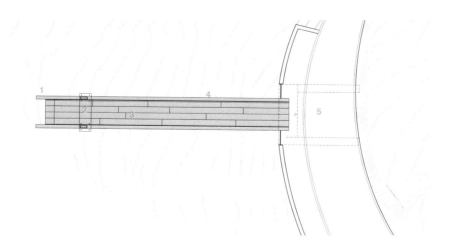

39.03
Plan
1:500
1 Timber balustrade
2 Glass balustrade
3 Timber platform
4 Timber balustrade
5 Approach road
  and footpath

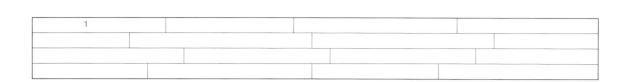

39.04
**Bridge Detail Plan
and Elevation
1:200**
  1 65 mm (2¹/2 inch)
thick pressure-treated
pine planks to lookout
walkway, screw fixed
to steel frame from
underside
  2 65 mm (2¹/2 inch)
thick laminated timber
balustrade
  3 Semi-circular joints
to balustrade cladding
members
  4 Rectangular hollow
section steel frame

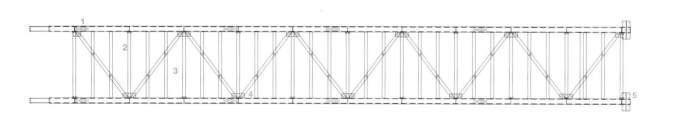

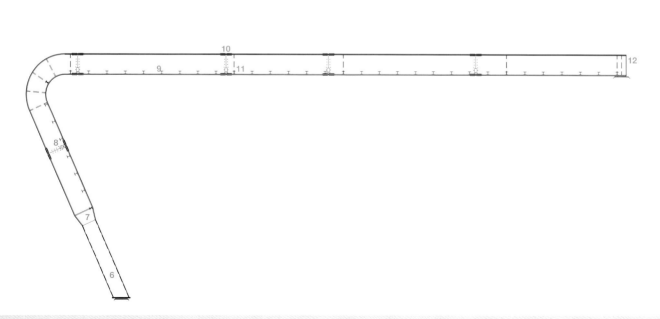

39.05
**Bridge Structural
Plan and Section
1:200**
  1 Bolted plate
connection between
beams
  2 Steel cross bracing
  3 45 degree steel
wind bracing
  4 Torsion stiffening
steel plate for
fastening cross
bracing
  5 Steel joint to
foundation at road
  6 Steel joint to
foundation below at
ground level
  7 Transition point
between beams of
differing size
  8 Steel cross bracing
  9 Steel cross bracing
  10 Steel joint between
two beams fastened at
top and bottom
  11 Steel cross bracing
  12 Steel joint to
foundation at road

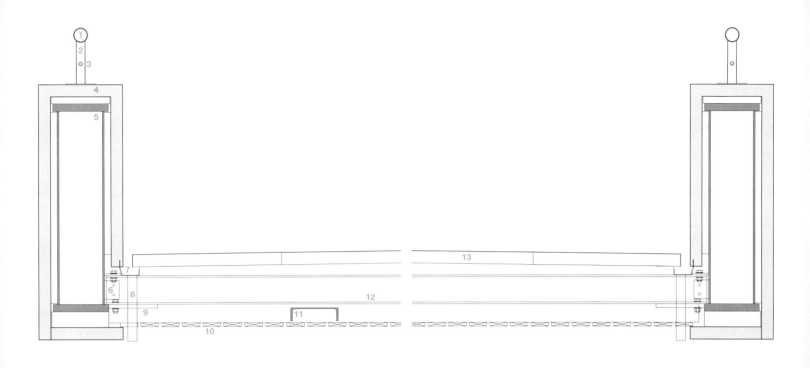

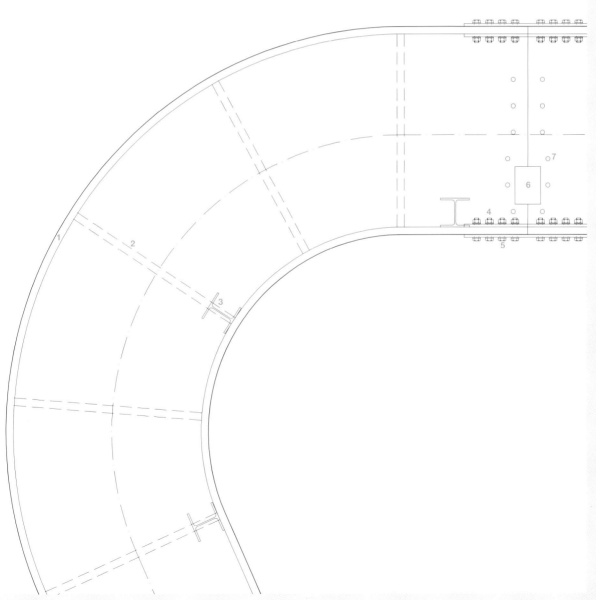

39.06
Bridge Platform
Section Detail 1
1:20
1 76 mm (3 inch) diameter horizontal steel handrail
2 48 mm (1⁹/₁₀ inch) vertical steel post for handrail
3 21 mm (⁴/₅ inch) horizontal secondary handrail
4 65 mm (2¹/₂ inch) thick laminated timber balustrade
5 300 x 1,100 mm (11 ⁴/₅ x 43¹/₃ inch) steel beam
6 Torsion stiffening steel plate for fastening cross beams
7 Drainage trough running the length of the platform
8 60 mm (2¹/₃ inch) long, 50 mm (2 inch) diameter drainage pipe
9 Joint plate for fastening cross beam
10 Timber slats
11 45 degree steel cross bracing
12 Steel cross bracing
13 65 mm (2¹/₂ inch) thick cross-laminated timber decking to platform surface

39.07
Bridge Platform
Section Detail 2
1:20
1 300 mm (11⁴/₅ inch) wide, 40 mm (1³/₅ inch) thick steel side beam
2 Steel stiffening plates
3 Steel cross bracing
4 Steel plates on top of beam bolted with 24 mm (1 inch) diameter bolts
5 Steel plates on bottom of beam bolted with 24 mm (1 inch) diameter bolts
6 Holes in steel to allow room for bolts to be mounted
7 24 mm (1 inch) diameter bolts

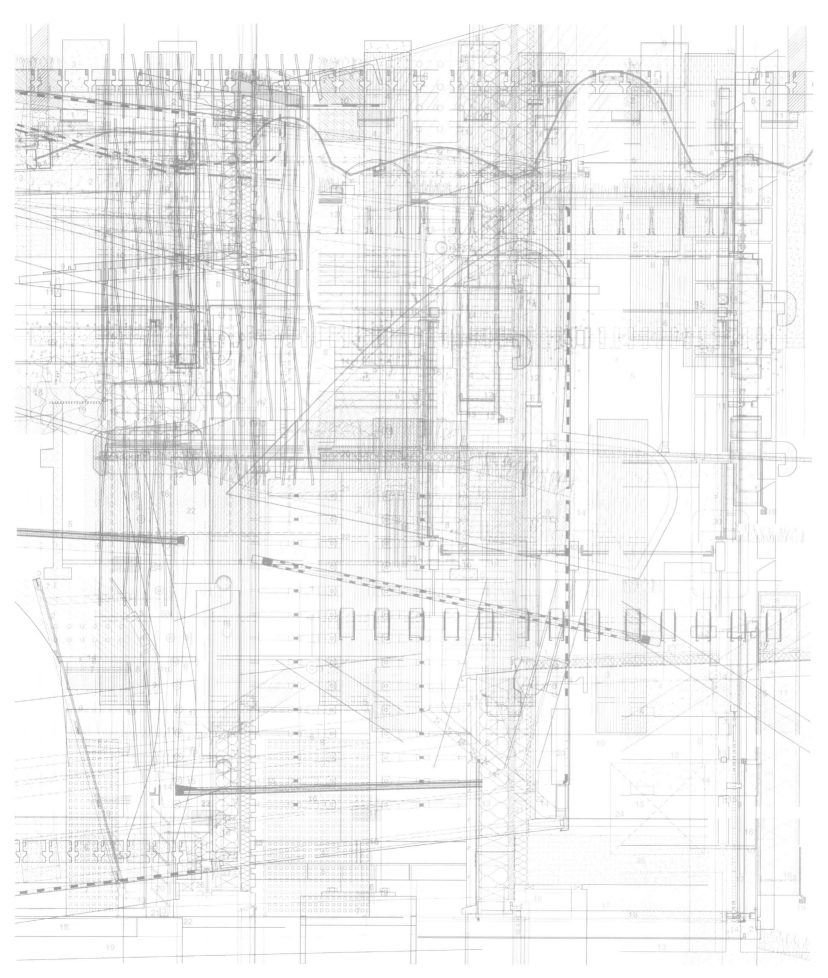

170

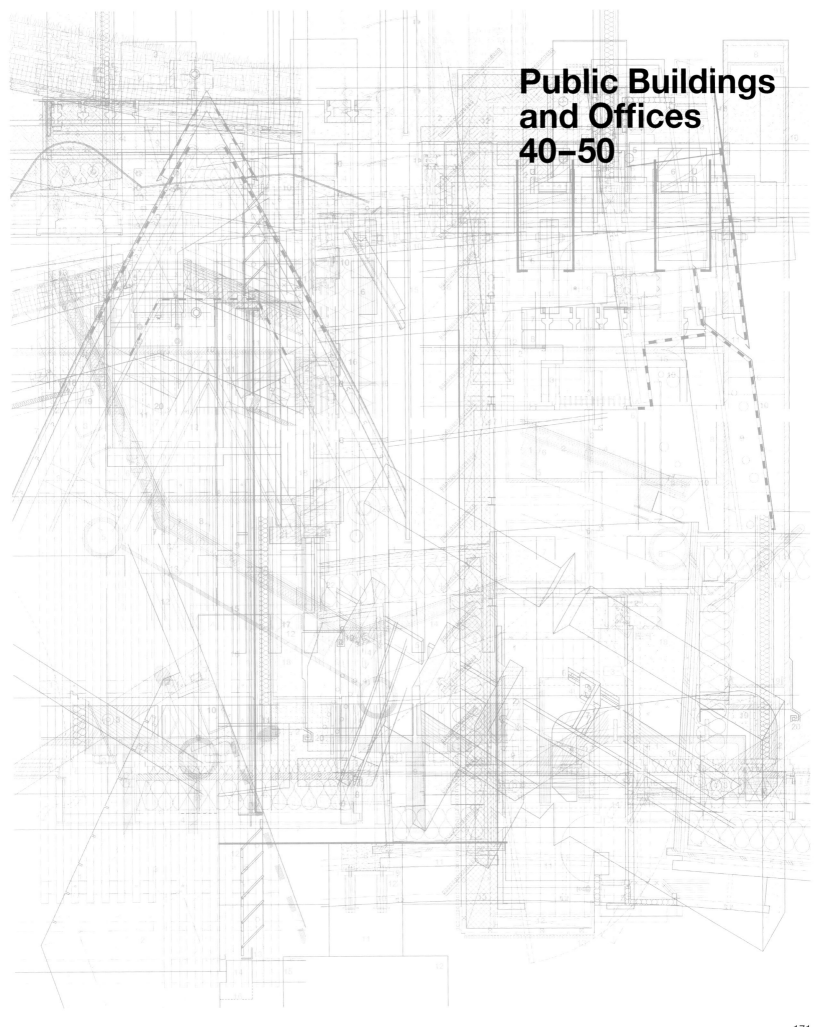

**Public Buildings
and Offices
40–50**

**British Council,
Lagos, Nigeria**

Client
British Council

Project Team
Paul Appleton, Victoria Thornton,
Gabor Gallov, Debola Ojo

Structural Engineer
Ove Arup and Partners

Main Contractor
Heraklion

In the summer of 2002 the British Council decided to relocate their Lagos headquarters to a site in the Ikoyi district. After an initial feasibility study by the British Council Architects to reorganize the site, Allies and Morrison were appointed to refurbish the existing buildings and develop the design of a new learning centre with information services, cafe, video conferencing and seminar facilities alongside new office accommodation. The British Council wanted, in their new building, to create a sense of accessibility and openness, as well as incorporating an appropriate level of security and screening from the equatorial environment.

The project responds by placing a semi-formal garden as a route to the new building. The protective front wall of the property has been replaced by an open metal screen, through which the garden and the building can be seen. The fully glazed main space of the reception building appears to be an extension of this garden to the inside. An external timber screen, which shades the interior, adopts the character of a garden trellis and creates a shaded colonnade in front of the building. Inside the building a large double-height reception area provides a visual introduction to all the functions of the British Council, continuing the sense of openness. The building is constructed of an in-situ concrete frame with block infill coated with a white textured render. This local vernacular is manipulated to invert the traditional closed impression and to reveal the activities of the British Council.

1 A timber screen, using locally sourced iroko, shades the building. It is separate from, but laterally supported by, the main structure.
2 The third screen, behind the first of the metal fence and the second of the timber screen, contains the entrance door, also made from iroko. It is a blast-resistant, double-glazed, bronze-anodized curtain wall.
3 A final internal screen, of exposed concrete and timber, veils the private office spaces.

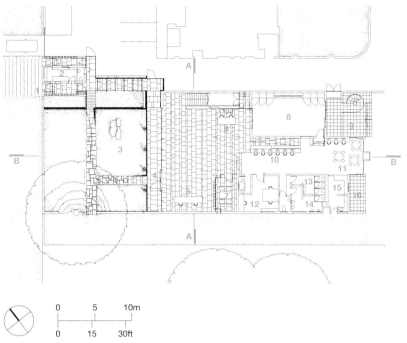

40.01
Ground Floor Plan
1:500

1 Street entrance
2 Security gatehouse
3 Garden
4 Building entrance
5 Reception
6 Reception
7 Meeting room
8 Multi-purpose
  audio-visual room
9 Stair to upper level
10 Information centre
11 Cafe
12 Process room
13 Female WC
14 Male WC
15 Kitchenette
16 Terrace

0   5   10m

0   15   30ft

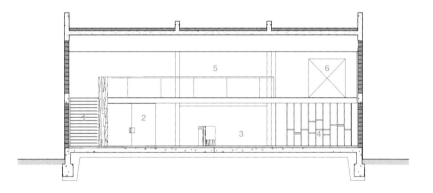

40.02
Section A–A
1:200

1 Stair to first floor
2 Doors to
  multi-purpose
  room
3 Information centre
4 Meeting room
  behind timber-
  framed glazed
  screen
5 Informal meeting
  area
6 Laminated glass
  panel

40.03
Section B–B
1:200

1 Timber screen
2 Entrance loggia
3 Reception
4 Stair to first floor
5 Mezzanine
6 Offices
7 Information centre
8 Cafe

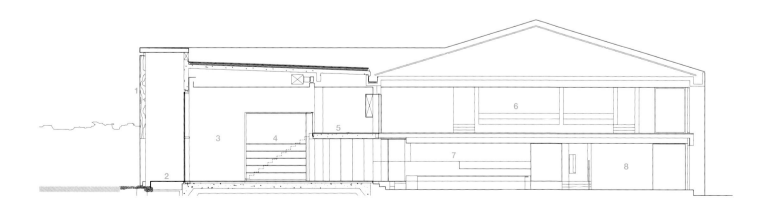

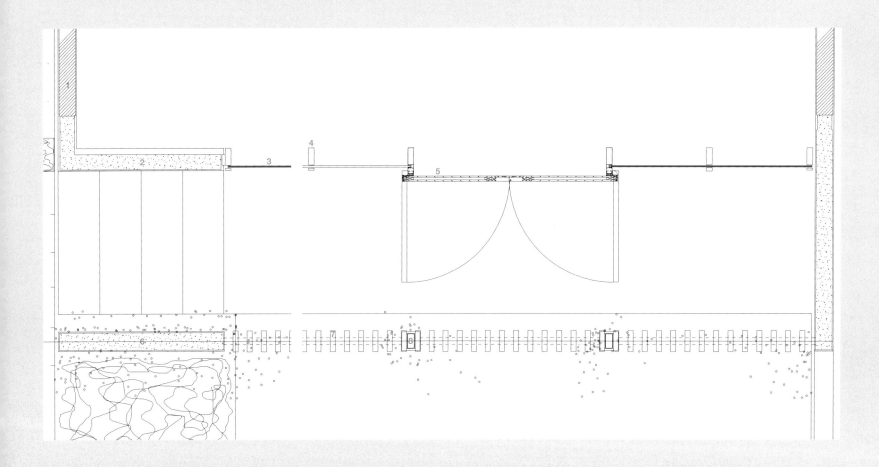

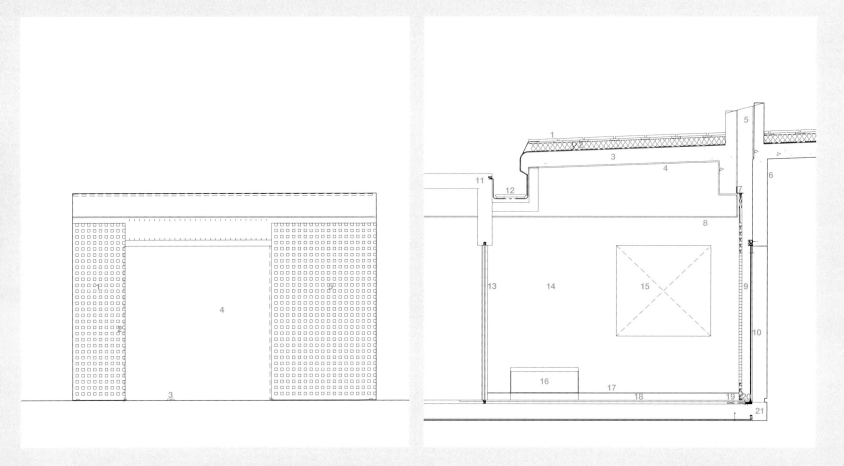

40.04
**Iroko Timber Screen
Plan Detail
1:50**
1 230 mm (9 inch)
thick rendered
blockwork wall
2 230 mm (9 inch)
thick rendered
reinforced concrete
wall
3 Double-glazed
screen with 6 mm
(^{1}/4 inch) thick clear
toughened outer layer,
12 mm (^{1}/2 inch)
airspace and 7.5 mm
(^{3}/10 inch) clear
laminated glass inner
layer
4 Anodized
aluminium mullion
5 Solid iroko timber
panelled door
6 230 mm (9 inch)
thick reinforced
concrete front wall
7 280 x 70 mm (11 x
2^3/4 inch) iroko timber
section to entrance
screen
8 200 x 100 x 5 mm
(7^9/10 x 4 x ^{1}/5 inch)
steel rectangular
hollow section

40.05
**Iroko Timber Screen
to Offices Detail
1:50**
1 40 mm (1^3/5 inch)
top-hung solid iroko
timber screen
comprised of timber
battens glued to form
37 x 37 mm (1^1/2 x 1^1/2
inch) square holes
2 Edge of screen
formed to complete
squares when closed
3 Intermittently
placed floor guides
4 Laminated
toughened glass
5 40 mm (1^3/5 inch)
top-hung solid iroko
timber screen
comprised of timber
battens glued to form
37 x 37 mm (1^1/2 x
1^1/2 inch) square holes

40.06
**Roof, Gutter and Wall
Section Detail
1:50**
1 300 x 300 mm
(11^4/5 x 11^4/5 inch)
clay pavers laid on
screed
2 100 mm (4 inch)
thick polyurethane
insulation
3 Reinforced
concrete beam
4 Emulsion paint on
render
5 Light slot
6 Fairfaced concrete
7 Steel angle fixed to
concrete upstand
8 Gypsum
suspended
plasterboard ceiling
9 40 mm (1^3/5 inch)
top-hung solid iroko
timber screen
comprised of timber
battens glued to form
37 x 37 mm (1^1/2 x
1^1/2 inch) square holes
10 Laminated
toughened glass
11 Existing concrete
roof
12 Existing roof gutter
13 Glazed screen
14 Emulsion paint on
rendered blockwork
wall
15 Fixed glazing with
concealed frame
16 Floor mounted split
unit air conditioning
17 15 x 100 mm (^{3}/5 x
4 inch) painted timber
skirting
18 Carpet on 50 mm
(2 inch) sand and
cement screed topping
over reinforced
concrete floor slab
19 Removable timber
floor board
20 Groove in bottom
rail with intermittent
guide
21 Reinforced
concrete floor slab

40.07
**Iroko Timber Screen
Elevation Detail
1:20**
1 Rendered wall
2 Bolt fixings
3 250 x 250 x 16 mm
(9^4/5 x 9^4/5 x ^{3}/5 inch)
thick steel end plates
4 280 x 70 mm (11 x
2^3/4 inch) iroko timber
section to entrance
screen
5 Bolt fixing through
steel rectangular
hollow section
6 200 x 100 x 5 mm
(7^9/10 x 4 x ^{1}/5 inch)
steel rectangular
hollow section
7 90 mm (3^1/2 inch)
diameter circular
hollow section
8 Cement bed
between steel
rectangular hollow
section upright and
steel end plate
9 250 x 250 x 16 mm
(9^4/5 x 9^4/5 x ^{2}/3 inch)
thick steel end plates
10 Bolt fixing between
steel end plate and
concrete footing
11 Reinforced
concrete footing

40.08
**Iroko Timber Screen
Plan Detail
1:10**
1 280 x 70 mm (11 x
2^3/4 inch) iroko timber
section to entrance
screen
2 12 mm (^{1}/2 inch)
steel plate welded to
rectangular hollow
section
3 200 x 100 x 5 mm
(7^9/10 x 4 x ^{1}/5 inch)
steel rectangular
hollow section
4 250 x 250 x 16 mm
(9^4/5 x 9^4/5 x ^{2}/3 inch)
thick end plates
5 280 x 70 mm (11 x
2^3/4 inch) iroko timber
section to entrance
screen

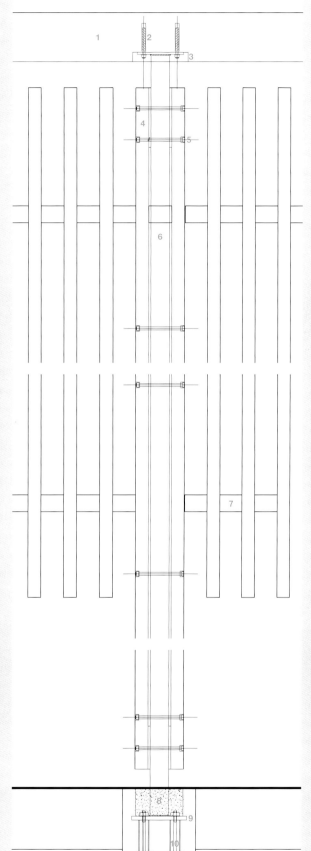
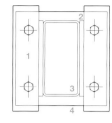
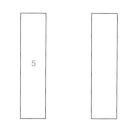

**Ballard Library and Neighborhood
Service Center
Seattle, Washington, USA**

Client
The Seattle Public Library

Project Team
Peter Q. Bohlin, Robert Miller, David
Cinamon, Steve Mongillo, Nguyen Ha,
Eric Walter, Daniel Ralls, Zeke Bush,
Stephen Gibson, Darren Lloyd

Structural Engineer
PCS Structural Solutions

Main Contractor
PCL Construction Services

The design of this new library and
service centre draws on Ballard's
Scandinavian and maritime roots, but
looks to the neighbourhood's future,
projected to be composed of a
younger, more diverse population.
The building forms a powerful civic
face with tapered metal columns
supporting a gently curving plane of
laminated timber beams and a planted
roof. The roof turns upwards at the
north and south edges, allowing light
into the building. Timber purlins
extend beyond the roof perimeter,
visually softening the edge. The entry
is pulled back from the street to make
a deep 'porch', tying together the
library and service centre under the
western edge of the roof. Metal
channels above the building's entry
mark the spine of the building. A pair
of red channels form a distinct line
leading through the lobby, over the
reference desk and terminating at an
enclosed glass quiet room. A pair of
blue channels parallel to the facade
lead to the lobby of the service centre.
Rectangular, cedar-clad boxes
containing support spaces are aligned
on east–west axes.

A periscope near the circulation
desk offers children views of the green
roof where the planting mimics the
natural spread of seeds by prevailing
breezes. The glazing in the curtain wall
includes a frit pattern of photovoltaic
film that produces shading for the
lobby. Anemometers, monitoring wind
speed and direction, are integrated on
the roof. Added to this data is
information about light, energy use
and rainfall, which is transmitted to
LED display panels as artwork,
making microclimatic conditions
created by the building visible.

1 Along the north
facade, the structural
timber purlins are
cantilevered out
beyond the facade to
create a feathered
edge to the building.
2 The main facade
features an aluminium
shingle-clad form
which accommodates
the public meeting
room.
3 The plywood
furniture, designed by
the architect, is
assembled utilizing a
series of notches and
tabs requiring no
mechanical fasteners.
4 This is the first major
building designed and
built within the new
Ballard Municipal
Center master plan.
The library and service
center are co-located
on a gently-sloping site
adjacent to a new city
park. This civic core is
easily accessible by
public transit, bicycles
and pedestrians.
5 The library's mission
offers an opportunity
to educate the
community in the
richness and benefits
of integrating green
design.

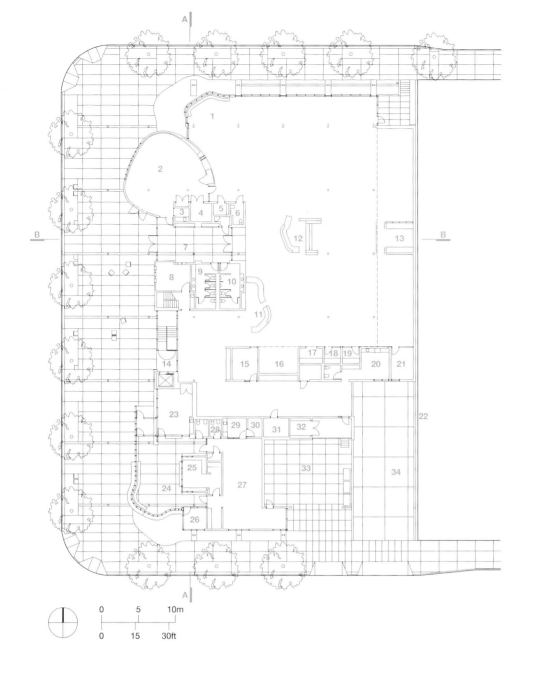

41.01
Ground Floor Plan
1:500

1 Children's library area
2 Multi-purpose room
3 Kitchen
4 Storage
5 Storage
6 WC
7 Main entrance
8 Book drop
9 Female WC
10 Male WC
11 Circulation desk
12 Reference desk
13 Quiet room
14 Stair and lift lobby
15 Branch manager's office
16 Reserves desk
17 Copy room
18 Quiet room
19 Quiet room
20 Kitchen
21 Quiet room
22 Future retail and housing development
23 Conference room
24 Neighborhood Service Center lobby
25 Neighborhood Service Center counter
26 Municipal Judge office
27 Service Center staff room
28 WC
29 Kitchen
30 Electrical room
31 Electrical room
32 Storage
33 Delivery and services
34 Driveway

41.02
Section A–A
1:500

1 Covered courtyard
2 Library collections
3 Quiet room
4 Parking garage
5 Office
6 Work room
7 Neighborhood Service Center WCs
8 Service Center
9 Office

41.03
Section B–B
1:500

1 Metal roof
2 Quiet room
3 Library collections
4 Lobby
5 Front porch

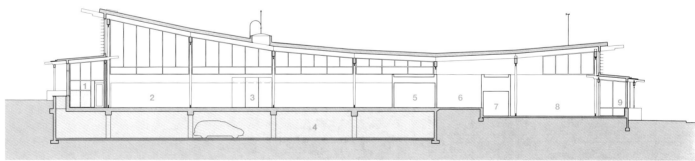

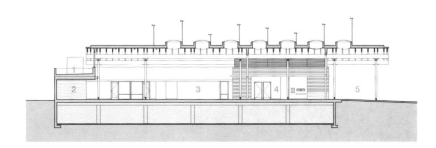

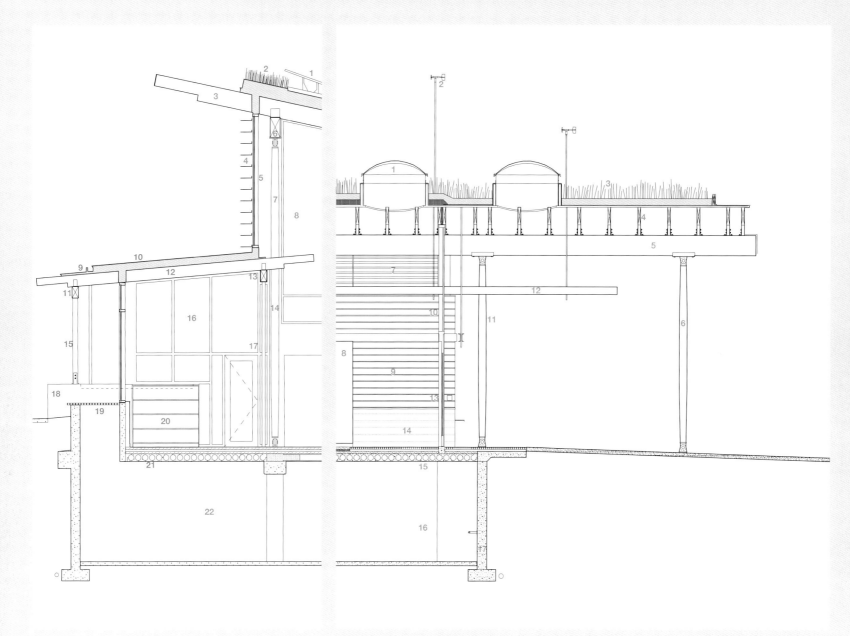

41.04
Detail Section 1
1:100
 1 Solar panels
 2 Green roof system
 3 Timber Glu-lam
purlin
 4 Aluminium louvres
 5 Aluminium curtain
wall system
 6 Timber Glu-lam
beam
 7 Tapered steel
column
 8 Glazing beyond
 9 Integrated rain
gutter
10 Metal roof
assembly
11 Timber Glu-lam
beam

12 Timber Glu-lam
rafter
13 Timber Glu-lam
beam
14 Tapered steel
column
15 Timber column
16 Glazing beyond
17 Steel pipe column
18 Board formed
concrete
19 Metal grating
20 Reading bay and
book shelves
21 Pre-cast concrete
plank floor structure
22 Parking garage

41.05
Detail Section 2
1:100
 1 Acrylic dome
skylight
 2 Anemometers
 3 Green roof system
 4 Timber Glu-lam
purlins
 5 Timber Glu-lam
beams
 6 Tapered steel
column
 7 Painted metal
louvres
 8 Entrance lobby
 9 Stained timber
siding
10 Aluminium curtain
wall system
11 Tapered steel

column
12 Steel channels for
LED art installation
13 Entry door
14 Board formed
concrete
15 Pre-cast concrete
plank floor structure
16 Parking garage
17 Reinforced
concrete structure

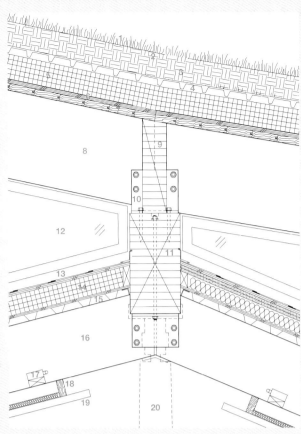

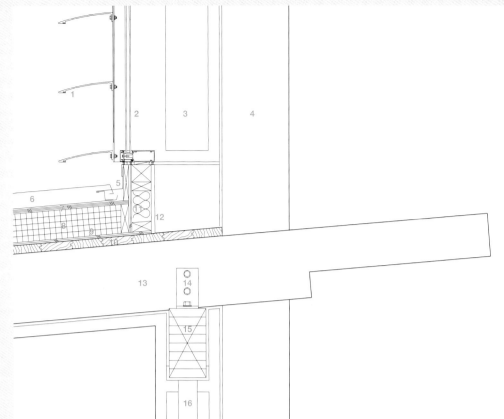

41.06
Roof Detail
1:20
  1 Planted roof
  2 Geotextile layer
  3 Top soil
  4 Hydrotech garden
roof system
  5 Roof insulation
  6 Plywood
  7 Timber decking
  8 Timber Glu-lam
purlins
  9 Timber Glu-lam
blocking
10 Metal brackets
11 Timber Glu-lam
beam
12 Clear glazed
window
13 Corrugated
galvanized metal
shingles
14 Insulation
15 Acoustical metal
decking
16 Timber Glu-lam
purlins
17 Lighting fixture
18 Timber trim
19 Timber slat ceiling
20 Tapered column
beyond shown dotted

41.07
Clerestory Glazing
Detail
1:20
  1 Metal louvres
  2 Aluminium curtain
wall system
  3 Window beyond
  4 Line of concrete
wall beyond
  5 Flashing
  6 Metal roof sheeting
  7 Plywood sheeting
  8 Roof insulation
  9 Plywood sheeting
10 Tongue and groove
timber decking with
chamfered edges up
11 Insulation
12 Gypsum wall board
13 Timber Glu-lam
beam
14 Metal bracket
15 Timber Glu-lam
beam
16 Steel pipe column

41.08
Library Window
Detail
1:10
  1 Metal siding wall
cladding
  2 Plywood sheeting
  3 Two layers of
gypsum wall board
  4 Metal wall studs
  5 Insulation
  6 Curved window sill
  7 Maple plywood
window reveal
  8 Stopped in glass
panel
  9 Recessed light
above
10 Glass door
11 Tackable fabric
panel
12 Pencil rail
13 Maple chair rail

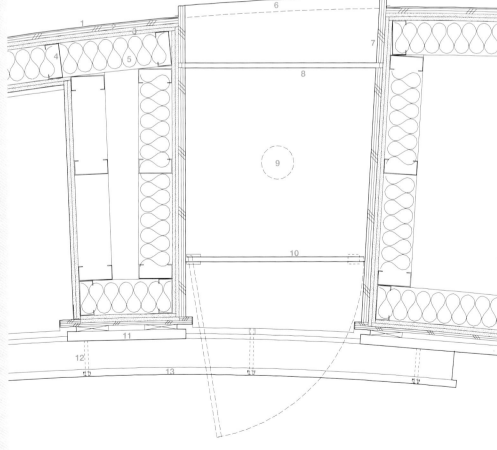

City of Melbourne / DesignInc

**CH2, Melbourne City Council House
Melbourne, Victoria, Australia**

Client
The City of Melbourne

Project Team
Rob Adams, Mick Pearce, Chris
Thorne, Stephen Webb, Jean-Claude
Bertoni, Chris Thorne

Main Contractor
Hansen Yuncken

The City of Melbourne aims to achieve zero emissions for the municipality by 2020. To this end, CH2 was designed to provide a working example for the local development market. The brief required a building that relied on passive energy systems while producing a premium grade building. Emissions are 64 per cent less than a five-star building, and when compared with the building that previously housed the council, is expected to reduce electricity consumption by 85 per cent, gas emissions by 87 per cent, reduce water mains supply by 72 per cent and produce only 13 per cent of the emissions. As a result, CH2 is the first new commercial office building in Australia to meet and exceed the six star rating system administered by the Green Building Council of Australia.

The building provides 100 per cent fresh air to all occupants with one complete air change every half hour. It also includes innovative practices and materials such as recycled concrete, recycled timber, timber windows, sewer mining and co-generating using natural gas. Shower towers and phase change material have been employed to produce and store cold water for use by chilled ceilings and beams, while wind turbines are used to extract air during a 'night purge'. Solar hot water heating and photovoltaics take advantage of good solar access as a result of CH2's location within the 40 metre (130 feet) height limit of Melbourne's central business district. The design follows a model that promotes a more interactive role between the city and nature, acting more like an ecosystem. Addressing concerns about environmental impacts and the health of occupants, CH2 has shown how simple ideas can produce impressive results.

1 The intelligent facade features a computer controlled timber louvre screen to neutralize western sun ingress.
2 The vegetation on the facades forms a 'green' microclimate. Windows that progressively narrow higher up the building, facilitate supply and exhaust air ducts located on the outside of the building that progressively widen towards the top to supply fresh air into, and move stale air out of each floor. 'Shower Towers' – five tubes of durable lightweight fabric – operate on low humidity hot summer days when a water shower will induce air movement and cool fresh air that will be fed into the cooling systems of the ground floor retail areas.
3 Hot stale air rises naturally and is discharged via the yellow and red vertical chimneys which are capped by wind-driven exhaust turbines.
4 The double-height entrance foyer features a boat-like reception desk made from recycled timber.

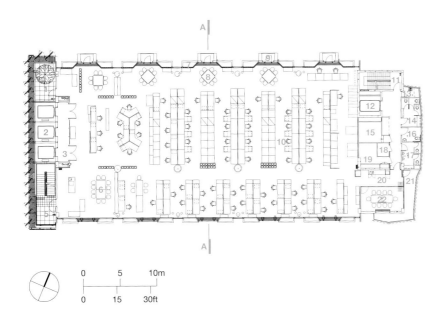

0   5   10m

0   15   30ft

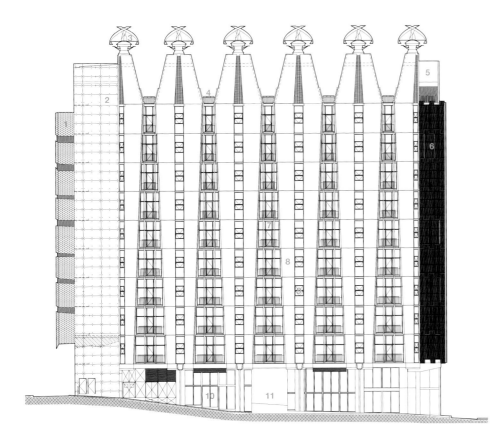

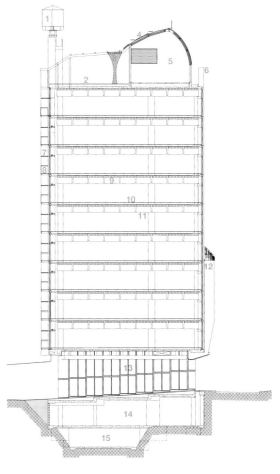

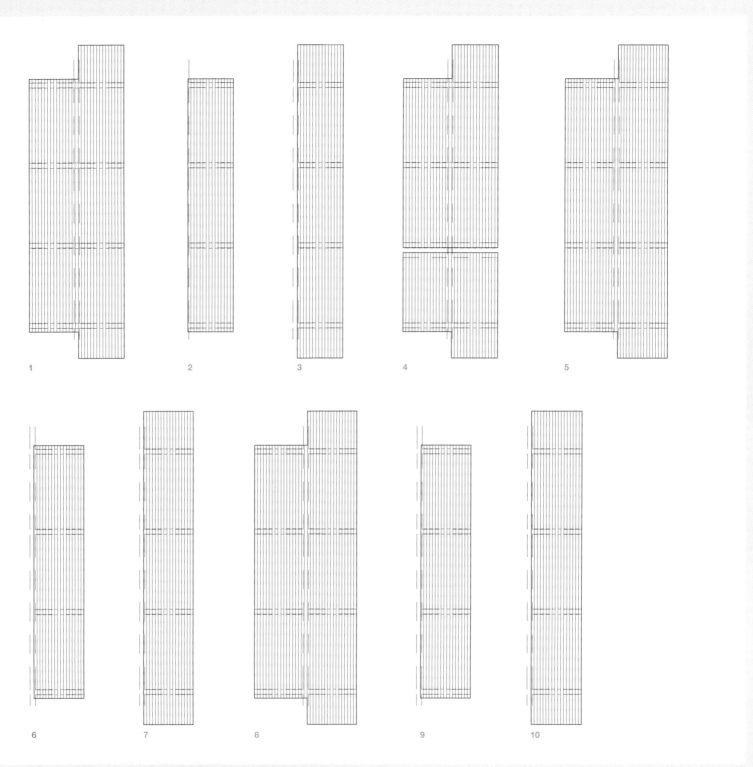

42.04
Timber Shutter
Schedule
1:50
 1 West elevation
pivotable timber
shutter, 1,294 mm (4
feet, 3 inches) wide by
4,150 mm (13 feet,
7 1/3 inches) high
 2 West elevation
fixed timber shutter,
625 mm (2 feet, 3/5
inches) wide by 3,350
mm (10 feet, 11 4/5
inches) high
 3 West elevation
fixed timber shutter,
625 mm (2 feet, 3/5
inches) wide by 4,150

mm (13 feet, 7 1/3
inches) high
 4 West elevation
timber shutter with
bottom section fixed
and top section
pivotable, 1,294 mm (4
feet, 3 inches) wide by
4,150 mm (13 feet,
7 1/3 inches) high
 5 North elevation
pivotable timber
shutter, 1,294 mm (4
feet, 3 inches) wide by
4,150 mm (13 feet,
7 1/3 inches) high
 6 North elevation
fixed timber shutter,
625 mm (2 feet, 3/5
inches) wide by 3,350

mm (10 feet, 11 4/5
inches) high
 7 South elevation
fixed timber shutter,
625 mm (2 feet, 3/5
inches) wide by 4,150
mm (13 feet, 7 1/3
inches) high
 8 South elevation
fixed timber shutter,
1,294 mm (4 feet, 3
inches) wide by 4,150
mm (13 feet, 7 1/3
inches) high
 9 South elevation
fixed timber shutter,
625 mm (2 feet, 3/5
inches) wide by 3,350
mm (10 feet, 11 4/5
inches) high

10 South elevation
fixed timber shutter,
625 mm (2 feet, 3/5
inches) wide by 4,150
mm (13 feet, 7 1/3
inches) high

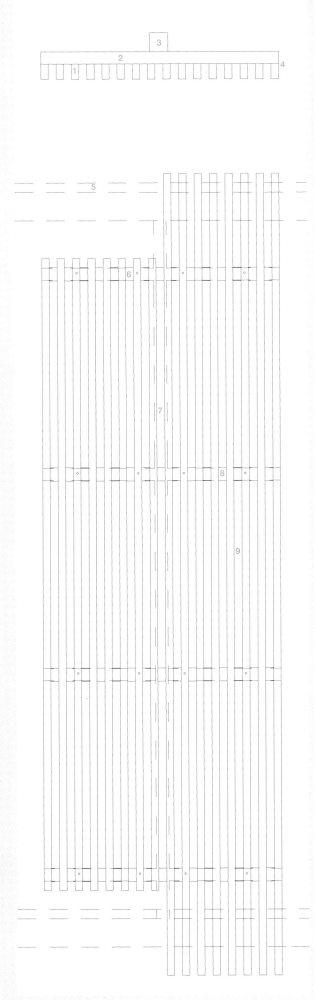

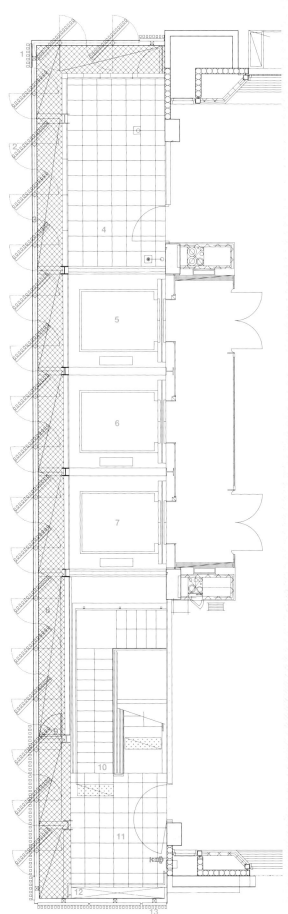

42.05
Timber Shutter Plan and Elevation Detail
1:20

1 80 x 40 mm (3^{1}/$_{8}$ x 1^{3}/$_{5}$ inch) recycled hardwood vertical timber battens

2 Through coach bolts between timber and back frame

3 100 x 100 mm (4 x 4 inch) square hollow section vertical pivot with thrust bearing and locator pin

4 Continuous punched rod through centre of timber battens with 70 mm (2^{3}/$_{4}$ inch) diameter timber 'doughnut' spacers and threaded rod ends for tightened recessed head bolts

5 200 mm (7^{9}/$_{10}$ inch) pre-formed concrete horizontal beam shown dotted for pivot support with 50 mm (2 inch) galvanized gangway flooring over

6 Continuous punched rod through centre of timber battens with 70 mm (2^{3}/$_{4}$ inch) diameter timber 'doughnut' spacers and threaded rod ends for tightened recessed head bolts

7 100 x 100 mm (4 x 4 inch) square hollow section vertical pivot with thrust bearing and locator pin, shown dotted

8 Continuous punched rod through centre of timber battens with 70 mm (2^{3}/$_{4}$ inch) diameter timber 'doughnut' spacers and threaded rod ends for tightened recessed head bolts

9 80 x 40 mm (3^{1}/$_{8}$ x 1^{3}/$_{5}$ inch) recycled hardwood vertical timber battens

42.06
Timber Screen Plan Detail
1:100

1 80 x 40 mm (3^{1}/$_{8}$ x 1^{3}/$_{5}$ inch) recycled hardwood vertical timber battens to fixed timber screen

2 80 x 40 mm (3^{1}/$_{8}$ x 1^{3}/$_{5}$ inch) recycled hardwood vertical timber battens to pivoting timber screen

3 Metal balustrade

4 Winter garden terrace

5 Elevator 3

6 Elevator 2

7 Elevator 1

8 Metal mesh walkway

9 Access gate

10 Fire stair

11 Summer terrace

12 Balustrade

13 80 x 40 mm (3^{1}/$_{8}$ x 1^{3}/$_{5}$ inch) recycled hardwood vertical timber battens to fixed timber screen

Hotel Remota en Patagonia
Magallanes, Patagonia, Chile

Client
Inmobiliaria Mares del Sur

Project Team
German del Sol, José Luis Ibañez,
Francisca Schuler, Carlos Venegas

Structural Engineer
Pedro Bartolomé

Main Contractor
Salfa Corp

This luxury hotel is located in a harshly
beautiful terrain of mountains, fjords,
glaciers and grassy plains near the
fishing village of Puerto Natales on the
edge of the Torres del Paine National
Park. The hotel is an elegant haven
offering visitors an opportunity to
experience the intensity of nature.
The inspiration for the design is the
region's farm buildings – barns (for
storing and drying sheepskins) along
with the shepherd's bothies, stables,
kennels and *estancias* that dot the
landscape. The new hotel appears as
a series of black barns. The concrete
structure of each is clad in insulated
plywood panels, finished with an
asphalt membrane and black gravel to
protect against the rain and wind.
    The hotel comprises guest wings
and a services building that includes
spaces for dining, entertainment and
administration. A small sauna and
pool block completes the composition.
Forming three sides of a rough square,
the main building and bedroom wings
enclose a large open courtyard. The
various parts are connected by
covered timber walkways, so guests
are exposed to the elements as they
move around the complex. The
principal wing, addressing the central
courtyard, contains generous lounge
areas and the entrance hall, while the
secondary wing, facing away from the
courtyard, is devoted to administration
and staff accommodation. The point
of intersection is marked by a
two-storey arrangement of dining
room, bar and kitchen at lower level,
with a conservatory, music room and
exhibition area above. The roof is
carpeted in Patagonian wild grasses,
and the rustic furniture was crafted by
local carpenters from large pieces
of dead lenga wood, the dark wood is
contrasting against native textiles.

1 The main building,
containing all of the
public functions
(foreground) is
connected at either
end to the bedroom
wings.
2 The hotel is
arranged around a
central courtyard that
opens onto the shore
of the lake.
3 Timber walkways
link the various parts of
the building, offering
guests an opportunity
to experience the
dramatic landscape as
they move about the
hotel.
4 Comfortable and
luxurious bedrooms
feature rough hewn
timber elements that
are contrasted with
smooth white plaster
walls and ceilings.
5 In the guest lounge,
an open grid of timber
with integrated lighting
creates a sculptural
ceiling.

43.01
Main Building Ground Floor Plan
1:500
1 Patio
2 Staff living room
3 Staff bathrooms and lockers
4 Staff bathrooms and lockers
5 Staff area access
6 Bathroom
7 Bathroom
8 Storage room
9 Bathroom
10 Ironing room
11 Linen store
12 Storage
13 Storage
14 Pantry

15 China store
16 Wine and liquor store
17 Reception store
18 Truck delivery access
19 Machinery room
20 Machinery room
21 Machinery room
22 Library storage

43.02
Main Building First Floor Plan
1:500
1 Offices
2 Offices
3 Offices
4 Offices
5 Offices
6 Offices
7 Offices
8 Bathroom
9 Bathroom
10 Staff dining room
11 Bakery
12 Dishwashing area
13 Kitchen
14 Storage
15 Storage
16 Dining room

17 Bar
18 Firewood store
19 Lounge area
20 Lounge area
21 Bathroom
22 Bathroom
23 Lounge area
24 Lounge area
25 Lounge area
26 Store
27 Hotel reception
28 Entrance lobby
29 Weather lobby
30 External entrance area

43.03
Section A–A
1:500
1 External stair access to second floor
2 Planted roof
3 Music room
4 Dining room
5 Pantry
6 Skylight
7 Fireplace
8 Lounge area
9 Dining room
10 Dining room
11 Storage room
12 Ironing room
13 Plywood panel facade

43.04
Section B–B
1:500
1 Vehicular access
2 Offices
3 Planted roof
4 Chimney
5 Staff dining room access
6 Staff dining room
7 Kitchen
8 Kitchen meeting room
9 Truck access to storage areas
10 Skylight
11 Dining room
12 Pantry

43.05
Section C–C
1:500
1 Plywood panel facade structure
2 Planted roof
3 Staff dining room
4 Library storage
5 Stair to staff dining room
6 Bathroom
7 Green roof skylight
8 Living room
9 Staff bathroom and lockers
10 Staff bathroom

43.06
Section D–D
1:500
1 Plywood panel facade structure
2 Chimney
3 Planted roof
4 Dining room
5 Washroom
6 Access to meeting room
7 Lounge area
8 Ramped access to meeting room
9 Staff bathroom and lockers
10 Lounge area
11 Chimney
12 Lounge area
13 Lounge area access
14 Weather lobby
15 Weather lobby
16 Vehicular access

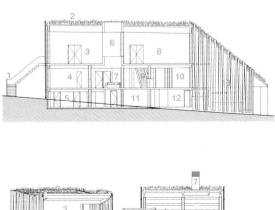

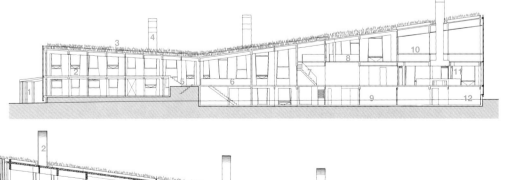

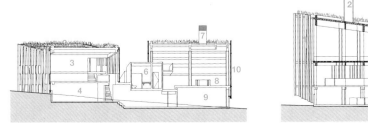

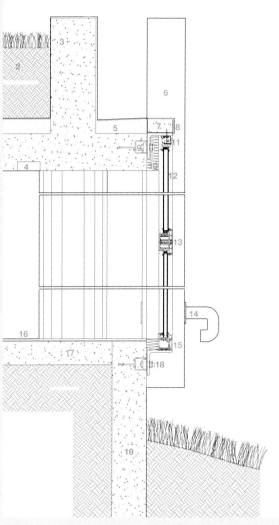

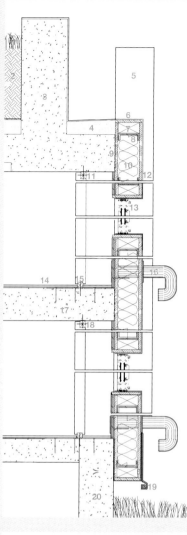

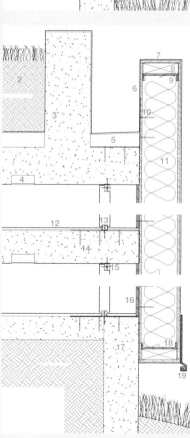

43.07
Bedroom Roof, Wall and Floor Detail 1
1:20
1 Local ovillo grass roof covering
2 Topsoil over synthetic asphalt membrane
3 Inverted reinforced concrete beam
4 Acoustic insulation
5 60 mm (2¹/3 inch) sloping cement screed
6 Timber facade panel beyond
7 Light concrete filling
8 U-shaped steel profile
9 Metal system anchoring window panel to concrete slab
10 Polyurethane foam insulation
11 PVC window frame
12 Double glazing with PVC film inner layer for ultra violet protection
13 PVC window frame
14 Ventilation duct
15 PVC window frame
16 Slate floor tiles
17 Reinforced concrete slab
18 100 x 100 mm (4 x 4 inch) profile for PVC frame
19 Reinforced concrete wall and footing with dry gunned synthetic asphalt membrane

43.08
Bedroom Roof, Wall and Floor Detail 2
1:20
1 Local ovillo grass roof covering
2 Topsoil over synthetic asphalt membrane
3 Acoustic insulation
4 Inverted reinforced concrete beam
5 60 mm (2¹/3 inch) sloping cement screed
6 Elastomeric waterproofing surface treatment
7 Brushed and polished timber beam
8 Stainless steel profile
9 Elastomeric waterproofing surface treatment, mineral asphalt membrane and 12 mm (¹/2 inch) oriented strand board panel
10 Foamed polyurethane insulation
11 Screw fixing between panel and steel plate
12 12 mm (¹/2 inch) oriented strand board
13 Ventilation duct
14 Slate floor tiles
15 Reinforced concrete slab
16 L-shaped steel plates for fixing external plates to concrete slab

17 Stainless steel profile
18 Galvanized aluminium drip moulding

43.09
Bedroom Roof, Wall and Floor Detail 3
1:20
1 Local ovillo grass roof covering
2 Topsoil over synthetic asphalt membrane
3 Inverted reinforced concrete beam
4 60 mm (2¹/3 inch) sloping cement screed
5 Timber facade panel beyond
6 Elastomeric waterproofing surface treatment, mineral asphalt membrane and 12 mm (¹/2 inch) oriented strand board panel
7 Brushed and polished timber beam
8 Stainless steel profile
9 Expanded polyurethane foam applied between slab and oriented strand board panel
10 Foamed polyurethane insulation
11 Timber fixings for vertical timber panels
12 Elastomeric waterproofing surface

treatment surface treatment, mineral asphalt membrane and 12 mm (¹/2 inch) oriented strand board panel
13 PVC window frame
14 Slate floor tiles
15 L-shaped steel plates for fixing external panels to slab
16 Ventilation duct
17 Reinforced concrete slab
18 Timber fixings for vertical timber panels
19 Galvanized aluminium drip moulding
20 Reinforced concrete wall and footing with dry gunned synthetic asphalt membrane

43.10
Bedroom Roof, Wall and Floor Detail 4
1:20
1 Local ovillo grass roof covering
2 Topsoil over synthetic asphalt membrane
3 Inverted reinforced concrete beam
4 60 mm (2¹/3 inch) sloping cement screed
5 Timber facade panel beyond
6 Elastomeric waterproofing surface treatment, mineral asphalt membrane and

12 mm (¹/2 inch) oriented strand board panel
7 Elastomeric waterproofing surface treatment, mineral asphalt membrane and 12 mm (¹/2 inch) oriented strand board panel
8 Brushed and polished timber beam
9 Stainless steel profile
10 Screw fixing between panel and steel plate
11 Foamed polyurethane insulation
12 Slate floor tiles
13 Timber fixings for vertical timber panels
14 Reinforced concrete slab
15 Timber fixings for vertical timber panels
16 Screw fixing between panel and steel plate
17 Reinforced concrete slab
18 Stainless steel profile
19 Galvanized aluminium drip moulding

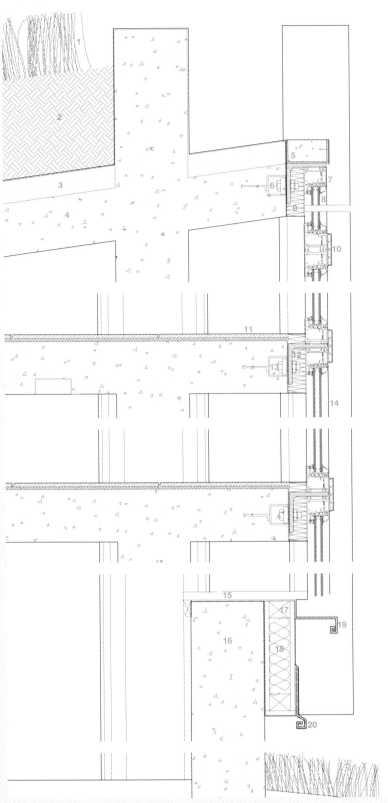

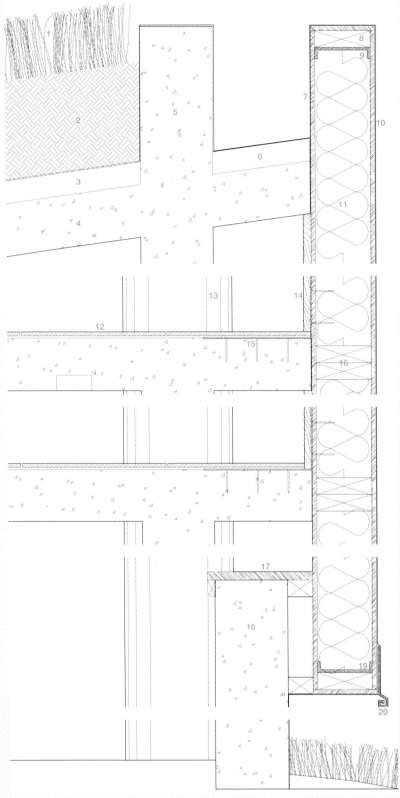

43.11
Main Building Roof,
Wall and Floor
Detail 1
1:12.5
1 Local ovillo grass
roof covering
2 Topsoil over
synthetic asphalt
membrane
3 60 mm (2¹/3 inch)
sloping cement screed
4 Reinforced
concrete roof slab
5 Metalcom stainless
steel U-profile with
lightweight concrete
filling
6 Expansion screws
anchoring windows to

reinforced concrete
slab
7 PVC window frame
8 Double glazing with
PVB film interlayer for
UV protection
9 Insulation
10 PVC window frame
11 Slate floor tiles over
flooring screed on
reinforced concrete
slab
12 Steel angle
13 Expansion screws
anchoring windows to
reinforced concrete
slab
14 Double glazing with
PVB film interlayer for
UV protection

15 Oriented strand
board
16 Concrete wall and
footing with dry
gunned synthetic
asphalt membrane
17 Timber framing to
support lower wall
panel
18 Insulation
19 Galvanized
aluminium drip
moulding
20 Galvanized
aluminium drip
moulding

43.12
Main Building Roof,
Wall and Floor
Detail 2
1:12.5
1 Local ovillo grass
roof covering
2 Topsoil over
synthetic asphalt
membrane
3 60 mm (2¹/3 inch)
sloping cement screed
4 Reinforced
concrete roof slab
5 Inverted reinforced
concrete beam
6 60 mm (2¹/3 inch)
sloping cement screed
7 Expanded
polyurethane foam

applied between
concrete upstand and
oriented strand board
cladding
8 Brushed and
polished timber beam
9 Metalcom stainless
steel profile
10 Exterior wall from
protective membrane
with elastomeric
waterproofing surface
treatment, mineral
asphalt membrane,
foamed polyurethane
insulation, oriented
strand board and
gypsum board panel
with white pained
plasterboard finish

11 Protective
membrane with
elastomeric
waterproofing surface
treatment, mineral
asphalt membrane and
foamed polyurethane
insulation
12 Slate floor tiles over
flooring screed on
reinforced concrete
slab
13 Circular reinforced
concrete column
14 Oriented strand
board and gypsum
board panel with white
painted plaster finish
15 L-shaped steel
plates for fixing

external panels to
concrete upstand
16 Double timber
bearer at floor level
17 Oriented strand
board
18 Reinforced
concrete wall and
footing with dry
gunned synthetic
asphalt membrane
19 Metalcom stainless
steel profile
20 Galvanized
aluminium drip
moulding

**Centennial Park Amenities
Sydney, New South Wales, Australia**

Client
The Centennial Park and Moore
Park Trust

Project Team
Andrew Nimmo, Annabel Lahz,
Andrew Lamond, Peter Titmuss

Structural Engineer
D.W. Knox + Partners

Main Contractor
Les Moore Projects

The brief for this project was to create
a generic amenities building which
could be built throughout the park
with minimal adaptation. The design
strategy involved creating a linear
building which could adhere to
existing pathway systems or act as a
backdrop to the landscape beyond.
The male and female programme was
divided into two pavilions linked by a
roof. The space between the pavilions
acts as a central entry point to the
toilets. The washbasins are also
located in this communal space with a
view out over the park.

The form of the building is driven by
a masonry section of honed pre-cast
concrete wall panels protecting and
housing the cisterns and plumbing,
juxtaposed with a lightweight steel
and glass structure that introduces an
abundance of natural light and fresh
air. A timber and weathered steel
screen is then added to both protect
the glass and provide an iconic
element that signals the structures as
public amenities. The majority of the
building components were fabricated
off-site, allowing for finer tolerances
and rapid on-site assembly. Building
within Sydney's historic Centennial
Park was very sensitive, thus it was
critical that the design deferred to the
primacy of the landscape as well as
the existing monuments and pavilions
within the park. In response to these
issues the design strategy establishes
a hierarchy of spatial relationships by
creating a distinction between
pavilions and monuments which sit as
objects within the Victorian landscape
and other ancillary structures such as
the amenities buildings.

1 The central entrance
area features a single
communal washbasin
where users enjoy
views over the park.
The timber screen
(right) signals the
entrance point.

2 The verticality of the
timber screen acts as a
juxtaposition to the
predominantly
horizontal elements of
the zinc roof, the
boxed out ceiling and
the wash basins.

3 The vertical
elements of timber
used to form the
screen – each one
consisting of a square
section sandwiched
between two flat
weathering steel

sections – are
connected using
circular hollow
sections, which in turn
are attached to the
building using steel
plate fins.

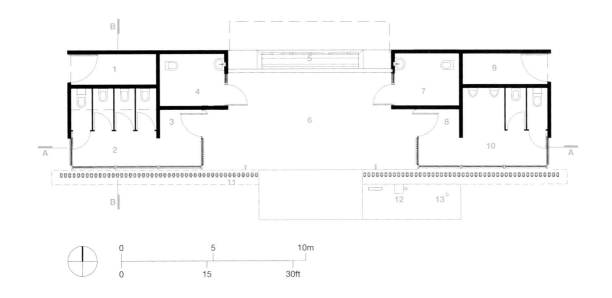

44.01
Floor Plan
1:200
1 Service store
2 Female WC
3 Female WC
 entrance
4 Disabled WC and
 parents' room
5 Washbasins
6 Breezeway
7 Disabled WC and
 parents' room
8 Male WC entrance
9 Service store
10 Male WC
11 Timber screen
12 Dog bowl and post
13 Bicycle parking

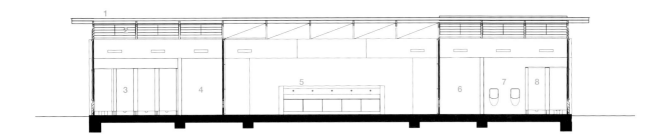

44.02
Section A–A
1:200
1 Zinc roof
2 High level louvres
3 Female WC
4 Female WC
 entrance
5 Washbasins
6 Entrance to Male
 WC
7 Male urinals
8 Male WC

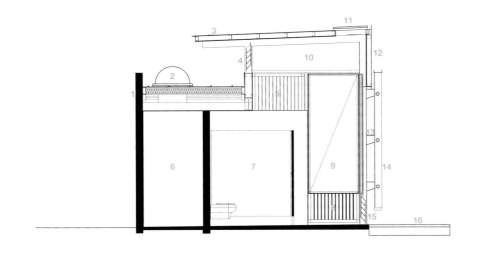

44.03
Section B–B
1:100
1 Pre-cast concrete
 wall panels
2 Polycarbonate
 dome skylight
3 Zinc roof
4 High-level steel
 ventilation louvres
5 Steel flat grille
6 Service store
7 WC
8 Steel flat grille to
 protect glass
 screens
9 Translucent
 laminated glass
 privacy screen
10 Open
11 Skylight
12 Zinc panel
13 Steel plate
 connectors
14 Timber screen
15 Low-level steel
 ventilation louvres
16 Concrete
 entrance path

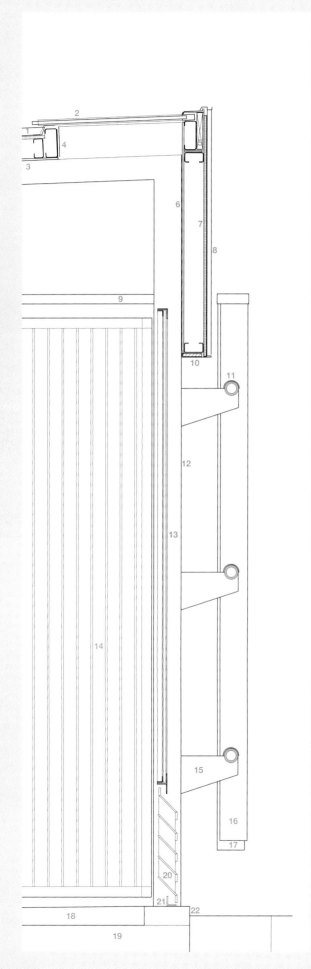

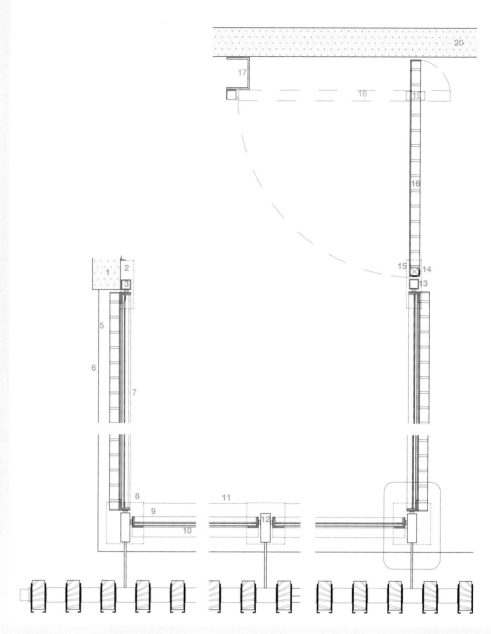

44.04
Detail Section Through Screen, Glazing and Fascia 1:20
1 Zinc roof sheeting on plywood substrate and C-purlins
2 Toughened glass and extruded aluminium frame skylight assembly
3 Set and painted fibre cement lining
4 Set and painted fibre cement lining to skylight shaft
5 Timber packing for wall sheeting
6 Set and painted fibre cement ceiling lining
7 Plywood substrate for zinc cladding
8 Zinc sheeting
9 50 mm (2 inch) square hollow section door head beam
10 Folded zinc capping to bottom edge of fibre cement lining

11 76 mm (3 inch) half circular hollow section capping over screen join
12 150 x 150 mm (6 x 6 inch) hot dipped galvanized rectangular hollow section portal frame with paint finish
13 Glazing panel 'A' screw fixed at 450 mm (17³/4 inch) centres along vertical edges to rectangular hollow section posts
14 Glazing panel 'B' screw fixed at 450 mm (17³/4 inch) centres along vertical edges to square hollow section and rectangular hollow section posts with steel protection grille from vertical steel flats
15 Steel support bracket for screen out of profiled 12 mm (1/2 inch) thick steel sheet
16 3 mm (1/10 inch) thick weathering steel sandwiched over timber

17 150 x 70 mm (6 x 2³/4 inch) Australian hardwood fins
18 Reinforced concrete topping laid to fall at 1:100
19 Reinforced concrete slab
20 Low-level louvre panel screw fixed at ends to rectangular hollow section posts below glazing panel
21 50 mm (2 inch) aluminium angle on bed of mastic and anchored to reinforced concrete upstand
22 100 mm (4 inch) high concrete upstand formed over structural slab as a level edge at finished floor level

44.05
Screen Glazing Detail 1:20
1 150 mm (6 inch) precast concrete wall panel with honed finish
2 Base plate for post under concrete

topping
3 Square hollow section post with base plate bolted to structural slab below and shop welded to square hollow section head beam over
4 Mastic bead between square hollow section and pre-cast panel
5 Edge of upstand set back 30 mm (1¹/5 inch) from edge of reinforced concrete slab
6 Edge of reinforced concrete slab under
7 Translucent glazing panel screw fixed at 450 mm (17³/4 inch) centres
8 Base plate for post under concrete topping
9 Glazing panel screw fixed along vertical edges at 450 mm (17³/4 inch) centres
10 Louvre panel screw

fixed at its ends to rectangular hollow section posts below glazing panel
11 100 mm (4 inch) high concrete upstand formed over structural slab as a level edge at finished floor level
12 Rectangular hollow section portal frame
13 Square hollow section post with slot and strike plate with corresponding slot for bolt
14 Deadlock mounted in end of grille door
15 Base plate for post under topping
16 Fabricated steel grille door
17 200 mm (7⁹/10 inch) high steel channel anchored to pre-cast concrete panel
18 Door in open position shown dotted
19 Floor pivot bearing anchored to floor
20 Honed concrete panel

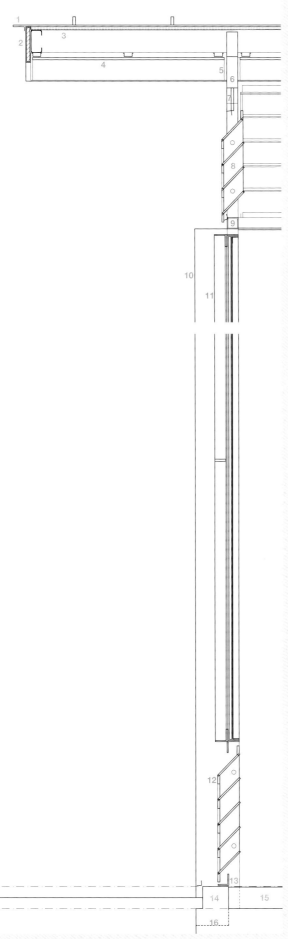

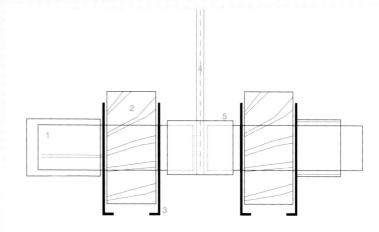

44.06
Glass Louvre Detail
1:20
1 Galvanized capping to end of circular hollow section
2 Zinc barge capping folded over 18 mm (7/10 inch) waterproof plywood
3 150 x 70 mm (6 x 2³/4 inch) timber
4 Set and painted soffit lining on furring channels
5 Set and painted fibre cement soffit lining to form shadow line at back edge of barge and rectangular hollow section roof structure
6 Rectangular hollow section portal frame and cleat plates for purlins
7 10 mm (2/5 inch) fillet plate welded to centre line of rectangular hollow section
8 Louvre panel from 10 mm (2/5 inch) steel plate bolted to rectangular hollow section steel posts at each end
9 Square hollow section head beam fully welded to rectangular hollow section posts
10 Line of 150 mm (6 inch) pre-cast concrete wall panel
11 Glazing panel screw fixed along vertical edges via frame to square hollow section and rectangular hollow section posts at 450 mm (17³/4 inch) centres
12 Louvre panel screw fixed along vertical edges to square hollow section and rectangular hollow section posts at 450 mm (17³/4 inch) centres. Inside of panel edge to align with inside face of square hollow section post
13 50 mm (2 inch) angle on a bed of mastic and anchored to reinforced concrete upstand
14 100 mm (4 inch) high concrete upstand formed over structural slab as a level edge for reinforced concrete topping
15 Reinforced concrete topping laid to fall at 1:100
16 Reinforced concrete slab

44.07
Timber Fin Plan Detail
1:5
1 Horizontal screen rails from 60 mm (2¹/3 inch) galvanized circular hollow sections
2 Screen blades from 70 x 150 mm (2³/4 x 6 inch) dressed hardwood

3 3 mm (1/10 inch) pre-weathered steel plate
4 Steel fin plate
5 Half round 76 mm (3 inch) circular hollow section as cap epoxy glued over join

44.08
Blade Assembly Detail Plan
1:2
1 150 x 70 mm (6 x 2³/4 inch) hardwood blade
2 Cap outline above from 3 mm (1/10 inch) weathering steel with preparation and finish to match sandwich plates
3 Stainless steel countersunk screws
4 Three 65 mm (2¹/2 inch) diameter holes at 975 mm (38¹/3 inch) centres for circular hollow section rail
5 3 mm (1/10 inch) folded weathering steel sandwiching plates fixed to hardwood blades at 325 mm (12⁴/5 inch) vertical and 80 mm (3¹/8 inch) horizontal centres with stainless steel countersunk screws, with the steel drilled, pressed and pre-weathered prior to screw fixing

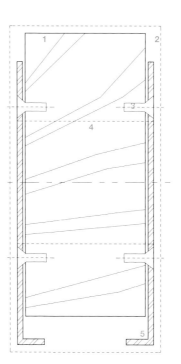

**Hugo Boss Industries Building
Coldrerio, Switzerland**

Client
Hugo Boss Industries

Project Team
Florian Köhler, Michael Catoir, Bruno
Franchi, Julia Leinfelder

Structural Engineer
Merz Kaufmann Partner

Main Contractor
Berlinger Holzbau

This building rises in the middle of
the Swiss countryside, its shell
structure of intertwined timber
elements covering a transparent
structure of glass and steel.
Transparency and lightness are the
essential ingredients of the formal
language of this building. The bent
timber lattice screen is designed to
express the weft and warp of the
textiles that are the core business of
Hugo Boss, as well as protecting the
construction from bad weather and
solar ingress. The structure is
comprised of steel, timber and
concrete with the maximum possible
use of prefabricated elements, which
allowed speed and precision during
the construction process. This
construction system made it possible
to achieve large spans as well as a
flexible division of interior spaces.

The roof is constructed using a
translucent membrane which is
composed as a sandwich structure of
EFTE (ethylene tetrafluoroethylene, a
fluorocarbon-based polymer) and
textile, in order to make the most of
the natural light inside the building.
The facade is comprised of three
layers. An external layer of a timber
diamond construction acts as a shell
structure for protection against the
weather. The middle layer consists of
a balcony that wraps around the
building, allowing occupants to enjoy
the landscape. The third internal layer
is a glass curtain wall. The five-storey
building is arranged with two
basement levels with parking, which
are followed by public spaces and
offices on the ground floor. On the first
and second floors are the main office
spaces, which are distributed around
a luminous central atrium.

1 The project fulfils the
highest standards of
comfort, thanks to
highly developed
integrated
management systems,
without neglecting the
importance of
architectural
aesthetics, which is
apparent in the timber
lattice facade screen.
2 Detail view of the
timber lattice screen
which encircles the
upper two storeys of
the three levels that are
above ground.
3 Behind the timber
screen, steel balconies
with steel mesh floors
wrap around the
building.
4 View of the staff
restaurant on the
ground floor. Robustly
detailed timber is used
extensively for furniture
and joinery items
throughout the
building, along with
custom-designed
fabrics and leather for
the loose furniture.

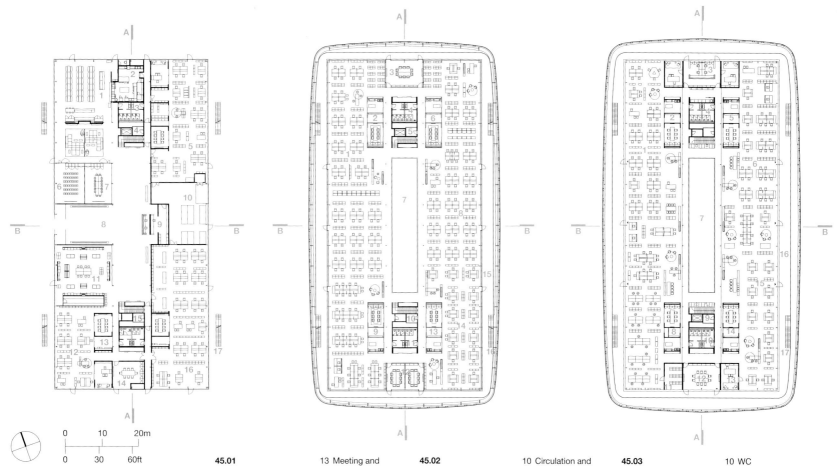

45.01
Ground Floor Plan
1:1000
 1 Staff restaurant
 2 Kitchen
 3 WC
 4 Circulation and
   storage
 5 Open-plan offices
 6 Audio-visual room
 7 Conference room
 8 Entrance
 9 Reception
 10 File store
 11 Library
 12 Open-plan offices
 13 Meeting and
   ancillary spaces
 14 Meeting room
 15 Circulation and
   storage
 16 Open-plan offices
 17 Escape stair

45.02
First Floor Plan
1:1000
 1 Open-plan offices
 2 Meeting and
   ancillary spaces
 3 Conference room
 4 WC
 5 Circulation and
   storage
 6 Meeting and
   ancillary spaces
 7 Atrium
 8 Open-plan offices
 9 Meeting and
   ancillary spaces
 10 Circulation and
   storage
 11 WC
 12 Meeting rooms
 13 Meeting and
   ancillary spaces
 14 Open-plan offices
 15 Balcony
 16 Escape stair

45.03
Second Floor Plan
1:1000
 1 Open-plan offices
 2 Meeting and
   ancillary spaces
 3 Private offices
 4 WC
 5 Meeting and
   ancillary spaces
 6 Open-plan offices
 7 Atrium
 8 Meeting and
   ancillary spaces
 9 Circulation and
   storage
 10 WC
 11 Archive
 12 Conference room
 13 Private office
 14 Meeting and
   ancillary spaces
 15 Open-plan offices
 16 Balcony
 17 Escape stair

45.04
Section A–A
1:1000
 1 Timber screen
 2 Balcony
 3 Private offices
 4 WC
 5 Circulation and
   storage
 6 Atrium
 7 Circulation and
   storage
 8 WC
 9 Conference room
 10 Balcony
 11 Timber screen
 12 Conference room
 13 WC
 14 Circulation and
   storage
 15 Circulation and
   storage
 16 WC
 17 Meeting rooms
 18 Kitchen
 19 Circulation and
   storage
 20 Entrance lobby
   and reception
 21 Circulation and
   storage
 22 Meeting room
 23 Basement level 1
 24 Basement level 2

45.05
Section B–B
1:1000
 1 Timber screen
 2 Balcony
 3 Open-plan offices
 4 Atrium
 5 Open-plan offices
 6 Balcony
 7 Timber screen
 8 Open-plan offices
 9 Open-plan offices
 10 Entrance lobby
 11 Reception
 12 File store
 13 Basement level 1
 14 Basement level 2

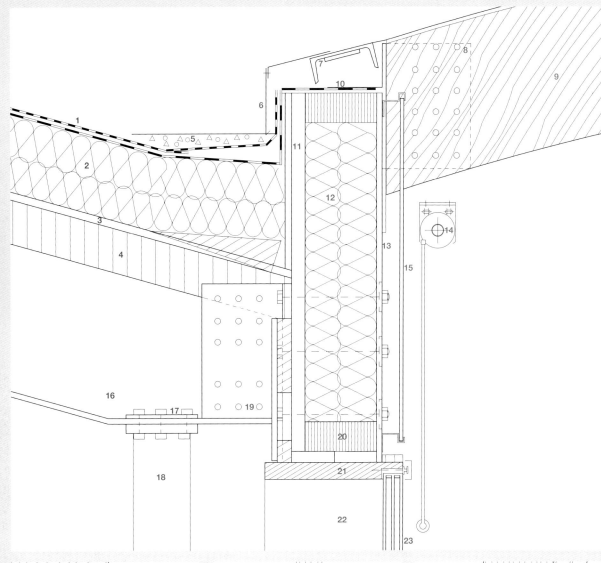

45.06
Roof, Timber Screen and Glazing Detail
1:10
1 Double layer of bitumen
2 200 mm (7⁹/10 inch) rockwool insulation
3 18 mm (7/10 inch) PVC
4 115 mm (4¹/2 inch) thick laminated timber structure
5 Gravel coating to roof drainage system
6 Aluminium sheet flashing
7 Steel channel
8 Perforated connection plate shown dotted
9 140 x 400 mm (5¹/2 x 15³/4 inch) primary structure
10 Waterproof membrane
11 Air cavity
12 200 mm (7⁹/10 inch) rockwool insulation
13 15 mm (3/5 inch) metal plate cladding
14 External shading system
15 8 mm (3/10 inch) glass spandrel panel over 50 mm (2 inch) shadow gap
16 Steel beam
17 Steel connection plate
18 159 mm (6¹/4 inch) circular steel column
19 Perforated connection plate
20 Timber bottom plate
21 Timber window head
22 Plasterboard window reveal
23 Triple glazing unit

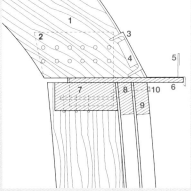

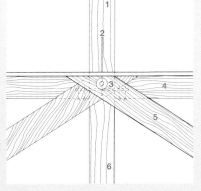

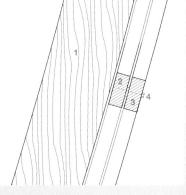

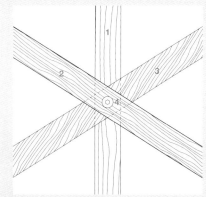

45.07
Timber Screen Upper Connection Section Detail
1:20
1 140 x 400 mm (5¹/2 x 15³/4 inch) primary structure
2 Perforated connection plate
3 Steel channel
4 Steel stiffening plate
5 Metal drip profile
6 Steel plate connection
7 Pressure lock
8 60 x 140 mm (2¹/3 x 5¹/2 inch) impregnated larch timber to screen
9 60 x 140 mm (2¹/3 x 5¹/2 inch) impregnated larch timber to screen
10 Bolted connection

45.08
Timber Screen Upper Connection Elevation Detail
1:20
1 140 x 400 mm (5¹/2 x 15³/4 inch) primary structure
2 Steel plate connection
3 Perforated connection plate
4 60 x 140 mm (2¹/3 x 5¹/2 inch) impregnated larch timber to screen
5 60 x 140 mm (2¹/3 x 5¹/2 inch) impregnated larch timber to screen
6 140 x 300 mm (5¹/2 x 11⁴/5 inch) impregnated larch timber to screen

45.09
Timber Screen Mid Connection Section Detail
1:20
1 140 x 300 mm (5¹/2 x 11⁴/5 inch) impregnated larch timber to screen
2 60 x 140 mm (2¹/3 x 5¹/2 inch) impregnated larch timber to screen
3 60 x 140 mm (2¹/3 x 5¹/2 inch) impregnated larch timber to screen
4 Bolted connection

45.10
Timber Screen Mid Connection Elevation Detail 1
1:20
1 140 x 300 mm (5¹/2 x 11⁴/5 inch) impregnated larch timber to screen
2 60 x 140 mm (2¹/3 x 5¹/2 inch) impregnated larch timber to screen
3 60 x 140 mm (2¹/3 x 5¹/2 inch) impregnated larch timber to screen
4 Bolted connection

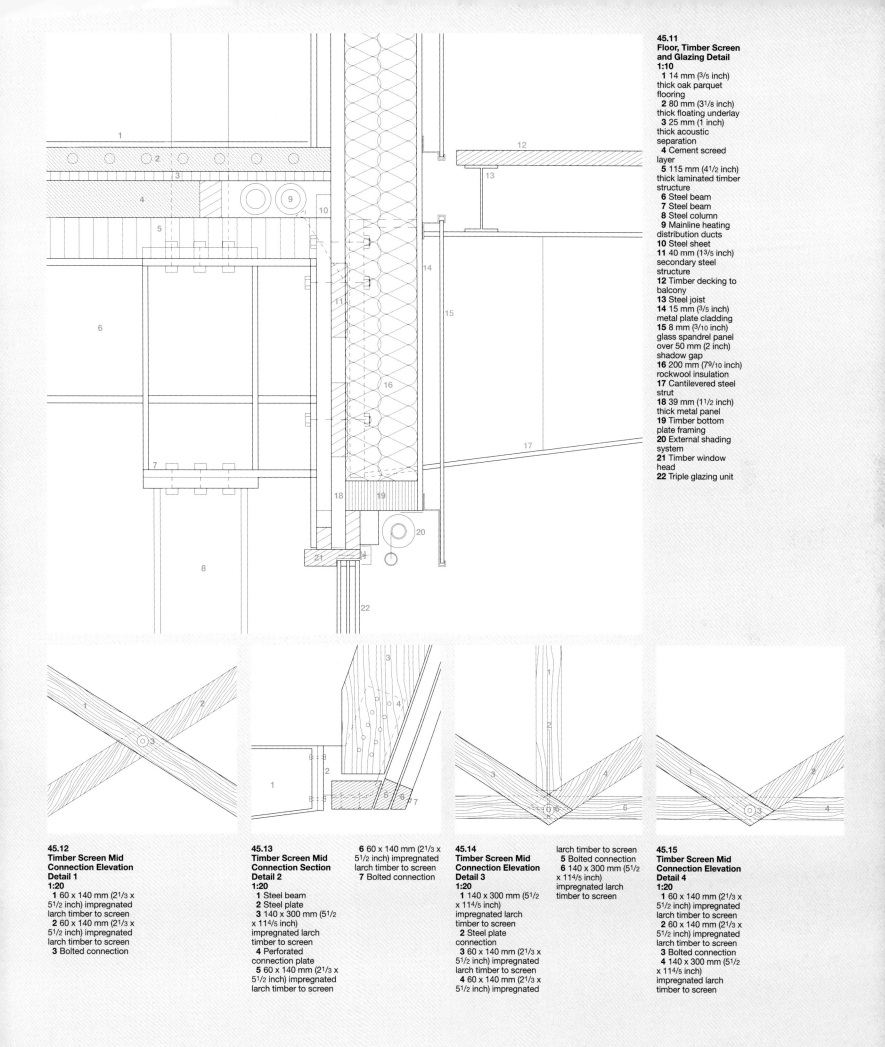

45.11
Floor, Timber Screen and Glazing Detail
1:10
1 14 mm (³/₅ inch) thick oak parquet flooring
2 80 mm (3¹/₈ inch) thick floating underlay
3 25 mm (1 inch) thick acoustic separation
4 Cement screed layer
5 115 mm (4¹/₂ inch) thick laminated timber structure
6 Steel beam
7 Steel beam
8 Steel column
9 Mainline heating distribution ducts
10 Steel sheet
11 40 mm (1³/₅ inch) secondary steel structure
12 Timber decking to balcony
13 Steel joist
14 15 mm (³/₅ inch) metal plate cladding
15 8 mm (³/₁₀ inch) glass spandrel panel over 50 mm (2 inch) shadow gap
16 200 mm (7⁹/₁₀ inch) rockwool insulation
17 Cantilevered steel strut
18 39 mm (1¹/₂ inch) thick metal panel
19 Timber bottom plate framing
20 External shading system
21 Timber window head
22 Triple glazing unit

45.12
Timber Screen Mid Connection Elevation Detail 1
1:20
1 60 x 140 mm (2¹/₃ x 5¹/₂ inch) impregnated larch timber to screen
2 60 x 140 mm (2¹/₃ x 5¹/₂ inch) impregnated larch timber to screen
3 Bolted connection

45.13
Timber Screen Mid Connection Section Detail 2
1:20
1 Steel beam
2 Steel plate
3 140 x 300 mm (5¹/₂ x 11⁴/₅ inch) impregnated larch timber to screen
4 Perforated connection plate
5 60 x 140 mm (2¹/₃ x 5¹/₂ inch) impregnated larch timber to screen
6 60 x 140 mm (2¹/₃ x 5¹/₂ inch) impregnated larch timber to screen
7 Bolted connection

45.14
Timber Screen Mid Connection Elevation Detail 3
1:20
1 140 x 300 mm (5¹/₂ x 11⁴/₅ inch) impregnated larch timber to screen
2 Steel plate connection
3 60 x 140 mm (2¹/₃ x 5¹/₂ inch) impregnated larch timber to screen
4 60 x 140 mm (2¹/₃ x 5¹/₂ inch) impregnated larch timber to screen
5 Bolted connection
6 140 x 300 mm (5¹/₂ x 11⁴/₅ inch) impregnated larch timber to screen

45.15
Timber Screen Mid Connection Elevation Detail 4
1:20
1 60 x 140 mm (2¹/₃ x 5¹/₂ inch) impregnated larch timber to screen
2 60 x 140 mm (2¹/₃ x 5¹/₂ inch) impregnated larch timber to screen
3 Bolted connection
4 140 x 300 mm (5¹/₂ x 11⁴/₅ inch) impregnated larch timber to screen

Castleford Bridge
Castleford, Yorkshire, England, UK

Client
City of Wakefield District Council

Project Team
Renato Benedetti, Jonathan
McDowell, Philip Schone, Roland
Karthaus

Structural Engineer
Alan Baxter and Associates

Civil and Hydrological Engineers
Arup

The new bridge in Castleford unites the north and south of Castleford's riverside, connecting Aire Street to Mill Lane. The 130-metre (426-foot) long S-shaped bridge curves in response to the mill, the weir and an old wrecked barge, giving users maximum experience of these landmarks and the lively flow of white water over the weir apron. Anchored by only three V-shaped supports, the deck structure appears to hover over the river. The streamlined timber deck is designed as a generous public space as well as a route, with the structure rising through the deck to create four curving benches on which to sit and enjoy the panoramic views.

Materials include untreated Cumaru timber for the bridge decking and handrail, stainless steel for the balustrades, tension cables, bench panels and a central grille in the timber deck to mark the midpoint of contra-flexure. The curved Cumaru timber boards have been sourced from sustainable forests in Brazil and were chosen for their durability. The decking boards run longitudinally along the bridge and over the benches (with anti-slip strips on the edge) and are fitted together by a unique concealed clamped-fixing system, tailor-made for the project. The system presents the maximum timber surface to walk on, while allowing the wood to expand, contract and weather naturally. Lighting is embedded under the Cumaru handrails, which run the length of the bridge. The bridge is a new focal point for the town and is the first phase of a riverscape masterplan which will act as a strong catalyst for future regeneration projects.

1 The three white bridge supports minimize visual impact and disruption of river flow. Twinned double steel columns branch off foundation caps in a V-formation, spreading the load at bridge level.
2 Lighting is embedded under the Cumaru handrails. Balustrade posts are curved to reduce climb-ability.

3 A series of stainless steel marker plates sit flush with the deck and rise up from the benches to create armrests that define personal space and also discourage any skateboarders from 'edge grinding'.

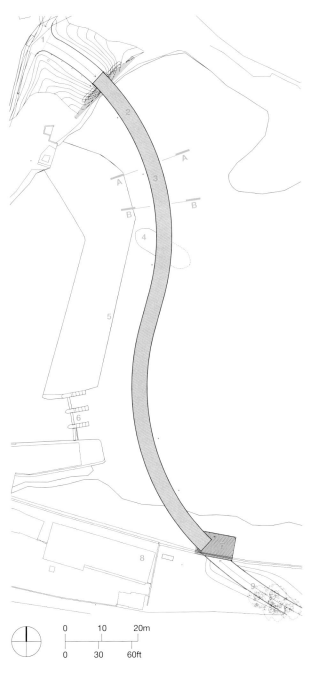

46.01
Site Plan
1:1000
1 Riverside path
2 Timber bridge
  decking with rising
  timber benches
3 Bridge deck
4 Barge wreck
5 Weir apron
6 Sluice gates
7 Boardwalk
8 Mill
9 Path from Aire
  Street

46.02
Partial Bridge Plan
1:200
1 Stainless steel
  marker
2 Access panel
3 Stainless steel
  armrest
4 Timber bench
5 Timber bridge
  deck
6 Standard
  balustrade post
7 Anchor balustrade
  post

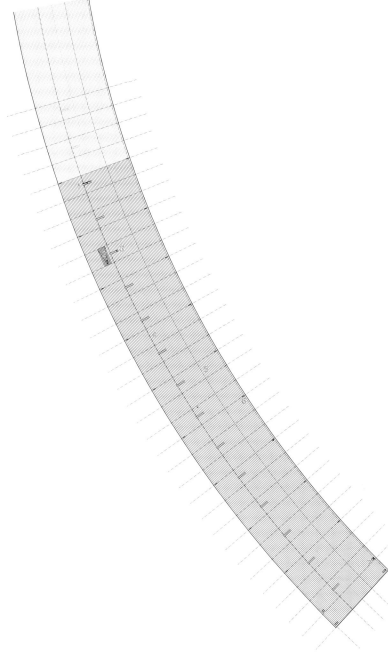

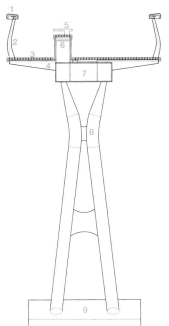

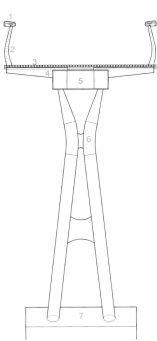

46.03
Cross Section A–A
1:100
1 Cumaru timber
  handrail
2 Stainless steel
  balustrade upright
3 Cumaru timber
  bridge deck
4 Stainless steel fin
  connectors
5 Stainless steel
  armrest
6 Cumaru timber
  bench
7 Steel box beam
8 Steel V supports
9 Concrete
  foundation

46.04
Cross Section B–B
1:100
1 Cumaru timber
  handrail
2 Stainless steel
  balustrade upright
3 Cumaru timber
  bridge deck
4 Stainless steel fin
  connectors
5 Steel box beam
6 Steel V supports
7 Concrete
  foundation

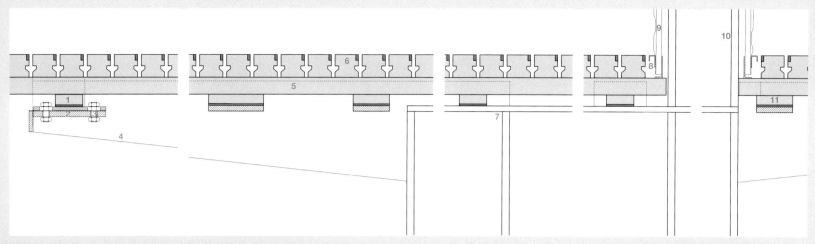

46.05
Bridge Deck
Connection Detail
1:10
 1 Timber spacer
 2 Connection plate
 3 Connection bolt
 4 Structural steel fin
 5 Timber bearer
screw fixed to decking
boards above
 6 60 mm ($2^1/_3$ inch)
deck board

 7 Composite steel
box beam
 8 Stainless steel trim
 9 Stainless steel
panelling
 10 Composite steel
box beam
 11 Timber spacer

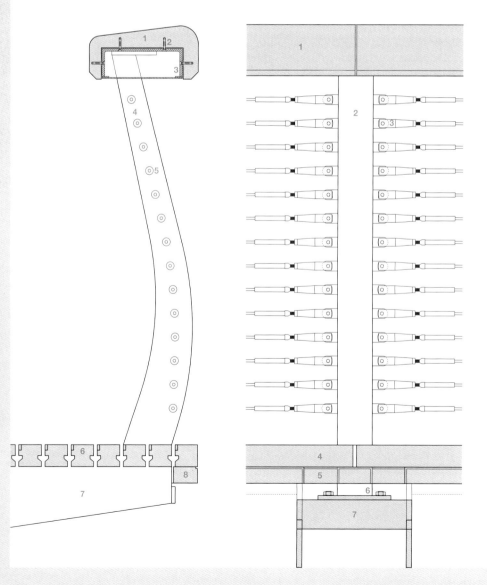

46.06
Balustrade Section
Detail
1:10
 1 300 x 150 mm
($11^4/_5$ x 6 inch)
handmade laminated
solid timber handrail
 2 Stainless steel
screw fixings
 3 Structural channel
 4 Standard stainless
steel balustrade post
 5 6 mm ($1/_4$ inch)
tensioned stainless
steel cables attached
to fork section
 6 60 mm ($2^1/_3$ inch)
deck board
 7 Structural steel fin
 8 Timber edge piece
screw fixed to decking
boards above

46.07
Balustrade Elevation
Detail
1:10
 1 300 x 150 mm
($11^4/_5$ x 6 inch)
handmade laminated
solid timber handrail
 2 Standard stainless
steel balustrade post
 3 6 mm ($1/_4$ inch)
tensioned stainless
steel cables attached
to swaged fork section
 4 60 mm ($2^1/_3$ inch)
deck board
 5 Timber edge piece
screw fixed to decking
boards above
 6 Connection bolt
 7 Connection plate
face

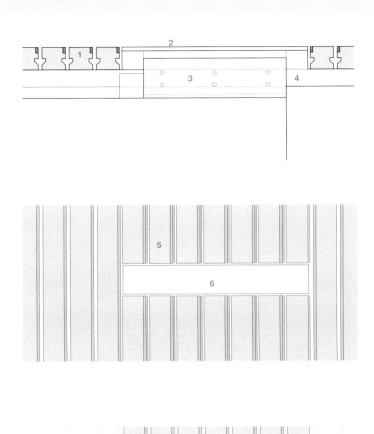

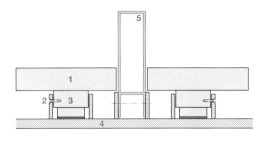

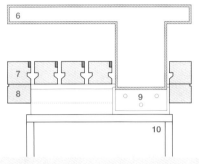

46.08
**Sections Through
Bench Showing
Marker Connection /
Marker Plan Detail /
Armrest Plan Detail
1:10**
1 60 mm (2^1/$_3$ inch)
deck board
2 Stainless steel
marker flush with deck
3 Steel flat welded to
main structure of
bridge for fixing of
stainless steel marker
4 Hardwood bearer
5 60 mm (2^1/$_3$ inch)
deck board
6 Stainless steel
marker flush with deck
7 60 mm (2^1/$_3$ inch)
deck board rising to
form bench
8 Stainless steel
armrest
9 Fixing post

46.09
**Section Details
Through Armrest
1:10**
1 60 mm (2^1/$_3$ inch)
bench deck board
2 Steel fixing lugs
3 Timber bearer
4 Composite steel
box beam (top part)
5 3 mm (^{1}/$_{10}$ inch)
stainless steel armrest
6 3 mm (^{1}/$_{10}$ inch)
stainless steel armrest
7 60 mm (2^1/$_3$ inch)
bench deck board
8 Timber edge piece
screw fixed to decking
boards above
9 Arm rest fixings
10 Composite steel
box beam

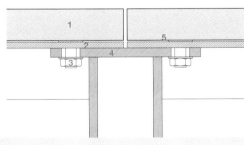

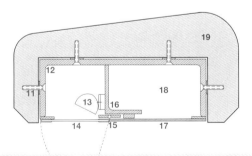

46.10
**Handrail Connection
to Anchor Balustrade
Post Detail / to
Standard Balustrade
Post / Through Light
and Access Panel
1:5**
1 300 x 150 mm
(11^4/$_5$ x 6 inch)
handmade laminated
solid timber handrail
2 Neoprene gasket
3 Bolt fixing
4 Wide balustrade
post
5 3 mm (^{1}/$_{10}$ inch)

thick nylon gasket
6 300 x 150 mm
(11^4/$_5$ x 6 inch)
handmade laminated
solid timber handrail
7 Neoprene gasket
8 Bolt fixing
9 Standard
balustrade post
10 3 mm (^{1}/$_{10}$ inch)
thick nylon gasket
11 Screw fixing
through 3 mm (^{1}/$_{10}$
inch) thick nylon
gasket
12 230 x 76 mm (9 x 3
inch) steel channel

13 LED lighting unit
14 Hinged, lockable
acrylic access panel
15 Hinge
16 Angle mounting for
lights
17 Stainless steel
cover panel
18 Cable space
19 300 x 150 mm
(11^4/$_5$ x 6 inch)
handmade laminated
solid timber handrail

Santa Caterina Market
Barcelona, Spain

Client
Foment de Ciutat Vella

Structural Engineer
Robert Brufau

Structural Engineer (Roof)
Jose Maria Velasco

Structural Engineer (Housing)
Miquel Llorens

The Santa Caterina Market, which dates from 1848, is located in the Ciutat Vella (old city) of Barcelona. A major refurbishment project involved the retention of three of the market's historic facades, the creation of a truck loading area, additional car parking spaces, an organic waste depository, and, most notably, a dramatic new roof canopy to unite all of the market facilities. The undulating laminated timber roof structure rests on large steel lattice girders that are supported on concrete portals. On three sides of the building the original archways with their more classic trusses were retained.

The geometry of the new arches combines straight segments with different lengths and radii of curvature. As a result, no two arches are the same, which made it impossible to use standard templates, moulds or presses to shape them. In addition, none of the arches are symmetrical – both in whole arches and in those divided into two halves, the left half is always different from the right half. The shape of some of the arches are extraordinarily complex, some having more than 10 or 12 different segments for the curvature, and the same number again for the unique transition points from some segments to others as well as the final cuts and central articulations. Ultimately, each arch is a unique timber sculpture. To build the arches, the architects used a solution based on the techniques of laminated wood, combined with building and computer-based procedures to solve the problems resulting from the huge variety of shapes and the complexity of their production. This involved using a computer-based calculation system to find the geometry and exact position of the more than 20,000 parts that form the immense puzzle of the structure.

1 The 5,500 square metre (1.36 acre) roof is clad in a spectacular arrangement of colourful tessellated tiles, making it just as sculptural from above as below.
2 A massive steel beam dissects the building, and it is from this that most of the lower market infrastructure is hung.
3 Inside, the ceiling's abundant laminated timber arches thrust upwards, reminiscent of upturned boats. Below the canopy, market stalls can be reconfigured as demand requires.

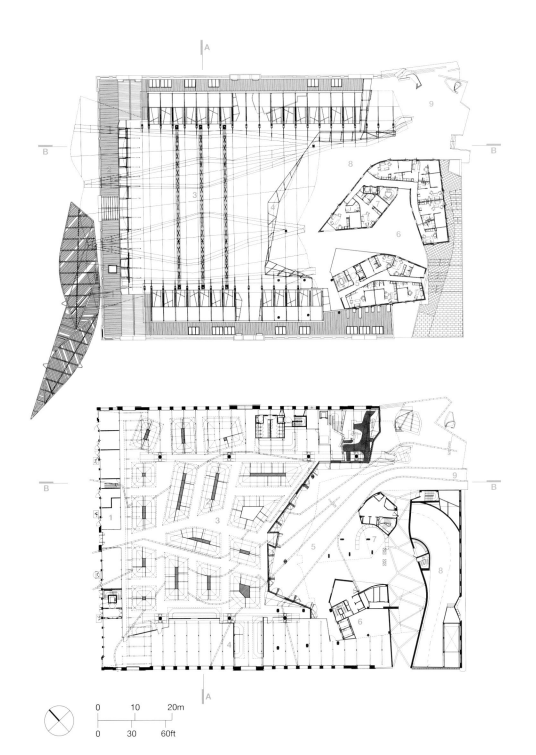

47.01
First Floor Plan
1:1000
1 Canopy
2 Mezzanine offices
3 Steel structure
4 South facade
5 Housing
6 Courtyard
7 Housing
8 Public space
9 Light well over
   existing ruins

47.02
Ground Floor Plan
1:1000
1 Retail unit
2 Food stalls
3 Interior public
   circulation
4 Restaurant
5 Public space
6 Supermarket
7 Public space
8 Market parking
   access
9 Public space

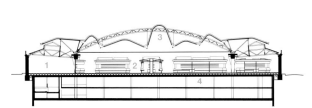

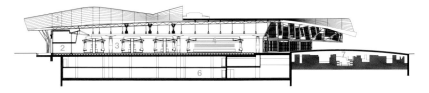

47.03
Section A–A
1:1000
1 Restaurant
2 Food stalls
3 Timber roof
   structure
4 Underground
   parking

47.04
Section B–B
1:1000
1 Roof
2 Retail unit
3 Food stalls
4 Roof to food stall
   area
5 South facade

6 Underground
   parking
7 Preserved
   archeological ruins

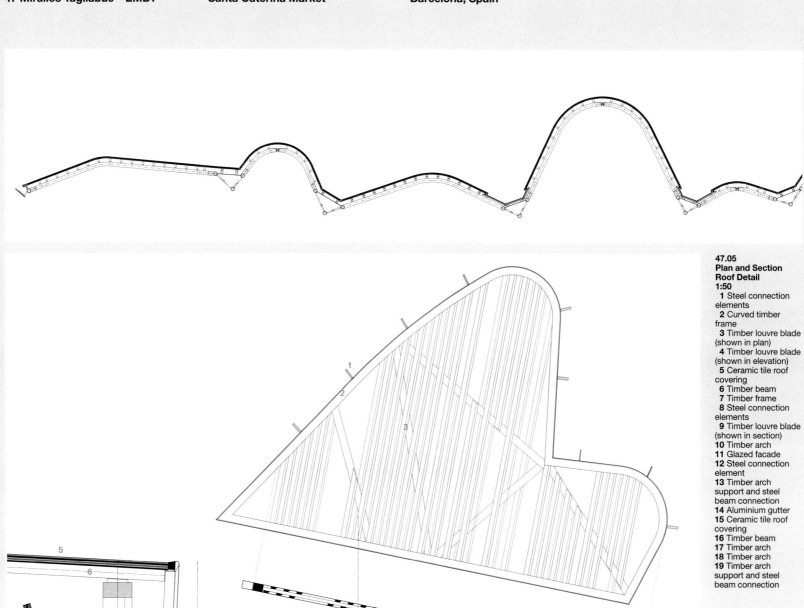

47.05
Plan and Section
Roof Detail
1:50
 1 Steel connection elements
 2 Curved timber frame
 3 Timber louvre blade (shown in plan)
 4 Timber louvre blade (shown in elevation)
 5 Ceramic tile roof covering
 6 Timber beam
 7 Timber frame
 8 Steel connection elements
 9 Timber louvre blade (shown in section)
 10 Timber arch
 11 Glazed facade
 12 Steel connection element
 13 Timber arch support and steel beam connection
 14 Aluminium gutter
 15 Ceramic tile roof covering
 16 Timber beam
 17 Timber arch
 18 Timber arch
 19 Timber arch support and steel beam connection

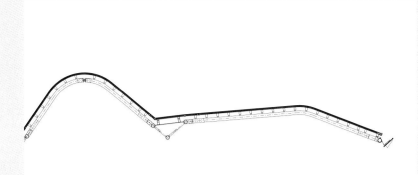

47.06
**North-East South
-West Section
Through Roof
1:200**
The curved shape of
the roof cover is
achieved by timber
arches. The timber is
structural, and its
cross-section is 200 x
400 mm ($7^9/_{10}$ x $15^3/_4$
inch) and acts as a flat
beam. The arches
differ in length and
shape and are
comprised, in general,
of two straight sides
and one curved part
above flat aprons and
one curved higher
part. The arches are
articulated at the base
to prevent transmitting
movement between
the timber parts and
the steel beams.

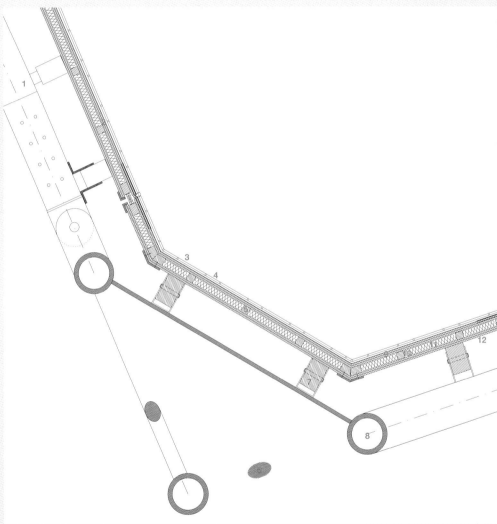

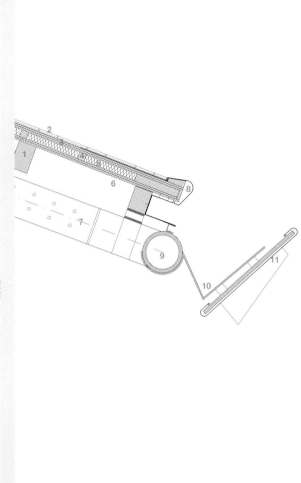

**47.07
Roof Detail 1
1:20**
1 Arch constructed
from individually
assembled 200 x 400
mm ($7^9/_{10}$ x $15^3/_4$ inch)
red spruce timber
boards
2 Perimeter
galvanized sheet metal
3 Ceramic tile pieces
grouted with one part
polymer modified
cement mortar
4 Ceramic tile pieces
fixed with Sicabond
5 Timber battens
6 Structural steel
tube structure
7 Timber beam
8 Structural steel

tube structure
9 70 x 10 mm ($2^3/_4$ x
$2/_5$ inch) double
dovetail crossed
panels
10 40 x 40 mm ($1^3/_5$ x
$1^3/_5$ inch) timber
battens at 300 mm
($11^4/_5$ inch) centres
11 Impermeable sheet
membrane and
insulation
12 10 mm ($2/_5$ inch)
thick tongue and
groove timber planks

**47.08
Roof Detail 2
1:20**
1 Timber beam
2 Ceramic tile pieces
grouted with one part
polymer modified
cement mortar
3 70 x 10 mm ($2^3/_4$ x
$2/_5$ inch) double
dovetail crossed
panels
4 40 x 40 mm ($1^3/_5$ x
$1^3/_5$ inch) timber
battens at 300 mm
($11^4/_5$ inch) centres
5 Impermeable sheet
membrane and
insulation
6 10 mm ($2/_5$ inch)
thick tongue and
groove timber planks

7 Arch constructed
from individually
assembled 200 x 400
mm ($7^9/_{10}$ x $15^3/_4$ inch)
red spruce timber
boards
8 Galvanized sheet
metal end capping
with grey metallic
oxidized paint
9 Structural steel
tube structure
10 Folded galvanized
sheet metal gutter
11 Galvanized sheet
metal-wrapped
plywood gutter
stiffener

**St Henry's Ecumenical Art Chapel
Turku, Finland**

Client
St Henry's Chapel Association

Project Team
Matti Sanaksenaho, Pirjo
Sanaksenaho, Sari Lehtonen, Enrico
Garbin, Teemu Kurkela, Juha
Jääskeläinen, Maria Isotupa, Jaana
Hellinen, Jari Mänttäri, Kain Tapper

Structural Engineer
Kalevi Narmala

Main Contractor
Hartela Oy

In the island landscape of Hirvensalo, forested hills rise from the flat fields. The chapel is aligned east–west on the top of one of the hills in order to focus on the landscape. Nearby existing buildings, which form part of a service centre for cancer patients, form a village from which the chapel rises. The copper surface of the chapel will become green over time and so the building will be in harmony with the colour of the surrounding trees. The form of the chapel expresses the intention to create a large landscape-sculpture and a small building. The path to the chapel travels up the hill to meet the entrance to the chapel through a small foyer. The foyer leads to the large hall, which metaphorically represents the belly of a fish, the fish being an important Christian symbol.

The gallery and the chapel are one space, with the gallery to the rear and the chapel at the front, with the altar at the termination of the axis. In the gallery the benches can be removed to accommodate art exhibitions. The interior is lined entirely in pine, creating a contrasting play of light and shadow that powerfully articulates the space. The exposed pine structural ribs are lit by spotlights, while indirect natural light enters from both ends of the chapel. The altar window includes an art work created by the Finnish artist Hannu Konola. The exhibition of art and religious ceremonies coexist within the same space, echoing the symbiosis of art and ceremony in Renaissance churches.

1 The copper-clad exterior is interrupted at the altar end of the chapel to include a panel of translucent glazing.
2 The entrance opens into a foyer, which leads to the gallery and chapel via a ramp. All of the facilities, including bathrooms and storage, are housed in timber-lined boxes on either side of the ramp.
3 Detail view of the timber ribbed structure. The spaces between the ribs are lined with pine boards.

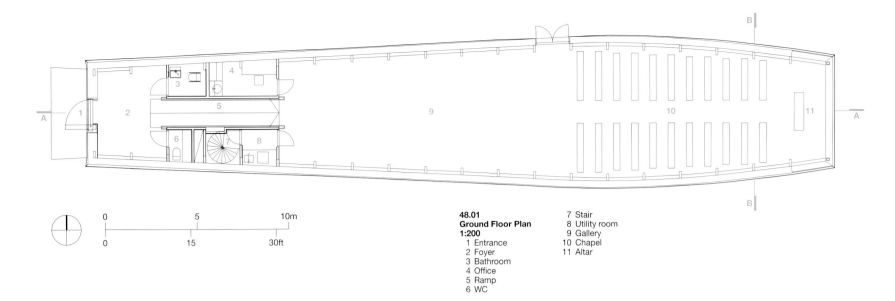

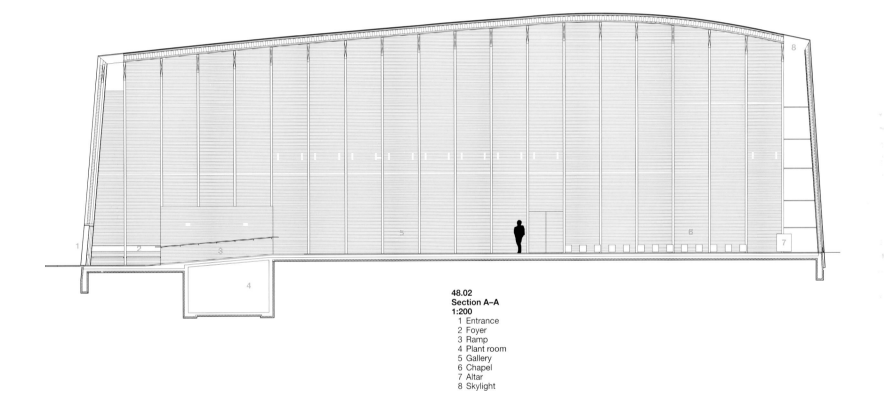

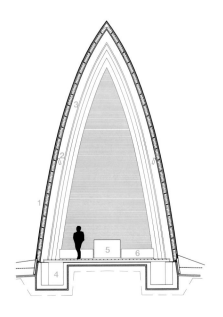

48.01
Ground Floor Plan
1:200
1 Entrance
2 Foyer
3 Bathroom
4 Office
5 Ramp
6 WC

7 Stair
8 Utility room
9 Gallery
10 Chapel
11 Altar

48.02
Section A–A
1:200
1 Entrance
2 Foyer
3 Ramp
4 Plant room
5 Gallery
6 Chapel
7 Altar
8 Skylight

48.03
Section B–B
1:200
1 Copper-clad
  exterior
2 Light fixtures
3 Exposed timber
  structure
4 Heating ducts
5 Altar
6 Timber bench

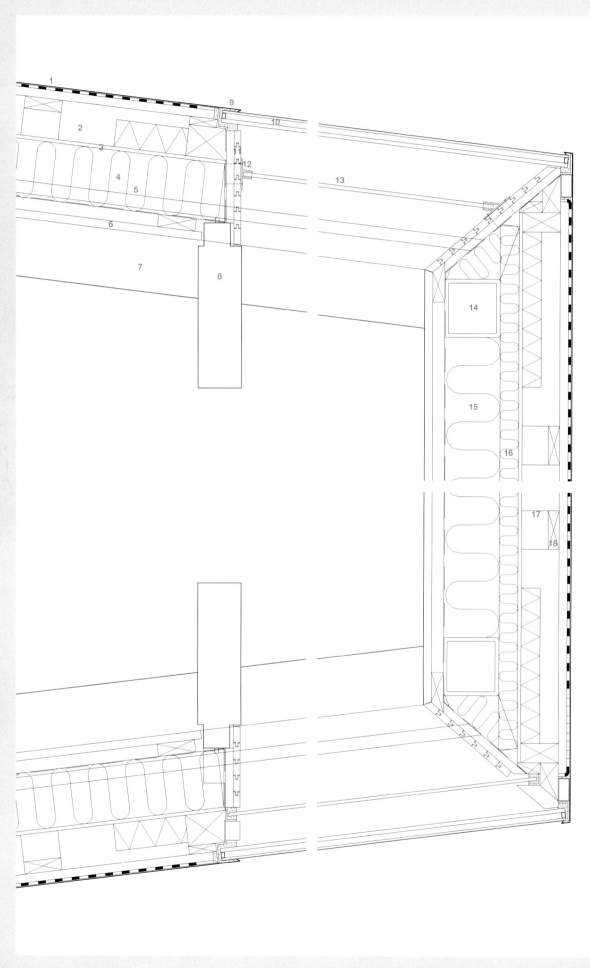

48.04
Chapel Window Plan Detail
1:10
 1 Copper sheet exterior cladding
 2 Ventilation cavity
 3 Bituminous waterproof layer
 4 Wool insulation
 5 Timber boarding
 6 Pine panelling to ceiling
 7 Floor level ventilation shaft
 8 Exposed timber structure
 9 Silicone joint
10 Fixed double-glazed window
11 Pine panelling to window reveal
12 Steel beading section
13 Fixed art glass
14 Steel rectangular hollow section structure
15 Wool insulation
16 Wool insulation
17 Timber structure
18 Timber panel

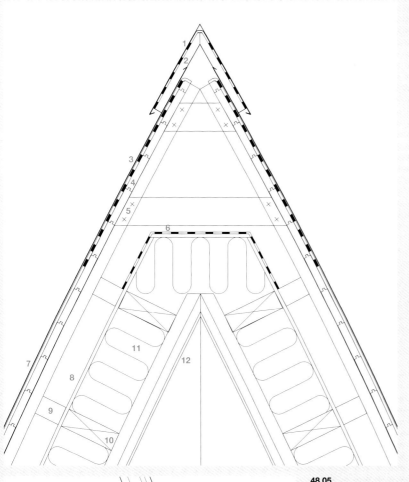

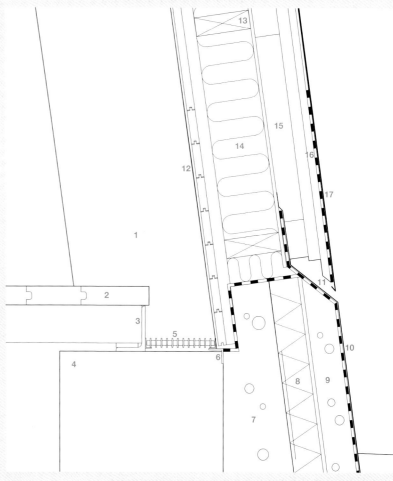

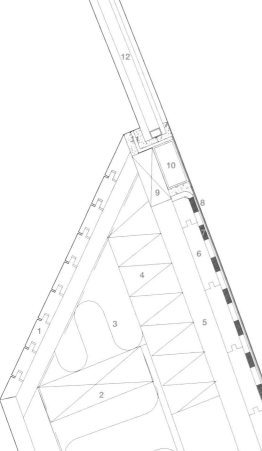

48.05
Roof Apex Detail
1:10
1 Copper sheet
exterior cladding
2 Ventilation shaft
3 Copper interior
lining
4 Pine panelling to
ceiling
5 Structural steel
plate
6 Bituminous
waterproof layer
7 Copper sheet
exterior cladding
8 Ventilation cavity
9 Timber framing
structure for exterior
cladding
10 Timber framing
structure
11 Wool insulation
12 Exposed timber
structure and pine
ceiling panelling

48.06
Floor / Wall Junction
Detail
1:10
1 Exposed timber rib
structure
2 Timber tongue and
groove flooring
3 Steel angle
4 Reinforced
concrete foundation
5 Copper grille
6 Steel angle
7 Reinforced
concrete foundations
8 Rigid insulation
9 Reinforced
concrete foundations
10 Copper sheet
exterior cladding
11 Air gap
12 Pine wall panelling
13 Timber framing
structure
14 Wool insulation
15 Ventilation cavity
16 Pine substrate for
copper cladding
17 Copper sheet
exterior cladding

48.07
Window Detail
1:5
1 Pine panelling to
interior
2 Timber framing
structure
3 Wool insulation
4 Wool insulation
5 Ventilation cavity
6 Pine substrate for
copper cladding
7 Bituminous
waterproof layer
8 Copper sheet
exterior cladding
9 Timber framing
structure
10 Steel rectangular
hollow section
11 Timber window
frame
12 Fixed double-
glazed window

**Federal Environmental Agency
Dessau, Germany**

Client
The Federal Republic of Germany

Project Team
Matthias Sauerbruch, Louisa Hutton,
Juan Lucas Young, Andrew Kiel

Structural Engineer
Krebs & Kiefer

Environmental Engineer
Zibell Willner and Partner

Site Supervision
Harms & Partner

Ecological requirements were an important consideration in the conception, planning and construction of the new office building for the Federal Environmental Agency (UBA) in Dessau. Standards for electrical and heat energy use are up to 50 per cent stricter than legally binding standards in Germany. These requirements formed an integral part of the brief. The Forum is a crescent-shaped space which draws the surrounding public park into the building and acts as a link between the public areas – such as the library, information centre and convention hall – and the offices themselves.

The interior and exterior facades of the building are organized into horizontal bands. On the outer facade, the spandrel areas are clad with larch planks, while transparent and coloured glass surfaces form a continuous strip in the window zone. The facade was prefabricated so that the cladding on the spandrel areas, the main structure itself and the window frames are constructed entirely from timber. This is the first time that a combination of high-tech, computer-assisted prefabrication with timber (traditionally a low-tech material) has been utilized on such a scale. Strategies of intelligent engineering and renewable energies play a central role in planning efforts. The offices have natural ventilation, when outside conditions are comfortable. In summer, night ventilation of the offices, together with the storage mass of ceilings and walls, exploit the day–night temperature difference to cool the working areas.

1 The interior and exterior facades of the Snake are organized into horizontal bands. On the outer facade, the spandrel areas are clad with larch wood planking, while transparent and coloured glass surfaces form a continuous strip in the window zone.
2 In the atrium, the timber spandrel areas between the window strips are sound absorbing, to improve the acoustic properties of this area.
3 and **4** Sixty per cent of the inner facade is glazed with transparent glass. The atrium roof is provided with solar protection, so the windows of the internal facade needed glare protection only. This takes the form of louvre blinds.

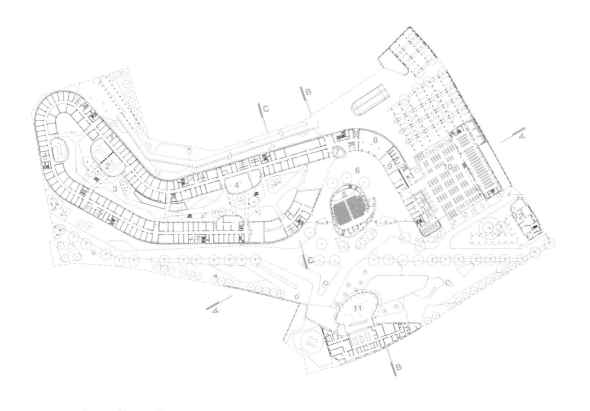

49.01
Ground Floor Plan
1:2000
1 Offices
2 Centralized
 depository
3 Atrium
4 Copy centre
5 Auditorium
6 Forum
7 Reception
8 Exhibition space
9 Information centre
10 Library
11 Cafeteria
12 Wörlitzer station

49.02
Section A–A
1:2000
1 Offices
2 Parking garage
3 Atrium
4 Glass roof
5 Bridge links
6 Forum
7 Library

49.03
Section B–B
1:2000
1 Cafeteria
2 Public park
3 Heat exchange
 system
4 Forum
5 Auditorium
6 Offices
7 Glass roof

49.04
Section C–C
1:2000
1 Public park
2 Heat exchange
 system
3 Air handling unit
4 Offices
5 Glass roof

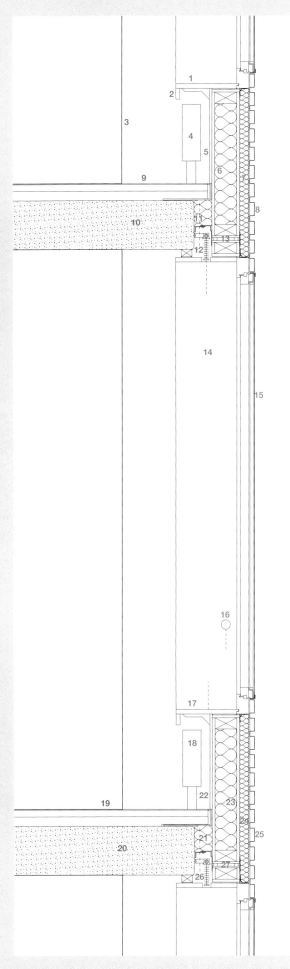

49.05
Typical Interior
Facade Section
Detail
1:20
1 Internal window sill
and reveal from larch
veneered timber board
2 Window sill
downstand from larch
veneered timber board
3 Cased concrete
column beyond
4 Radiator
5 Painted gypsum
board lining mounted
onto 16 mm (3/5 inch)
laminated chipboard
substructure
6 120 mm (43/4 inch)
cellulose fibre
insulation
7 50 mm (2 inch)
melamine resin
insulation
8 Larch cladding with
fire protection coating
on all sides
9 Linoleum flooring
10 Reinforced
concrete floor slab
11 Insulation
12 25 mm (1 inch)
manually operated
blinds for glare
protection
13 Separation joint
between facade
elements
14 Larch window
reveal
15 Casement window
from larch-veneered
timber frame with
double-glazing
colour strip inside,
colour enamelled
screen print outside
integrated opening
limiter
16 Stainless steel tube
guard rail
17 Internal window sill
and reveal from
larch-veneered timber
board
18 Radiator
19 Linoleum flooring
20 Reinforced
concrete floor slab
21 Insulation
22 Painted gypsum
board lining mounted
onto 16 mm (3/5 inch)
laminated chipboard
substructure
23 120 mm (43/4 inch)
cellulose fibre
insulation
24 50 mm (2 inch)
melamine resin
insulation
25 Larch cladding with
fire protection coating
on all sides
26 25 mm (1 inch)
manually operated
blinds for glare
protection
27 Separation joint
between facade
elements

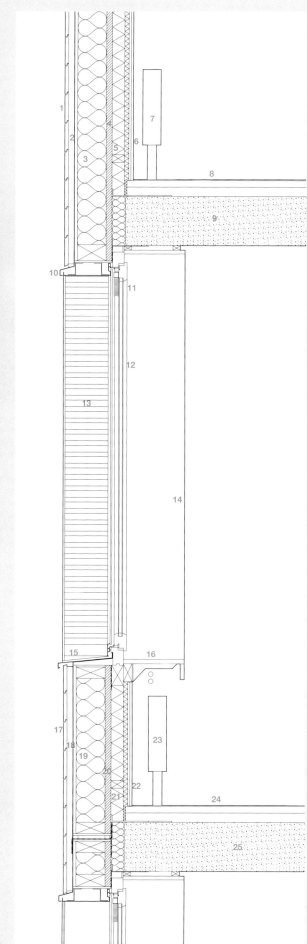

49.06
Typical Exterior
Facade Section
Detail
1:20
1 Spandrel panel
from larch cladding
with fire protection
coating on inner side
2 40 mm (13/5 inch)
ventilation gap and 15
mm (3/5 inch) gypsum
fibre board
3 160 mm (63/10 inch)
cellulose fibre
insulation
4 29 mm (11/10 inch)
fibre board
5 90 mm (31/2 inch)
cellulose fibre
insulation
6 25 mm (11/10 inch)
painted gypsum board
over 63 mm (21/2 inch)
timber substructure
with 27 mm (11/10 inch)
metal fixings
7 Radiator
8 Linoleum flooring
9 Reinforced
concrete floor slab
10 Tin-coated sheet
copper external
window sill
11 25 mm (1 inch)
manually operated
blinds for solar
protection with light
refraction feature
between casement
window and security
glazing
12 Larch-veneered
timber-framed double
window composed of
double-glazed
casement window
(internal) and single
leaf security glazing
(external)
13 Powder-coated
aluminium ventilation
grille with free section
allowing 70 per cent air
transmission
14 Larch-veneered
timber window reveal
15 Tin-coated copper
external window sill
16 Larch-veneered
timber board internal
window sill
17 Spandrel panel
from larch cladding
with fire protection
coating on inner side
over 40 mm (13/5 inch)
ventilation gap
18 15 mm (3/5 inch)
gypsum fibre board
19 160 mm (61/3 inch)
cellulose fibre
insulation
20 Laminated timber
frame
21 90 mm (31/2 inch)
cellulose fibre
insulation
22 25 mm (1 inch)
painted gypsum board
over 63 mm (21/2 inch)
timber substructure
with 27 mm (11/10 inch)
metal fixings
23 Radiator
24 Linoleum flooring
25 Reinforced
concrete floor slab

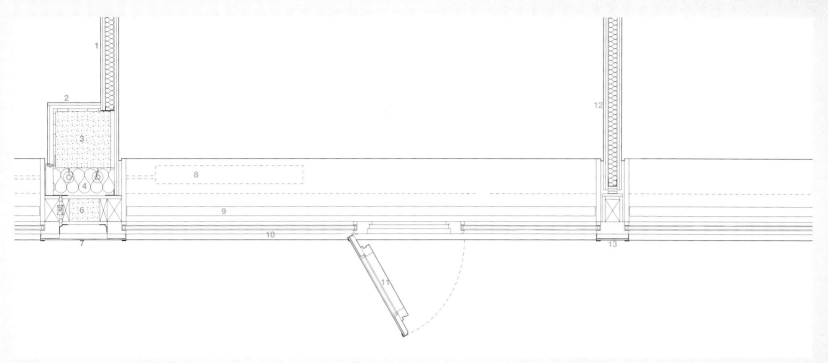

49.07
Typical Interior
Facade Plan Detail
1:20
  1 Insulated and
painted gypsum board
interior wall lining
  2 Painted gypsum
board lining mounted
onto 16 mm (^{2}/$_3$ inch)
laminated chipboard
substructure
  3 Reinforced
concrete column
  4 Insulation

  5 Separation joint
between facade
elements
  6 120 mm (4^3/$_4$ inch)
cellulose fibre
insulation
  7 Exterior skin from 8
mm (^{3}/$_{10}$ inch) single
sheet safety glazing
with colour screen
print on outer surface,
vertical substructure
and all round channel
fixing
  8 Radiator below sill

shown dotted
  9 Stainless steel tube
guard rail
  10 Larch-veneered
timber-framed
casement window
  11 Larch-veneered
timber-framed window
with double glazing
colour strip inside and
colour enamelled
screen print outside
with integrated
opening limiter
  12 Insulated and

painted gypsum board
interior wall lining
  13 Exterior skin from 8
mm (^{3}/$_{10}$ inch) single
sheet safety glazing
with colour screen
print on outer surface,
vertical substructure
and all round channel
fixing

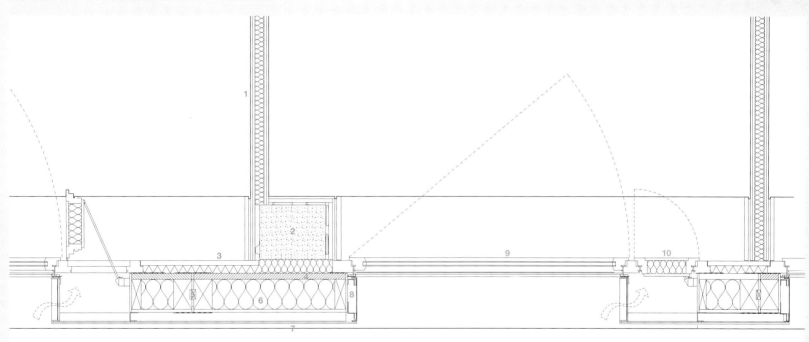

49.08
Typical Exterior
Facade Plan Detail
1:20
  1 Insulated and
painted gypsum board
interior wall lining
  2 Reinforced
concrete column
  3 Larch-veneered
timber board interior
wall lining
  4 29 mm (1^1/$_8$ inch)
fibre board
  5 Separation joint

between facade
elements
  6 160 mm (6^3/$_{10}$ inch)
cellulose fibre
insulation on 15 mm
(^{3}/$_5$ inch) gypsum fibre
board
  7 Coloured glass
facade panel from 10
mm (^{2}/$_5$ inch) single
sheet safety glazing,
colour enamelled on
reverse side, held in
place top and bottom
by aluminium

U-profiles over 52 mm
(2 inch) ventilation gap
  8 Powder-coated
steel plate window
reveal
  9 Larch-veneered
timber-framed double
window composed of
double-glazed
casement window
(internal) and single
leaf security glazing
(external)
  10 Automatically
operated ventilation

panel for night cooling
from 14 mm (^{3}/$_5$ inch)
timber-framed
larch-veneered panel
with moisture
protection and 70 mm
(2^3/$_4$ inch) cellulose
fibre insulation

**United States Census Bureau
Suitland, Maryland, USA**

Client
U.S. General Services Administration

Project Team
David Childs, Gary Haney, Stephen
Apking, Peter Magill, Elias Moubayed,
Nazila Shabestari-Duran, Anthony
Fieldman, Rod Garrett, Nestor
Santa-Cruz, Mark Igou, Elizabeth
Marr, Aybars Asci, Kim VanHolsbeke,
Nicholas Cotton, Donald Holt, Dale
Greenwald, Mary Broaddus, Catherine
Haley, Cynthia Mirbach

Structural Engineer
Skidmore, Owings & Merrill

Situated on a wooded site near
downtown Washington, D.C., the new
headquarters for the U.S. Census
Bureau exemplifies the very latest
thinking on architecture and the
corporate workplace. To minimize this
necessarily large building's presence,
the office programme is limited to
eight storeys and uses a variety of
architectural and sustainable design
strategies to reduce the impact on the
site. Two separate buildings grow from
one single mass, cleaved apart to
create a central garden that integrates
the building with its landscape. By
eroding the mass, and developing
materials to camouflage the edges of
the enclosure, SOM developed a
concept that breaks down the
enormous scale of this building,
blurring the boundaries between
building and landscape.

The curved office buildings have
two enclosures. The facade facing the
woods is covered in a brise soleil of
laminated timber elements that create
dappled patterns of shadow and
warm light inside the offices, allowing
the occupants to view the outside
while sheltered from the sun. The
marine-grade white oak is harvested
according to sustainable guidelines.
The facades facing the courtyard are
fully glazed to maximize daylight with
a veil of curving lines that echo the
timber sunshades. The designers
incorporated various sustainable
techniques, including water reclamation,
recycled building materials, minimal
energy consumption and use of
natural light, into the design.

1 The ground floor is
arranged as a series of
timber-clad elements
that read as
independent volumes
that house shared
facilities such as the
cafeteria and fitness
centre. Above these,
the office
accommodation with
its textured timber
brise soleil appears to
float above the anchor
of the shared facilities
while unifying the
various elements of the
programme.
2 Detail view of the
timber-clad facade.
3 Throughout the
interior, open
workspaces with low
partitions surround the
perimeter to allow for
natural light exposure
and easy
communication.

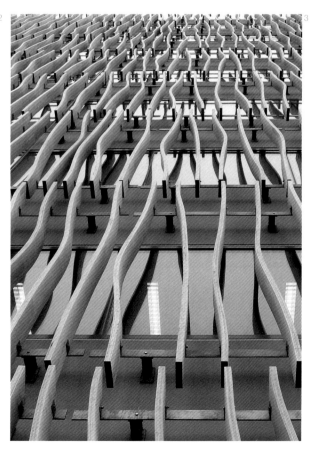

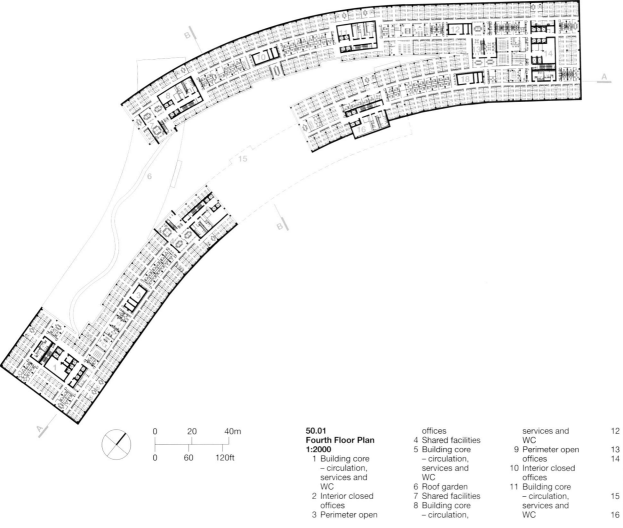

50.01
Fourth Floor Plan
1:2000
1 Building core
  – circulation,
  services and
  WC
2 Interior closed
  offices
3 Perimeter open

offices
4 Shared facilities
5 Building core
  – circulation,
  services and
  WC
6 Roof garden
7 Shared facilities
8 Building core
  – circulation,

services and
WC
9 Perimeter open
  offices
10 Interior closed
  offices
11 Building core
  – circulation,
  services and
  WC

12 Interior closed
  offices
13 Shared facilities
14 Building core
  – circulation,
  services and
  WC
15 Line of building
  over shown dotted
16 Building core

  – circulation,
  services and
  WC
17 Perimeter open
  offices
18 Interior closed
  offices

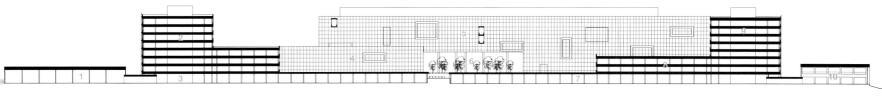

50.02
Section A–A
1:2000
1 Remote delivery
  facility
2 Offices
3 Cafeteria
4 Training centre
5 Bridge

6 Central courtyard
7 Fitness centre
8 Offices
9 Offices
10 Library

50.03
Section B–B
1:2000
1 Auditorium
2 Offices
3 Courtyard
4 Centre circulation
  spine
5 Offices

6 Underground
  parking
7 Parking pavilion

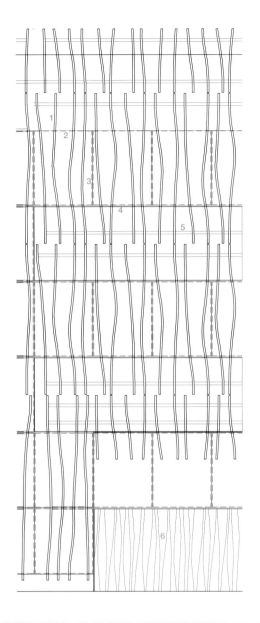

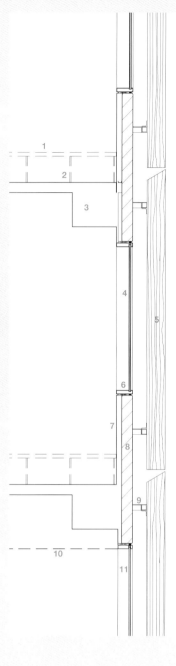

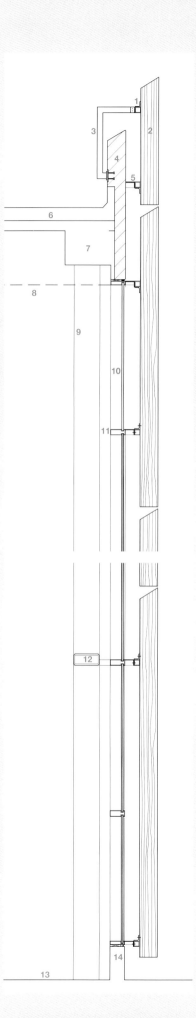

50.04
Timber Facade
Elevation Detail
1:100
 1 Laminated timber
blade to external
screen wall
 2 Insulated glass
 3 Mullion
 4 Pre-cast concrete
facade spandrel panel
 5 Stainless steel
panel frame
 6 Textured precast
concrete

50.05
Timber Facade
Section Detail
1:50
 1 Finished floor level
 2 Raised floor
structure
 3 Concrete perimeter
beam
 4 Insulated glass
facade
 5 Laminated timber
blade to external
screen wall
 6 Window mullion
 7 Plasterboard lining
to interior wall

 8 Pre-cast concrete
spandrel panel
 9 Stainless steel
panel frame
10 Line of suspended
ceiling shown dotted
11 Insulated glass
facade

50.06
Typical Wall Section
Detail
1:50
 1 Stainless steel
panel frame
 2 Laminated timber
blade to external
screen wall
 3 Stainless steel
panel frame
 4 Pre-cast concrete
facade element
 5 Stainless steel
panel frame
 6 Roof system
 7 Concrete perimeter
beam
 8 Line of suspended
ceiling shown dotted
 9 Concrete column
beyond
10 Insulated glass
facade

11 Window mullion
12 Steel rectangular
hollow section frame
13 Finished floor level
14 Wall base

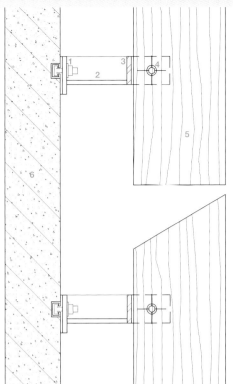

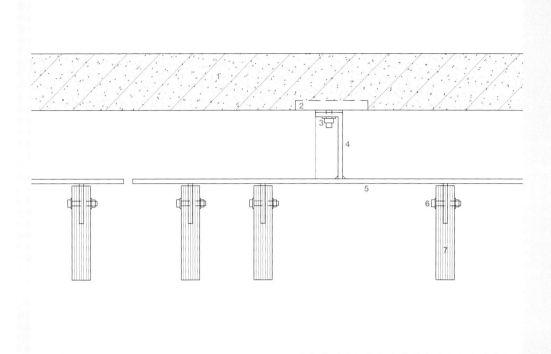

50.07
Exterior Wall Section Detail
1:10
  1 Cast-in anchor connection
  2 Stainless steel hanging clip
  3 Stainless steel panel frame
  4 Through bolt connection
  5 Laminated timber blade to external screen wall
  6 Pre-cast concrete facade spandrel panel

50.08
Exterior Wall Plan Detail
1:10
  1 Pre-cast concrete facade spandrel panel
  2 Cast-in anchor connection
  3 Bolt connection
  4 Stainless steel hanging clip
  5 Stainless steel panel frame
  6 Through bolt connection
  7 Laminated timber blade to external screen wall

50.09
Exterior Wall Axonometric Detail
Not to Scale
  1 Pre-cast concrete facade spandrel panel
  2 Laminated timber blade to external screen wall
  3 Through bolt connection
  4 Stainless steel tab
  5 Stainless steel panel frame
  6 Cast-in anchor connection
  7 Stainless steel hanging clip

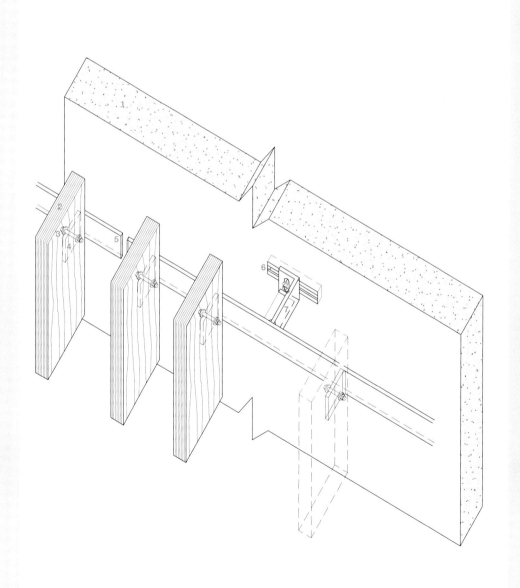

Directories
of Details and
Architects

Directory of Details

Balustrade Details

18.06 Jackson Clements Burrows
46.06 McDowell + Benedetti
46.07 McDowell + Benedetti

Bench Details

46.08 McDowell + Benedetti
46.09 McDowell + Benedetti

Bridge Details

28.04 Seth Stein Architects
28.05 Seth Stein Architects
28.06 Seth Stein Architects
39.04 Saunders Wilhelmsen
39.05 Saunders Wilhelmsen
39.06 Saunders Wilhelmsen
39.07 Saunders Wilhelmsen
46.05 McDowell + Benedetti
46.10 McDowell + Benedetti

Ceiling Details

36.05 Hopkins Architects

Cladding Details

20.06 Knox Bhavan Architects

Column Details

01.07 Bohlin Cywinski Jackson
01.08 Bohlin Cywinski Jackson
01.09 Bohlin Cywinski Jackson
01.10 Bohlin Cywinski Jackson
03.04 Francis-Jones Morehen Thorp
03.05 Francis-Jones Morehen Thorp
03.06 Francis-Jones Morehen Thorp
03.07 Francis-Jones Morehen Thorp
03.09 Francis-Jones Morehen Thorp
03.10 Francis-Jones Morehen Thorp
34.04 Frank Harmon Architects
36.08 Hopkins Architects
36.09 Hopkins Architects
44.07 Lahz Nimmo Architects
44.08 Lahz Nimmo Architects

Door Details

07.11 Hunters
16.05 Hudson Architects
21.04 Lake Flato Architects
26.06 Saia Barbarese Topouzanov
          Architectes
27.07 Boran Ekinci Architects
27.08 Boran Ekinci Architects
29.05 Stutchbury and Pape
29.06 Stutchbury and Pape
29.07 Stutchbury and Pape

Eaves Details

03.08 Francis-Jones Morehen Thorp
09.06 Lassila Hirvilammi Architects
16.04 Hudson Architects
25.05 Rooijakkers + Tomesen
          Architecten
31.07 Allies and Morrison

Facade Details

04.08 FORMA 6
04.09 FORMA 6
04.11 FORMA 6
04.12 FORMA 6
24.05 Ofis Arhitekti and Jelka
          Šolmajer
24.06 Ofis Arhitekti and Jelka
          Šolmajer
27.04 Boran Ekinci Architects
27.05 Boran Ekinci Architects
27.06 Boran Ekinci Architects
27.09 Boran Ekinci Architects
28.07 Seth Stein Architects
28.08 Seth Stein Architects
28.09 Seth Stein Architects
32.07 António Portugal & Manuel
          Reis, Architects
32.08 António Portugal & Manuel
          Reis, Architects
32.10 António Portugal & Manuel
          Reis, Architects
49.05 Sauerbruch Hutton
49.06 Sauerbruch Hutton
49.07 Sauerbruch Hutton
49.08 Sauerbruch Hutton
50.04 Skidmore, Owings & Merrill
50.05 Skidmore, Owings & Merrill

Floor Details

12.07 SHoP Architects
33.07 Cowper Griffith Architects
34.06 Frank Harmon Architects
48.06 Sanaksenaho Architects

Glazing Details

02.09 Dannatt, Johnson Architects
33.11 Cowper Griffith Architects
35.06 Glenn Howells Architects
35.08 Glenn Howells Architects
36.10 Hopkins Architects
38.04 McChesney Architects
44.05 Lahz Nimmo Architects
44.06 Lahz Nimmo Architects

Gutter Details

18.04 Jackson Clements Burrows
18.05 Jackson Clements Burrows
22.05 Localarchitecture
23.06 MACK Architects
33.06 Cowper Griffith Architects
33.09 Cowper Griffith Architects
38.08 McChesney Architects

Lighting Details

11.05 OBRA Architects
11.06 OBRA Architects
11.07 OBRA Architects
11.08 OBRA Architects

Louvre Details

20.05 Knox Bhavan Architects
33.10 Cowper Griffith Architects
33.12 Cowper Griffith Architects
33.13 Cowper Griffith Architects
36.07 Hopkins Architects

Pool Details

11.03 OBRA Architects
11.04 OBRA Architects

Roof Details

05.04 Gareth Hoskins Architects
05.05 Gareth Hoskins Architects
06.08 Hérault Arnod Architectes
06.09 Hérault Arnod Architectes
08.07 Jarmund/Vigsnæs AS
          Architects
09.04 Lassila Hirvilammi Architects
09.05 Lassila Hirvilammi Architects
12.05 SHoP Architects
14.07 Bercy Chen Studio
14.08 Bercy Chen Studio
15.04 Seth Stein Architects
17.03 Innovarchi
17.04 Innovarchi
21.05 Lake Flato Architects
21.07 Lake Flato Architects
22.04 Localarchitecture
24.07 Ofis Arhitekti and Jelka
          Šolmajer
24.08 Ofis Arhitekti and Jelka
          Šolmajer
25.04 Rooijakkers + Tomesen
          Architecten
31.08 Allies and Morrison
34.03 Frank Harmon Architects
34.04 Frank Harmon Architects
35.04 Glenn Howells Architects
38.05 McChesney Architects
38.06 McChesney Architects
40.06 Allies and Morrison
45.06 Matteo Thun & Partners
47.05 Miralles Tagliabue – EMBT
47.06 Miralles Tagliabue – EMBT
47.07 Miralles Tagliabue – EMBT
48.05 Sanaksenaho Architects

Screen Details

Skylight Details

Wall Details

Window Details

Directory of Architects

Australia

DesignInc
Melbourne Central Tower, Level 51
360 Elizabeth Street
Melbourne, Victoria 3000
melbourne@designinc.com.au
T +61 3 9654 9654
F +61 3 9654 4321
www.designinc.com.au
42 CH2 Melbourne City Council House

Francis-Jones Morehen Thorp
Level 5, 140 George Street
Sydney, New South Wales 2000
media@fjmt.com.au
T +61 2 9251 7077
F +61 2 9251 7072
www.fjmt.com.au
03 Chancellery and Business School, Edith Cowan University

Innovarchi
Level 1, 12–20 Argyle Street
The Rocks, Sydney
New South Wales 2000
architects@innovarchi.com
T +61 2 9247 6191
F +61 2 9247 6148
www.innovarchi.com
17 Future House

Jackson Clements Burrows
One Harwood Place, Melbourne
Victoria 3000
jacksonclementsburrows@jcba.com.au
T +61 3 9654 6227
F +61 3 9654 6195
www.jcba.com.au
18 Cape Schanck House

James Russell Architect
118 Brookes Street
Fortitude Valley
Brisbane, Queensland 4006
james@jamesrussellarchitect.com.au
T +61 4 2770 4288
www.jamesrussellarchitect.com.au
19 Brookes Street House

Lahz Nimmo Architects
Suite 404 Flourmill Studios
3 Gladstone Street
Newtown, New South Wales 2042
info@lahznimmo.com
T +61 2 9550 5200
F +61 2 9550 5233
www.lahznimmo.com
44 Centennial Park Amenities

Stutchbury and Pape
5/364 Barrenjoey Road
Newport, Sydney
New South Wales 2106
info@stutchburyandpape.com.au
T +61 2 9979 5030
F +61 2 9979 5367
www.stutchburyandpape.com.au
29 Bangalay House

Canada

Saia Barbarese Topouzanov Architectes
339 Saint-Paul Street
Montreal, Quebec H2Y 1H3
sbt@sbt.qc.ca
T +1 514 866 2085
F +1 514 874 0233
www.sbt.qc.ca
26 Maison Goulet

Taylor Smyth Architects
354 Davenport Road
Suite 3B, Toronto
Ontario M5R 1K6
mtaylor@taylorsmyth.com
T +1 416 968 6688
F +1 416 968 7728
www.taylorsmyth.com
30 Sunset Cabin

Chile

Germán del Sol Architects
Camino las Flores 11441, Las
Condes, Santiago
germandelsol@entelchile.net
T +56 2 214 1214
F +56 2 214 1147
www.germandelsol.cl
43 Hotel Remota en Patagonia

Finland

Lassila Hirvilammi Architects
Hakalankatu 10 B, FIN-60 100
Seinäjoki
info@lh-ark.fi
T +358 6 4141 225
F +358 6 4141 225
www.lh-ark.fi
09 Kärsämäki Church

Sanaksenaho Architects
Tehtaankatu 27-29 D, 00150 Helsinki
ark@sanaksenaho.com
T +358 9 177 341
F +358 9 630 636
www.kolumbus.fi/sanaksenaho
48 St Henry's Ecumenical Art Chapel

France

FORMA 6
6 bis rue de l'Ouche de Versailles
B.P. 30209
44002 Nantes Cedex 1
forma6@forma6.net
T +33 2 40 29 47 25
F +33 2 40 29 40 50
www.forma6.net
04 Médiathèque René Goscinny

Hérault Arnod Architectes
16, rue Thiers
38 000 Grenoble
zzz@herault-arnod.fr
T +33 4 76 12 94 94
F +33 4 76 86 11 44
www.herault-arnod.fr
06 Cultural, Sports and Congress Centre

Germany

Sauerbruch Hutton
Lehrter Strasse 57
10557 Berlin
pr@sauerbruchhutton.com
T +49 30 397821 25
F +49 30 397821 30
www.sauerbruchhutton.com
49 Federal Environmental Agency

Italy

Matteo Thun & Partners
Via Appiani 9 - I 20121
Milano
info@matteothun.com
T +39 02 655 6911
F +39 02 657 0646
www.matteothun.com
45 Hugo Boss Industries Building

Japan

Kengo Kuma
2-24-8 BY- CUBE 2-4F
Minamiaoyama Minato-ku
Tokyo 107- 0062
kuma@ba2.so-net.ne.jp
T +81 03 3401 7721
F +81 03 3401 7673
www.kkaa.co.jp
37 Onsen Hotel

Norway

Jarmund / Vigsnæs AS Architects
Hausmanns Gate 6, 0186 Oslo
jva@jva.no
T +47 22 99 43 43
F +47 22 99 43 53
www.jva.no
08 Svalbard Science Centre

Saunders Wilhelmsen
Vestre torggate 22
NO-5015 Bergen
post@saunders.no
T +47 55 36 85 06
F +47 97 52 57 61
www.saunders.no
39 Aurland Lookout

Portugal

António Portugal & Manuel Reis Architects
76 Rua da Bandeirinha, 4050-088
Porto
info@aportugal-mreis.com
T +351 22 600 7847
F +351 22 600 7850
www.aportugal-mreis.com
32 Brufe Restaurant

Slovenia

Ofis Arhitekti and Jelka Šolmajer
Kongresni TRG 3
1000 Ljubljana
info@ofis-a.si
T +386 1 4260085
F +386 1 4260085
www.ofis-a.si
24 Shopping Roof Apartments

Spain

Miralles Tagliabue – EMBT
Passatge de la Pau, 10 bis, pral.
08002 Barcelona
info@mirallestagliabue.com
T +34 93 412 53 42
F +34 93 412 37 18
www.mirallestagliabue.com
47 Santa Caterina Market

Switzerland

Localarchitecture
Case postale / CH 1002 Lausanne
local@localarchitecture.ch
T +41 21 320 06 86
F +41 21 320 06 86
www.localarchitecture.ch
22 Cow Stables

The Netherlands

Rooijakkers + Tomesen Architecten
WG-plein 105
1054 SC Amsterdam
architectenbureau@rooijakkers-
tomesen.com
T +31 20 615 22 62
F +31 20 612 78 84
www.rooijakkers-tomesen.com
25 Light-Catcher

Turkey

Boran Ekinci Architects
boranekinci@gmail.com
T +90 0216 425 16 22
F +90 0216 425 16 24
www.boranekincimimarlık.com
27 Lakeside House

UK

Alison Brooks Architects
Unit 610 Highgate Studios
53–79 Highgate Road
London NW5 1TL
natalie@alisonbrooksarchitects.com
T +44 20 7267 9777
F +44 20 7267 9772
www.alisonbrooksarchitects.com
13 Salt House

Allies and Morrison
85 Southwark Street
London SE1 0HX
info@alliesandmorrison.co.uk
T +44 20 7921 0100
F +44 20 7921 0101
www.alliesandmorrison.co.uk
**31 WWT Welney Visitor Centre and
Footbridge**
40 British Council

Cowper Griffith Architects
15 High Street
Whittlesford
Cambridge CB22 4LT
architects@cowpergriffith.co.uk
T +44 1223 835998
F +44 1223 837327
www.cowpergriffith.co.uk
33 Anglesey Abbey Visitor Centre

Dannatt, Johnson Architects
52c Borough High Street
London SE1 1XN
david.johnson@djarchitects.co.uk
T +44 20 7357 7100
F +44 20 7357 7200
www.djarchitects.co.uk
02 Battle Visitor Centre

Gareth Hoskins Architects
Charlotte House, 78 Queen Street
Glasgow G1 3DN
mail@hoskinsarchitects.co.uk
T +44 141 221 0600
F +44 141 222 2770
www.garethhoskinsarchitects.co.uk
**05 Culloden Battlefield Visitor
Centre**

Glenn Howells Architects
321 Bradford Street
Birmingham
B5 6ET
mail@glennhowells.co.uk
T +44 121 666 7640
F +44 121 666 7641
www.glennhowells.co.uk
35 The Savill Building

Hopkins Architects
27 Broadley Terrace
London NW1 6LG
mail@hopkins.co.uk
T +44 20 7724 1751
F +44 20 7723 0932
www.hopkins.co.uk
36 Norwich Cathedral Refectory

Hudson Architects
49–59 Old Street
London EC1V 9HX
info@hudsonarchitects.co.uk
T +44 20 7490 3411
F +44 20 7490 3412
www.hudsonarchitects.co.uk
16 Cedar House

Hunters
Sussex Business Village
Lake Lane, Barnham
West Sussex, PO22 0AA
l.denby@hunters.co.uk
T +44 1243 558750
F +44 1243 554923
www.hunters.co.uk
07 Crawley Down Primary School

Knox Bhavan Architects
75 Bushey Hill Road
Camberwell
London SE5 8QQ
mail@knoxbhavan.com
T +44 20 7701 3108
F +44 20 7277 0751
www.knoxbhavan.com
20 Holly Barn

McChesney Architects
1A Iliffe Street, London SE17 3LJ
design@mcchesney.co.uk
T +44 20 7703 1133
F +44 20 7692 7833
www.mcchesney.co.uk
38 Avenham Park Pavilion

McDowell + Benedetti
Karen House
1–11 Baches Street
London N1 6DL
email@mcdowellbenedetti.com
T +44 20 7253 2807
F + 44 20 7490 2399
www.mcdowellbenedetti.com
46 Castleford Bridge

Seth Stein Architects
15 Grand Union Centre, West Row
Ladbroke Grove, London W10 5AS
admin@sethstein.com
T +44 20 8968 8581
F +44 20 8968 8591
www.sethstein.com
15 Beach House
28 Pencalenick House

USA

Bercy Chen Studio
1111 East 11th Street, Suite 200
Austin, Texas 78702
info@bcarc.com
T +1 512 481 0092
F +1 512 476 7664
www.bcarc.com
14 Lago Vista Lake House

Bohlin Cywinski Jackson
1932 First Avenue, Suite 916
Seattle, Washington 98101
hnelson@bcj.com
T +1 206 956 0862
F +1 206 956 0864
www.bcj.com
**01 Grand Teton Discovery and
Visitor Center**
**41 Ballard Library and
Neighborhood Service Center**

Frank Harmon Architects
706 Mountford Avenue
Raleigh, North Carolina 27603
frank@frankharmon.com
T +1 919 829 9464
F +1 919 829 2202
www.frankharmon.com
**34 Prairie Ridge Ecostation for
Wildlife and Learning**

Lake Flato Architects
311 3rd Street
San Antonio, Texas 78205
info@lakeflato.com
T +1 210 227 3335
F +1 210 224 9515
www.lakeflato.com
21 Lake Tahoe Residence

Machado and Silvetti Associates
560 Harrison Avenue, 3rd Floor
Boston, Massachusetts 02118
info@machado-silvetti.com
T +1 617 426 7070
F +1 617 426 3604
www.machado-silvetti.com
**10 Provincetown Art Association
and Museum (PAAM)**

MACK Architects
2343 Eastern Court
Venice, California 90291
office@markmack.com
T +1 310 822 0094
F +1 310 822 0019
www.markmack.com
23 Judenburg West Housing

OBRA Architects
315 Church Street, 4th Floor
New York, New York 10013
jennifer@obraarchitects.com
T +1 212 625 3868
F +1 212 625 3874
www.obraarchitects.com
11 BEATFUSE!

SHoP Architects
11 Park Place Penthouse
New York, New York 10007
studio@shoparc.com
T +1 212 889 9005
F +1 212 889 3686
www.shoparc.com
12 Mitchell Park Camera Obscura

Skidmore, Owings & Merrill
14 Wall Street
New York, New York 10005
somnewyork@som.com
T +1 212 298 9300
F +1 212 298 9500
www.som.com
50 United States Census Bureau

Picture Credits

All architectural drawings are supplied courtesy of the architects.

Photographic credits:
In all cases every effort has been made to credit the copyright holders, but should there be any omissions or errors the publisher will be pleased to insert the appropriate acknowledgment in any subsequent editions of the book.

10   Nic Lehoux
14   © Peter Cook / VIEW
18   © John Gollings
22   Patrick Miara **1, 2, 4**
22   Courtesy Forma 6 Architects **3**
26   © Andrew Lee **1, 2, 4**
26   © Ewen Weatherspoon **3**
30   © André Morin
34   Courtesy Hunter and Partners
38   Nils Petter Dahle
42   © Jussi Tiainen
46   © Anton Grassl / ESTO
50   Elsa Ruiz. Courtesy P.S.1 Contemporary Art Center **1**
50   Courtesy OBRA Architects **2, 3, 4**
54   © Seong Kwon
60   © Cristobal Palma
64   © Pettyjohn Photography
68   © Richard Davies
72   © Steve Townsend / www.stownsend.com
76   © Richard Glover / VIEW **1, 2, 4**
76   Courtesy of Innovarchi **3**
80   © John Gollings
84   © Jon Linkins
88   © Dennis Gilbert / VIEW
92   Jeff Dow
96   © Milo Keller / www.twinroom.net
100 © Manfred Seidl, Vienna
104 Tomaz Gregoric
108 Luuk Kramer Fotografie
112 Marc Cramer
116 Riza Tansu **1, 3**
116 Cemal Emdem **2**
120 © Richard Davies
124 © Michael Nicholson
128 © Ben Rahn. A-Frame Inc
134 © Dennis Gilbert / VIEW
138 © Luis Ferreira Alves
142 © Peter Cook / VIEW
146 © Tim Hursley
150 The Royal Landscape www.theroyallandscape.co.uk / Warwick Sweeney
154 © Paul Tyagi / VIEW **1**
154 © Peter Mackinven / VIEW **2, 3**
154 © Nick Guttridge / VIEW **4**

158 Daici Ano Architectural Photography / Forward Inc
162 © Peter Cook / VIEW
166 Courtesy Todd Saunders
172 © David Grandorge
176 Nic Lehoux **1, 2, 3**
176 Ben Benschneider **4, 5**
180 © Dianna Snape
184 Courtesy Germán del Sol Architects
188 © Brett Boardman Photography
192 © Klaus Frahm / Artur
196 © Tim Soar
200 © Alex Gaultier
204 © Jussi Tiainen
208 © Paul Raftery / VIEW
212 Fig 1: © Eduard Hueber / archphoto.com
212 Figs 2 + 3: Courtesy Skidmore, Owings & Merrill LLP

About the CD

The attached CD can be read on both Windows and Macintosh computers. All the material on the CD is copyright protected and is for private use only.

All drawings in the book and on the CD were specially created for this publication and are based on the architects' original designs.

The CD includes files for all of the drawings included in the book. The drawings for each building are contained in a numbered folder. They are supplied in two versions: the files with the suffix '.eps' are 'vector' Illustrator EPS files but can be opened using other graphics programs such as Photoshop; all the files with the suffix '.dwg' are generic CAD format files and can be opened in a variety of CAD programs.

Each file is numbered according to its original location in the book: project number, followed by the drawing number(s), followed by the scale. Hence, '01_01_200.eps' would be the eps version of the first drawing in the first project and has a scale of 1:200.

The generic '.dwg' file format does not support 'solid fill' utilized by many architectural CAD programs. All the information is embedded within the file and can be reinstated within supporting CAD programs. Select the polygon required and change the 'Attributes' to 'Solid', and the colour information should be automatically retrieved. To reinstate the 'Walls'; select all objects within the 'Walls' layer/class and amend their 'Attributes' to 'Solid'.

Acknowledgments

Thanks above all to the architects who submitted material for this book. Their time, effort and patience is very much appreciated. Special thanks to Hamish Muir, the designer of this book, and to Sophia Gibb for her indomitable dedication in researching the pictures. Sincere thanks to Philip Cooper and Gaynor Sermon at Laurence King, to Justin Fletcher for editing the drawings, and to Vic Brand for his technical expertise. And finally, special thanks to Tom Redpath, Jim McInulty, Oscar and Holly.